THE LIVES OF THE POPES

VOL. XIII.

Reproduced from Ciaconius.

Vitae RR. PP.

THE
LIVES OF THE POPES
IN THE MIDDLE AGES

BY THE

RT. REV. MONSIGNOR HORACE K. MANN, D.D.

"De gente Anglorum, qui maxime familiares Apostolicæ Sedis semper
existunt" (*Gesta Abb. Fontanel.*, *A.D.* 747–752, ap. M.G. SS. II. 289).

RECTOR OF THE COLLEGIO BEDA, ROME; CORRESPONDING MEMBER OF THE ROYAL ACADEMY OF
HISTORY OF SPAIN; MEMBER OF THE ACCADEMIA D'ARCADIA AND OF THE R. SOCIETÀ ROMANA
DI STORIA PATRIA.

THE POPES AT THE HEIGHT OF THEIR
TEMPORAL INFLUENCE
Innocent II. to Blessed Benedict XI.
1130–1305

(A) THE POPES AND THE HOHENSTAUFEN, 1130–1271

VOL. XIII

Honorious III. to Celestine IV., 1216–1241

LONDON:
KEGAN PAUL, TRENCH, TRUBNER & CO., LTD.
ST. LOUIS, MO.: B. HERDER BOOK CO.
1925

1886

Printed in Great Britain by Stephen Austin & Sons, Ltd., Hertford.

PREFACE

SINCE the appearance of the twelfth volume of my *Lives of the Popes in the Middle Ages*, ten years have elapsed—years in some respects the most memorable through which mankind has ever passed. During them has been fought the most awful war ever waged, a war in which it may be said, with but little exaggeration, that every man, woman, and child in the world was engaged, a war which brought three great Empires to a sudden and disastrous end. Small wonder that " the world is out of joint," and that its energy and its resources are still reeling after so terrible a shock. Every peaceful industry is crippled, and none more so than the printing press. " Silent leges inter arma," which we may well translate " Amid the din of arms, the voice of letters cannot make itself heard." Nor would this further effort of mine ever have had a chance of making its appeal to the English-speaking public had it not been helped. That this thirteenth volume is now printed, is due to the liberality of the same old and tried friend through whom the first volume saw the light, to Alderman Weidner of the City of Newcastle-on-Tyne. To him, therefore, do I owe especial thanks. Still, I must not forget warmly to thank also the Rev. C. Hart, and Mr. F. F. Urquhart, of Balliol College, Oxford, for the care with which they have once more read through the proof sheets of the hundreds of pages which make up this new volume.

H. K. MANN.

Rome, 1925.

A LIST OF THE PRINCIPAL ABBREVIATIONS USED IN THIS VOLUME.

Potthast . . . = *Regesta Pontificum Romanorum*, ed. A. Potthast, 2 vols., Berlin, 1874.

Reg. . . . . = One of the volumes of the *Registres des Papes* in course of publication by the French Schools of Athens and of Rome, ed. Fontemoing, Paris.

L. P. . . . . = *Liber Pontificalis*, 2 vols., ed. L. Duchesne, Paris, 1886.

M. G. H. or Pertz . . = *Monumenta Germaniæ Historica*, either *Scriptores* (M. G. SS.), or *Epistolæ* (M. G. Epp.) or *Poetæ* (M. G. PP.).

P. G. . . . . = *Patrologia Græca*, ed. Migne, Paris.

P. L. . . . . = *Patrologia Latina*, ed. Migne, Paris.

R. I. SS. . . . = *Rerum Italicarum Scriptores*, ed. Muratori, Milan, 1723 ff., or the new ed. in course of publication.

R. F. SS. . . . = *Recueil des Historiens des Gaules*, ed. Bouquet and others, Paris, 1738 ff.

R. S., following an edition of a book = The edition of the Chronicles, etc., of Great Britain and Ireland, published under the direction of the Master of the Rolls.

Rymer or Foedera . . = *Foedera, Literæ, etc., ab anno* 1101 *ad nostra usque tempora*, accurante T. Rymer. Unless the contrary is stated we quote from the original ed., London, 1704 ff.

Other abbreviations will be readily understood by reference to the *Sources* prefixed to each biography.

The sign † placed before a date indicates that the date in question is the year of the death of the person after whose name the sign and date are placed. The sign * placed before the title of a book indicates that the author of these volumes has seen the book in question well spoken of, but has not examined it himself.

TABLE OF CONTENTS

LIST OF ILLUSTRATIONS

Honorius III.

From a copy made by Grimaldi from a frescoe of the Church
of S. Bibiana.

(Photo) by kind permission of the British School of Rome.

HONORIUS III.

A.D. 1216–1227.

Sources.—The best source for the biography of Honorius is his register, which, contained in the Vatican archives in five large parchment tomes, has been splendidly printed in an abridged form by Dr. P. Pressutti (2 vols. folio, Rome, 1888). As is well known, the existing papal *Regesta* do not contain all the letters which issued from the Pope's chancellary, and Pressutti has endeavoured from other sources to make his *Regesta Honorii* as complete as possible. He began to edit the *Regesta* in 1884 in a modest octavo volume (Rome, 1884) ; but fortunately the munificence of the late glorious Pontiff Leo XIII. came to his aid, and he was enabled to publish them in a more satisfactory manner. His two folio volumes give us the analysis, not always, we are bound to say, made with judgment, of over 6,250 bulls and briefs.[1] Horoy had already in 1879 published in five volumes, Paris, 1879–82, all the works, sermons, and letters which he could find. He has printed the letters in full. C. Rodenberg did the same for the documents of Honorius that concerned Germany, in the first volume of *Epistolæ Sæculi XIII e regestis PP. RR. (M. G. Epp.)*, Berlin, 1883, as did Bouquet, *R.F. SS.*, t. xix, for those concerning France. B. Hauréau in the *Notices et extraits des MSS.*, t. xxi, part ii, Paris, 1865, also published with valuable notes a number of letters of Honorius, till then inedited, dealing with France. The briefs that relate to England are to be found analysed in the *Calendar of entries in the Papal Registers*, R.S. i, London, 1893. References to Honorius also occur in the *Registri dei cardinali Ugolino d'Ostia e Ottaviano degli Ubaldini*, edited by G. Levi, Rome, 1890.

No full contemporary biography of Honorius is known to exist, but a brief notice of him is given in a contemporary catalogue

[1] The Registers of Honorius, like the earlier papal biographies in the *Liber Pontificalis*, note at the end of each year the bishops whom Honorius consecrated in person. Many of his bulls bear the words : " Perfice gressus meos in semitis tuis," Psalms xvi, 5.

which has been assigned to a certain Italian named Gilbert, who wrote in Rome, and may possibly have been a Dominican, ap. *M. G. SS.*, xxiv, p. 135–6. Other pontifical catalogues (ap. *ib.* and elsewhere) and many of the contemporary chronicles give other facts concerning him. Muratori printed a *Life* of him by Bernard Guidonis,[1] in *R. I. SS.*, iii, pt. i, p. 568 ff., and, in the second part of the same vol., p. 387 ff., a second *Life* by another fourteenth century author Amalricus (Aimeric or Amaury) Auger of Béziers. He was an Augustinian canon and chaplain to Blessed Urban V (1362–70), to whom he dedicated his *Actus Pontificum Roman.* He brought his work, which is compiled with commendable accuracy, down to the year 1321 in the pontificate of John XXII.[2]

Modern Works.—The *Life* of Honorius by Bishop Simon Majolus, printed by Horoy (vol. ii, p. 397 ff.), rests only upon sixteenth century authorities. Dr. J. Clausen (*Papst Honorius III*, Bonn, 1895) has furnished us with a full and appreciative biography of Innocent's successor. He does not, however, treat the affairs of England adequately, and is said to be in great measure superseded by W. Knebel, * *Kaiser Friederich II und P. Hon. III in ihren gegenseitigen Beziehungen*, 1220–7, Munster, 1905.

See also F. Vernet, *Étude sur les sermons d'Hon. III*, Lyons, 1888, a pamphlet of which only a small number of copies were printed, and now entirely out of print ; E. Caillemer, *Le P. H. III et le droit civil*, Lyons, 1881 ; G. Digard, *La Papauté et l'étude du droit romain au XIII e siècle* (an extract), Paris, 1890, and M. Fournier, *L'église et le droit romain au XIII e siècle*, ap. " Nouvelle Rev. hist. et droit," Jan. 1890, p. 80 ff. *I pontefici Onorio III, Gregorio IX ed. Innocenzo IV a fronte dell' imp. Federico II*, by P. T. Masetti, Rome, 1884, is an academic dissertation of 23 pp., in which its author seeks to establish that the contest between these Popes and Frederick was one of right against might.

---

[1] † 1331, *cf. supra*, vol. x, p. 284 f.

[2] The edition in Eccard's *Corpus*, vol. ii, is not very accurate.

CONTEMPORARY SOVEREIGNS.

EMPEROR OF THE ROMANS.	KING OF ENGLAND.	EASTERN EMPERORS.	KINGS OF FRANCE.
Frederick II., Stupor Mundi, the World's Wonder, 1212-50.	Henry III., 1216-72.	Peter of Courtenay, 1216-19. Robert, 1219-28. Theodore Lascaris I., at Nicæa, 1204-22. John Vatatzes, at Nicæa, 1222-55.	Philip II., Augustus, 1180-1223. Louis VIII., 1223-6. St. Louis IX., 1226-70.

CHAPTER I.

CENCIUS SAVELLI. HE BECOMES HONORIUS III. HIS
LITERARY WORKS.

The Savelli. AMONG the most formidable of the early foes of Rome were the Samnites or Sabines or Sabelli—all men of the same tribe. When, in process of time, the tribal became a family name, a certain Sabellus gave his name to the picturesque little hill just below Albano. It seems to stand out as a sentinel of the Alban mountains, and is known as Monte Savello. Falling at length into the hands of the Crescentii of the Aventine, it gave a special name to that branch of the family which acquired it, and we hear at length in the twelfth century of the Savelli of Rome. Hence, some of the bulls of Celestine III. are *given* by Cencius *de Sabello*, cardinal deacon of St. Lucia in Orphea or in Selci, the subject of this biography.

The town house of the Savelli was on the lonely Aventine, close to the Church of Sta. Sabina, and was built on the foundations of the old temples of Juno Regina and Libertas.[1]

Cencius "of the Savelli." Here, we may suppose, was born, somewhere before the middle of the twelfth century, Cencius " of the Savelli," [2] as he is expressly called by St. Antoninus.[3] Later writers give his father's name as Aimeric, but they do not profess to know that of his mother.[4] Educated, no doubt, in

---

[1] All this is ably proved by Tomassetti, *La Campagna Romana*, ii, § 7, p. 127 ff. Cf. Pressutti, *Regest.*, p. xii ; Lanciani, *Ruins and Excavations of Ancient Rome*, p. 544 ; and especially E. Celani, *De Gente Sabella*, Rome, 1892.

[2] According to Pressutti, relying on the researches of Panvinio († 1568), he was born *c.* 1130.

[3] Anton. († 1459), *Chron.* iii, p. 106, "Natione Romanus, de Sabellis."

[4] Again, Pressutti from Panvinio.

the Lateran, as " he was brought up from his earliest years by the Holy Roman Church," [1] he became in due course canon of St. Mary Major's, and then *camerarius* under Popes Clement III. and Celestine III.[2] Of these pontiffs he appears to have been more attached to Pope Celestine, whom he calls his father,[3] and to whom, when he was cardinal Hyacinth, he had been procurator.

Burchard, from whom we learn this fact, gives us a pretty little story connected with Cencius' duties as procurator. His master, cardinal Hyacinth (or Jacinthus) had been ordered by Pope Clement to go as his legate to Spain. In want of money the cardinal bade his procurator borrow some for him. Money, however, seems to have been hard to get, and the procurator was walking along with a worried look on his face, when he was met by an aged and venerable man, who kindly inquired into the reason of his anxiety. On learning its cause the old man bade him cease from troubling as his master would not be going to Spain. " How knowest thou this ? " asked Cencius. " The present Pope will die, and your master will take his place," was the reply. And so it came to pass. When the procurator returned home, word had come that the Pope had fallen ill and had counter-manded his instructions to Hyacinth. A few days after-wards he died, and cardinal Hyacinth was elected to succeed him. Accordingly, adds Burchard, many, seeing how the prophecies of the old man had been fulfilled, judged him to have been St. Peter.

A legend of Cencius the procurator.

[1] So he tells us himself in the prologue to his *Liber Censuum.*

[2] *Cf.* the Prologue. Burchard, *Chron.*, an. 1216, calls him " camerarius cardinalium," and, in recognition of his peculiar integrity in that position, adds that he distributed their dues to the cardinals with the greatest exactness : " pecunias ipsis collatas inter eos fideliter et provide distruebat." Under Innocent III. he was succeeded by a certain Richard as Camerarius.

[3] Ep. i, 304 ; Reg., n. 524.

**Cardinal
and
auditor.**

On March 3, 1193, Cencius was certainly cardinal deacon of the old Church of St. Lucy in Selci or in Orphea, and he held the post of vice-chancellor of the Holy See from November 6, 1194 to September 10, 1197. Pope Innocent III. named him cardinal priest of SS. John and Paul, in 1201,[1] and his signature attached to bulls shows that he was with that Pope every year till his death. Whilst holding these distinguished offices, he was often appointed as *auditor*, to decide some of the innumerable cases which were brought before the Holy See.[2]

Camerarius.

Perhaps the most responsible of the posts held by Cencius was that of Camerarius (chamberlain, later known as Cardinal Camerlengo). Since the decay in the eleventh century of the offices of Vestararius, of Vicedominus (the modern Majordomo), and of Archdeacon of the Roman Church, that of the Head of the " Apostolic Chamber," the Camerarius, had increased in importance, and he was at this period the treasurer, majordomo, vicar of the Pope in Rome, and his first minister in civil affairs.

**Literary
works of
Cencius
Camerarius.
(*a*) The Liber
Censuum.**

It was whilst attending to the financial affairs of the Holy See in his capacity of treasurer that Cencius felt

---

[1] Speaking of Saints John and Paul, Honorius says that he had a special devotion to them "utpote qui ad eorum titulum sacerdotii gradum accepimus." Ep. ii, 302. Reg., n. 1454.

[2] " In qua questione nos fuimus auditores dum eramus in minori officio constituti." Reg., n. 91. The *auditores* appear to have replaced the *judices palatini* in the course of the twelfth century. *Cf.* A. de Boüard, " Les notaires de Rome au Moyen Age," ap. *Melanges d'archéol. et d'hist.*, June, 1911, p. 291 ff. Hence we read of cardinal Gualo, " the most learned of all the cardinals in civil law," being appointed *auditor* of a case. *Chron. abbat de Evesham*, p. 191 R.S. On the strength of some words of Frederick in a charter addressed to Honorius, it has been argued that he had been that monarch's tutor. But the words refer to the " Roman Church " and not to the Pope personally, as is clear from the fact that the said charter (ap. Theiner, *Cod. Dipl. Domin. Temp.*, i, p. 51, or Huillard-Bréholles, *Hist. Dip.*, i, pl. ii, p. 675 f.) is a verbatim repetition of the one addressed to Innocent III. on July 12, 1213, ap. H.-B., *ib.*, i, pt. i, p. 269.

the want of an accurate and up-to-date list of tax-payers
of the Roman Church. The old account books of the
Roman Church—the Polyptycus of Gelasius I. as re-edited
by St. Gregory I. and in use in the days of John VIII.—
would seem to have perished. Eugenius III., the Englishman Hadrian IV., and others had indeed drawn up notes [1]
of more or less value on the subject. But there was no
complete and orderly list whence it could be discovered
at a glance who had fulfilled their pecuniary obligations
to the Holy See, and who had not. To meet this difficulty,
which had already caused considerable loss to the Apostolic See, Cencius drew up his famous *Liber Censuum*,
which he presented to " his father " Celestine III., in
1198.[2]

His manuscript (Vaticanus 8486), as it was engrossed
under his eye and direction by William Rofio, of St. John
d'Angély, a clerk of the " Apostolic Camera," and scribe
(scriptor) of the papal chancellary, is still extant. An
examination of it shows that, to his list of tax-payers,
arranged under different countries and provinces,[3] Cencius
added a list of bishoprics and monasteries directly
dependent on the Holy See, a copy of the *Mirabilia Urbis
Romæ*, an *Ordo Romanus*, two chronicles of the Popes,
one up to Celestine III., and the other up to Eugenius III.,

[1] " Quædam memorialia, semiplena tamen, nec authentice scripta,
seu ordinata in scriptis." Prologue to the L.C. *Cf. supra*, vol. ix,
p. 231. It is to one of these documents that Alexander III. referred
in a letter of Oct. 11, 1163–4. " Invento in quodam scripto librorum
nostrorum, quod Lateranensi palacio ecclesia vestra . . . unciam
deberet auri persolvere." Ap. Loewenfeld, *Epp. Rom. Pont.*, pp. 134–5.
[2] *Prolog.* It is cited by Celestine's successor the great Innocent.
Ep. i, 535. " Inspectione libri censualis cameræ nostræ." Honorius
himself refers to it. *Cf.* Potthast, 5816, or Pitra, *Epp. RR.PP.*,
pp. 528–9.
[3] He set down only those properties over which, in his judgment,
the Holy See had the *altum dominium*, and of which the owners (on
payment of a tax) enjoyed the usufruct.

and lastly, a Cartulary. The manuscript also shows that additions were made to the original work of Cencius up to the end of the thirteenth century ; [1] for Cencius had left blank spaces in his manuscript that it might be useful "to the end of the world." [2] The Cartulary, containing copies of donations, wills and the like, showed whence the dues of the Roman Church had their origin. Its introduction into a Tax-book is thus easily accounted for ; but the connexion between " The Marvels of the City of Rome " (the *Mirabilia*), together with brief papal biographies, and the Tax-book is not so clear. The reason of their insertion, however, has been admirably explained by Fabre, the late learned editor of the *Liber Censuum*. " The titles of Rome," he says, " to the government of Christendom (chrétienté) are the splendour of its past, and the uninterrupted series by which we ascend, pontiff by pontiff, to St. Peter. Hence, the description of the Wonders of Rome, and the list of the Popes who have succeeded one another in the chair of Peter seem to have their well-defined place in a collection of the rights and prerogatives of the Holy See. It is a way of representing in a concrete form the abstract idea of the preeminence of Rome, and of setting forth its historic rights side by side with its diplomatic title deeds." [3] Though the book of Cencius, who made such a mark as papal treasurer that the title of treasurer (camerarius) is often given him as a surname (Cencius Camerarius), did not remain in use till " the end of the world," it did remain in use till the sixteenth century. In that age, when so much that was venerable was swept away, the old systems of papal taxation and many of the sources of the papal

---

[1] *Cf.* the Introduction to Fabre-Duchesne's ed. of the *Liber Censuum*. Their ed. is much more complete than the one given by Horoy, vol. i.
[2] Prologue.
[3] *Étude sur le Liber Censuum*, p. 9, Paris, 1892.

revenues were abolished, and the *Liber Censuum* of Cencius became merely an historical monument, most useful for studying the finances of the mediæval Popes, but of no further utility for the controllers of the pontifical exchequer.[1]

Like his predecessor, Honorius contributed (*c.* 1226) to the Corpus Juris Canonici by his so-called *Quinta Compilatio*. This collection in five books of his decretal letters[2] Honorius dispatched to Master Tancred, with an instruction to cause it to be used in the law courts and in the schools.[3] It was incorporated along with the similar work of Innocent III. in the collection of Decretals made by St. Raymund of Pennafort for Gregory IX., and hence has not attracted the attention which would otherwise have been accorded to it.

(b) Quinta Compilatio.

Although, then, Honorius III. was a lawgiver himself, he is thought by some to have been ill-disposed towards a branch of law with which he was not directly concerned. He is said to have endeavoured to crush civil, i.e., Roman, law, inasmuch as it was supposed to run counter to the rights or pretensions of the Church. This idea is based upon his Decretal known as " Super specula "[4] which forbade, under severe penalties, any one to give or to listen to lectures in civil law in the city of Paris or in any place near it.

The Decretal " Super specula," 1219.

---

[1] In Horoy the *Liber C.* is followed by a *Life* of Gregory VII. But this *Life* is the work not of Cencius but of Boso reproducing Bonizo's *Liber ad Amicum*, and was added with other papal biographies to a MS. of the *Lib. C.* between the years 1254 and 1265. *Cf.* Duchesne, *Lib. Pont.*, ii, p. 351.

[2] Ap. Horoy, i, p. 95 ff.

[3] Tit. i, c, 1, ap. *ib.*, p. 114.

[4] *Quinta Compil.*, l. v, c. 3 ap. Hor., i, p. 364. In the collection of the Decretals of Gregory IX. it may be read ap. Freidberg, *Corpus juris can.*, vol. ii, p. 660. See also Potth., n. 6165. It is an extract from an encyclical (" Super speculam Domini ") of Nov. 16, 1219, ep. iv, 53, ap. Hor., iii, p. 347 ff., or ap. Denifle, *Chartularium Univer. Paris.*, i, n. 32.

Apart, however, from any special considerations which may have influenced Honorius at the moment of his issuing this prohibition, the course of previous legislation is quite enough to explain his action. We have seen the council of Clermont (1130) forbidding religious to devote themselves to the study of civil law and medicine, and we have observed that this decree was confirmed by the Lateran Council (1139).[1] The cause of this legislation is not far to seek. It was framed with a view to the improvement of ecclesiastical discipline. Honorius also published his decree partly for the same object. But he had also other reasons for his action. He explained in the first place, that there was no necessity for the study of Justinian's Code in Paris. In and about Paris, that is in France proper, that Code was not in vogue,[2] and ecclesiastical cases could as a rule be settled by the Canon Law.[3] The Church, he continued, did not indeed despise the service of the civil laws,[4] but it was better for all ecclesiastics, in Paris at least, not to devote their time to the study of them.

That the main aim of Honorius was to preserve for the University of Paris its theological character is brought out by the action of his successor, who readily gave permission for the study of law in another city of France,

[1] *Cf. supra*, vol. ix, p. 26 n., and p. 61. The same prohibition was also decreed by the Council of Tours (1163). *Supra*, x, p. 66.

[2] This was pointed out by the famous Roger Bacon in his attack on the abuses of the civil law. *Cf. Opus Tertium*, p. 419 *R.S. Cf. ib.*, p. 84.

[3] " In Francia et nonnullis provinciis, laici Romanorum imperatorum legibus non utuntur, et occurrunt raro ecclesiasticæ causæ tales, quæ non possint statutis canonicis expediri." Ep. iv, 53.

[4] " Sancta Ecclesia legum sæcularium non respuat famulatum." *Ib.* Hence he directs his legate at Constantinople to proceed in certain cases according "to Canon and Civil Law." *Quinta Compil.*, l. i, tit. 20, c. 1. Moreover, he and his successor gave their patronage to Bologna and Montpellier, where civil law and medicine were studied.

namely, in Orleans, by all except ecclesiastics having the cure of souls.[1]

Besides the guide of previous legislation just mentioned, Honorius had also to influence him a complaint from the Bishop of Poitiers to the effect that priests of his diocese, neglecting the duties of their sacred calling, had for the sake of gain, devoted themselves to legal affairs. Such scandals must be stopped, as it was not becoming " for priests who were set aside for the mystery of the Body and Blood of Christ, to be fond of the noise and wrangling of lawsuits." [2]   Furthermore, the schools of Paris were essentially schools of theology and literature, and even there the study of the latter was being ruined by the eager pursuit of legal studies. Geraldus Cambrensis, writing not long before Honorius published his decretal, avers that the love of gain was causing literature to be suffocated by the Justinian Code, and that he had himself heard Master Mainerius maintain in his school at Paris that there was then being fulfilled that prophecy of the Sibyl which declared " The days will come, and woe be to them, when laws will blot out the science of letters." [3]   Hence, especially as the spread of heresy rendered the study of theology and literature so important, it was felt that those faculties must not be interfered with by the study of civil law.

It was under the influence of such ideas, and in the hope of lessening the notorious litigiousness of the monks, and not because, after the manner of many of our country-

[1] Ep. of Jan. 17, 1235, ap. Denifle, *Chartular. Univer. Paris.*, p. 156. See a similar remark by the professors of Toulouse about works on natural science. *Ib.*, p. 131.

[2] See the reply of Honorius to the bishop, ap. *Quinta Compil.*, l. iii, tit. i, c. 1, Horoy, i, pp. 265–6.

[3] *Gemma eccles.*, D. ii, c. 37, Op. ii, p. 349 R.S.   *Cf.* R. Bacon, *l.c.*, and Pætow, *The battle of the Seven Arts*, p. 44 ff.

men,[1] he mistrusted Roman law as unfavourable to liberty, that Honorius issued his Decretal against the study of the Code Justinian.

It appears, however, that even from the fiist it was not unusual for dispensations to be granted in connexion with the decretal " Super specula." " It is the rule," says a contemporary, " that those who read law at Paris are excommunicated unless they have obtained a dispensation." [2] Moreover, as time went on, and it was found that Frederick II., like his grandfather Frederick I., waged war on the Church with the aid of the lawyer as much as with that of the soldier, it was felt to be necessary to remove the restrictions in the way of clerics devoting themselves to the study of civil law. The Church must have trained lawyers to meet those of the State.

Accordingly, Gregory IX. began by *interpreting* the " Super specula." " We declare," he decreed, " that such as have the simple cure of souls are not bound by the constitution *Super Specula.* Now we call those having the simple cure of souls such as hold parish churches, unless they be *plebania,* i.e., unless they have chapels, with clergy attached, subject to them." [3]

---

[1] This antipathy of our countrymen is well brought out by Digard, *La Papauté et l'étude du droit,* p. 28 ff. Matth. Paris, for instance, denounces the pride of the "lawyers and decretalists." *Chron. maj.,* v, 79.

[2] *Cf.* Digard, *l.c.,* p. 26 n., quoting *Questiones disputate Andegavis* (Paris, MS. lat., n. 11724, fol. 102*a*). " De consuetudine est Parisius quod omnes ibi leges legentes excommunicantur, *nisi dispensatus fuerit de aliquo.*"

[3] " Declaramus, quod illi qui habent simplices curas animarum non tenentur illa constitutione *Super specula* Etc." Cited by Freidberg in connexion with a confirmation by Boniface VIII. of this exemption which that Pope assigned to Clement IV. He, however, appears to have merely confirmed the exemption granted by Gregory IX. *Cf.* Freidberg's note to the *Sexti decret.,* lib. iii, tit. 24, c. 1, vol. ii, pp. 1064-5. See also a dispensation granted by Innocent IV., ap. *Regist.,* n. 7116 ed. Berger.

This important exemption was confirmed by Gregory's successors; and Innocent IV., to make headway against the lawyers of Frederick II., found it necessary directly to encourage the study of civil law in the university which he founded in connexion with his court, when he was living at Lyons.[1] His action, we may well suppose, did not pass unobserved at the time ; at any rate a distinguished canonist, John Andrew, of a somewhat later date (c. 1270–1348), remarked what a strange thing it was that civil law could be read in the Roman Curia, and not in Paris and its neighbourhood.[2]

If then, Honorius III., in no "narrow spirit of hostility to legal or to secular studies in general," [3] forbade the study of civil law in Paris, and if an attempt was made about his time to prevent the great mass of the clergy from devoting themselves to its study, his successors found themselves compelled by the necessities of their position to grant ample dispensations from the law.

About the year 1220, Pope Honorius dedicated the (c) Sermons. collection of his sermons to the Dominicans ; and somewhat later the Cistercians were equally honoured.[4]

[1] His biographer, Nicholas de Carbio, ap. R. I. SS., iii, pt. i, p. 5928, says : " Secundo anno sui pontificatus apud Lugdunum in sua curia generale studium ordinavit tam de theologia quam in decretis, decretalibus pariter et legibus." Cf. a section of the bull of foundation cited ap. Sexti decret., lib. v, tit. vi, c. 2, ap. Freidberg, ii, pp. 1083–4. This alone is enough to prove that the bull Dolentes (among the Additamenta of Matthew Paris, vol. vi, p. 293 R.S.) by which Innocent IV. is supposed to have renewed the Super Specula, is not genuine. See Denifle, Chartular. Univer. Paris., i, p. 262 n.

[2] As quoted by Digard, p. 26 n.

[3] This is the language of the first English authority on the mediæval Universities, Canon Rashdall. He writes (The Universities of Europe, i, p. 323) : " It should be added that the study of the Civil Law was forbidden in 1219 by Honorius III., not (as is sometimes represented) in a narrow spirit of hostility to legal or to secular studies in general, but because it threatened to extinguish the study of Theology in the one great theological School of Europe."

[4] Ep. viii, 73, c. An. 1223, vol. iv, p. 491, Horoy.

In sending the volume of his sermons to the abbot
and brethren of Citeaux, he tells them that, " casting off
the dust of vain glory, and setting aside all idea of earthly
gain, he must from charity alone so water the parched
hearts of those subject to him, that in his work the
spirits of evil may not be able to find any part. Although
then," he continued, " I am weighed down by the in-
firmities of my body, overwhelmed by the burden of the
pontifical office and distracted by the flood of cares that
rushes upon me from every quarter so that I am scarce
able to collect my mind . . . and give even a little time
to reading or meditation, still, in order that the time
which I can snatch or rather steal from my daily occupations may not be wasted, I have been at pains to gather
together in one volume the sermons which from time to
time[1] I have preached to the clergy and people of Rome,
that they may be of use to the present and even to future
generations."

With regard to the book he is sending them, he asks
their prayers in return for it, and tells them to take care
of it lest the excommunication, which he has decreed
against such as venture to alienate in any way the sacred
vessels or ornaments which he has presented to different
churches, may fall upon them.[2] However, from the
dedication of these same sermons to the Dominicans, it is
clear that Honorius did not suppose that taking care of a
book excluded the idea of lending it. He expressly begs
them to lend copies of his sermons to such as might like
to have them, in order that, " whilst he was in the taber-

[1] From the dedication to the Dominicans it is clear that, if some of
the sermons were preached while their author was Pope, some of them
were preached before he received that title. " Hoc nimirum sermonum
opus a nobis in minori officio constitutis sub sola spe gratiæ cœlestis
incœptum, etc." Ap. Horoy, *Introduction*, i, pp. xiv–xv.

[2] Ep. viii, 73.

nacle of the body, and after he had laid it down, they might have him in their memory." [1]

The topical allusions which occur in them show that most of the extant sixty-seven sermons were preached after he became Pope.[2] They were addressed to the clergy more than to the laity, and were delivered at the *stations*.[3] As he is constantly denouncing long sermons, we must suppose that he considered a sermon of half an hour's duration a short one. At any rate, it is said that his sermons would occupy a little over half an hour in delivery.

In an age when so many of the clergy had a remarkably accurate knowledge of the Bible, his sermons show that his close acquaintance with its words was well nigh as profound as that of St. Bernard. He does not often cite pagan authors, but he gives evidence of some knowledge at least of Greek and Hebrew. In his treatment of the Sacred Scriptures he is naturally like the other writers of his age. He elaborates, and at times even abuses their spiritual or mystical sense. Search for mystical meanings and antitheses often causes him to be too subtle, and his habit of constantly dividing his subject makes his discourses at times more like those of a theologian than of an orator. But, despite these tendencies which are those of his age, he could also at times rise to real oratory, and it

---

[1] Ap. Horoy, *l.c.*, p. xv.

[2] *Cf.* his sermon on the Golden Rose, the origin of which he assigns to St. Gregory the Great. Serm. 19 de temp., ap. H., i, p. 797. He notes that in blessing it the Pope wears the golden mitre, and " mitra aurea frigiata est cœlestis regni gloria."

[3] Honorius is said to have been the first to hold a station at Sta. Maria in Trastevere on the octave (Jan. 1, 1224) of the Nativity, and to have prescribed that his successors should do the same. See a marginal note to the martyrology of Sta. Maria now in the British Museum, ap. *M. G. SS.*, xix, 273. But it does not appear from later *Ordines Romani* that his successors ever obeyed his behest. I can only find that a station was held at Sta. Maria T. on the Thursday of the second week in Lent. *Cf. Ord. Rom.*, xvi, ap. *P.L.*, t. 78, p. 1369.

is to be reckoned to his credit that he was a preacher in an age when, strange to say, there was a great dearth of preachers, as he himself has left on record.[1] Hence, he continued to preach as Pope, both to give an example to others, and because he was deeply convinced of the necessity under which ministers of the Gospel lay of preaching the Gospel.[2] Both in his sermons and in his letters he was very careful of his style, and attached so much importance to correct expression that he is said [3] to have deposed a bishop for not paying sufficient attention to his Donatus.

Election as
Pope, 1216. On the death of Innocent, if the solitary authority of Martinus Polonus can be relied on, the citizens of Perugia inaugurated a new method of dealing with the cardinals in order that they might elect a new Pope with as little delay as possible. On the very day after the death of Innocent they practically imprisoned the cardinals (July 18).[4] As a result of this prompt action " the learned and aged " cardinal " Camerlengus " was, " after much discussion," elected on the following day.[5]

His election ultimately took place by what is called the method of *Compromise*. The cardinals made over their powers to the bishops of Ostia and Preneste, and " they placed the apostolical pallium on our shoulders.

---

[1] " Quia etsi sunt qui Sacram Scripturam velint audire, desunt prædicatores qui eam exponant." Serm. 22 ap. Hor., ii, p. 258.

[2] *Cf.* the same sermon, p. 248 ; and Serm. 19 ap. *ib.*, p. 226.

[3] By a late thirteenth century authority, the *Memoriale Potestatum Regiensium*, ap. *R. I. SS.*, viii, p. 1083. " Deposuit episcopum qui Donatum (the authority on Grammar) non legerat."

[4] " Perusinis causa electionis pape cardinales strictissime artantibus." Martinus Pol., *Chron.*, ap. *M. G. SS.*, xxii, p. 438.

[5] *Cf.* Chron. de Mailros, an. 1216 ; Codagnellus, *Annales*, 1216, " qui vocabatur Zinzius camarlengus " ; *Ignot. mon. Cist., Chron.*, an. 1216. " Cincio . . . assumptus (est) in papam Honorium die tertio post obitum predecessoris sui." See also Honorius' own account of his promotion ap. *Reg.*, n. i, Vol. I, p. i.

forcing us to undertake a burden which we would have gladly avoided." [1]

Less than a week later he was consecrated bishop in the ancient basilica attached to the monastery of St. Peter (July 24) ; [2] and on the following day he announced his accession to the Catholic world, begging the prayers of all good men to enable him to bear the great load which had been thrust upon his unwilling shoulders. [3]

In these, his first letters, he made very plain his high idea of his predecessor, " a man in all things Catholic," [4] and his intention of following in his footsteps, especially in the matter of the Crusade. Innocent, he said, merited indeed so to be called because " of the merits of his life, and the greatness of his wisdom . . . And though we doubt not that he is a saint in heaven . . . still we implore the Divine clemency which constituted him a father and a teacher on earth, to cleanse him of any venial fault into which human frailty may have caused him to fall." [5] On the very day after his consecration he wrote to the King of Jerusalem, John de Brienne, that he was animated by the same ardent desire for the liberation of the Holy Land as his predecessor ; [6] and, before many more days had elapsed, he had dispatched letters to a considerable number of the nobility of France, urging them not to delay to fulfil their vows of proceeding to the Holy Land, but to set out forthwith. [7]

Consecrated.

Honorius proclaims the virtues of Innocent III., and his intention to work for the Crusade.

[1] Ep. i, 6, or *Reg.*, n. 8.

[2] *Ann. Ceccan. (Fossæ N.)*, an. 1216, ap. *R. I. SS.*, vii, 893. A year or two later (May 17, 1218) Honorius granted certain indulgences to the monastery, adding : "nosque olim assumpti ad apostolatus apicem consecrationem recepimus in eodem." *Reg.*, n. 1341, i, p. 222.

[3] *Reg.*, nn. 1–9.

[4] Honor. : "senior venerandus," succeeded we are told Innocent, "viro per omnia catholico." *Notæ S. Emmerammi*, ap. *M. G. SS.*, xvii, 574.

[5] i, 7 ; *Reg.*, n. 9.

[6] Ep. i, 1.

[7] i, 11, Aug. 7.

Towards the close of August when the summer heats had begun to abate a little, Honorius left the charming breezy hill town of Perugia, and by way of Narni betook himself to Rome.

Just before reaching the Ponte Molle, the papal party left the great north road (the Via Flaminia), and turning to the right, proceeded to the chapel which had been comparatively recently erected by Gregory VIII. It stands at the foot of Monte Mario (ad radicem montis Mali), was originally dedicated to St. Mary Magdalene, and is now known as S. Lazzaro dei Lebbrosi.[1] Here the Pope assumed his cope (pluviale) and mitre, remounted his horse and rode towards the Porta Angelica in the walls of the Leonine City, about a mile distant. On his way he was met in triumphal procession by the Jews bearing a copy of the Bible, and by all the clergy of the city carrying crosses, banners, and thuribles. After being incensed by the clergy of each of the churches in turn, the Pope passing through the Porta, entered the covered portico which led from the castle of St. Angelo to the steps of St. Peter's. There he was met by the arch-priest and the canons of St. Peter, and to the chant of hymns was escorted to the doors of the basilica by the prior of the canons on the one hand, and the prior of the cardinals on the other. At the door the place of the prior of the canons was taken by another cardinal, and when they reached the middle of the church, the cardinal priests intoned the *Protector noster aspice Deus Etc.* Then, whilst the Pope prayed by the altar of St. Peter, the canons sang the *Te Deum.* When they had finished, the Pope arose, said the versicle *Sit nomen Domini,* and after kissing the altar, offered thereon some cloth of gold.[2] He was then

[1] *Cf.* Armellini, *Le chiese di Roma*, pp. 841–2.
[2] The *Ordo Romanus XIII*, n. 11, ap. *P. L.*, t. 78, p. 1113, which we are here following adds that it was the rule for the Pope to offer silk

conducted to a prominent seat behind the altar, and thereon solemnly enthroned by the prior of the cardinal deacons. After his feet and cheeks had been duly kissed by the cardinals and deacons in order, he retired to the palace.

He had reached St. Peter's and taken up his abode in the Vatican on the last day of the month. Thence, on 4th September, he went in solemn procession with the ceremonies already described [1] to take possession of the Lateran, and, somewhat as usual, "all who saw the cavalcade declared that not one of his predecessors had been received with such joy and respect, with such honour and delight." [2]

when he approached the altar of any Church for the first time. This *ordo* was drawn up by order of Gregory X. (1271–6) to clear away doubts as to what was wont to be done by the Popes on state occasions. It was drawn up : " Ad cautelam præsentium, et memoriam futurorum," n. 1.

[1] *Supra*, vol. xi.
[2] *Chron. Cec., l.c.*

CHAPTER II.

EASTERN POLICY—(THE CRUSADES).

Sources.—Röhricht, *Regesta Regni Hierosol.*, gives an analysis of the letters of Honorius III., etc., regarding the Holy Land.

The first and last thought of Honorius III., the delivery of the Holy Land.

THE pontificate of Honorius was literally an echo, a powerful echo indeed, but simply an echo, of that of his great predecessor. No new question was agitated during his reign, and he took up the same attitude towards the questions he had to face as had been taken up by the man whom he revered as a saint.[1] He did not, however, always use the same bold and determined methods as Innocent in pushing his policy. He was essentially a man of peace, almost a man of peace at any price. His love of peace was deepened both by his great age and by his natural gentleness in excess of that of his family.[2] He was prepared to sacrifice almost everything that peace might be kept by every Christian people, so that there should be no obstacle in the way of the Crusade. He ordered his days in peace [3] so that the one desire of his heart, the delivery of the Holy Land from the power

---

[1] In his first letter (i, 1) he speaks of him : " ad regionem sanctorum spirituum, ut credimus, evocato." *Cf. Ignoti mon. Cist., Chron.,* 1216. "Ad cujus tumulum, sicut dicitur, ceci . . . et aliis infirmitatibus detenti . . . sanati sunt."

[2] " Pietatis et misericordiæ singularis." *Chron. Turon.,* ap. *M. G. SS.,* xxvi, p. 476. A later writer, James Stephaneschi, a nephew of Boniface VIII., in his account of that Pope, calls the Savelli family "mild or gentle," "sabellia mitis." Lib. ii, c. 5, ap. *R. I. SS.,* iii, pt. i, p. 648.

[3] " Dies suos in pace disposuit " says a catalogue of the Popes regarding him, ap. *M. G. SS.,* xxii, p. 370.

of the infidel, might be accomplished.   His pronounced
love of peace is noted by chronicler after chronicler.[1]   He
sent his letters and his legates in the cause of peace into
every land, especially into the north of Italy, where the
material resources of the cities which might be used for
the good of the Holy Land were only equalled by the
fierce rivalries and enmities of the cities themselves
towards one another.   Accordingly into the north of
Italy he sent Ugolino Conti, the grandnephew of Innocent,
the most distinguished of his cardinals, " A man," he
wrote, "after our own heart, a man pleasing both to God
and to his fellow-men, a man powerful in work and word,
the chief member of God's Church, a man whom we
love with a most particular affection."[2]   Ugolino was
to preach the Crusade which had been proclaimed by the
Lateran Council (1215), and to promote peace.   The
cardinal's labours were not in vain.   The *Annals of
Cremona* tell us that, through his exertions, their city,
along with Parma, made peace with Milan and Piacenza
(1218);[3] and a document is extant in which the Podestà
of Siena declares that " with the full and free consent of
the whole council of Siena, duly assembled by the sound
of the bell, he gives and grants to the lord Ugolino, bishop
of Ostia and Velletri, legate of the Apostolic See, through
reverence for God, for the remission of their sins, and in
answer to the request of the lord Honorius, supreme

---

[1] " Pacifice vixit."   Salimbene, *Chron.*, ap. *M. G. SS.*, xxii, p. 36 ;
" Ecclesiam Dei in pacem gubernavit."   John de Deo, *Chron.*, ap.
ib., xxxi, p. 324 ; "In diebus suis pacem fovit," a contemporary
Chronicle, ap. *ib.*, xxiv, p. 154.

[2] See his letter addressed to all the superior clergy and laity and to
all the faithful "in Lombardy and Tuscany."   Ep. i, 167, *Reg.*,
n. 272, Jan. 23, 1217.   *Cf.* v, 292, March 14, 1221, where he calls
Ugolino "as it were a cedar of Lebanon in the garden of the Church,
etc."

[3] Ap. *M. G. SS.*, xxxi, p. 14.

Pontiff, and of the lord Frederic, Emperor, six solidi of Siena from every hearth in our Commune." [1]

Exertions for peace in the interests of the Crusade.

The letters of Honorius everywhere supported the work of his numerous legates in the cause of peace. The people of Milan are first tenderly exhorted not to wage war against Pavia,[2] and then, when they persisted in so doing, all Lombardy is informed that they are excommunicated for breaking the decree of the Lateran Council which proclaimed a four years' truce.[3] He prescribed conditions of peace between Pisa and Genoa,[4] which he had the happiness of seeing accepted in the Lateran by the envoys of both cities.[5] He exhorted his legate, Roderick, archbishop of Toledo, to induce the Kings of Spain to keep the peace among themselves, in order that they might be the better ready to attack the Moors ;[6] and he instructed his legate, cardinal Bertrandus, in Languedoc, to compel King James of Aragon not to wage war on Simon de Montfort who was striving " to exterminate heretical depravity in Provence." [7]

Especially, however, did he exert himself to bring about and to preserve peace between England and France.

---

[1] Ap. Huill.-Bréh., ii, p. 143 n., or ap. *Regist. dei card. Ugo.*, p. 7, March 26, 1221. The letter of Honorius (March 13, 1221) alluded to is cited by Ughelli, *Italia Sacra*, iii, 552, and that of Frederick (Feb. 10, 1221) by H.–B., ii, p. 122 ff. Frederick named Ugolino his vicar in Lombardy and Tuscany : " vobis imperialis celsitudinis auctoritatem plenam concedimus, etc." The people of Florence acted in a similar way to those of Siena for like reasons. *Cf. Reg. Ugol.*, nn. 9–10 ; and nn. 17–28 for corresponding engagements made by the people of Milan, Lodi, Brescia, Verona, etc. See Levi, "Documenti del Regist. del Card. Ugolino," ap. *Archivio Rom. di storia pat.*, vol. xii (1889), p. 241 ff.

[2] *Reg.*, n. 22, Aug., 1216.

[3] *Ib.*, 27. *Cf.* n. 1244, Apr. 20, 1218 ; and 1520–1, July 12, 1218.

[4] *Ib.*, n. 896, Dec. 1, 1217.

[5] *Ib.*, sub. n. 898.

[6] *Reg.*, n. 1042 f., Jan. 30, 1218.

[7] *Ib.*, n. 842, Oct. 23, 1217.

To this he was particularly bound not merely in the interests of the Holy Land, but in those of his youthful vassal Henry III.[1] Letter after letter was dispatched by him to the King and bishops of France with the object not only of promoting peace in that country itself,[2] but of preventing war between France and England.[3] And with the same end in view did he watch over Henry's Continental subjects,[4] and beg Louis VIII. at least to make a truce with Henry for four years,[5] reminding him that it was the general belief that the exceptionally long period of prosperity which had been enjoyed by France was due to the fact that it had had " Kings who were conspicuous by their faith and piety, and by their special devotion to the Holy Roman Church, which, by the will of God, is the mother and mistress of all Christians."[6]

Besides making unceasing efforts to maintain the peace of Europe in the interests of the Crusades, Honorius made equal efforts to raise money for the same purpose. He insisted that all [7] should pay the twentieth for three years prescribed by the Lateran Council, commanding the moneys collected to be paid over as usual to the Templars. The order of Cluny must subscribe the twentieth,[8] so must all clerics,[9] even those " in the

The Pope raises and grants money for the Crusades.

---

[1] His father, King John, died Oct. 19, 1216. Before John's death the Pope tried to preserve the peace in his Continental possessions. *Cf. Reg.*, n. 34, Sept. 16, 1216.

[2] *Reg.*, nn. 35, 386.

[3] *Ib.*, 1989, Apr. 1, 1219 ; 2056, May 10.

[4] *Reg.*, n. 615, June 10, 1217.

[5] *Reg.*, n. 4792, Feb. 21, 1224.

[6] *Ib.*, 5102, Aug. 3, 1224, or ap. *Royal Letters, Henry III.*, i, p. 541, ed. Shirley, *R. S. Cf.* a similar prohibition addressed to Henry, ap. *ib.*, p. 545.

[7] He raised the first tax in Hungary for a Crusade. *Cf.* Theiner, *Mon. Hungar.*, i, p. 3.

    Reg., 101–2, Nov. 12, 1216.

    See the encyclical, *Reg.*, 111, Nov. 21, 1216.   " Ut juxta decretum

Spains," as only so can the requirements of the Crusaders be met.[1] And yet, bearing in mind the needs of the poor, he exempts from payment " the provost and canons" of Mons Jovis (the Great St. Bernard), since they are already burdened with debt owing to the help they give to the poor pilgrims who cross over the dread pass.[2]

Not content, however, with compelling others to give of their substance to the Crusades, Honorius not only exhausted his treasury in the sacred cause, but even borrowed money that he might have the wherewithal to give.[3] Hence, his Register is full of letters in which he notifies different authorities in the Holy Land that he is sending them money which he would have spent " by the advice of the Patriarch of Jerusalem and its King, the Masters of the Templars, Hospitallers, and Teutonic Knights, and the Prince of the army of the Romans." [4]

Despite his general meekness, however, the aged Pontiff got very angry if anyone questioned his right to apportion the twentieth as he thought fit ; and so we find him ordering a certain canon of Aix and others to be sent to Rome as blasphemers and excommunicated persons because they declared that he had no right to divert it from the Holy Land to the Albigensian war.[5] On the

Conc. Lat. omnes clerici, tam subditi quam prælati vicesimam ecclesiasticorum proventuum usque ad triennium . . . solvant in subsidium Terræ Sanctæ." *Cf. ib.*, 381, Feb. 28, 1217 ; 1359 (*re* Holland), May 21, 1218.

[1] *Ib.*, nn. 337, 1116, 1634.

[2] *Ib.*, n. 1458, June 21, 1218.

[3] *Reg.*, 1634, Oct. 5, 1218. " Camera nostra pene penitus sit exausta." *Cf. ib.*, 1783, Jan. 4, 1219 ; 1808, Jan. 17, 1219 ; 4005, May 28, 1222 ; 2620, Aug. 18, 1220. " Cum nuper quidquid habuimus in Camera misimus in subsidium Terre Sancte propter quod multis tenemur debitis obligata." The Pope's greatest personal expenses seem to have been over the Crusaders from Rome itself.

[4] *Reg.*, 2195, Sept. 7, 1219. *Cf.* n. 1824, Jan. 23, 1219 ; 2114, June 15, 1219.

[5] *Reg.*, 3658, Dec. 23, 1221.

other hand, he was ready to allow his liegemen in Tuscany to help the Senator of Rome even against vassals of the Church, if they attempted to divert corn which would be required for the Crusade.[1]

The first effort of Honorius was to bring to a successful head the Crusade which had been inaugurated by Innocent and the Lateran Council. When Frederick was crowned at Aachen (1215), he had spontaneously assumed the Cross, and had induced others to follow his example,[2] so that Honorius, and those who had taken the Cross, naturally looked to him to take the leading part in the new Crusade. But there was no sincerity in Frederick, except in the pursuit of his own personal interests,[3] and these interests were comprised in his resolve, despite all promises to the contrary, to unite the crowns of Germany, Italy, and the Sicilies in his own person, and to make the imperial crown hereditary in his own family.

The so-called fifth crusade.

The Lateran Council had decided that the Crusaders should assemble at Brindisi and Messina by the first of July, 1217, and Innocent had promised to be present at the latter port so that " by our advice and authority " the expedition might be properly organized.[4] Accordingly, in reply to Frederick's congratulations on his accession, Honorius had called his attention to the position of affairs regarding the Holy Land,[5] as he had already reminded the faithful at large and of France in particular that the time fixed by the Council for the expedition to the Holy Land was drawing near, and must not be prorogued.[6]

Frederick's first failure to fulfil his obligations.

[1] *Ib.*, 569, May 10, 1217.

[2] *Cf. supra*, vol. xi, p. 193 ff.

[3] It has been said of him that " il avait la ruse d'un Cromwell avec l'absence de scrupules et la cruauté d'un Robespierre." Blondel, *Frédéric II.*, p. 15.

[4] *Cf.* the decree regarding the Crusade ap. Hefele, *Concil.*, viii, p. 154 ff.

[5] Ep. i, 289, Apr. 8, 1217.

[6] Potth., nn. 5380–1, Dec. 5, 1216.

" Take up then your arms like men, sharpen your swords, haste ye, soldiers of Jesus Christ, so that when the time comes you may cross over all together." [1]

Honorius was not, however, probably much surprised when he learnt that Frederick had no intention of going to the Holy Land with the other Crusaders in 1217. He had the excellent excuse that his rival Otho IV., if crushed, was still alive, and might prove dangerous if the King of the Romans left the country. It cannot be denied that there was some force in the excuse, but it may be noted now [2] that throughout the whole pontificate of Honorius, Frederick did nothing but make and break engagements to fulfil his vow. Whether there was any substance in his excuses or not was matterless to Frederick. He had no intention of keeping his promise to fight for the recovery of the Holy Land ; nor had he any concern whatever either for the disappointment and loss of time and money which his tergiversations brought on intending Crusaders, or for the want of success in which his failure to provide his promised co-operation involved those who actually proceeded to the Holy Land or to Egypt.

Meanwhile, Honorius continued to exert himself in the cause to which Frederick proved so false. The Crusaders were exhorted to meet Andrew, King of Hungary, in Cyprus,[3] and the faithful were urged to pray for the success of the expedition, and were told that, from advices received from the Holy Land, the Moslems had never been in such straits before. He himself, with the clergy and people of Rome, carrying the heads of the Apostles Peter and Paul, went barefoot in solemn procession of intercession from the Lateran to St. Mary

---

[1] *Ib.*, n. 5380.

[2] We shall return to the subject when speaking about Honorius' imperial relations.

[3] *Reg.*, nn. 672-3, July 24, 1217.

Major's.[1] Unfortunately, however, the Crusade which,
led by the Kings of Hungary, Cyprus, and Jerusalem,
landed on the coast of Palestine in 1217 effected nothing.
Andrew of Hungary returned home, and the King of
Cyprus died. However, on the arrival of fresh reinforcements in the following year, the King of Jerusalem, John
de Brienne, resolved to put into execution a plan which
had long been thought likely to produce the best results.
It was to attack the Moslems in Egypt. He accordingly
sailed thither, and laid siege to the strongly fortified
seaport of Damietta, which Honorius described as " the
gate and the protection of Egypt " (May, 1218),[2] and
which was situated on one of the eastern branches of the
Nile.

With the object of promoting concord among the leaders
and peoples who were encamped before Damietta, Honorius sent to them as his legate, Pelagius, cardinal bishop
of Albano. All were instructed to obey him, and were
urged to bring down God's blessing on the Christian army
by the virtue of their lives.[3]

In the midst of the conflicting accounts regarding
Pelagius which have reached us, it is not easy to discern
his real character. After balancing them, we may perhaps
correctly conclude that, while he was a man of upright
and virtuous character, he was a little disposed to believe
that his very position gave him a knowledge of military
affairs and political conditions. At any rate, even allowing
that the sending of cardinal Pelagius was a doubtful
boon to the Crusaders, there can be no doubt that the
exhortations which the Pope scattered broadcast were
advantageous to them. They brought them fresh recruits.
The papal letters hurried forward the embarkation at

[1] *Ib.*, n. 885, Nov. 24, 1217.
[2] *Reg.*, n. 4330.
[3] *Reg.*, 1350, May 18, 1218.

Genoa of the English cardinal Robert de Courçon, and
his Crusaders from France,[1] and brought them further help
from England.[2]

At length, in September 1219, El-Kamil, the Sultan
of Egypt, after having made vain attempts to relieve the
beleaguered city, endeavoured to come to terms with the
Christians. He is even said to have offered almost the
whole kingdom of Jerusalem in exchange for Damietta.[3]
But his offers were rejected, and the exhausted city was
stormed in November.

The Pope, who had been kept well informed of the
progress of the siege by Jacques de Vitry,[4] and others,[5]
wrote to congratulate the Crusaders as soon as he heard
of their success. He offered the most heartfelt thanks to
God for their victory, and assured the Christian host that
he would strive by his legates and his letters to animate
the faithful to hasten to their aid, in order that they might
be able to hold the possession which they had so gloriously
won.[6]

The Moslems
recapture
Damietta,
Sept., 1221.

Disheartened by the loss of Damietta, El-Kamil again

[1] *Reg.*, nn. 1580–1, Aug. 1218.

[2] *Ib.*, 1716, Nov. 1218. *Cf.* Roger of Wendover, *Flores hist.*, an.
1218, and *Memoriale Potestat. Regien.*, an. 1219, ap. *R. I. SS.*, viii,
p. 1088, where a full account of the siege of Damietta is to be found.

[3] By the Scholastic Oliverius, *Hist. Damiatina*, c. 16. This *Hist.*
is sometimes erroneously made to do duty as the third book of Jacques
de Vitry's, *Hist. Hierosol.* Mr. Stevenson, *The Crusaders in the East*,
p. 304 n., is convinced that "the alleged offer to restore (nearly) the
whole kingdom of Jerusalem must be an exaggeration." Our historian
Roger of Wendover, *l.c.*, an. 1219, iii, p. 58, puts down the rejection
of these terms to the legate ; but both Oliverius and Jacques de Vitry
(ep. to Master John and others, and ep. 4 to Hon.), who wrote on the
spot, show that the Templars, Hospitallers, and those with most
experience thought with the legate.

[4] *Cf.* four letters of his to Hon., ap. Martène, *Thesaurus novus*, iii.

[5] *Cf.* Walter of Coventry, *Memor.*, an. 1219, ii, 242, R. S. ; Röhricht,
Regest. Hier., n. 1217, etc.

[6] Ep. iv, 86, Feb. 24, 1220.

offered to make peace with the Crusaders on such favourable terms as the surrender of Jerusalem, Ascalon, and other important cities. In accordance with his instructions,[1] Pelagius communicated the proposed terms to the Pope. In his reply, although he expressed regret at the great loss of Christian life that the war had entailed, and at the labour and expense it had brought upon himself and others, he nevertheless declared that he was induced by the fresh undertaking which Frederick had just given that he would sail to the East in the near future to advise that the terms should not be accepted.[2] Honorius also made it clear that his decision had been influenced by the rumours that had reached him concerning the doings of *Prester John*.[3] He had been informed by Pelagius " that King David, who is called Prester John (presbyter Johannes) a God-fearing man," was threatening Bagdad " which is said to be the chief seat of the Caliph whom the Saracens call their high priest." This action of King David had had the effect of compelling the Saracens to divert their attention from the Crusaders in Egypt.[4] But as a matter of fact, Honorius had really heard of the exploits of Chingiz Khan and his terrible Tartars. They were to prove to be, as Alberic, whom we are here quoting,

[1] Ep. of Jan. 2, 1221, to Pelagius, ap. Rodenberg, i, p. 112.

[2] " Utilius consilium nobis videtur, adhuc manum misericordiæ Dei expectare, quam hujusmodi pactionibus inclinari." A postscript to a letter of June 21, 1221, to Pelagius, ap. Rod., p. 123.

[3] " Sicut dicitur, orientis se pluribus accingentibus ad subsidium Terre Sancte." *Ib. Cf.* ep. of Jacques de Vitry, ap. Giles, *Incerti auct. de rebus in sacro bello gestis*, p. 40 ff.

[4] Alberic Trium Font., *Chron.*, an. 1221, ap. *M. G. SS.*, xxiii, 911. *Cf.* the legate's account of " King David," ap. Eccard, *Corpus*, ii, 1451 ff. The account closes with a request that all Christians should pray for the continued success of David " because he was obedient to God and to Holy Church." See also *Ann. de Dunstap.*, pp. 66 and 69, ed. *R. S.*; and R. Coggleshall, *Chron.*, p. 190 *R. S.*

assures us that already some had averred them to be,
"neither Christians nor Saracens,"[1] but terrible foes of both.

The loss of Damietta.

Frederick also by letter after letter forbade the exchange
of Damietta for Jerusalem.[2] Acting on these orders, and
relying on the coming of the emperor,[3] Pelagius not only
rejected the terms of peace offered by El-Kamil, but with
many others, urged an advance against Cairo. Unfortunately, their exhortations were listened to. The Christian
host advanced along the right bank of the Nile, and, as
Pope Gregory IX. asserts, through the non-arrival of the
galleys promised by Frederick,[4] it was caught in a trap
in the midst of the branches and canals of the Nile " like
a fish in a net," and, to save itself from annihilation, had
to deliver up Damietta and agree to a peace for eight
years, or till the arrival of a Western Prince—presum-
ably Frederick II. (September 8, 1221).[5]

The loss of Damietta cast a gloom over Christendom,
similar to that caused by the failure of the second Crusade.
And now, as then, there were those who threw all the
blame for the disaster upon the Pope. Huon of St.
Quentin in his *La complainte de Jérusalem contre la cour
de Rome*,[6] was one of these ignorant or vicious critics.

---

[1] Alberic, *l.c.*

[2] See the letter of Gregory IX. (1228) against Frederick, ap.
Wendover, *l.c.*, iii, p. 163.

[3] " Il oïrent que li emperere avoit porté corone, et qu'il fasoit
grant apareillement de passer et d'als secorre." Ernoul et Bernard,
Chron., c. 38.

[4] " Qui ('the Christian army,' and not 'he,' i.e., the emperor, as
in the translation of Giles, ii, p. 503) etiam non fuisset in manibus
paganorum inclusus, si galeiarum subsidium, ut ex parte sua
(Frederick's) promissum fuerat . . . subsecutum esset." Wendover, *l.c.*

[5] On this see various letters in Wendover, an. 1222, *l.c.*, p. 75 ff. ;
Makrizi (†1441–2), *Hist. d'Égypte*, p. 336 ff., ed. Blochet; Oliverius,
ap. Eccard, ii, 1438 ; Ernoul et Bernard, *Chronique*, c. 39.

[6] Ap. K. Bartsch, *La langue et la littérature françaises*, p. 373 ff.,
Paris, 1887.

Grim must have been the smile of the Pontiff, whose exchequer had been ruined by the Crusade, if the " unjust and violent " [1] lines of the troubadour about the avarice of Rome ever met his eye. The poet even accuses Rome at this juncture of making men give up their intention of taking the Cross for money :

> " Rome, on set bien a escient
> que tu descroisas por argent
> ciax qui por dieu erent croisie."

Other singers, however, were wiser, and assigned the blame to the proper quarter. " Emperor," wrote one of them,[2] " Damietta (lost by your fault) is waiting for you (Frederick) ; and day and night the white tower weeps for your eagle whom a vulture drove away—dastard is the eagle that is conquered by a vulture ! Shame have you for that, but the Sultan has honour ; and besides the shame, you all receive such hurt that our religion suffers."

Honorius, however, had enough of the spirit of Innocent III. in him not to lose heart, as did Eugenius III. under similar circumstances. Up to the end of his life he continued to exert himself to set on foot another Crusade. He could not resist the heart-broken cries which, on behalf of the Christians in Egypt, were addressed " to the supreme pontiff of the most holy Roman Church and the universal Pope " by Nicholas, " humble patriarch of the See of Alexandria." The Patriarch told the Pope how dire was the persecution of the Christians by the infidel—the heavy taxes thay had to pay, the degrading occupations which

Renewed efforts of Honorius to the day of his death.

---

[1] The criticism of Gaston Paris, *La littérature française au Moyen Age*, p. 139. He adds that the *Besant de Dieu* of William, the Clerk of Normandy, on this same subject displays more moderation and more genuine enthusiasm.

[2] Peirol (†1225), ap. Raynouard, iv, p. 101, cited by J. H. Smith, *The Troubadours at Home*, ii, p. 394, New York, 1899.

they were forced to undertake, the limitations imposed on the practice of the Christian faith, and the indignities to which they were exposed. "As the Saints before the coming of Christ awaited the redemption which the Saviour was to bring, so do we long for the coming of your son the Emperor." [1]

As the want of a recognized leader had been one of the causes of the failure of the fifth Crusade, Honorius devoted himself especially to the task of inducing Frederick to fulfil his vow, and to lead a fresh Crusade against the infidel. At an interview with him at Ferentino (March, 1223), he obtained from him a promise on oath that he would set out in two years.[2] Of this the whole Christian world was at once informed by the Pope, and all were exhorted to get themselves ready for a new campaign.[3] With this in view, he strove to promote peace between England and France.[4] He moreover entered into correspondence with Georgia to secure the support of its warlike people for Frederick,[5] and with the King of Hungary regarding what he had heard of the doings of King David or Prester John. The Hungarian, however, replied that he could not understand the conduct of the Tartars.[6]

---

[1] Ep. ap. Rodenberg, i, p. 162, summer of 1223. Neale, *A hist. of the pat. of Alex.*, ii, p. 294, translates the whole letter. The eagerness with which the Crusaders expected Frederick is also clear from another chronicler. After the loss of Damietta, "expectant (the Crusaders) Frederici . . . adventum, quem summo desiderio sperant venturum." Reiner, *Annal.*, an. 1220, ap. *M. G. SS.*, xvi, p. 678.

[2] Ric. of San. Germ., an. 1223. *Cf.* Böhmer, *Reg. Imp.*, p. 303 ; and ep. Hon., *c.* Apr. 27, 1223, ap. Rod., i, p. 153.

[3] *Reg.*, 4262, March–Apr., 1223 ; 4903, March, 1224 ; 4919, Apr. 4, 1224. *Cf. Chron. reg. Colon.*, cont. iv, an. 1223, p. 252.

[4] Ep. ap. Rodenberg, i, p. 192.

[5] *Cf.* Raynaldus, *Ann. Eccles.*, an. 1224, nn. 17–19, or Rod., i, p. 178 ff.

[6] Ric. of S. Germ., *Chron.*, an. 1223. " Quod sit eorum (the men of King David) propositum nescitur," wrote the Hungarian monarch. There was evidently suspicion arising in the West as to the intentions of the Tartars.

Fresh efforts were also made to raise money both from the clergy and from the laity—the latter being asked to give every month for three years one *Turonensis* (denarius) or its equivalent.[1] With a view to deepening the interest of Frederick in the Holy Land, the Pope induced him to agree to marry Isabella (or Yolande), the only child of John de Brienne and heiress of the Kingdom of Jerusalem.[2]

But when the appointed day (June 24) in the year 1225 arrived for setting out, there came another request to delay the Crusade in order that he might first marry Isabella.

This time, however, he bound himself to set out in the August of 1227, under pain of excommunication. Isabella became his child-wife in November, and Frederick declared to the world his intention of sailing to the Holy Land in the August of 1227.[3]

Convinced that Frederick was at last in earnest, the aged Pontiff spent the last months of his life in rousing Europe by letters and by legates to prepare to accompany the emperor in August, 1227.[4] Prayers, processions, and collections were ordered everywhere.[5] But it was with Honorius as with his great predecessor. The Crusade which he actually launched, failed, and he did not live long enough to see the departure of the second one for which he had made such great exertions.

[1] *Ib.*, 4263 and 4329, Apr. 26, 1223.

[2] *Ignot. Cist.*, *Chron.*, an. 1224, p. 38, ed. Gaudenzi.

[3] Ric. of S. G., an. 1225. If he failed in his undertaking " ecclesia Romana sententiabit in ipsum et in terram suam de spontanea voluntate et jam prestito consensu imperatoris ejusdem." p. 117, ed. Gaudenzi. This is an extract from the encyclical letter of Fred. himself, which, sealed with a golden bull, he issued from San Germano in July, 1225, ap. H.–B., i, pt. ii, p. 501 f.

[4] *Reg.*, 6155-7, Jan., 1227. The success of the preaching of some of his legates was remarkable, especially, for instance, of Conrad, cardinal-bishop of Porto. He was sent to Germany. *Cf. Ann. S. Trudperti*, ap. *M. G. SS.*, xvii, 293 ; and *Ann. Neresheimenses*, ap. *ib.*, x, 23, " Et infinita millia hominum signata sunt."

[5] *Chron. Turon.*, an. 1226, ap. *M. G. SS.*, xxvi, p. 472.

CHAPTER III.

IMPERIAL POLICY.

Sources.—The documents concerning the reign of Frederick II. have been collected, as we have noted already, in the magnificent *Hist. diplom. Fred. II.*, of Huillard-Bréholles (H.-B.). See also Böhmer, *Regesta Imperii*, vol. v, parts i and ii, etc., supra, vol. xi, pp. 5 and 139.

Works.—To the works on Frederick II. by Huillard-Bréholles (in his fine *Introduction* to his *Hist. Dip.*), by T. L. Kington (Oliphant) and Blondell, cited in vol. xi, add essays on him by E. A. Freeman (" The Emperor Frederick II." ap. *Historical Essays*, first series, London, 1871) ; G. Audisio (*Sistema politico e religioso di Federico II.*) ; Dora G. McChesney (" Roger II. and Frederick II., a study in kinship " ap. *Dublin Review*, Apr., 1910) ; and B. Mitrović (*Federico II. e l'opera sua in Italia*, Trieste, 1890).[1]

See also on Frederick's great chancellor, Peter della Vigna, G. de Blasiis, *Della vita et delle opere di Pietro della Vigna*, Naples, 1860, and A. Huillard-Bréholles (H.-B.), *Vie et correspondance de Pierre de la Vigne*, Paris, 1865.

The imperial policy of Honorius. THE policy of Honorius III. towards the Empire and towards him who in his pontificate became its chief, was so completely dependent upon his policy towards the Holy Land as practically to be inseparable from it. He was prepared to make any sacrifice if he could free from the infidel the country which had been hallowed by the touch of the Saviour.

He knew better than anyone else that it was a principle with the Holy See that the Empire was never to be

---

[1] How narrow is the point of view of the last-named author may be inferred from his assertion : " Fino ai giorni nostri l'ira partigiana ha dichiarato Federico tiranno e nemico della Chiesa, perché si oppose all'apertà usurpazione con cui questa volle sotto la sua signoria ruinite le due podestà," p. 125.

allowed to become the heirloom of a family, and that it was the fixed and generally understood policy of his predecessors never to agree that the crowns of the Empire and of Sicily should be united in the same person. And yet, with hardly a word of protest, he beheld Frederick successfully take the first steps towards rendering the Empire the heritage of his family, and towards the firm welding of Sicily to the Empire. In the hope that the day would surely come when Frederick would fulfil his vow, and sail for the deliverance of Palestine, Honorius patiently suffered him over and over again to break his solemn engagements. Even when, through his delays, Damietta had been lost, and countless disappointments and troubles of every kind [1] had been inflicted on thousands of Crusaders in every land owing to reliance having been placed on a word which was repeatedly broken, either with cynical indifference or, more probably, with calculated selfishness, even then Honorius still relied on the broken reed, and went to his grave firmly trusting that the emperor would yet lead a Crusade against the Saracen. Neither the passionate outburst of the betrayed Crusader nor the calm reasoning of the more thoroughgoing among the cardinals could induce him to take any strong measures against Frederick.

Completely cognizant of the Pope's frame of mind, Frederick took every advantage of it ; for, if he was anything, he was utterly selfish.[2] For this his education was perhaps largely responsible, as he saw little of the

Frederick's relations with Honorius.

[1] As an instance of the loss to the cause of the Crusades brought about by Frederick's action we may note that, when in 1217 it was found that Frederick was not going to proceed to Palestine, the Count of Holland and others did not continue their journey thither. *Chron. reg. Colon.*, contin. iii, an. 1217, p. 240.

[2] Stubbs characterizes him as a "man of unbounded ambition . . . who never did a great or kingly act, or followed any but a selfish aim." *Lectures on Medieval and Modern hist.*, p. 199, Oxford, 1887.

unselfish devotion of loving parents, but passed all his childhood and youth in the midst of men who had no other thought than that of taking every advantage of his childish and youthful helplessness. Their conduct, far from inspiring him with disgust, only served him as an example. He resolved to profit by his instruction and to better it.[1]

Towards Honorius, Frederick had no cause to display his blacker qualities. Without serious opposition from him, and by the aid of some lying and perjury,[2] he succeeded in getting his son Henry elected King of the Romans, in securing the imperial crown and his hold both on the Empire and on Sicily, and in grasping the title of King of Jerusalem.

Frederick's appearance.

The man whose ambition was to be the ruin of his family, and of the imperial power,[3] and who was to do more than any other civil ruler in the Middle Ages to wreck the temporal influence of the Papacy, was a man of middle height, and, before advancing age brought on corpulence, of well-shaped body. His features were

[1] Abbot Menko (abbot from 1237–77) calls attention to Frederick's copying the "ways of the gentiles : Et heu, mores gentilium, quos apud eos didicit, ac ydolatriam et consortia eorum nimis diligens, etc." *Chron.* ap. *M. G. SS.*, xxiii, p. 553. He had, however, as his guardian for many years Gregory de Galgano, cardinal-priest of Sta. Anastasia. *Cf.* ep. Greg. IX. of Apr. 7, 1239, ap. Rodenberg, *Epp. Rom. Pont.*, i, p. 637.

[2] "Throughout his transactions with the Popes his conduct was a tissue of perfidy or violence, as best suited his immediate advantage." This is the verdict of the author of *The Germanic Empire*, i, p. 201, in the *Cabinet Cyclop.* With the gentle Honorius Frederick found perfidy sufficient.

[3] "His great charters to the spiritual and temporal princes of Germany dealt the death-blow to the Imperial power." Freeman, *The emp. F. II.*, p. 284. Hence, our old chronicler Capgrave, as Freeman notes, says that in Frederick's time "the empire, in maner, sesed here . . . for after that tyme that F. was deposed, the eleccion was dyvyded." *Chron.*, p. 149 *R. S.*

regular and pleasant, displaying, however, a sensual mouth. His complexion was fair ; and his hair like that of his father and grandfather, somewhat reddish. At least this is the description given of him by Western writers ; but an Arab writer who saw him during his Crusade of 1229 when he was thirty-five years of age, does not give anything like such a flattering description of the famous Frederick. Iafeï, who is here citing a contemporary, Ibn-giouzi, says that he was red, bald, small in stature, and of weak sight, and that, if he had been sold as a slave, he would not have fetched two hundred drachmas.[1]

Well favoured in body, as we must believe that Frederick was, despite Iafeï, he was also well favoured in mind. His understanding was clear, his knowledge considerable, and his accomplishments, many. His devotion to the study of mathematics was so pronounced as to cause Leonardo Fibonacci, the first Christian student of Algebra, to dedicate to him his *Treatise on Quadratics*.[2] The development at this period of the ancient medical school of Salerno certainly owed much to Frederick's interest in medicine, even if that interest did not lead him to write medical works himself.[3] From Ricobaldi of Ferrara we learn that he had a good knowledge of languages,[4] and according to a somewhat later historian, Giovanni Villani (†1348), he was " acquainted with the Latin tongue, and with our vernacular (Italian), with German, Greek, and Arabic." [5] In the most whole-hearted fashion did he devote himself to develop

His abilities and character.

[1] Given by Michaud, *Bibliothèque des Croisades*, iv, p. 430 f. *Cf.* Salimbene, *Chron.*, an. 1250, p. 349.

[2] H.–B., *Introd.*, p. Dxxxiii f. *Cf.* Salimbene, *Chron.*, pp. 203, 341 ff., 591 f.

[3] *Ib.*, p. Dxxxviii.

[4] *Hist. imp.*, an. 1250, ap. *R. I. SS.*, ix, p. 132.

[5] *Chron.*, l. vi, c. i.

all the Greek and Arabic civilization which he found around him, and, as a great help thereto, caused books to be translated from these languages into Latin by such men as Michael Scott.[1]

Frederick a patron of art. Of art in all its forms he was a lover and a patron. Whether he wrote poems in Latin may be doubtful, but his verses in Italian won for him from Dante the title of the father of Italian poetry. They sang not merely of love, like the Provençal lays of which they were imitations, but what was rarer then, of the beauties of nature.[2] At the court of this royal poet which, as again we learn from Dante, was the meeting-place of all the most distinguished men from far and near,[3] we may be sure were poets from Provence ; for the praises they bestowed upon him " prove that he must have been very gracious to them." [4] And it may be that it was from them that he learnt to set his poems to music.

Frederick a builder. Like all rulers of magnificent aims and views, Frederick was a collector of art treasures, and was particularly keen to have his name attached to imperishable monu-

---

[1] *Cf.* Fred.'s own letters of Aug. 9, 1232, etc., ap. H.–B., iv, pp. 381–6. See especially p. 384.

[2] H.–B., *l.c.*, p. Dxl f.

[3] The impression that Frederick made upon his age may be estimated from the frequency with which his name is connected with the popular stories current in Italy in the thirteenth century. Apparently about the beginning of the fourteenth century an unknown author collected together a hundred such stories (*Cento novelle antiche*) some of which seem to date from the twelfth century, but most of which are of the thirteenth. Many of these stories tell of the sayings and doings of Frederick. The very first *novella* (p. 27) says that he was truly " specchio del mondo. in parlare ed in costumi, ed amò molto delicato parlare " ; and in the seventeenth we read that men of talent in all the arts flocked to him (troubadours, artists, and even *necromancers*), because he treated men of this sort very generously. *Cf.* L. Cappelletti in his ed. of the *Novelle*, Firenze, 1884 ; Gaspary's *Italian Literature*, p. 164 ; Gebhart, *L'Italie mystique*, p. 159 ff.

[4] Gaspary, *Italian Literature*, p. 51 ff.

ments in stone. The remains of his palaces and castles at Foggia, Capua, Castel del Monte, etc., show him to have had no little taste for architectural beauty.[1] Combining, moreover, what writers have told us of the works which he caused to be executed with existing remains of some of them, we may conclude in a word that he practised himself to no slight extent, and largely encouraged in others, all those arts and sciences which in his day were used by men in improving or brightening the conditions under which they lived.[2]

Frederick was also deeply interested in Natural History, a science which, except at the hands of Albertus Magnus, did not receive much attention in the Middle Ages. To facilitate study in this direction he formed a regular menagerie with which, to the great wonder of the people, he sometimes paraded the country.[3] He proved, too,

He is interested in Natural History.

[1] H.–B., *l.c.*, p. Dxlvi. *Cf.* G. Villani, *Chron.*, vi, i (Selfe's trans.). " He raised in all the chief cities of Sicily and Apulia strong and rich fortresses which are still standing . . . and he made the park for sport on the marsh of Foggia in Apulia, and the hunting park near Gravina and Amalfi in the mountains." It may again be noted that by Apulia is meant the continental portion of the kingdom of the two Sicilies. Frederick's faithful justiciar, Thomas of Gaeta, exhorts his master not to oppress the poor for the sake of the castles which he is everywhere erecting, but rather to put up churches and monasteries which will benefit the poor. He reminds him also that if he wins the love of his subjects, there is no need for him to build lofty castles, nor to crown high hills with walls and turrets. *Cf.* a letter of his to F. ap. his *Briefbuch*, p. 55 f.

[2] " Omnium artium mechanicarum, quibus animum advertit. artifex peritus." Ricobaldi, *l.c.* *Cf. re* painting, F. Pipinus, *Chron.*, l. ii, c. 39, and see his coins (his *Augustales*) and his golden bullæ.

[3] H.–B., p. cxciii. Salimbene, *Chron.*, an. 1235, p. 35, says he himself saw the emperor's elephants, leopards, etc., at Parma. One of the chronicles records the death of one of his animals, " the beast which is called an elephant, bestia quæ vocabatur elephans." *Chron. de rebus in Italia gest.*, p. 215, ed. H.–B. His treatise on hawks has been published : " Reliqua librorum de arte venandi cum avibus . . . de falconibus, etc.," Aug. Vindelicorum, 1596. *Cf.* C. H. Haskins on this work in the *Eng. Hist. Rev.*, July, 1921.

by the work he wrote on hawks, and by the assistance he gave to one of his officials who composed a work on horses, that he had more than a visual knowledge of these animals.[1]

A law-giver.

Whether Frederick may be called a great soldier may be doubted. Villani[2] describes him as " courageous and prudent in arms," and certain it is that he was constantly at war. But, if he was only an " indifferent soldier," his clear mind enabled him to be a good law-giver. His *Constitutions* of 1231 were indeed but another expression of his determination to be lord and master, but they were of enormous advantage to the masses of the various peoples who inhabited the two Sicilies. They made Lombards, Normans, Greeks, and Saracens all equal before a common law. Opposed alike to the privileges of the nobles and of the communes, they protected the poor and the peasant.[3]

But, Frederick was a false friend.

In common with other great men, Frederick had the faculty of picking out great men to serve him. But, seeing that in all that he did he had only self in view, he threw them aside as soon as, from any cause, they ceased to be useful to himself. He only nourished pigs, he is reported to have said, that at some time he might have their fat.[4]

Frederick attracts great men.

Meanwhile, however, his magnificence, his need of men for his various enterprises, and the belief that he

---

[1] H.–B., p. DXXXV ff. ; Kington, i, 462 f.

[2] *L.c.*

[3] *Cf.* Kington, i, 363 ff., and Curtis, *Roger the Great*, p. 443 ff. Speaking of Frederick's opposition to the quasi independent commonwealths which were springing up in various parts of the Empire, Freeman says : " It is sad to see Frederick everywhere interfering to check this new birth of freedom." *The Emp. F. II.*, p. 299.

[4] " Imperator nullius amicitiam conservare sciebat, quin immo gloriabatur, quod numquam nutrierat aliquem porcum cujus non habuisset axungiam." Salimbene, *Chron.*, an. 1247, ap. *M. G. SS.*, xxxii, p. 199.

selected his dependents by their worth and not by their
birth,[1] brought gifted men to his court in crowds.[2]
He needed, for instance, men for his new University of
Naples which he founded by royal charter in 1224, in
order that those in his kingdom who were athirst for
knowledge might be able to find all learning at home
and might not have to beg for it elsewhere.[3] Inspired
by his example, and encouraged by his liberality and
courtesy, literary men, artists, lawyers, and soldiers
exerted themselves in his behalf ; and everywhere
throughout the two Sicilies the greatest intellectual
activity prevailed.

In many ways, then, as a man and a monarch Frederick *He was a moral failure.*
II. was a great success.[4] Morally, however, he was a
failure. His ambition was of that kind which o'er-
leaps itself, and his unbridled lust made him, as it ever
makes its slaves, savagely cruel. To gain his ends he
accounted no means too base, and to have the means
of gratifying his passions, whether of mind or body,
he never shrank from wringing money from his subjects.

As though he were a Sultan, Frederick kept a harem *He was impure.*
at his Saracen colony at Lucera. Not content with this,
he caused one to travel about with him on his military
expeditions, and was more distressed, we are told, at
the capture of one of them than at the loss of his troops

[1] " Jamsilla," *Hist.*, ap. *R. I. SS.*, viii, p. 522.

[2] *Ib.*, p. 495 f.

[3] E.g., in such a papal city as Bologna. He instituted at Naples
professors of all the faculties "ut . . . famelici doctrinarum in ipso
Regno inveniant unde ipsorum aviditatibus satisfiat, etc." See the
Charter, ap. Ric. de S. G., an. 1224. *Cf.* documents ap. H.–B., ii,
p. 447 ff. The University of Naples, however, was merely " a creation
of despotism," and was never a success as a University. *Cf.* Rashdall,
The Universities of Europe, ii, pt. i, p. 22 ff.

[4] Fisher, *The Medieval Empire*, ii, 61, regards him as " The most
gifted administrator of the Middle Ages, with . . . a passionate
enthusiasm for civilization . . . and a consuming thirst for work."

and treasure.[1]   To one who does not forget the women
of his harems and his other concubines there is no
need to prove at length that the emperor treated his
wives shamefully.   There is little doubt that he shortened
the lives of his last two wives, Isabella (or Yolande)
of Brienne and Isabella, sister of our Henry III., by the
jealous confinement under a guard of black eunuchs
to which they were submitted.[2]

He was cruel, and an un-believer.   Sensual without restraint, he was naturally cruel
without measure, and that, too, especially to women.[3]
Cruel to his wives, he was, like Henry VIII. of England,
cruel to those who had once been his favourites, and who,
unhappily for themselves, had served him better than

---

[1] For the authorities for these statements see H.–B., *l.c.*, p. cxc ff.
The references to Matthew Paris in the *R. S.* ed. are *Chron. maj.*,
an. 1243, iv, p. 268 ; an. 1244, iv, p. 357.   Many respectable writers
accuse him of still greater impurities ; and it may be that their accusations are well founded.   It is beyond all question that excessive
indulgence in one form of impurity begets satiety, and a consequent
craving for other and baser means of impure gratification.   Albert
von Behaim cites (n. 39, p. 124 ff.) a ballad which sings of Frederick's
grief for the loss of his harem at the great defeat inflicted on him at
Parma in 1248.

"Impius a facie fugit subsequentis,
Relictis amasiis subsequendo lentis,
De quo plus turbatus est status suæ mentis,
Quam de gente perdita vel auri talentis."

[2] *Ib.*, p. clxxxix.   With reference to Isabella, Matthew Paris says,
Hist. Angl., ii, 381 *R. S.*, "Deputavit (Fred.) . . . imperatricem
inclusam . . . spadonibus, et Mauris ementulatis et vetulis larvis
consimilibus, nocte dieque strictissime custodiendam."   *Cf.* Albert
von Behaim ; n. 5, p. 78 : "Cruelty, treachery, and lewdness are the
three blots that can never be wiped away from the memory of
Frederick II."   Kington, i, 474.

[3] To Salimbene, *l.c.*, pp. 31, 197 ff., 348 f., and the other authorities
cited by H.–B., pp. cxcvi ff. and cdlxxxvii, I will only add the Roman
continuation of the so-called *Chron. of Hugh of St. Victor*, an. 1220,
ap. *M. G. SS.*, xxiv, p. 99 f. ;   Mat. Par., *Chron. maj.*, an. 1247, iv,
613, and an. 1249, v, p. 60 ff. *R. S.*   The references to the biographer of
Gregory IX. are cc. 33 and 34 of Fabre-Duchesne's ed.

they had served their God.[1] Want of money for the
gratification of his vices or of his expensive tastes also
had its share in hardening the heart of Frederick.[2]
When he found that the confiscation of property for
treason was a convenient way of filling his coffers he
cared not who was made to suffer for that elastic " crime."[3]
" The last five years of the Emperor's life," says Kington,[4]
"are indeed a mournful spectacle ; his temper had been
soured by the sentence at Lyons and by the Apulian con-
spiracy ;   thenceforward he suspected everybody.[5]   In
despair he quoted the text :   ' They that were sometime
my counsellors have abhorred me ; and he whom I
loved most is turned against me.'   Job, xix, 19."[6]

The cruel husband, the faithless friend, was also the
treacherous politician[7] ; and the man of cynical impiety[8]
paid a childish heed to the utterances of astrologers.[9]
In formal documents addressed to St. Louis, King of
France, or to the whole world, Pope Gregory IX. declared
that it could be demonstrated that Frederick held views
which were incompatible not merely with Christianity

[1] H.-B., p. cxcv.

[2] For his ways of raising money by debasing the coinage, robbing
the church, etc., see cc. 31–7 of Gregory's biography just cited.

[3] H.-B., ib. Cf. Salimbene, Chron., p. 200. " Interficiebat enim
consiliarios et principes et barones suos, imponendo eis quod proditores
essent."

[4] Fred. II., ii, p. 452.

[5] Cf. Salimbene, Chron., an. 1247, p. 198.   On p. 200 we read :
" Faciliter enim turbabatur tunc temporis imperator, eo quod ab
imperio fuisset depositus, etc."

[6] Ib., p. 200.

[7] H.-B., ib., p. cxciv.

[8] Cf. n. 1 infra.

[9] Ib., pp. ccii, Dxxxi f.   Cf. Salimbene, Chron., an. 1250, p. 350 ff.
Blessed Jordan of Saxony, addressing Frederick II. especially, declares
that he put faith in auguries : " Dicitur autem de vobis quod Ecclesias
gravatis, sententias contemnitis, auguriis intenditis . . . Vicarium
Christi et b. Petri successorem . . . non honoratis." Vita Jord.,
c. 8, n. 52, ap. Acta SS., Feb. 13, vol. ii, Feb., p. 733 ; or c. 31 in the
Lives of the Brethren, Eng. trans., p. 109.

but with any form of revealed religion. " That pestilential
King," wrote the Pope, " presumed categorically to
affirm that—to use his own words—the whole world had
been deceived by three impostors, to wit, Jesus Christ,
Moses, and Mahomet . . . and that a man ought not to
believe anything except what he can prove by his natural
powers." [1]

Frederick was one of those who, in the words of the
Psalmist, would not understand. In order that he
might follow after the desires of his heart, he had
said therein, if not in his understanding, there is
no God.

With reference to all that is affirmed against the
moral character of Frederick, it has been said that,
as his public deeds were great and glorious, his private
conduct should be left to take care of itself. But against
this view Blondel has correctly urged that a man does
not possess two consciences, and that " history has not

---

[1] Ep. Greg. IX., June 21, 1239, ap. H.–B., *Hist. Dip.*, v, p. 239 f.
" Iste rex pestilentie a tribus baratoribus . . . Christo Jesu, Moyse
et Mahometo, totum mundum fuisse deceptum . . . mentiri pre-
sumpsit . . . et homo nihil debet aliud credere nisi quod potest vi et
ratione nature probare." *Cf.* his letter to St. Louis, Oct. 21, 1239,
ap. *ib.*, p. 457 ff. " No wonder," wrote Albert von Behaim, or at
any rate the author of a pamphlet against Frederick in 1245, " that
he holds the lives of men of no account . . . and heedlessly piles one
heinous sin on the top of another since he holds that (at death) the
soul is dissipated like a breath of wind." *A. v. B.*, ed. Höfler, p. 64.
Salimbene, *Chron.*, p. 344, following Innocent IV.'s bull of deposition,
says he caused the name of Mahomet to be invoked (decantari) "in
the Temple of the Lord " at Jerusalem. Menko, *Chron.*, an. 1241,
ap. *M. G. SS.*, xxiii, p. 536, says he had " multa signa incredulitatis."
" In that age there existed one great authority which operated powerfully on the side of the Pope, and fought against Frederick—this was
the power of *public opinion* . . . In addition to which, Frederick's
rash and capricious wit had too often thoughtlessly attacked sacred
objects ; whilst his life was stained with the excesses of sensuality.
Accordingly he sank more and more in general estimation, and it was
this that embittered the latter period of his life." F. Kohlbransch,
A Hist. of Germany, p. 239, London, 1844.

offered us a single example of a sovereign whose political
conduct has not been in strict correlation with his
private morality."[1]

However, whatever may have been Frederick's But he
religious belief as a man, as a king he inculcated the publicly
professed
strictest orthodoxy. This was to have been expected orthodoxy.
from him ; for he knew that by the very laws of the
Empire he could be at once deposed for any public
profession of heresy.[2] The Empire was fundamentally
Christian and Catholic in spirit and in form, in underlying
principle, and in outward organization. Frederick was
too wise to dream of attempting to change its constitution.
To destroy its Catholicity would have been to kill it,
and not even the powerful and unscrupulous Frederick II.
was strong enough for that. At the head, therefore,
of an Empire that was Catholic, Frederick made public
profession of the orthodox faith ; and, as far as in him
lay, took care that all subject to him should do the same.
He increased the severity of the laws against heretics,
at least against such anti-Christian and anti-govern-
mental sects as the Albigenses ; and he saw that the
laws against them were put into execution.[3] This he

[1] *Fréd. en Allemagne*, p. 12.

[2] The *Sachsenspiegel* of Eike von Repgow (see *supra*, vol. ix, p. xxvi,.
n., and p. 262 n.) teaches " that no one can be King who is under the
ban of the Church, and the ban of the Church may be lawfully imposed
if the emperor break his promise or abandon his lawful wife or destroy
God's house." By the "destruction of God's house " is meant
"heresy," as may be gathered from the words of a contemporary
evidently having these causes in his mind. Speaking of the deposition
of Otho IV., a writer states that "the emperor can only be excommunicated for three causes : Desertion of his wife, diminution
of imperial honour, heresy." *Disp. carm. conscript. inter Romam et
Papam de Ottonis IV. destitutione*, ap. Leibnitz, *SS. Rer. Bruns.*, ii,
530. Fisher, from whom we have drawn this note, adds that the
Sachsenspiegel " was antipapal, so much so indeed that many of its
provisions were subsequently condemned by the Pope." *Medieval
Empire*, ii, 58.

[3] H.–B., *Introd.*, p. cdlxxxviii ff.

did, not from any excessive zeal for the Catholic faith, but simply because those who held opinions, and practised customs condemned by the laws of the Empire, were not submissive to the head of that Empire, and therefore were by chastisement to be brought to due subjection and obedience.

Frederick aims at being supreme in matters spiritual as in matters temporal.

However, in process of time, and as his aims unfolded, Frederick found it convenient to give a more or less unobtrusive support to those sectaries who made a greater profession of zeal for a reformation of morals than for a renovation of doctrine. He gradually made it plain that he was aiming at being the whole and sole head of the Empire, the source of all power temporal and spiritual, the supreme governor of the Church and State. He wished for the absolute civil and ecclesiastical dominion of the Byzantine Basileus, and he strove to acquire what the Protestant Princes succeeded in securing in the sixteenth century, control over both the temporal and the religious life.[1]

Hence he strives to make himself regarded as specially sacred.

Accordingly, in imitation of the Cæsars of Constantinople, whom he heartily congratulated on their two-fold power, he endeavoured to engender the idea that his person was especially sacred. He constantly alluded to his *miraculous birth*,[2] called his mother *divine*,[3] and spoke of Iesi where he was born as " our Bethlehem . . . whence has gone forth the great leader, the Prince of the

[1] According to Huillard-Bréholles, *l.c.*, p. cdxcv, Frederick's supreme aim was " de régner sur les âmes comme il régnait sur les corps d'établir une Église indépendante dont il eût été le chef, et non seulement de se substituer au pape dans le gouvernement spirituel des États siciliens, mais aussi de faire triompher chez les États voisins la suprématie religieuse du pouvoir laïque."

[2] So says Benvenuto of Imola († 1391), Dante's commentator, *Excerpta historica ex commentariis B. de I. super Dantis . . . comœdias*, i, p. 1236, ed. Muratori, *Antiq. Ital. Cf.* H.–B., *ib.*, p. clxxviii.

[3] He speaks of Iesi " ubi nos diva mater nostra eduxit in lucem." H.–B., *Hist. dip.*, v, p. 378.

Roman Empire, to rule and protect his people " ! [1]
Hence, rebels against himself were properly to be accounted
" rebels against the empire of heaven." [2] He addressed
his son Conrad as " the divine offspring of the blood
of Caesar," [3] and in turn Conrad always spoke of himself
as " the son of the divine Augustus." [4] He is even said
to have usurped the homage due to the Pope as the Vicar
of Christ, by causing his feet to be kissed in the
church by the clergy and by commanding that
he was to be spoken of as holy. [5] The author of the
Life of Gregory IX. goes even further, and declares that
his constant intercourse with Greeks and Arabs resulted
in his regarding himself as a god in human guise, and
in believing that he could excel Moses, Jesus, and
Mahomet in founding a new religion, inasmuch as he
was already superior to them by his birth, power, and
glory. [6]

Further, he never lost an opportunity, when the He causes
contest between the Church and himself was at its himself to be extolled.
height, of extolling himself or of having himself extolled,
and of bringing humiliation on the Church. With his
connivance, *prophecies* anent the approaching collapse

[1] *Ib.*
[2] Ep. Fred. ap. *ib.*, p. 368.
[3] Ep. of Fred. (*c.* 1244), ap. *ib.*, vi, p. 245.
[4] See his letters, ap. *ib.*, v, p. 1172 ff.
[5] Alb. von Beh., *l.c.*, p. 62.
[6] C. 39 ed. Fabre-Duchesne in the *Lib. Cens.*, ii, p. 33. " At cum
eos (Moses, etc.) genere, prudentia, viribus, et honore precedere
publice protestetur . . . facile reputat novis ritibus eos superare
(et) culturam . . . apostolicæ sedis . . . sua superstitione delere."
Cf. Cronica minor Erpher., an. 1245.   In one of the *prophecies* mentioned
below there is a line to the effect that there shall be but one
hammer of the whole world (" Totius mundi malleus unus erit," *Mat.
Par.*, an. 1239), and another reading of the same prophecy makes
it clear that Frederick was to be that one hammer.   " Totius et subito
malleus orbis ero."   Ap. Richer († *c.* 1267) *Gesta eccles. Senon.*, c. 9,
ap. *M. G. SS.*, xxv, p. 304.

of the papal power were circulated, and even written up
in the Pope's bedchamber; [1] and men traversed Germany
bidding the people pay no heed to heretical Popes or
sinful prelates, priests, and monks, but only to them,
seeing that they were the sole repositories of truth.
Men were taught to think no more of the Pope, but to
pray for the Emperor Frederick and Conrad his son.
" They alone are the perfect and the just." [2]   In Rome
itself, where Frederick supported a party, his partisans
on the occasion of a religious function in which the image
of our Lord was being carried in procession, cried out :
" Behold, our Saviour cometh !   Let the Emperor (now)
come." [3]

Peter della Vigna, unable, so he writes, to praise
Frederick sufficiently, does not hesitate to apply to him
the words which the prophet applies to the Saviour—
" Let the clouds rain the just " [4]—speaks of him as the
" overseer " (antistitem) desired by reason, and prays
that " the name of Frederick the holy " may ever live
among the people. [5] A master Salvus declares that
Frederick " is God's vicar on earth " . . . and that his
" divine mind is in the hands of God." [6]

Similarly, as his partisans compared Frederick to
our Lord, so they likened his minister, Peter della Vigna,

---

[1] " Aliud scriptum quod videtur procurasse imperator.   Fertur
tamen pro vero quod inventi sunt hi versiculi in cubiculo Papæ
scripti."   *Mat. Par.*, an. 1239, iii, p. 550 f., *R. S.*

[2] Alb. Stadensis, *Chron.*, an. 1248.

[3] " Ecce Salvator," veniat imperator !   *Vit. Greg. IX.*, c. 42.   *Cf.*
from a *prophecy* of this period :   " Erit unus Deus, id est, monarcha.
Secundus Deus adiit."   Ap. Mat. Par., *Chron. maj.*, an. 1239, iii,
538 *R. S.*

[4] Isaias, xlv, 8.

[5] No. 107 among the letters, etc., of Peter, ap. H.–B., *Pierre de la
Vigne*, p. 425 f.

[6] " Cujus (Frederick) divina mens in manu Dei est."   No. 109,
ap. *ib.*, p. 428.

to the Lord's apostle Peter,[1] spoke of him as the rock
on which the imperial Church was founded,[2] and assured
him that he had been appointed by the Prince, " the
sight of whom surpassed all the joys of Paradise," " the
true vicar " to oppose the false one, i.e., the Popes.[3]

Frederick's aspirations to be as supreme in the spiritual
world as in the temporal, to be, as our Henry VIII.
subsequently became, " the supreme governor " of
Church and State, could not escape the notice of the
Popes. Gregory IX. often reproached him for interfering
with things spiritual,[4] for raising himself above God,
despising the privileges of Peter, taking possession
of the Patrimony of Peter as a sign of his universal
dominion, and for threatening to overthrow the chair
of Peter and to seat himself in the temple as a priest.[5]
Gregory's successor, too, Innocent IV., declared that
Frederick reckoned that he was possessed of but little

The Popes note Frederick's ecclesiastical aspirations.

[1] Nos. 108, 110, *ib.*

[2] " Unde non immerito me movet hæc externa relatio quod Petrus
(della Vigna) in cujus petra fundatur imperialis Ecclesia cum augustalis
animus roboratur in Cœna cum discipulis, tale verbum potuit edixisse
quia dum me facerem eligi, faceretis subsequenter in vacante ecclesia
promoveri." No. 111, *ib.*, p. 433. *Cf.* S. Mat., xvi, 18. " Tu es
Petrus, etc."

[3] No. 110, *ib.*, p. 431. " Ideo vos (the Peter who loved him)
constituit dominus in faciem nunc prælati sed prævaricantis Ecclesiam,
ut ubi dudum falsus Christi vicarius commissum sibi vicariatum
depravans . . . multos fama, rebus et corpore deformavit, verus
Petrus vicarius justicia regat."

[4] Ep. ap. H.-B., *Hist. dip.*, iv, 919 f.

[5] Ap. *ib.*, v, p. 777. " Super omne quod dicitur Deus aut colitur
elevatus . . . Christi claves et Petri privilegium vilipendens,
irreverenter divinis interesse presumit . . . patrimonium Petri . . .
ditioni suæ in signum universalis dominii reservavit, Petri sedem
evertere minatur et fidem ad gentilitatis ritus subrogare priores, et
velut in templo sedens sacerdotis usurpat officium." Frederick himself, in writing to our King Henry III., says that Gregory accused him
of endeavouring to overthrow the Roman Church : " quod nos ad
eversionem R. ecclesiæ . . . procedere nitebamur." Ep. ap. *Mat.
Par.*, an. 1239, iii, p. 637 *R. S.*

if he were only first in things temporal, and if the things of the soul escaped his jurisdiction.[1]

That the Popes were not mistaken in their estimate of Frederick's aims in the world of spirit, is rendered almost certain by that monarch's language to the Greek emperor of Nicæa, John Vatatzes. In his letters to him and to other Eastern potentates, he made it plain that he envied the absolute power of the Greek emperors in Church and State alike. He impressed upon John that all the princes of the world have reason to hate the prelates of the Church. All of them are eager for " a pestiferous liberty," [2] and those of the West are even secretly aiming at " making shipwreck of our life." " Happy Asia ! Happy potentates of the East who have no reason to fear either the arms of your subjects or the machinations of your priests." [3]

Moreover, as on the one hand he strove to encourage the idea of his own sacred character and exalted position even in the domain of the Church, so on the other hand, did he endeavour to eradicate from the minds of his contemporaries their high opinion of the power of the Popes and of the sacredness of their persons. Speaking, for instance, of Innocent IV., he alludes to him as " that

---

[1] Ep. Inn. IV., Dec. 7 or 8, 1248, ed. Höfler, p. 215, or ap. H.-B., ib., vi, p. 678.

[2] Ep. ap. H.-B., ib., vi, p. 685. " Illi quidem pestifere libertatis abusum ambiunt."

[3] Ib. Here, indeed, we have one despot writing to another. Frederick, like all other despots, knew well that the surest way to enslave the State is to enslave the Church. Cf. his boast in another letter to Vatatzes : " A nobis omnia juxta mandata nostra diriguntur et gubernantur." Ep., May to June, 1250, ap. ib., p. 772. I would venture to quote with approval the following from Miss A. Gardner's excellent little work The Lascarids of Nicæa, p. 173 n. " Recent critics are disposed to think that Huillard-Bréholles overrates the importance of Frederick's ecclesiastical ideals. But his views seem to derive confirmation from a study of Frederick's correspondence with Vatatzes."

man " (iste) " who is called the Prince of the Priests,"
and he assures the Greek emperor, John Vatatzes, that
the bishops, no doubt in his mind the Bishops of Rome
especially, were " not pontiffs of the Church of Christ,
but ravening wolves, savage beasts who devour Christ's
people." [1]

Writing to different princes after his excommunication,
first in 1227 by Gregory IX., and then in 1245 by Innocent
IV., Frederick denounced the Pope and the various
members of the Roman Church as men wholly taken
up with extorting money, oppressing the free, and
disturbing the peaceful, and as completely devoid of
the evangelical virtues, and wallowing in wealth and
luxury. [2] Accordingly he called on all Princes to help
him to do his duty, which was to reform the Church
by furnishing it with more worthy ministers. [3]

As time went on there was no limit to his pretensions Frederick
and to his cruelties. For he did not allow his ideas strives to
to remain in the land of theory and literature. Becoming his view.
more and more irritable as time went on, and as he met
with more and more uncompromising opposition to his
despotic ideas with regard to Church and State from
the Pope and the cities of Lombardy, he proceeded as
far on the road of schism as he was permitted " by

[1] One of four of Frederick's letters to Vatatzes which exist in a Greek
translation, and have been edited by N. Festa, *Le Littere greche di
Federigo II.*, Florence, 1898. We quote from H.-B.'s Latin version,
Hist. Dip., vi, 772 f. *Cf. ib.*, p. 760.

[2] *Cf.* his letter to Henry III. (Dec., 1227) *as given by Matthew Paris*
in an abbreviated form of his own, ap. H.-B., *Hist. D.*, iii, p. 48 ff. ;
and that to all princes (Feb., 1246), ap. *ib.*, vi, p. 390 ff. " Isti (the
Pope, and the greater churchmen) seculo dediti et ebriati, deliciis,
Deum postponunt, quorum ex affluentia divitiarum et opum omnis
religio suffocatur."

[3] Ep. of March, 1249, " to all the Princes," ap. *ib.*, p. 705 ff.
" Assistite nobis . . . ut ipsorum omnino supercilium deprimentes
sacrosanctam Ecclesiam . . . dignoribus fulciendo rectoribus . . . in
melius reformemur."

the state of feeling at the time and by the secret opposition of his own subordinates." [1] About a year before
he died, he issued orders to his officials in the kingdom
of Sicily actually to commit to the flames such as
introduced papal letters into the kingdom, spoke or
acted against him in the name of religion, or deviated
from a code of conduct laid down by himself. Those
of his subjects who killed such persons " at sight " were
not to be troubled. [2]

Frederick
more
moderate
during the
pontificate
of Honorius.

However, whilst the mild Honorius was Pope, Frederick
had no cause to display towards the Church the violent
side of his character. For one reason he was engaged
in consolidating his power in Germany and in his kingdom
of the two Sicilies, and for another, he was able to get
his way with the aged Pontiff by chicanery and perjury.
But if he did not make serious attempts " to corrupt
the unity of the faithful," [3] i.e. to establish a national
Church till after the Council of Lyons (1245), he very
early gave every indication of his desire to absorb the
Church in the State. The Popes, therefore, had from
the very beginning every right to oppose Frederick,
if not for his personal immorality and his private unbelief,

---

[1] H.-B., *Introduc.*, p. ᴅi.

[2] " Quos libet . . . si a capitulorum forma quam tibi dirigimus
interclusam aliquo modo compereris detorsisse . . . submissis torturis
igneis, in bona sequacium puniri facias." Ap. *Hist. Dip.*, vi, p. 701.
Cf. the foll. letter. As early as 1243 he had hanged two Franciscans
for carrying letters which were said to contain exhortations to certain
nobles to take up arms against the emperor. Mat. Par., *Chron. maj.*,
an. 1243, iv, p. 256 *R. S.* See also *ib.*, p. 278, for the ferocious doings
of his son Conrad at the same time.

[3] Salimbene, *Chron.*, an. 1283, p. 438, avers that Frederick
attempted " subvertere ecclesiasticam libertatem, et corrumpere
fidelium unitatem." Freeman, in his essay on Frederick, p. 310,
does not go quite far enough when he says that the emperor's main
object was " the depression of the spiritual, and the exaltation of the
temporal, power " ; but he does on p. 313, when he shows that
Frederick's aim was the establishment of a European Caliphate.

if not for his attacks on their proprietary rights, at least for his overt attempts to enslave the Church.[1]

We may perhaps now with advantage briefly recapitulate all that we have said of Frederick II. by means of the short, safe summary of Salimbene, saying with that worthy gossip, that " if he had been a good Catholic, and had loved God, the Church and his own soul, there would have been very few emperors to equal him." [2] As it was, however, his great lack of moral fibre left Frederick II. all too small to wear the imperial crown with honour.[3] "Frederick," says Freeman, "founded nothing, and he sowed the seeds of the destruction of many things." [4]

Though much distressed, as he said, at the death of Innocent, Frederick lost no time in congratulating his successor on his accession, and in professing his devotion towards him. While thanking the King for his courtesy, Honorius assured him that he was anxious for " his exaltation," informed him that he was sending him a legate to treat of the needs of the Holy Land, and urged him to remain true to the Roman Church in order that its zeal in his behalf might never lessen.[5]

Efforts of Honorius in behalf of Frederick.

---

[1] There is nothing to be learnt about Frederick's character or policy from Theodore II. Lascaris' funeral oration on him. It is in the main rather an apology for rulers in general, on the lines that the good they do is buried with them, whereas any evil they may have done lives after them. " Καὶ τὰ μὲν οἱονεί τάφῳ στελλονται τὰ ἐσθλά, τροπαίῳ δὲ φαυλισμοῦ ὑψοῦνται τὰ στυγητά." The oration is printed by J. P. Pappadopoulos at the end of his life of *Théodore II. Lascaris*, Paris, 1908.

[2] *Chron.*, an. 1250, p. 349. *Cf.* pp. 591–2.

[3] As a mere matter of fact, the imperial crown was too large for Frederick. Salimbene, who once held it in his hand, and who, comparing it to a jar, says it was of more use as a piece of valuable treasure than as an ornament for the head, assures us that, but for a special contrivance, it would have covered Frederick's whole head and face. *Chron.*, p. 203.

[4] *Essay*, p. 284.

[5] Ep. i, 289, Apr. 8, 1217.

As evidence of this zeal, the Pope sent, on the very next day, a letter " to all the princes both ecclesiastical and secular of Germany (Alamannie)," in which he exhorted them to stand fast in their fidelity to Frederick " the King of Sicily and Emperor elect," as it was the Pope's intention " to forward his advancement to the best of his ability." [1]

The coronation of Peter of Courtenay, 1217, Apr. 9. Honorius was very soon to be called upon to give proofs of his intention to promote the honour of Frederick. Henry of Flanders, the Latin Emperor of Constantinople, had died in 1216, and its barons had then at last elected to succeed him the grandson of Louis VII. of France, Peter of Courtenay, count of Auxerre. On his way to the East, Peter and his wife Isabella (or Jolanda) went to Rome to receive the imperial crown at the hands of the Pope.

There was then in Rome Ulric, abbot of St. Gall, the head of the embassy which Frederick had sent to congratulate Honorius on his accession.[2]

In the interest of his master, whom he wished to see sole lord of the East and West, Ulric endeavoured to prevent the coronation of Peter. He maintained that he could not be made emperor except with the consent " of the Prince of Princes." Though Honorius would not hearken to this assertion, Ulric succeeded in inducing him not to crown Peter within the. city, nor to permit him to wear his crown in the city. The new aspirant to the Empire had, therefore, to be content with a coronation in S. Lorenzo fuori-le-mura.[3]

After the ceremony, Honorius wrote to Gervase, patriarch of Constantinople, telling him of what he had done,

---

[1] Ep. of Apr. 9, 1217, ap. Rod., p. 22.

[2] Ep. ap. H.-B., *Hist. Dip.*, i, p. 504.

[3] Conrad de Fabaria, *Casus S. Galli*, c. 8, ap. *M. G. SS.*, ii ; *Ann. Cavenses*, ap. *ib.*, iii, 193 ; Renier, ap. *ib.*, xvi, 675. Peter never saw Constantinople. He was captured in Greece and killed in prison.

and assuring him that he had performed the ceremony in consequence of the earnest request of Peter, and without prejudice to the rights of the patriarch of Constantinople, to whom it normally belonged to crown the Byzantine emperors. [1]

We may here still further interrupt the course of our narrative in order to conclude the relations of Honorius with the ill-starred Latin Emperor. After his coronation Peter sailed from Brindisi to Durazzo, accompanied by John Colonna, cardinal priest of Sta. Prassede, who had been attached to him by the Pope " as a guide and defender on his journey," according to the phrase of the Chronicle of Ceccano. [2] By a vain attempt to seize Durazzo for the Venetians, Peter had the misfortune to offend Theodore Comnenus, the ambitious Despot of Epirus, through whose dominions he had to march, and who claimed that city as his own. [3] By treachery the Despot succeeded in seizing the emperor and the legate and in killing or dispersing his small army. [4] The Pope was naturally very much distressed, and at once wrote (July 28, 1217) to Andrew, King of Hungary, to the Prince of Achaia, to the Governor (Baiulus) of Constantinople and to the Doge of Venice begging them to work for the release of the emperor and the Legate. [5] He also wrote to the Archbishop of Thessalonica and to Theodore himself, pointing out what an outrage it was for a Prince who professed to be a Catholic to seize a legate of the Roman Church. [6] As the Despot paid no heed to the remonstrances either of the Pope

[1] Ep. of Apr. 12, 1217, ap. Horoy, ii, p. 360.

[2] Or of *Fossanova*, as it is otherwise called, ap. *R. I. SS.*, vii, p. 895. See also the letters of Honorius addressed to the clergy and laity of Constantinople and Achaia (Apr. 21, 1217). *Reg.*, n. 526.

[3] Robert of Auxerre, *Chron. Contin. II.*, ap. *M. G. SS.*, xxvi, p. 282.

[4] "Proditionaliter captos," say the Pope, *Reg.*, n. 684, and the Chroniclers just cited.

[5] *Reg.*, nn. 684–5, 688–9.

[6] *Ib.*, nn. 687 and 691 of about the same date.

or of anyone else, Honorius ordered a Crusade to be preached against him in France for the delivery of his august prisoners.[1] This, or the fact that Peter died in prison (1218),[2] resulted in the release of the cardinal.[3] Isabella, who had gone to Constantinople by sea from Brindisi, ruled in her husband's stead, but did not long survive him.

Death of Otho IV. This year, too, Frederick's rival, the emperor Otho IV. died (May 19, 1218), after he had been absolved from excommunication by the bishop of Hildesheim,[4] and had ordered his brother Henry, duke of Brunswick, to give up the imperial insignia, " the Holy Cross, the Lance, and the Crown, to whomsoever the princes should elect as emperor." [5] Henry, however, showed himself unwilling to hand them over to the duly elected Frederick, who at once appealed to the Pope for his assistance to recover the regalia.   In his letter to Honorius on the subject, Frederick inaugurated the policy which he pursued throughout all his dealings with him.   He put forward all his requests under cover of the interests of the Crusades.   Accordingly, in this case, he professed the greatest anxiety at the dangerous position of the Christian army in Egypt, assured the Pope of his firm resolve to succour the Holy Land,[6] and, while acknow-

---

[1] *Ib.*, n. 859, Nov., 1217.

[2] Ernoul, *Chron.*, pp. 391–3, ed. Mas Latrie ; P. Mouskes, *Chron.*, v, 23016 ff. ; Pipinus, *Chron.*, i, 38 ; Ric. of S. G., *Chron.*, 1217 ; Dandolo, *Chron.*, l. x, c. 4, n. 28.

[3] From ep. Hon., March 17, 1228, n. 3863, it is clear that the legate was free in 1218.

[4] *Ann. Stad.*, an. 1218, ap. *M. G. SS.*, xvi. *Cf. ib.*, p. 299. Honorius confirmed the absolution. *Cf.* Chounradi Schirensis *Annal.* an. 1218, ap. *ib.*, xvii, p. 632 ; Richer, *ib.*, xxv, p. 296 ; *Chron., princip. Brunsvic.*, n. 7, ap. *M. G. SS.*, xxx, p. 24 f.

[5] Kington, i, p. 167, quoting from Otho's will.

[6] " Firmum propositum de succursu Terræ Sanctæ cordi nostro diutius reservatum . . . firmius roboratum, etc." Ep. Jan. 12, 1219, ap. H.-B., i, p. 584 ff.

ledging that he held the Empire " by the grace of God
and of the Roman Church," begged the Pope to threaten
with excommunication those Crusaders who should not
have set out by the feast of St. John the Baptist (June 24).
Then he inserted his request that the Pope would by
excommunication and interdict compel Henry of
Brunswick to yield up the imperial insignia to him.[1]
He brought his letter to a close by urging the Pope to
prompt action, lest any failure in the matter of the Crusade
should be attributed to him.[2]

But though Honorius at once complied with Frederick's
requests, bidding Henry give up the insignia of empire [3]
(which were consequently duly handed over to him),[4]
and issuing the required threats of excommunication,[5] he
had soon cause to make known his suspicions that the
emperor-elect had no intention of taking the Cross,
but was pursuing his own interests. He was working,
it was said in the papal curia, to have his son elected
King of the Romans, a thing which he had promised
not to do ; he was conniving at an attempt of Raynald,
son of Conrad, once duke of Spoleto, to possess himself
of the patrimony of the Church, by allowing him to
assume the title of duke ; and he was attacking ecclesiastical

Marginal note: Frederick's appeals for delays regarding the Crusade, 1219-20.

[1] " Petens ut comitem Heinricum de Brunswick pro eo quod
coronam, lanceam, et alia insignia sibi non resignaverit . . . ex-
communicari . . . faciat." *Ib.*
[2] In a note to this letter, H.-B., citing the *Chronicle* of *Ursperg*
(an. 1218), observes that in the preceding year (1218) certain German
Crusaders had been hindered in Apulia from proceeding to the help
of their brethren, that this hindrance was naturally ascribed to
Frederick, and that hence there seems " good reason to doubt of his
good faith."
[3] Ep. Feb. 8, 1219, ap. Rod., i, n. 92, p. 66 ; or H.-B., i, 591.
[4] Albert Stad., *Chron.*, an. 1219, ap. *M. G. SS.*, xvi. *Cf. Ann. S.
Trudperti*, an. 1218, ap. *ib.*, xvii, p. 293.
[5] *Cf.* his letters of Feb. 11, 1219, Nos. 1867-9, ed. Pres. ; or ed.
Rod., i, p. 67 f. " Semper nocuit differe paratis," he reminded
Frederick.

freedom by interfering with elections. To these charges Frederick gave evasive answers. With regard to the first charge, he replied that he was merely providing for the good government of the empire in his absence "in the service of Christ." As for the second charge, it was, he urged, quite customary in Germany to give the title of duke to the son of a duke even if he had no fief, and finally he declared that he did not interfere in ecclesiastical elections. He only made suggestions.[1]

The sinister rumours which reached the Pope about Frederick's doings came hand in hand with one request after another from Frederick himself for deferring the date fixed for the departure of the Crusade. Honorius agreed first to its being put off till the feast of St. Michael (September 29)[2]; then till after Frederick's coronation; then again,[3] under threat of excommunication in case of failure to keep the engagement, till the feast of St. Benedict (March 21), in 1220;[4] and on the day before that feast arrived (March 20) he agreed, "not without many misgivings," to get a further delay till May 1.[5]

Frederick's excuses and promises, 1219–20.

Meanwhile, assuring the Pope that he could never thank him enough for his goodness to him, and at the same time asking for the imperial crown, he denies that he has made any grants of the lands of the Church,[6] declares to the Pope that he has ordered his agents to respect papal rights in Ferrara,[7] and renews to Honorius at Hagenau the promises he had made to Innocent III. at Egra in Bohemia on July 12, 1213. He also renewed

---

[1] See a document of May, 1219, ap. Rod., i, p. 69.

[2] No. 2071, Pres.

[3] No. 2195, *ib.*

[4] *Ib.*, n. 2207, ep. of Oct. 1, 1219.

[5] *Ib.*, n. 2372.

[6] H.-B., i, 636, June 16, 1219.

[7] *Ib.*, i, 673 f., ep. of Sept. 6, 1219. " Revera civitas Ferarie Romani pontificis est et terra ecclesie," says Salimbene, *Chron.*, p. 165.

the oath he had taken on the same occasion.[1] A few
months later, " as he owed everything to the Roman
Church,"[2] he told Honorius that he had sent his envoys
to impress upon the Roman people his devotion to the
Pope, and to induce them to show proper respect to his
Holiness.[3] Then, while hinting that the steps he is taking
regarding the Crusade may delay his departure beyond
the appointed day, he expresses a hope that the Pope
will allow him to keep the kingdom of Sicily during his
lifetime.[4] And if indeed it be true that he has issued
orders to papal cities, he did it in ignorance that they
were under the jurisdiction of the Roman Church.[5]
About the same time, too, he gave orders that his subjects,
whether in the Empire or in Sicily, should put pressure
upon the people of Spoleto and Narni should they be
unwilling to obey the Pope.[6]

Under cover of these suave professions of honourable
conduct, Frederick was steadily pursuing his own ends,
which at the moment were to secure for his son recognition
as King of the Romans, and for himself the reception
of the imperial crown. In April, by winning over the
ecclesiastical princes by promises of privileges,[7] he contrived to bring about the election at a Diet in Frankfort
of his firstborn son Henry as King of the Romans.

The young Henry is recognized as King of the Romans, 1220.

[1] Documents of Sept., 1219, ap. H.-B., i, p. 657 ff.

[2] Ep. of Feb. 19, 1220. " Humbly inclining before the Pope's feet,
utpote qui per Romane Ecclesie et vestre paternitatis grata subsidia
et favorem reminiscimur nos adeptos quidquid honoris et glorie
possidemus." H.-B., i, p. 741 ff.

[3] *Ib.*

[4] *Ib.* If the Pope granted his petition : " Quis fidelior, quis accepti
beneficii magis memor ? "

[5] Ep. of Feb. 29, 1220, ap. Theiner, *Cod. Dip.*, i, p. 49.

[6] Ep. of Feb. 28, 1220, ap. *ib.*

[7] See his decree in their favour of Apr. 26, 1220, ap. H.-B., i, 765 ff.,
in return for the assistance they had given him in gaining the empire,
" et demum filium nostrum Heinricum in regem . . . concorditer
elegendo."

No doubt with a view to placating the Pope, the assembled princes renewed the assurance already made that the Empire should not be united to Sicily,[1] and seriously discussed the question of the Crusade, inasmuch as, says the monk Reinerius of Liège, Frederick was, by reason of his power in Apulia and Sicily, in a better position to save the Oriental Church than any other King.[2] Pressure, too, was put upon those who had taken the cross to set out at once, and it was decided that Frederick should proceed to Rome to receive the imperial crown.

Frederick prepares the way for his coronation, 1220.
To prepare the road for the " Rome-journey," Conrad, bishop of Metz, was dispatched to Italy as imperial legate in order to receive the oaths of fidelity from the various dignitaries, ecclesiastical and civil, and to make peace.[3] Some time before giving Conrad his commission, the emperor-elect had written to secure the goodwill of the Roman Senate, and to urge upon them the need of making peace with the Pope; and he had received from them an answer in which he had been

[1] *Cf.* their proclamation, ap. *ib.*, p. 763 f., Apr. 23. They made the declaration : " quod imperium nihil cum dicto regno habeat unionis vel alicujus jurisdictionis in ipso," to take away all occasion of discord between the Church and State : " ut tollatur de medio omnis materia scandali, dissensionis . . . inter ecclesiam et imperium." They were renewing the undertakings of Hagenau, Sept., 1219.

[2] *Chron.*, an. 1220, ap. Böhmer, *Fontes*, ii, 386, or *M. G. SS.*, xvi, p. 678. Reiner (†1230) continued the annals of Lambert the Little. He is an excellent authority. *Cf. Chron. reg. Col.*, 1220, p. 251, ed. Waitz.

[3] See Frederick's announcement of Conrad's appointment to all the officials of Italy. He was sent " ut ipse fidelitates et alia jura a vobis recipiat et discordiis tolendis nobis viam planam faciat, quatenus adire ad coronam possimus." Apr. 17, 1220, ap. H.-B., i, 753. Frederick afterwards declared that Conrad had also been instructed to inform the Pope about the election of Henry as King of the Romans. Ep. of July 13, 1220. If that were so, it would seem as if the Diet of Frankfort had been held before Apr. 17.

thanked by them for the affection which he had manifested to the Roman Republic. They had also thanked him, " who had been brought up on the milk of the Church . . . and was its advocate and defender," for his words to them regarding the devotion they owed to the Roman Church "which had been established (fundata) in the City not by men but by Jesus Christ." They had assured him that they would do their best to preserve the bond of peace which ought to exist between them, and that they would make the greater effort to preserve it, inasmuch as they desired that " the solemnity of his coronation might be conducted by the supreme Pontiff in peace and quiet." [1]

On April 10, probably before the holding of the Diet of Frankfort, Honorius promised to crown Frederick and to send a legate into Germany to keep it in peace, and free " from heretical depravity." [2] But on hearing of the action of the Diet, and finding that the King was not ready for the Crusade,[3] Honorius began to be more than ever suspicious of his good faith. Letter after letter, however, reached Rome from Frederick in which he assured the Pope that Henry had been elected King of the Romans in his father's absence, in a wholly unexpected manner, for the sake of the peace of the empire, and that he himself, inasmuch as the election had been made without any consultation with the Pope,[4] had refused to sanction it unless each elector drew up an account of his action, and sent one of their

Frederick quietens the suspicions of the Pope.

---

[1] March, 1220, ap. H.-B., i, p. 747 ff. The letter concluded thus : " Quicquid commodi vel honoris ipsi (the Roman Church) feceritis, nobis qui sumus Ecclesie catholici filii, reputabimus esse collatum."

[2] Ep. ap. Pressutti, *Reg.*, i, n. 2392.

[3] Ep. ap. *ib.*, nn. 2468-9, May, 1220.

[4] " Sicut fuerat celebrata (the election of Henry) absque vestra notitia seu mandato sine quo nihil presumimus nec volumus aliquid attentare, ipsi electioni contradiximus consentire." Ep. of July 13, 1220, to Hon., ap. H.-B., i, p. 802 ff.

number to the Pope with the full story of the election
in order to win his approval.[1] Owing to the sickness
en route of the imperial envoy,[2] and to other reasons
which Frederick promised to explain to the Pope when
they met, word of all this had hitherto failed to reach
him. He had no doubt, he continued, that the Pope
was only concerned about the election from fear lest
Sicily should be united to the empire.[3] That union
he earnestly impressed on the Pope should never take
place. He would always so act that the Church should
ever rejoice that she had begotten such a son.[4]

This deceitful letter concluded with the enumeration
of the *reasons* which had forced him to delay his departure
for the East, and with a declaration that he would be
starting soon " in accordance with his own wish and that
of the Pope."

Arrangement
for
Frederick's
coronation.

Shortly after this it was arranged that Frederick
should first be crowned in the autumn, and should only
sail to the help of the Holy Land after the conclusion
of the ceremony.[5] In the interim the Pope occupied
himself in endeavouring on the one hand to secure
tranquillity in Germany in Frederick's interest,[6] and on

[1] *Ib.*

[2] There is extant a letter of this envoy (the legate Conrad) addressed
to the Pope from Mantua (July 31, 1220) in which, after declaring
that serious illness prevented him from prosecuting his journey,
he excuses the election on various grounds, and asserts that, though he
could not obtain any reply from the Holy See when he had consulted
it long ago on this very election question, he had heard from a cardinal
friend of his that the Pope had declared that he had nothing to do with
the election of a King of the Romans. Ep. of Conrad, bp. of Metz,
ap. H.-B., i, p. 803 n.

[3] " Videtur nobis . . . non ob aliud promotionem nostri filii gravem
fertis, nisi quia de unione regni cum imperio dubitatis." Ep. of July 13,
p. 803 f.

[4] *Ib.*

[5] See the Pope's letter to his legate Pelagius, July 13, 1220, ap.
Rodenberg, i, 89 f.

[6] *Cf.* nn. 2630, 2637–8, in Pressutti, *Reg.*

the other in vain efforts to obtain from bishop Conrad, the imperial legate in Lombardy, or from Frederick himself, the restitution of the lands of the Countess Matilda in accordance with the latter's promises.[1] Frederick on his side continued to send the Pope letters full of thanks and promises of devotion.[2] He also made a pretence at least of endeavouring to compel certain barons to give up the lands held by them which formed part of the territory of the Countess Matilda and which belonged to the Roman Church.[3]

It was in the month of September that Frederick crossed the Brenner Pass, and entered Italy with a comparatively small army.[4] When he reached Bologna, he sent envoys to the Pope to announce his speedy arrival in Rome, and as the bearers of a letter in which he again expressed his devotion and gratitude to the Roman Church, which would never have cause to regret having brought him up at her breast, and promised that she should soon pluck the fruit from the tree which it had so carefully cultivated (Oct. 4).[5] But the movements of Frederick were slow ; he had to deal with the cities of the Lombard plain. At length, however, he came to terms with Milan and her allies, received armed support from them,

Frederick enters Italy 1220.

---

[1] Cf. ep. 119, ap. Rodenberg, and nn. 2598, 2608, 2683, 2732, in Pres. In view of the difference between Frederick's promises and his performances, one can appreciate the instruction of Honorius to his legates to endeavour to find out the King's real mind regarding the union of the Empire with Sicily and regarding the Crusade. Ep. of Nov. 10, ap. H.-B., i, 880 f.

[2] H.-B., i, pp. 827, 863 (Oct. 4).

[3] See his order, ap. *ib.*, p. 855, Sept. 24. He speaks " comitatus, terre et poderis quondam comitisse Mathildis " which belonged to the Roman Church " pleno jure."

[4] Tolosanus, *Chron.*, an. 1220, p. 709. Reiner, *l.c.*, and Ric. of San Germano, ad. an., say that Fred. set out with a large host.

[5] Ap. Raynaldus, *Ann. eccles.*, an. 1220, § 18.

and resumed his march towards Rome.[1] Whilst still on his way, he was met by Nicholas, cardinal bishop of Tusculum, and the sub-deacon Alatrinus, who had been specially commissioned to present to him the terms (capitularia) on which he was to receive the imperial crown, and which, recognized as part of the law of the empire, were to be proclaimed on his coronation day. The envoys were also to endeavour to find out his real intentions with regard to Sicily, pointing out to him that he was acting against his own undertakings in causing his son, who had been crowned king of Sicily, to be also elected King of the Romans ; in dealing with the spiritual and temporal lords of Sicily by virtue of his imperial power ; and in again exacting from them oaths of fidelity. By these means, insisted the Pope quite in the spirit of prophecy, an effort is being made to bring about the union of Sicily with the Empire which will end in great loss both to the Apostolic See and to Frederick's own posterity.[2]

They were also to impress upon the King that it was the universal opinion that the success of the Crusade absolutely rested upon him.[3]

Frederick, however, had no intention of revealing

---

[1] Reiner, l.c. A late author, Galvaneus Flamma († 1344), whose reputation for sense and veracity is of the poorest, nevertheless declares that, " when Frederick asked the Milanese that he might be crowned with the iron crown of Lombardy (preserved at Monza) which his grandfather and father before him had received in the splendid old basilica of St. Ambrose, the Milanese flatly (ore rotundo) refused his request." Manipulus Florum, c. 253, ap. R. I. SS., xi, p. 668. At any rate, there is no record of Frederick having been crowned at Milan.

[2] Ap. Rodenberg, i, p. 103, Lateran, Nov. 10, 1220. " Per que (the means noted in the text) in sedis apostolice nec non posteritatis sue dispendium videtur prefata unio (of the Empire and Sicily) procurari."

[3] Ib.

his real mind any further than he had already done by his actions. He had previously shown himself ready enough to comply with the Pope's request that he should in every way support the Church against the heretics of North Italy,[1] and he now solemnly declared, from his camp on Monte Mario overlooking the city, that the empire had no jurisdiction over Sicily, that he himself held it in virtue of the rights of his mother, though it belonged to the Roman Church, and that he would never be a party to its being withdrawn from the propriety of the Roman Church, or to its being united to the empire. Moreover, to remove any suspicion of any attempt being made to effect this union, he undertook to keep separate in every way the affairs of the empire and the kingdom, and for that purpose only to employ officials of the kingdom for the work of the kingdom.[2]

After such an explicit declaration, Honorius had no excuse for refusing to bestow on Frederick the imperial crown. Some difference with the Romans is supposed to have been the cause why he had left Rome in January, 1220. However that may be, he returned to the city in October, 1220, as some say through the influence of Frederick, and, according to others, even through his armed intervention.[3] At any rate, on Sunday, November

The coronation of Frederick II. Nov. 22, 1220.

---

[1] See the Pope's letters of Sept., 1220, ap. Pres., nn. 2732 and 2766, and Frederick's action, ap. H.-B., i, 854, Sept.

[2] " Profitemur Imperium nihil prorsus juris habere in regno Siciliæ . . . et nos ipsi tenemus (the kingdom of Sicily), ejus regni proprietatem eidem recognoscentes Ecclesiæ." See the full decree (Nov.), ap. Balan, *Storia di Gregorio IX.*, i, p. 130, Modena, 1872 ; or apud *Notices et extraits des MSS.*, t. xxi, pt. ii, p. 353. *Cf.* n. 27, p. 354. Huillard-Bréholles, who published this document from the Rouleaux de Cluny, notes that it is dated " Mons Gaudii," and adds that the place is evidently Monte Mario or in Latin " Mons Malus," and that Frederick has here changed the name of evil omen into one of good omen.

[3] Alberic Trium Font., *Chron.*, an. 1220, ap. *M. G. SS.*, xxiii, p. 911.

22, on the feast of Sta. Cecilia, he received Frederick and Constance [1] at St. Peter's ; and husband and wife, " surrounded by a splendid gathering of archbishops, bishops, abbots, counts, and barons from Rome, Germany, Sicily, Apulia, and the Terra di Lavoro, were crowned in the midst of such peace and glory as is not remembered to have happened in the case of any other emperor." [2]

Then, as we learn from the Pope himself,[3] while all present held lighted candles in their hands to be brusquely extinguished at the close of the ceremony, he solemnly excommunicated all heretics and their supporters, including all who should attempt in the future to preserve the *customs* which had been introduced contrary to ecclesiastical liberty, or who should not remove them from their Statute Books in the course of the two months following the promulgation of this decree.

On his side Frederick gave many presents to St. Peter's, again took the cross at the hands of cardinal Ugolino,[4] promising to set out for the East in the following August,[5] and, like the Pope, condemned all laws issued by communes or others against the privileges of the Church, and all heretics, as well as all such as should injure the persons or property of shipwrecked persons or of travellers

---

[1] It was through his influence that Constance was also crowned. *Cf. Reg.*, n. 2650, ed. Pres.

[2] *Ignot. mon. Cister.*, an. 1220, p. 37, ed. Gaudenzi. *Cf.* ep. Hon. of Dec. 15 to card. Pelagius : " Nos . . . cum inestimabili alacritate ac pace civium Romanorum solemnissime (Frederick) coronasse." Yet the well-informed Reiner declares that the Romans received Frederick "more from motives of fear than love." Ann., 1220, ap. *M. G. SS.*, xvi, p. 678. *Cf.* other authorities ap. Potthast, sub. 6407, and the Pope also ap. *Quinta compilatio*, i, c. 2.

[3] *Q. comp.*, *l.c.* *Cf. Reg.*, n. 2945.

[4] Burchard and Ric. de S. Germ., an. 1220, and Richer, *Gesta*, iv, c. 4, ap. *M. G. SS.*, xxv, p. 301.

[5] *Reg. Hon.*, nn. 2796, Nov. 27, and 2866, Dec. 15, 1220.

or of agricultural labourers.[1] Both Pope and Emperor
ordered the universal publication of the imperial decrees ;
and that they should be inscribed in the law-books
in use at Bologna, and commented on in the schools.[2]

Though the coronation ceremonies, which we have Difficulties
elsewhere described at length,[3] and the negotiations arise, 1220-1.
immediately following them, were in the main conducted
in a manner satisfactory to both the parties,[4] it was not
long before fresh difficulties sprang up between the Pope
and the Emperor.

Frederick remained on Monte Mario three days after Frederick
his coronation. He then proceeded through Campania goes to Sicily, 1220.
into Sicily, and at once began to assert his authority by
revoking grants made by himself or his father.[5] He

[1] His decrees, ap. H.-B., ii, p. 2 ff., "in die qua de manu
sacratissimi patris nostri summi pontificis recepimus imperii diadema."
In ordering the confiscation of the goods of heretics, the emperor
gives as a reason that it is far worse to offend the divine than human
majesty. " Cum longe sit gravius eternam quam temporalem offendere
majestatem." In 1224 Frederick went further, and sent an order
to his legate in Lombardy to cause heretics to be burned or deprived
of their tongues. Cf. ep. of March, 1224, ap. H.-B., ii, 421 f. As
Freeman noted in his essay on Frederick (p. 308) : " the heretic is
one who has cast off his allegiance to the Church ; he is a spiritual
rebel to be chastised as unsparingly as a temporal rebel. This principle
was acted on throughout the middle ages."

[2] Reg., n. 3506, March 25, 1221 ; H.-B., ii, p. 7.

[3] Vol. x, 391 ff.

[4] Cf., e.g., the letter of Honorius (Dec. 13) to the prelates of the
kingdom of Arles urging them to support William Marquis of
Montferrat, whom the emperor had appointed governor of that
kingdom, and who had declared to the Pope that it was his wish
to consolidate it " in loyalty to the empire and devotion to the Church."
Ap. H.-B., ii, 81. On the other hand, see a charter of Frederick
renewing, at the request of Pope Honorius, the privileges of the
monastery of St. Zeno at Verona, because " ex concesso nobis a Deo
imperio ecclesiis et personis ecclesiasticis teneamur adesse." Ap.
H.-B., ii, 93, Jan. 2, 1221.

[5] Chron. ignot. Cist., an. 1220, p. 36, ed. Gaudenzi ; Ric. de S. Germ.,
Chron., ad. an., and Chron. Suessanum, ap. H.-B., ii, 83. Somewhat
later, ep. March 3, 1221, he explained this line of conduct to the Pope,
ap. ib., p. 139.

also complained to Honorius that he had had difficulty in procuring in the pontifical territory the *fodrum* (purveyance) which was his due. In his reply the Pope averred that he had instructed his chaplain, the subdeacon Alatrinus, a man wholly devoted to the emperor, to see to it that the *fodrum* (or *procurationes*) should be duly furnished him throughout all the parts of Tuscany "subject to our sway." Moreover, he had even ordered, he added, "the rector" of Campania and the Maritima to do likewise, though the emperor had no right to the *fodrum* there, inasmuch as he did not pass through those territories on his way to Rome for his coronation.[1]

Satisfied with this reply, Frederick renewed the promises he had made at his coronation about Sicily,[2] and in 1219, at Hagenau regarding the papal rights over various territories, even over those that had belonged to the countess Matilda. This he did by a charter to which was attached a golden bulla bearing "the effigy of our majesty."[3]

In this matter the undertakings of the emperor were not merely empty words, for although the Pope had to ask Frederick to cause his bailiff to cease from exacting tolls from the citizens of Benevento, as that city belonged to the Roman Church,[4] still he recovered rights in the lands of Matilda, the Duchy of Spoleto, and the March of Ancona, and ruled "the whole patrimony of Blessed Peter from the bridge of Ceprano to Radicofani in peace and quiet."[5]

[1] Ep. of Dec. 11, 1220, ap. H.-B., ii, 79 ff. *Cf. Reg.*, n. 2857.

[2] Ep. of Dec., 1220, at Naples. He affirmed that the empire had no right to Sicily, and promised not to do anything to submit or unite it to the empire. Ap. H.-B., in *Notices des MSS.*, t. xxi, pt. ii, p. 354.

[3] Ap. H.-B., ii, 108, Jan., 1221. "Aurea bulla typario nostre majestatis impressa, firmatum." *Cf. ib.*, p. 109.

[4] *Reg.*, n. 3378, May 14, 1221.

[5] The Pope managed to recover the territories : "quamquam infinitis et arduis essemus negociis inevitabiliter occupati." He

For a brief space also, at this period, Frederick mani- Frederick's
fested great zeal in behalf of the Crusade, and dispatched delays cause
the loss of
various letters to Lombardy, urging all to follow his Damietta,
1221.
example in taking the Cross, " for now the victorious
eagles of the Roman Empire have come forth." He
expressed the greatest pleasure that the Pope had appointed a man of the character of Ugolino, cardinal-bishop
of Ostia, as his legate in Lombardy;[1] and to facilitate the
cardinal's work in behalf of the Cross, he named him his
vicar also in Lombardy.   Moreover, he assured the
various cities of Lombardy and Tuscany that he was
preparing ships on a great scale to convey speedy help to
the Crusaders.[2] This was in February, but in June (13)
Honorius had to urge him to send off some of these ships
to Egypt at once, as men were beginning to believe that
he intended again to put off the fulfilment of his vow, and
to blame the Pope himself for suffering him to do so.[3]

Forty galleys were accordingly ordered to sail forthwith ; but, as the Pope told the emperor at the time
(July 20), they should have sailed before.[4] Nevertheless,

describes the lands of Matilda thus : " de toto comitatu et podere
ac terris comitisse Mathildis." He invested the marquis of Este
with the March of Ancona by means of a banner in the presence of
the emperor, while feudal lords acknowledged his suzerainty by
presenting him with hawks " unum asturem et duos braceos." Ep.
Hon., ap. H.-B., ii, 128 ff. In this letter he also speaks of recovering
" castrum Procenum," and the *Annals of Orvieto* (ad. an. 1220, ap.
M. G. SS., xix, p. 269) say that " commune Urbevetanum dedit
ei Procenum."

[1] He calls Ugolino (afterwards Gregory IX.) " vir fama integer,
religione perspicuus, vita purus, facundia eloquentissimus et claris
virtutum et scientie titulis circumspectus." Ep. of Feb. 10, ap.
H.-B., ii, p. 125. *Cf. ib.*, ii, 110.

[2] *Ib.* " Preparando magnifice galeas et naves . . . de festino
succursu die ac nocte . . . cogitamus."

[3] Ap. H.-B., ii, p. 190.   " Dilationem voti nobis precipue im-
putantes."

[4] *Cf.* Coggeshall, *Chron.*, p. 189, R. S., regarding their non-arrival
in Egypt in time.

Honorius thanked him for sending the ships, and again begged him not to allow his devotion to the affairs of Sicily to prevent him from fulfilling his vow of sailing himself in August. Men were everywhere saying that the Pope was deferring too much to him.[1]

August came, and Honorius had to complain towards the end of it that Frederick had failed to fulfil his undertakings not merely with regard to the Holy Land, but also with regard to episcopal elections. Despite the promises he had made to Innocent, and to his successor, he had begun to interfere with the freedom of episcopal elections. The Pope felt compelled to speak severely, as many, both within and without the Roman Church, were accusing him of undue complacency towards the emperor. He reminded Frederick that it was due as much to the Pope as to the emperor that his son was reigning in peace in Germany, and that he " who had the eyes and ears of many," could, if he saw fit, cause many things to be done in every part of the empire and kingdom which Frederick would not like. The emperor would therefore be well advised not to meddle with the elections.[2]

On September 8, 1221, Damietta, in the capture of which the Christian army had suffered so much, was regained by the Saracens, and on October 25 the emperor expressed great indignation to the Pope that " the puppies of the synagogue " (catuli *synagoge*, as he calls a mosque) have put to flight the sons of the Church, and he professed to be more grieved than others at the loss of

---

[1] Ep. ap. Rod., i, p. 123 f. " Pro te igitur contra nos *graviter* acclamatur; dicitur enim . . . quod illum ad personam tuam habeamus affectum, ut contra Deum et negotium suum non dubitemus tibi deferre." Blondel, *Fréd. II. en Allemagne*, p. 381 n., takes notice that it was not the Popes only but other contemporaries who accuse him of indifference in connexion with the affair of Damietta.

[2] Ep. Aug. 21, ap. *ib.*, p. 124 ff., or H.-B., ii, 200.

the city, inasmuch as he was just about to set out to its assistance.[1]

The news of the fall of Damietta sent a thrill of anguish throughout the West, and the Pope was much blamed for not having compelled Frederick to keep his vow. Of this Honorius informed the emperor,[2] and, reminding him that it was reliance on his promises that caused the Christian leaders to reject the offers of peace made them by the Moslems,[3] solemnly assured him that, if he did not show real zeal for the fulfilment of his vow, he would no longer set his advantage before that of the papacy and of the whole Christian people, but would publicly excommunicate him.[4]

It was clearly advisable for the emperor to pacify the Pope and Christendom. Accordingly, a conference was proposed, and Honorius and Frederick met at Veroli on April 12, 1222, and after an exhaustive discussion lasting fifteen days, it was resolved to hold a great Diet at Verona in November. The emperor professed greater zeal than ever for the cause of the Cross,[5] and at the same time

Interview between the Pope and the Emperor at Veroli, 1222.

[1] Ap. H.-B., ii, 206 f.

[2] Ep. of Nov. 19, ap. Rod., i, 128 ff. "Clamante contra nos universo populo Christiano . . . eo quod te . . . transire non compulimus."

[3] A letter preserved by Roger of Wendover shows how much hope was placed on the coming of the emperor to the help of the Crusaders, and the loss to the cause which resulted from his faithlessness. The Grand Master of the Templars wrote from Acre : "We have long expected the arrival of the emperor . . . If we are deceived in our hope . . . Syria and Egypt will be placed in a doubtful position." An. 1221, iv, p. 72 ff., ed. Coxe. He wrote on Sept. 20, 1221, before he had heard of the loss of Damietta.

[4] The Pope's letter of Nov. 19. Cf. epp. of Dec. 10 and 19, ap. ib., pp. 130–1.

[5] Ep. Hon. of Apr. 25, 1222, ap. H.-B., ii, 240. Cf. Ric. of S. Germ., an. 1222, and other authorities ap. Potthast, sub. 6812. Both Gregory IX. (ep. ap. Roger of Wendover, an. 1228) and Frederick himself (ep. ap. Mat. Par., an. 1239) refer to this conference at Veroli, and to the subsequent one at Ferentino.

satisfied the Pope on the subject of his action with regard
to the episcopal elections, issuing an order to his officials in
the kingdom of Sicily to refrain from interfering with the
clergy or their privileges.[1]

Illness, however, prevented the Pope from being able
to take the journey to Verona.[2] Still there was the
greatest anxiety on the part of many[3] to bring the
Pope and emperor together, as various things had
happened which caused many to fear their estrangement.
To further his plans for making the empire hereditary,
and for uniting Sicily permanently to the empire,
Frederick caused his youthful son to be solemnly crowned
(May 8, 1222).[4] Then before the same year was out, the
emperor's standard-bearer, Gunzelinus, had seriously
interfered with the rights of Rainerius, cardinal-deacon of
S. Maria in Cosmedin, who was the governor (rector) of
the Duchy of Spoleto. In various parts of the Duchy and
of the March of Ancona he had expelled the papal
officials (balivi), and appointed his own in their stead.[5]

Interview at Ferentino, 1223.

Frederick, however, readily found excuses for the
coronation of his son, and vigorously repudiated the
conduct of Gunzelinus. Those, therefore, who were in

[1] At least with such immunities as they had enjoyed in the days
of William II. See his letter of Apr. 23, 1222, ap. H.-B., ii, 239.

[2] Cf. H.-B., ii, p. 241 n. He was so ill that his death was commonly
reported. Chron. Mont. Sereni, ad. an. 1222, ap. M. G. SS., xxiii,
p. 200. Cf. Annal. Mediol. brev., ap. ib., xviii, p. 391.

[3] Cf. the letter of bishop Conrad to the officials of his diocese of
Hildesheim. Ap. ib., p. 317, Feb. 18, 1223. He was waiting in Rome
for the meeting of the Pope and the emperor " de successu Terre
Sancte et pace generali tracturi."

[4] Cf. Giles of Orval, Chron. ad. an. " Ipso patre consentiente et
procurante." Ap. M. G. SS., xxv, p. 119. The ceremony was
performed by St. Engelbert, the archbishop of Cologne, regent of
Germany. Cf. his Life, c. 5, by Cæsarius, ap. Böhmer, Fontes, ii, 299 ;
and Burchard, Chron., p. 107.

[5] Cf. a series of documents of Nov. and Dec., 1222, ap. Theiner,
Cod. diplom. domin. temp., i, pp. 71-5, and H.-B., ii, 272, 283, 286-7.

earnest regarding the Holy War, John of Brienne, the King of Jerusalem, and the Grand Masters of the Military Orders, managed to bring about an interview between the sick Pope and the emperor at Ferentino, March 23, 1223.[1] To obtain further delay, Frederick was able to plead his difficulties with the Saracens in Sicily, and the loss of his wife Constance († June 23, 1222).[2] He promised, however, to go to the help of the Holy Land in two years.[3] It was further arranged, with a view to interesting the emperor still more in the Holy Land, that he should in due course marry the child Isabella (Yolande or Iolanthe), daughter of John de Brienne, the titular King of Jerusalem.[4]

In the interim, Honorius earnestly devoted himself to furthering whatever might be to the advantage of the coming Crusade. Among other things, he succeeded in bringing about peace between Thomas, count of Molise and Celano, Raynald of Aversa with other rebel Apulian nobles on the one hand, and Frederick on the other. The emperor sent a copy of the treaty between himself and the rebels to the Pope, " because," as he wrote, " we wish to bring to your knowledge whatever with God's help we

Relations between the Pope and Frederick, 1223-5.

---

[1] Ric. of S. Germ., ad. an. 1223. " Qui (the Pope) tunc graviter patiebatur in crure." It was in connexion with the differences between Frederick and Honorius that the Grand Master of the Teutonic Knights, Herman von Salza, first began to mediate between Popes and Emperors. Cf. Peter de Dusburg, *Cronica Prussie*, ap. *SS. RR. PP.*, i, p. 32.

[2] Cf. H.-B., ii, p. 254.

[3] Ric. of S. G., *l.c.* Cf. epp. Hon. of Apr. 18, etc., ap. *Reg.*, nn. 4262, 4304, 4321, and 4330. Quoting from the last-named letter : " Juravit (Frederick) se in festo b. Johannis Baptistæ primo futuro post biennium iter arrepturum transfretandi."—June 24, 1225.

[4] *Ib.* Cf. *supra*, p. 25. According to Honorius, the marriage was arranged at the suggestion of the patriarch of Jerusalem " and other Orientals." See his letter to Philip of France, *c.* end May, 1223, ap. H.-B., ii, 375 ff. He granted Frederick a dispensation to marry Isabella, who was related to him in the fourth degree of consanguinity, *Reg.*, 4460, Aug. 5, 1223.

succeed in bringing to a conclusion." [1] He, moreover, solemnly promised the Pope to abide by the treaty.[2]

Frederick, then, was very deferential towards the Holy See when deference was to his advantage, and served to forward the consolidation of his power. When, however, deference would not suit his purpose, he assumed a different attitude. Nothing was more calculated to serve his absolutism than to have the episcopal sees in the hands of his creatures. He accordingly nominated a number of persons for the sees of Capua and Aversa, and sent the *Judex* of Bari to request the Pope to select two from among them to fill the said sees. When, however, owing to the absence of some of his counsellors, Honorius felt unable to give a decisive answer at the moment, and gave the *Judex* letters for the emperor to that effect, that functionary not only refused to accept them, but, wrote the Pope to the emperor, " used language in your name which ought not to have been used even if you had been grievously injured by us." [3]

The envoy declared that the Pope's protection was a sham, and rather tended to the ruin of the King and his kingdom ; and that, if the King's nominees were not accepted, certainly no candidates of the Pope would be allowed to take possession of the sees in question. If, urged the Pope in the letter to the emperor, which is the sole source of our knowledge of this incident, you authorized the use of such language, you evidently wish to break the bond of affection between us. And if you do so, you will find that there are only too many ready to take advantage of any breach between us. It behoves you to reflect that, if a quarrel has to spring up between us, no cause of quarrel could be imagined more likely

[1] Ep. of Apr. 25, 1223, ap. H.-B., ii, 357–60.
[2] *Ib.*, and Ric. of S. Germ., *Chron.*, ad. an. 1223.
[3] Ep. June 27, 1223, ap. H.-B., ii, 384 ff.

to bring general discredit on you and to enlist sympathy for us than a tyrannical attempt to overthrow the liberty of the Church. "Are we not to have that jurisdiction and authority in the kingdom of Sicily that we have in France, England, Spain, and the other Christian countries, and in the empire itself?" The fire of youth and evil counsel, suggested the Pope, were leading the emperor astray.[1]

It would appear that for the moment the emperor did not actively press his claims, seeing that for some time after this we hear of nothing discussed between him and the Pope but the Crusade. He was very far, however, from abandoning the position which both his mother and he himself had agreed to surrender, and the number of vacant sees in the two Sicilies increased. At length, however, in September, 1225, Honorius on his own account (motu propriæ voluntatis) nominated and consecrated five candidates for the vacant sees of Capua, Aversa, Conza, Brindisi, and Salerno.[2] For a time, however, the emperor would not suffer one of them to occupy his see.[3] Indeed, in a document which is thought to belong to this period (c. April, 1226) he is said to have declared that he would rather give up his crown than lose the rights concerning episcopal elections held by his predecessors.[4] Apropos of this quarrel regarding the five bishops, between the "all-enduring Honorius" and the emperor, Döllinger remarks that "if Frederick had not hitherto been acting the part of a hypocrite, we must suppose that at this time his religious opinions underwent

---

[1] Ib.

[2] Reg., nn. 5654-5, 5668, of Sept. 25 and 27, 1225.

[3] Ric. of S. Germ., Chron., an. 1225, says in general terms that the emperor would not allow them to hold their sees. "Quos imperator in prejudicium juris promotos sui, in ipsis ecclesiis recipi non permisit."

[4] Ap. H.-B., ii, 932.

that change by which alone we can explain many circumstances that followed."[1] However this may be, we must remember that, after his failure to coerce Lombardy in the year 1226, he accepted all the five bishops,[2] and that this quarrel did not, as certain later authors have supposed, lead to his excommunication by Honorius.[3]

Meanwhile, Frederick informed the Pope of the extensive preparations he was making for the forthcoming Crusade, and even complained that the preachers of the Crusade were not exerting themselves.[4] Whether or not inspired in turn by the seeming zeal of the emperor, Honorius, at any rate, made earnest attempts to secure support for him throughout Europe.[5] This he continued to do even when another seditious outbreak of the Romans forced him to betake himself to Tivoli (April, 1225).[6]

Frederick again not ready, 1225.

Despite all his professions, however, the emperor was not prepared to fulfil his engagements when the feast of St. John the Baptist drew near. Whilst the Pope was still at Tivoli, imperial envoys, in the persons of the King and of the Patriarch of Jerusalem, appeared before him and asked for further delay.[7] They no doubt alleged their master's persistent difficulties with the Saracens of

[1] *Hist. of the Church*, iv, pp. 36–7, London, 1842.
[2] Ric. of S. G., an. 1226. " Omnes . . . in suis ecclesiis recipiuntur."
[3] " Perchè . . . (Frederick) uzurpava la chiesa, Honorio P. scomunicò (him)." G. Sercambi, *Cron.*, c. 35, vol. i, p. 18, ed. Borgi.
[4] Ep. of March 5, 1224, ap. H.-B., ii, 409. In gratitude to God for his favours to him "obsequio Sancte Crucis obtulimus nosmet ipsos . . . substantiam, etc." He was preparing among other things fifty transports (usseria), each of which was to carry forty men and forty horses.
[5] *Reg.*, nn. 4903–4, March, 1224, and 4919–23, of Apr. 4, ap. vol. ii, pp. 232, 235 f. ; 5575, an. 1225.
[6] Ric. of S. Germ., *Chron.*, ad. an.
[7] *Ib.* " Pro dilatione passagii obtinenda."

Sicily,[1] his work for the development of the University of Naples,[2] the fact that the Kings of England and France had not yet agreed to that peace which the Pope and emperor had ordered,[3] and the advisability of the marriage taking place between Isabella and Frederick before he set out for the Holy Land.

In reply to this request, the Pope sent cardinals Pela- *Renewed undertaking of the emperor, 1225.* gius and Gualo to Frederick,[4] before whom he swore to set out for the Holy Land in two years from the following August, and in the meantime to maintain a thousand soldiers there. To these and other conditions he bound himself under pain of excommunication, July, 1225.[5]

A few months after this solemn renewal of his pledges *He marries Isabella, 1225.* to lead an army to the Holy Land, Frederick married Isabella, or Yolanda, the daughter of John of Brienne (November 9). And now, as though he had obtained all he wanted, Frederick began to show himself in his true colours. He proved false to his young wife, to her father, and to the Pope. Besides being untrue to Isabella, he so ill-used her that she died soon after giving birth to Conrad ; [6] he deceived his father-in-law by at once claiming

---

[1] *Cf.* Ric. of S. Germ., *Chron.*, ad. an. 1225.

[2] See documents in H.-B., ii, 447 of *c.* July, 1224.

[3] Ep. Hon. ap. Rod. i, p. 192 (*c.* Feb., 1225) to Louis VIII. of France : "Contempto . . . statuto de pace . . . quod . . . fecimus in colloquio inter nos et . . . Fredericum imperatorem."

[4] Ep., ap. *Reg.*, n. 5566, July 18, 1225 ; or ap. H.-B., ii, 498 ; Ric. of S. Germ., *l.c.* *Cf.* ep. of Fred., ap. H.-B., ii, 500.

[5] Ap. H.-B., ii, 501 ff. " Lata ex nunc excommunicationis sententia in quam incidemus si non transfretaverimus . . . Si antem defecerimus . . . Ecclesia Romana sententiabit in nos . . . de . . . consensu nostro." *Cf.* Codagnellus, *Chron.*, an. 1226, p. 84 f., ed. Holder-Egger., though his narrative is here much condensed and inaccurate.

[6] Ernoul, *Chronique*, c. 39, p. 451 ff., ed. Mas Latrie. The account given in the French continuation of Will. of Tyre (L. XXIV., c. 84, f. p. Pat. Lat., t. 201) is practically the same as that in Ernoul. *Cf.* another contemporary French Chron., ap. H.-B., ii, 921 ff. ; *Chron. Turon.*, ap. *R. F. SS.*, xviii, 311.

the kingdom of Jerusalem in right of his wife, the heiress
of that kingdom, though he had promised to leave it to
John during his life;[1] and he showed himself ungrateful
to the Pope by the efforts which he, not content with the
lands which he had inherited, now began to make in order
" to usurp the patrimony of Blessed Peter." [2] You, the
advocate or defender of the Church, wrote the Pope to
Frederick in a strong letter upbraiding him for his
ingratitude, have seized and still hold Arquata and other
possessions belonging to our loyal subjects.[3] Moreover,
it appeared that, without any reference to the Pope, he
had ordered the men of the Duchy of Spoleto to accompany him to the Diet which he was about to hold in
Lombardy.[4]

[1] " Le jour meismes des noces li empereres . . . li (King John)
requist que il le deust saisir dou roiaume de Jerusalem . . . Jehan . . .
fu moult esbahis ; car Hermans (Frederick's great friend Hermann
von Salza, the Grand Master of the Teutonic Knights) . . . qui avoit
pourchacié le mariage, li avoit fait entendant que li empereres li
lairoit tenir li roiaume de Jerusalem toute sa vie." Chron., ap. H.-B.,
ii, p. 922, and cf. epp. Hon., ap. ib., pp. 596 and 708. Jordan, Chron.,
ap. Raynaldus, Ann. Eccles., an. 1226, n. 11 ; and the biographer
of Gregory IX., c. 10 : " Quem (John de Brienne) per imperatoris
versutiam contra justitiam publice honestatis de regno dejectum,
etc." Already in Dec., 1225, Frederick styles himself : " imperator
. . . Jerusalem et Sicilie rex." Ap. H.-B., ii, p. 526. Honorius
did what he could for the disinherited King. Not content with urging
Frederick to treat John as a father-in-law should be treated (ep. of
Jan. 27, 1227, ap. H.-B., ii, 708), he came to his help practically by
making him governor of all the papal territory between Radicofani
and Rome, " except the March of Ancona, the Duchy of Spoleto
Rieti, and the Sabina " (ep. of Jan. 27, 1227, ap. Reg., n. 6203). Cf.
Ric. of Germ., an. 1226 ; and Alberic Trium Font., Chron., an. 1226,
ap. M. G. SS., xxiii, p. 919.

[2] Cf. epp. Hon. of April to May or June, 1226, ap. H.-B., ii, p. 552 ff.,
and p. 588 ff. In the latter letter especially the Pope upbraids
Frederick for his ingratitude. According to Salimbene, Chron.,
p. 383, this famous letter, which begins " Miranda tuis sensibus,"
was drawn up by Cardinal Thomas of Capua, who was one " of the
most polished dictators of the Curia."

[3] The last cited letter.

[4] Ric. of S. Germ., an. 1226, p. 122.

Frederick, who had written a very sharp reply [1] to the Pope's first letter of remonstance, found it convenient when he was in the midst of the warlike Lombards to send a mild answer [2] to the Pope's long and strong second remonstrance.

Overtly, with the object of promoting the Crusade, but no doubt covertly with the intention of definitely establishing his power in Lombardy, Frederick had ordered all the Counts and Podestàs of Lombardy to meet him at Cremona on the Easter Sunday of the year 1226.[3] His son was also instructed to join him with an army from Germany.

Frederick began his march towards Lombardy in February, 1226. But he was not destined to find the Lombards unprepared. They had heard of his highhanded treatment of John de Brienne, and of the Pope, they knew that the men of Cremona and Pavia were betraying them into his hands, and they resolved that he should not lord it over them in the same way as he was lording it over southern Italy. Dissensions among them largely ceased, and the Lombard League was renewed near Mantua, March 2, 1226.[4] The *Rectors* of Lombardy,

Frederick in Lombardy, 1226.

The second Lombard League, 1226.

[1] Ap. H.-B., ii, p. 932.

[2] Ap. Winkelmann, *Acta inedita*, i, p. 261. Hence Ric. of S. Germ., *l.c.*, after speaking of the Pope's second sharper letter (the *Miranda*), says, " propter quod imperator ut ipsius placaret animum, rescribit humiliter in omni subjectione." *Cf.* Böhmer, *Reg. imp.*, v, p. 336, July, 1226.

[3] Ric. of S. Germ., *Chron.*, an. 1225, c. August, 1225 ; *Chron. reg. Colon., contin. IV*, an. 1226, p. 258 ; and ep. *c.* March, 1226, ap. H.-B., ii, p. 548.

[4] Tolosanus, *Chron.*, 1226. " Omnes fere Lombardi contra Imperatorem conjuravere se invicem juvaturos, dummodo Imperator . . . aliquem vellet pertractare injuste." *Cf.* Codagnellus, an. 1226, p. 74 ff., who bursts into verse on this story of the new Lombard League, and the series of documents regarding the formation of the League, ap. H.-B., ii, 924. The chief parties to the League were Milan, Bologna, Brescia, Mantua, Padua, Vicenza, and Treviso. See Butler, *The Lombard Communes*, c. ix.

says the canon of Faënza, remembered the evils they had suffered at the hands of the first Frederick, and wished to guard themselves against worse evils at the hand of the second Frederick.

The League hinders Henry from joining his father, 1226. On the emperor's arrival in Lombardy, aggressive action would appear to have been begun by the League. At any rate, the men of Faënza who afterwards joined the League slew an envoy of the emperor under the impression that he was the emperor himself,[1] and it is certain that troops of the League so firmly held the defiles between Trent and Verona that the German princes, unable to enter Italy, were compelled to return home.[2] The emperor's officials retorted by plundering all they met with on the high roads, even those who were simply going to or returning from Rome, and even, " with damnable presumption," [3] dared to read such papal letters as they found in the possession of any of the pilgrims.

The League is excommunicated by Frederick's party. All hope, therefore, of holding a peaceful Diet at Cremona in connexion with the Crusade was now at an end. Frederick's supporters accordingly advised him to cause the members of the League to be excommunicated on the strength of letters from the Pope in which Conrad, bishop of Hildesheim, was authorized to

[1] *Chron. de rebus in Italia*, an. 1226, p. 148, ed. H.-B. According to the verses of Codagnellus, sub. an. 1225, the Emperor advanced with the usual " Teutonic fury " :—

> " Mox incepit advenire
> Cum furore sue ire
> More Theothonico."

[2] He had come " with a terrible army " in order to help his father, " aided by the men of Cremona and some others," to maintain his rights. Tolosanus, *l.c.*, p. 719. *Cf.* Frederick's own letter of June 1236, ap. H.-B., iv, pt. ii, p. 874.

[3] See the Pope's letter to Frederick complaining of this gross violation of the rights of travellers. Ep. *c.* June, 1226, ap. H.-B., ii, 633 ff.

excommunicate any who should venture to interfere with the imperial rights whilst Frederick was engaged on the work of the Cross.[1] Their advice was taken, and on July 11, at Borgo San Donnino, the members of the League were placed under the ban of the Church and of the Empire.[2] The concessions of the Treaty of Constance[3] were revoked, and, no doubt with special reference to Bologna, " the schools and studies " were to be removed from the cities of the League in perpetuity.[4]

As this action had no effect on the League, Frederick in great wrath left Lombardy, and on his return to Apulia, appealed to the Pope. He declared that he had gone into Lombardy with peaceful intention in order to forward the interests of the Crusade, threw all the blame for the failure of the Diet of Cremona on the Lombards, and submitted the whole affair to the final decision of the Holy See. He could, indeed, he averred, punish the cities for the injuries they had done him, but he would not hinder " the business of the redemption " which he had taken on his shoulders.[5]

Anxious above all things for peace for the sake of the Crusade, Honorius applied himself to effect a reconciliation

Frederick submits the dispute with the League to the Pope, 1226.

---

[1] Cf. a document in connexion with an assembly of the emperor's advisers at Parma, June 10, ap. H.-B., ii, 609 ff.

[2] Ric. of S. Ger., an. 1226 ; the verses of Codagnellus, sub. an. 1225 ; and especially a letter of Frederick of July 11, ap. H.-B., ii, 641 ff.

[3] Cf. supra, vol. x, p. 247.

[4] Ep. of Fred., July 11, 1226, ap. H.-B., ii, 641 ff. " Scholas et studia ab eisdem civitatibus statuimus . . . perpetuo removeri." Cf. Chron. reg. Colon., an. 1226, p. 258. Ann. S. Rudberti, an. 1226, ap. M. G. SS., ix.

[5] Ep. of Aug. 20, 1226, ap. ib., p. 675 ff. " Hujusmodi causam inter nos et Lombardos ordinationi . . . vestræ . . . duximus libere committendam." Cf. epp. Fred. ap. ib., p. 678 ff. ; and 691. In the latter letter Frederick endeavours to allay the natural suspicion of the Pope that the emperor, in referring the dispute to him, had no other end in view than that of causing enmity between natural allies— the Papacy and the Lombard League.

between the League and the emperor.[1] He implored
" the rectors of the Community of Lombardy " to send
envoys to Rome by the Feast of All Saints (November 1),
in order to arrange a peace with Frederick for the sake of
the Crusade.[2] The rectors accordingly took the same line as
the emperor, and referred the whole question to the ultimate
decision of Honorius.[3] On January 5, 1227, the award of
the Pope was ready and was dispatched to Lombardy.
" The rectors of the society of Lombardy, the March, and
Romaniola " were to furnish the emperor with four
hundred soldiers for two years for service in the Holy
Land, to lay aside all ill-feeling against those who
had supported the emperor, to accept his decrees
against heretics and to withdraw all statutes against
the Church ; whilst the emperor, on his side, was to lay
aside all ill-feeling against them and to revoke the ban
issued against them, particularly his constitution
against the " studium " and the students of Bologna.[4]

A few days later (January 8) Frederick and his son
were solemnly taken under the protection of the Holy
See ;[5] and, as the misunderstandings between the
emperor and the Lombards had now, as the Pope
explained,[6] been smoothed over by him, he exhorted
the Princes of Germany and Hungary to be ready to
accompany Frederick to the Holy Land in August.[7]

[1] Cf. Annal. Cremonenses, an. 1226, pp. 14 and 188, ap. M. G. SS.,
xxxi.
[2] Ep. of c. Oct. 1, ap. Rodenberg, i, 234 ; cf. the foll. ep.
[3] " Ipso igitur imperatore ac vobis totum ipsum negotium in
nostra et fratrum nostrorum providentia . . . ponentibus," etc.
Ep. Hon., Jan. 5, 1227, ap. ib., p. 246 ff., or H.-B., ii, 733.
[4] Rod., ib. Cf. other documents, ib., p. 248 ff., nn. 328-31.
[5] Ib., p. 251. Cf. ep. p. 255.
[6] Ib., p. 253, Jan. 11, 1227. " Cum . . . super ipsa discordia per
studium nostrum . . . salubriter sit provisum."
[7] Ib. The emperor had informed the Pope " per sollempnes nuntios
et litteras " that he was going to set out for the Holy Land in August.

By letters dated from Catania on February 1, and duly He accepts dispatched to the Pope and to the rectors of the Lombard the Pope's award, 1227. League, Frederick declared his acceptance of the papal award " from reverence for Jesus Christ, and for the sake of the Holy Land." [1] But the Lombards were not so ready to accept in its entirety the decision of Honorius,[2] and one of the last acts of the long-suffering Pope was to write (March 10) to the Lombard rectors to express his annoyance at their delay in finally accepting his terms. The Lombards had endeavoured to excuse their tardiness by pretending that the document manifesting their acceptance of the papal settlement had fallen into the water, and had become unintelligible. Honorius would not, however, listen to their idle excuses, but, refusing their request for further delay, bade them sign and forward forthwith the prescribed terms of peace already accepted by the emperor.[3]

About a week after he wrote this letter in the interests of peace and of the Holy Land, Honorius closed his eyes in death without seeing any substantial effort made for the succour of the Holy Land, and without being able effectively to heal the breach between the emperor and the Lombards. Frederick never forgot the check he had received on this occasion and the outrages which he had had to endure. " The wars, the tribulations, the miseries, the seditions, the cruelties, which took place in Lombardy in the reign of the lord Frederick, emperor of the Romans," of which a contemporary undertook the narration,[4]

---

[1] Ep. ap. H.-B., ii, 712 ff.

[2] We say " in its entirety " because to judge from the words of Codagnellus, *Chron.*, an. 1226, the substance of his decision had been accepted by them. He writes : " De mense vero decembri pax et concordia facta fuit per summum pontificem inter imperatorem et ipsos Lombardos."

[3] Ep. ap. Rod., i, p. 259.

[4] The author of the *Chron. de rebus in Italia*, p. 147 f., ed. H.-B.

may be said to date from this time. And a later writer, Malvecius (fl. 1412), is probably not far wrong in assigning to this period the origin of the terrible factions of the Guelfs and Ghibellines. After telling how Frederick, " a man given up to wickedness of every kind," raised his hand against the Church and induced various peoples and cities of Italy to do likewise, he adds, " Thereupon a dreadful schism arose, not merely between the Cæsar and the Pope, but between the Cities of Italy, especially between those in Lombardy. Then were those pestiferous party factions (those of the Church and of the Empire which afterwards received the names of Guelf and Ghibelline) so rooted in our forefathers that they handed them down to their descendants as an indestructible heirloom." [1]

[1] *Chron. Brixianum*, c. 103, ap. *R. I. SS.*, xiv, p. 903.

HONORIUS III.

Parted per fess argent & or, a fess vert with a bar wavy of the second supporting a chief of the first charged with two lions rampant holding in their fore-paws a rose surmounted by a martlet all of gules, in base bendy of six or and gules.

CHAPTER IV.

DOMESTIC POLICY. ROME AND THE STATES OF THE CHURCH.

FROM the strong hands of his predecessor Honorius received a City at peace with itself and with its neighbours, and in peace it remained for a year or two.

In June of the year 1219, Honorius left Rome to avoid the summer heats, passed some months at Viterbo, and did not return to his capital till the end of December. He must have received a bad reception from the Romans, for we are told that they made themselves so disagreeable that he went back to Viterbo after a few days' residence at the Vatican.[1] To argue from subsequent events, we may suppose either that the Romans were jealous of the Pope spending so much time at Viterbo, or that Rome was not big enough for Honorius and the Senator Parenzi, a very different man from that other member of his family whom the Cathari murdered at Orvieto in the days of Innocent III. But at this time Frederick was desirous of receiving the imperial crown, and accordingly used his good offices to bring about an understanding between the Pope and the Romans.[2] Moved either by fear of Frederick's power, or by hope of profit from his coronation, the Romans came to some agreement with the Pope, and he returned to them in October (1220).

The reconciliation, however, did not last long. Trouble

---

[1] *Ric. S. Germ.*, an. 1219, and *Chron. Mont. Seren.*, an. 1219, ap. M. G. SS., xxiii, p. 195. The register of Hon., ap. Pres., i, shows that he was at Viterbo on Dec. 28, in Rome from Dec. 30 to Jan. 3, and again at Viterbo on Jan. 23, 1220.

[2] *Cf. supra*, pp. 60 and 65.

came from the renewal of that enmity between Rome and
Viterbo which Innocent III. had silenced for a time.[1]
In 1221, the Romans made a vain attack on their rival,
and renewed it with greater determination in the following
year. Naturally anxious that a city which had given him
hospitality should not be a prey to the ambition of the
Romans, Honorius appealed to the emperor. The troops
sent by him to the assistance of Viterbo caused the Romans
to leave their enemy in peace for the moment at least.[2]

Troubles in
Rome, 1225.

This action of the Pope no doubt rankled in the bosoms
of the Romans, and when Parenzi again became Senator
(1225), he brought about such a state of sedition that
Honorius had to leave Rome (c. end of April, 1225) for
Tivoli.[3] In this affair Parenzi was perhaps not wholly
to blame, for we hear of fierce faction fights between
Richard, count of Sora,[4] the brother of Innocent III.,
and the nephews of the Pope,[5] quelled, perhaps, by the
influence of cardinal Ugolino on his relative Richard.[6]
One thing at least is clear, Honorious was too gentle to
control parties in Rome. In some way, however, Parenzi
was forced to resign his office of Senator, and was replaced
by Angelo de Benincasa. Peace was restored, and at the

---

[1] Cf. supra, vol. xi, p. 73 ff.

[2] Le croniche di Viterbo, ann. 1221–2, p. 238, ed. Egidi, and, by the
same editor, " L'archivio della cattedrale di Viterbo, No. 112," ap.
Bullettino dell' Istit. storico Ital., n. 27, p. 122. See also Ric. of S.
Germ., an. 1222.

[3] Ric. of S. G., an. 1225.

[4] His register, n. 768, shows that Honorius was well disposed towards
Richard. Cf. n. 5886.

[5] Chron. S. Martin. Turon., an. 1225, ap. M. G. SS., xxvi, p. 471.
From a document in the Liber Censuum, i, pp. 258–9, we learn the names
of two of the Pope's nephews, the scriniarius John Cinthius and
Beneincasa, and from another in the Register of Honorius, n. 6203,
the name of Peter Caputius, a relative and Hostiarius of the Pope.

[6] At any rate we read in the life of Ugolino (Gregory IX.), c. 3 :
" Graves Romanorum discordias per quas multorum excidia timebantur
ad insperate pacis concordiam futurus pater . . . reducebat."

beginning of February (1226) Honorius returned to Rome,[1] where he was to remain till his death.

Whether or not the nephews of Innocent III. gave Honorius himself any particular trouble, their conduct did not lessen that Pope's admiration for his predecessor. In matters both of foreign and domestic policy he was fain to follow in his footsteps. Among the many institutions into which Innocent endeavoured to introduce reforms was the papal chancellary.[2] Honorius, who had himself been vice-chancellor, continued the work thus begun, and in 1220, according to the opinion of Muratori,[3] issued a decree regarding the receiving and dealing with " petitions " for favours or graces. Notaries were forbidden to receive petitions (except such rolls of them as had been accepted and bore a common date, or, as some suppose, had been accepted in the office known as the *Data Communis*),[4] unless they were presented by the Pope or a cardinal, or by the papal chaplain and the camerarius with the Pope's mandate.

Reforms in the papal chancellary.

On their own account no member of the chancellary (notaries, bullatores, breviatores, or scriptores) were to take up any petitions except such as concerned themselves, their relatives, or special friends, and such petitions were to be presented for admission to the Pope alone. Breach of this regulation was to be followed by dismissal.

Only the properly sealed letters of important personages, such as princes, bishops, abbots, and archdeacons, who were accustomed to use a seal, must be placed in the roll of petitions (in data communi). The notary must take care not to present forged letters, or he will be treated as a forger. He may, however, freely (libere ac licenter)

---

[1] Ric. of S. Germ., an. 1225, p. 118, ed. Gaudenzi.
[2] *Cf. supra*, vol. xi, p. 53.
[3] *Cf. Liber Censuum*, i, p. 461, n. 209.
[4] *Ib.* : " Nisi que fueriut in communi data recepte."

present the petitions of lowly, and especially of poor, persons, provided that he does not present an outrageous number (multitudo effrenata). All the petitions which he receives for presentation must be written on one sheet of parchment (in una carta) or on several sewn together (in the form of a roll), so that one notary shall be in charge of the petitions of one person.[1]

As a rule, each person was, in the first instance, to present his own petition, except in the case of a dignified personage, who might have a proctor. The petitioner might employ an intercessor (or backer), especially a cardinal.

Finally, Honorius laid it down very stringently that, where there was any question of justice or of obtaining a spiritual favour (pro spirituali negotio), both the giver and the receiver were to be severely punished if bribes were introduced. Noting now that this set of regulations speaks of " notaries, bullatores (officials who affixed the leaden bullas), breviatores, and scriptores," we will refer our readers to the document from which we are quoting,[2] for the few less important regulations which we have omitted.

Up to the time of Pope Honorius it would appear that

[1] The petitions were sewn together in rolls and the date on which they were granted was placed at the bottom of the roll. Later on the common date was ordered to be affixed to each of the petitions which went to make up a particular roll, except, of course, in the case of such as required a special date. The fourth rule of the regulations for the chancellary imposed by Pope Benedict XII. throws light on this subject : " Item mandavit servari quod data in fine rotulorum habentium in se plures petitiones signatas, apposita ponatur in litteris omnium gratiarum in eisdem rotulis contentarum, exceptis gratiis habentibus datas aliquas speciales in quibus apponitur data illa sibi contigua (congrua) et propinqua dumtaxat ; in aliis vero precedentibus et subsequentibus ut premissum est *data communis alia* (alias) apponatur." Ap. Ottenthal, *Regulæ cancellariæ apostolicæ*, p. 9 f., Innsbruck, **1888**.

[2] N. 209, ap. *Lib. Cens.*, vol. i. On this question of *Petitions*, see Bliss in his introduction to *Petitions to the Pope*, vol. i, London, **1896**, in the series *Calendar of entries in the Papal Registers*.

the ancient papal Archives were preserved more or less intact in the Lateran, but that after his time they in some way perished. His pontificate marks an epoch in the history of the papal chancery also from this fact that, after his time, no chancellor of the Roman Church was appointed, but only a vice-chancellor—the title *vice-cancellarius* coming into use about the middle of the thirteenth century.[1]

One of the last acts of Honorius was to find food for his starving people. In the winter of 1226–7 food became so scarce in Rome that a *rubus* of wheat could scarcely be bought for twenty soldi (shillings) ; [2] and in order to wring more money from the suffering multitudes many Roman dealers kept back the supplies which they had in their possession. Complaining bitterly of this inhumanity, Honorius wrote to Frederick begging him to supply the City's needs from the Sicilian granaries, as his predecessors had done for Popes Alexander and Lucius under similar circumstances.[3] The Pope's appeal was listened to, and the Justiciar, Henry de Morra, was ordered to furnish the necessary corn.

Famine in Rome, 1227.

Despite his difficulties and worries with the Roman people, Honorius found time and opportunity to develop those artistic tastes which he had cultivated before he became Pope.

Honorius and Art.

Some twenty miles south of Rome, and three from the

[1] *Cf.* R. L. Poole, *The Papal Chancery*, Cambridge, 1915. He gives an account of the chancery up to the time of Honorius.

[2] Ric. of S. Germ., an. 1227.

[3] Ep., *c.* end of January, ap. H.-B., ii, 710. In his great care for the poor, Honorius decreed that the papal almoner should every year pay to the Hospital of the Holy Ghost in Saxia " seventeen pounds of current money (usualis monetæ)," so that, on the day of the *station* held there, there might be 3 denarii for each one of three hundred inmates of the hospital, and of a thousand poor visitors. One of the denarii was to go to buy bread, another wine, and the third flesh meat. *Regest.*, n. 4416.

sea, there arises a rocky hill on which may be seen the miserable fever-stricken remnants of the once flourishing town of Ardea.   On an adjoining height, the *Civitavecchia* of ' ancient 'Ardea, stands a church dedicated to St. Marina, of whom the legend tells that she passed her life in a monastery of Benedictine monks who were quite unaware of her sex.   Above the doorway of this church is an inscription which runs thus :—-

C̄EC̄I EXCELSE 'E CANCELL URBIS
OBTULIT HĀC PORTĀ VIRGO MARINA †.

There is a doubt about the signification of 'E ; but Tomasetti [1] would appear to have best resolved it.   His reading of the inscription is this : " Cencius excelsæ te cancellarius urbis obtulit hanc portam virgo Marina tibi." He assumes the 'E to stand for *te* (i.e., fecit te hanc portam) and to have been inserted to make an hexameter verse. The inscription, therefore, sets forth : " Virgin Marina, Cencius, chancellor of the great City, offered this gate to thee."   It is supposed by many authors [2] that this offering was made by Cencius, afterwards Honorius III., but Cencius Camerarius is not known to have ever been " chancellor of the city."   The inscription then at St. Marina's must be assigned either to the same Cencius, " chancellor of the great City," i.e., Cencius Benedetti di donna Bona, who set up the inscription over the doorway of San Bartolomeo all'isola in Rome, and who was also at one time [3] confused with the Camerarius, or perhaps to a Cencius Bufalus who was chancellor about the year 1360.[4]

If, however, these inscriptions are of no avail to prove that Cencius Camerarius had any artistic taste, the same

---

[1] *La Campagna Romana*, ii, p. 457 f.
[2] E.g., Horoy, i, p. 34 f.
[3] *Ib.*
[4] *Cf.* Tomasetti, *l.c.*, pp. 450–1.

cannot be said of the legend on the bronze gates in the
Lateran Baptistery, of which an illustration has been
given in a previous volume.[1] The artists who made
them are thereon stated to have been acting under the
orders of the Camerarius Cencius.

The bronze gates also which lead to the other oratory
opening out of the Lateran Baptistery, namely, that on
the left, dedicated to St. John the Evangelist, likewise
bear an inscription stating that they were made by order
of Cencius, cardinal of St. Lucy, as may be seen in the
composite illustration in Ciaconius of the works of
Honorius (*Vit. Pont. Rom.*, vol. i, ed. Rome, 1630).

When the cardinal of St. Lucy became Pope, not only St. Paul's
may he be presumed to have patronized those elegant outside-the-
"parcel" mosaic workers, the Cosmati,[2] with one of walls.
whose names his name is linked in an inscription in the
cathedral of Anagni,[3] but he certainly brought from Venice
mosaic picture workers imbued with Greek traditions.
When he was adorning St. Paul's outside-the-walls, we
find him thanking the Doge of Venice for sending him a
mosaist for that work, and begging him to send him two
others.[4] Despite the fire of 1823, something of the apsidal
mosaic work which Honorius caused to be executed,
probably by these Venetians, still survives.   There can
still be seen, as our illustration shows, the Pontiff (with
his name by his side, "Honorius, PP. III.") in very minute
dimensions, embracing the feet of a Christ, much more
remarkable for its great size than for its artistic beauty.
The figures of this picture, though in general unpleasant,
are, according to Crowe and Cavalcaselle, "remarkable

[1] Vol. x, opp. p. 426.

[2] *Cf. supra*, ix, p. 1.

[3] Given by Crowe and Cavalcaselle, *Hist. of Painting*, i, p. 85 n., ed.
1903.

[4] Ep. of Jan. 23, 1218, ap. *Reg.*, i, p. 173.

for careful setting, a fair definition of light and shadow, a fine and accurate outline, and perfectly jointed cubes of mosaic." An inscription beneath the great mosaic tells us that the work, begun by Honorius, was brought to perfection by the abbot of St. Paul's, John *Caietanus* (John V., 1208–41), whose name also appears in the inscription :

> " Totius orbis honor, quod Honorius artis honore
> Papa prius fecit, fulget fulgente decore,
> Abbas post papam quem, Christus ad alta vocavit,
> Omne Joannis opus mira pietate beavit." [1]

St. Peter's.

Other basilicas also were adorned by Honorius. He spent more than two hundred marks of silvei on the *ciborium* of St. Peter's, and presented that basilica with a chalice weighing one hundred and sixty marks, and a silver lamp weighing one hundred and twenty.[2] He gave similar chalices to the Lateran and to St. Mary Majoi's.

St. Lawrence outside-the-walls.

The church of S. Lorenzo fuori-le-mura owes its present shape to Honorius III. Before his time there were two basilicas, one of Constantine and the other of Sixtus III., " one orientated and the other not, so that the apses met in the middle till they were thrown together by Honorius III." The ambos, the Cosmatic pavement, and the choir of the present church date from the same period, as does also the portico, on the narrow frieze of which may be seen a small half-figure of Honorius.[3] This mosaic frieze, if of no artistic value, is of considerable historic importance. Honorius is shown presenting a kneeling figure to

---

[1] Ap. *Lib. Pont.*, ii, p. 453 n. *Cf.* E. Bertaux, *Rome*, pp. 68, 71.

[2] *Cf.* the *Viterbo pontifical catalogue*, ap. *M. G. SS.*, xxii, p. 352. The work of Honorius disappeared when the ciborium was remade by Sixtus IV.

[3] *Cf.* T. G. Jackson, *Byzantine and Romanesque Architecture*, i, p. 193, and *L. P., l.c.* R. van Marle, *Peinture romaine au Moyen Age*, p. 195, has given a confused description of the work of Honorius in this portico.

St. Lawrence, the patron of the church. The red shoes of the kneeling figure enabled Canon Biasiotti to identify it as that of Peter of Courtenay, who was crowned emperor of Byzantium by the Pope in this basilica.

Passing over Honorius' restoration of the famous St. Bibiana. " basilica which is called Sancta Sanctorum,"[1] as his work seems to have quite disappeared in the course of the reconstruction of the sanctuary by Nicholas III.,[2] we may turn to the very old church of St. Bibiana. Built under Pope Simplicius in the fifth century, it was restored by Honorius III. and by Urban VIII. Although the last-named Pontiff thoroughly renovated the church, there may still be seen on its outer left wall traces of ancient pictures, among which is the portrait of a Pope, no doubt that of Honorius III.[3] In the days of Ciaconius an ancient inscription, too, could still be plainly read which set forth that in the month of March, on the Friday before Passion Sunday, in the *seventh* year of his pontificate, Pope Honorius, of happy memory, with great solemnity and reverence consecrated this church in honour of Blessed Bibiana, Virgin and Martyr, and granted an indulgence of three years and three quarantines to such as devoutly visited the church during the anniversary of the octave of its consecration.[4] Unfortunately, this inscription, though old, can scarcely be even approximately contemporary, as the notes of time given in it do not tally.[5]

[1] *Cf.* a Casinese catalogue, ap. *M. G. SS., ib.,* p. 363.

[2] *L. P., l.c.* We may also pass over his work at Viterbo and Casamari.

[3] It is reproduced in the composite illustration which we have given from Ciaconius.

[4] Ap. Ciaconius, *Vit. PP.,* i, p. 671. He took the words of the inscription : "ex veteris ecclesiæ demolitione." *Cf.* Armellini, *Le Chiese di Roma,* p. 804.

[5] In the seventh year of the pontificate of Honorius the day mentioned fell on April 7, but in the eighth year it fell on March 29 ; and on that day in that year (1224) Honorius was in Rome.

But it was not only the revival of the mosaic picture in Italy which Honorius helped forward ; he also fostered the advance of fresco painting, as may be seen in the frescoes which he caused to be executed in the portico of San Lorenzo fuori-le-mura. These were the production of Roman artists who, "unmoved by Byzantine influence," maintained their " old individuality " and traditions.[1] Although their works are partly much faded and partly restored out of all recognition, and though the figures in them are thin and long, still " in composition, distribution, and a certain animation of movement they now and then recall the antique, and . . . they are free from the exaggerated action which had already begun to mark the decline of Greek or Byzantine art." [2]

The States of the Church.

Value of the documents of the pontificate of Honorius for details of papal government. A number of documents, preserved either in the *Liber Censuum* (Tax Book), of which, as we have seen, Honorius himself drew up the best edition, or in his Register,[3] are of material help in dealing with the States of the Church at this period, inasmuch as they furnish us with a number of details of papal government. Beginning our notice of this government with a word or two on the personal rule of Honorius, we find from the documents that, as we should otherwise have expected, it was very paternal. The people of Centumcellæ (Civita Vecchia) were so

---

[1] Crowe and Caval., *l.c.*, p. 67 f.

[2] *Ib.*, p. 68. From what we have seen of the encouragement given to art by the Popes from Innocent II. to Honorius III., and from what we shall have to say on the same subject, of their successors to the end of the Hohenstaufen domination, we may safely affirm that, despite their struggles with that dynasty and with the Commune of Rome, "ecclesiastical Rome was the real staff and stay of young Italian Art " (Sedgwick).

[3] The documents of the Register have been published in full by Theiner, *Cod. diplom.*, vol. i.

touched by his paying off the debt contracted by their commune that they most solemnly renewed their allegiance to him (December 9, 1224). They declared that it was their wish that the Roman Chuich should have perpetual dominion over them for the sake of the great goodness and kindness with which the lord Pope Honorius III. had always treated them, and especially for his having, out of pure charity, relieved their city from the debts under which it was labouring." [1]

Anxious that the Roman Church should not fail on the side of strict pecuniary justice, Honorius, as receipts in the *Tax Book* (Liber Censuum) show, was constantly settling claims which were urged against her. Among these receipts there is an interesting one given by the Gandulfi (January 4, 1217), whose family name is perpetuated by Castel Gandolfo. For damages which their ancestors had received during the troubles between Alexander III. and the Romans, they received from Honorius " two hundred pounds of good provinois of the Senate." [2]

In his endeavours to keep his subjects " free both from the molestations of external foes and from internal dissensions," [3] Honorius aimed at making the feudal nobility respect the rights of the communes, [4] and the communes the rights of the nobles. [5] He also made a point of rewarding those cities which showed themselves specially devoted to the apostolic see. It was on this principle,.

[1] Ap. *Lib. Cens.*, i, p. 10* f., ed. Fabre-Duchesne. The document sets forth that the people were duly summoned by the sound of the bell, and that, in what they did, they were subject neither to force nor fraud.

[2] Ap. *ib.*, p. 255. *Cf. ib.*, p. 455, for a deed showing the purchase by Honorius of rights over Ariccia. On the money " of the senate "' see *supra*, ix, p. 151 f.

[3] Theiner, *Cod. dip.*, i, n. 82.

[4] *Cf. ib.*, n. 61. *Cf.* H. de l'Épinois, *Le Gouvernement des Papes*,. p. 55.

[5] *Ib.*, n. 67.

therefore, that he hearkened to the petition of the people of Fermo, and granted them the right of coining their own money.[1]

The way in
which the
states of the
Church were
ruled during
the thir-
teenth
century.
The great
rectors.

From this period onward for many ages, the States of the Church were divided into a number of great provinces. Of these the Pope appears to have at times kept in his own hands the suzerainty of the one known as " The Patrimony of St. Peter in Tuscany," i.e., the province from Radicofani to Rome, for they regarded this district as their special reserve.[2] But, as a rule, there was a *rector* over this as over the other provinces.[3] The province of Campania, including the Maritima, from Rome and Tivoli to Terracina and Ceprano, also had its rector, and in March, 1217, Honorius nominated for that office John of the title of Sta. Prassede,[4] bidding him " correct the

---

[1] Theiner, *l.c.*, n. 96, p. 61. " Habendi proprium cuneum ad cudendam monetam citra valorem Imperialium, liberam vobis auctoritate presentium concedimus facultatem." In the same way, along with an immunity from certain taxes, Gregory IX. granted the citizens of Gaeta the right of coining money. The coins were to bear on the one side the image of Blessed Peter and the name of the city, and on the other side the image of the Pope with his name running round it. *Cf. Reg. Greg. IX.*, i, p. 191. The right does not appear to have been exercised.

[2] " Hoc (patrimonium) est ejus peculiare pomerium ubi grate subjectionis flores colligit." *Reg. Alex. IV.*, i, p. 4.

[3] In the time of Innocent III. the rector of the Patrimony was his cousin the marshal James. Ep. xvi, 95, Inn. III. *Cf. Regest. Greg. IX.*, i, p. 946, ed. Auvray. We do not propose on this occasion to say anything about the rule of the " Popes in the lands of Matilda," as their control over them in this age was so uncertain. Suffice it to say here that Honorius made strenuous efforts to recover them (*Regest.*, nn. 2490, 2682–3, 2723, etc.), and that when parts of them were recovered, they were enfeoffed to nobles. *Cf. ib.*, 2831–2, 2859, 3110, 3964. Sometimes they were entrusted to towns (*cf.* n. 200) ; and so we have receipts granted to Modena for payment of the taxes due from it to the papal treasury (1219–21) for Carpi and Monte Baranzone. For one year the City had to pay the sum of 135 pounds " bononiensium " as the equivalent of 60 pounds " proveniensium Senatus."

[4] *Reg.*, n. 394.

unruly, encourage the pusillanimous, exalt the humble, and
repress the proud, and distribute rewards according to
merit." [1] The province of Spoleto, too, was in the days
of Honorius governed by a cardinal rector, as we learn
from his letter (August 3, 1220) naming Rainerius,
cardinal deacon of S. Maria in Cosmedin, " to the rectorship (rectoriam) of the said Duchy." [2]

But as the March of Ancona was much less under his
control than the other provinces just named, it was
enfeoffed by him to Azzo (or Aczolinus, etc.), marquis
of Este, for one hundred pounds of the money of Provins,
with the obligation of sending on demand a hundred
men for a month's service in the Patrimony every year.[3]
However, as the century progressed, the March of Ancona
had a rector like the other provinces.[4] Still less direct
control had Pope Honorius over the province of Romania
(Romaniola, Romagna). He had to leave it under the
spiritual and temporal sway of the archbishop of Ravenna,
whose authority was in turn often contested by imperial
nominees.[5] But certainly in the second half of the
thirteenth century, if not before, there were rectors of
Romaniola.[6]

[1] *Ib.*, n. 397. The Pope says he knows that he wishes to be loved
rather than feared, and so hopes he will rule not so much by power
as by love. Both these letters are given in full, ap. Theiner, *Cod.
dip.*, i, p. 47. John was apparently succeeded by Romanus, cardinal
deacon of St. Angelo. *Cf. Reg.*, n. 2350, March 6, 1220.

[2] Ap. Theiner, *l.c.*, p. 56.

[3] *Reg.*, n. 467, March 31, 1217. " Marchiam Anconitanam in rectum
tibi feudum concedimus." Ep. in full ap. Horoy, ii, p. 347. The
investiture was conferred by a banner. *Cf.* nn. 89 and 90, p. 58, ap.
Theiner, *l.c.*

[4] *Cf.* the *Regest.* of Inn. IV., n. 6557. " Rector Marchie Anconitane."
See also Theiner, *ubi infra*, p. 82, n. 138, and p. 93, n. 157.

[5] *Cf.* Huillard-Bréholles, *Hist. Dip.*, ii, pp. 74 and 186 ff.

[6] Theiner, *l.c.*, nn. 364, 374, 423, and 430. N. 374 is addressed by
Nicholas III. (1278) to Berthold Ursinus, " the rector in temporal

Of the papal states there now only remain for discussion the city and environs of Benevento, a sort of papal oasis in the kingdom of the two Sicilies. Over-looking the valleys of the Calore and the Sabato, the walled city of Benevento derived no little of its importance from its position at the point where the Appian Way in its course to the south bifurcated. Definitely acknowledged by Henry III. to belong to the Roman See,[1] it was always regarded by the Popes as one of their most important possessions. To this strategically placed and loyal stronghold Honorius at least was wont to nominate one of his chaplains as *rector*.[2]

Duration of the rectors' rule.

These great rectors held office at the will of the Pope who nominated them, but usually for as long as he lived. Each new Pontiff, however, as a rule appointed fresh rectors, and not unfrequently the same rector was entrusted with the rule of more than one province.[3]

The lesser rectors.

Officials with the same title of rector were also appointed to some of the cities and counties ; and so in the register of Honorius we read of the rector of Segni, of Umana and of Piperno,[4] and there is mention in the papal registers of a rector of Massa Trabaria, of the Terra Arnulphi, and the county of Bertinoro.

The powers of the rectors.

The rectors or governors of the provinces were, if clerics, often cardinals or high ecclesiastics who were their

---

affairs in Romandiola." " Te in predictis partibus generalem Rectorem in temporalibus duximus ordinandum . . . exequendi ea que ad nostram . . . pertinent jurisdictionem temporalem . . . necnon et rebelles temporali districtione . . . compellendi concessa tibi . . . plenaria potestate."

[1] *Cf. supra*, vol. vi, 117.
[2] *Reg.*, nn. 3718, 5663, 5699, etc.
[3] *Cf.* Savio, *Niccolo III.*, n. 3, pp. 35–7.
[4] *Ib.*, nn. 4156, 2715, 3888. *Cf.* Theiner, *Cod. diplom. S. Sedis*, i, p. 129, n. 236, where we find Innocent IV. granting the *rectorship* [rectoriam] of Radicofani to one Sarracenus.

rulers both in spiritual and temporal concerns ; [1] but
they were perhaps almost equally often only laymen,[2]
and in that case they were assisted by rectors who had
spiritual jurisdiction.[3]

Among other powers possessed by the rector was that
of nominating the different officials for the counties,
communes, and other places in his province, such as
lieutenants (balivos), judges, and notaries.[4] And among
their duties was that of summoning the people for the
purposes of peace or war, of raising the taxes, and
receiving appeals.[5]

The rectors of the provinces who sometimes had
control of more than one province [6] were appointed
by the Pope. In nominating the cardinal-deacon
Matthew " to the rectorship (rectoria) of the Patrimony
of Blessed Peter in Tuscany," Urban IV. thus addressed
him : " In full trust in your industry and prudence,
of which we have had long experience, we entrust to you
by the authority of these presents the rectorship of the
aforesaid Patrimony in matters spiritual and temporal.

Appointment of the rectors.

[1] *Cf.* Theiner, *l.c.,* p. 56, n. 82. This document shows Honorius III.
naming Cardinal Rainerius rector of Spoleto. " Ceterum ne quid tue
videatur auctoritati deesse, spiritualem et temporalem tibi concedimus
potestatem." *Cf. ib.,* p. 174, nn. 319-22, *re* a lay rector.

[2] *Cf. ib.,* p. 151, n. 279, where Urban IV. names " the noble, Guiscard
of Petrasancta, Captain and rector of the Patrimony." *Cf.* the Register
of Gregory IX., ii, p. 857, ed. Auvray.

[3] *Cf. Reg. Greg. IX.,* i, p. 59, n. 169 f., and *Reg. Nichol. IV.,* i, p. 453 ;
and ii, 939. Hence in the *Introiti e Esiti di P. Niccolo III.,* under the
year 1279, there is mention of the notaries " del vicario ispiritale."

[4] Innocent IV., writing to a new rector of the March of Ancona
(Jan. 25, 1251, ap. Rodenberg, *Epp. Rom. Pont.,* iii, p. 29), bids him
" ita quod balivos, judices, notarios in comitatibus, communantiis,
et locis aliis statuas et ordines, quemadmodum ibi faciebamus nos ipsi,
dum illius gerebamus regimen in minori officio constituti." He was
rector in 1239 and 1240.

[5] *Cf. ib.,* p. 107, ep. of Dec. 18, 1251.

[6] *Cf. Reg. Greg. IX.,* i, p. 325 f., n. 497 f., and *Reg. Urban IV.,*
ii, p. 305.

We grant to you full power to ordain for it whatever you
shall judge to be for the good of the church therein
and for the advantage of its people, and we moreover
concede to you, as the final court of appeal, the right of
proceeding by spiritual and temporal means against
any who may oppose your authority." [1]

It would appear also that the Popes themselves
nominated the treasurers of the Provinces, and gave
them seemingly a salary of over a hundred pounds
a year.[2] No doubt in appointing these greater Rectors
of the different States of the Church, the Popes were
in the habit of consulting the cardinals ; but it was not
till the days of Nicholas IV. that the right to be consulted
on this matter was formally accorded to them.[3] Nicholas
further decreed that they were also to be responsible
for the appointment and dismissal of the collectors
of the revenues of the said States.[4]

With regard to the lesser rectors, they were in some

[1] *Reg. Urban IV.*, ii, p. 425 f., n. 875 ff., ed. Guiraud. *Cf. Reg.
Alex. IV.*, i, p. 4, ed. de la Roncière for a similar appointment.
Alexander urges the new rector to betake himself to his province,
and so to use his power as to win grace from God, favour from the Pope,
and an illustrious reputation among men. *Cf. Epp. Inn. III.*, iii, 29,
and Theiner, *l.c.*, i, n. 82. Latini, *ubi infra*, c. 7, p. 586, says : " Ce
est li propres guerredons de seignorie (the rector or podestà) à conoistre
que il doit avoir la cure de la cité, et maintenir ses honors et ses dignitez,
et garder la loi, et faire droit ; et que toutes les choses sont bailliées
à sa foi."

[2] At any rate, Nicholas IV. named a treasurer for the March of
Ancona. See his *Register*, vol. ii, p. 957 ; and the account book of
Nicholas III. gives the yearly salary of a treasurer : " De'dare libre
cento solidi sei e denari sei di ravignani, per lo salaro del tesoriere,
per uno Anno." *Introiti ed esiti di P. Niccolo III.*, p. 111, ed. Palmieri.

[3] *Cf.* Ep. of July 18, 1289, ap. Theiner, *Cod. diplom.*, i, p. 304.
" Sancimus, ut institutio et destitutio Rectorum qui preerunt locis
et terris predictis, . . . fiat de consilio Cardinalium predictorum."

[4] *Ib.* The object of Nicholas in making these regulations was to
ensure to the cardinals for the future the half of the ecclesiastical
revenues which he had promised them.

cases named by the Pope,[1] but in many other cases
the communes had obtained the right of electing their
own rectors or podestàs or captains, along with their
subordinates, judges, notaries, etc., " under whatever
other names their officials might be designated." [2]

Even in the case of those cities which had acquired
the right to manage their own affairs, and whose chief
magistrates had civil and criminal jurisdiction,[3] their
rector or podestà had to be confirmed by the Pope ;
but in their case the confirmation was merely formal,
and had to be granted unless the candidate was " under
excommunication or was an enemy of the Church." [4]
Under those circumstances the Pope exercised a veto
over the appointment of the chief magistrate.[5] Moreover,
even the most privileged communes could not make
exactly what bye-laws they wished, nor impose taxes
at will.   To make new regulations or raise new taxes

---

[1] Innocent III., ep. ii, 256 ;   *Reg. Alex. IV.*, i, p. 33, n. 128.
Brunetto Latini, who tells us all about these podestàs, assures us that
" il avient sovent que li conseilleor establissent demander à mon
signor l'apostoile ou à l'empereor que il lor mande i bon governeor
cele année."   *Li Livres dou Trésor*, l. iii, pt. ii, c. 4, p. 582, ed. Chabaille.

[2] *Cf.* a concession of Gregory IX. to Civita Castellana, in which he
confirms to that city the same privileges as are enjoyed by " other
cities of the Patrimony " ;   " scilicet in eligendis et faciendis potestatibus
seu consulibus, judicibus, camerariis, et notariis, consulibus mercatorum
et omnibus aliis officialibus . . . quibuscumque nominibus censeantur."
Ap. Theiner, *l.c.*, n. 152, p. 88.   *Cf.* n. 188, p. 109, where Gregory IX.
grants the people of Assisi permission to elect their podestà and other
officials, " like the other cities of the Duchy of Spoleto."   See his
Register, ii, pp. 755–6.   These podestàs generally chose their own
officials, judges, notaries, etc.   Latini, *l.c.*, p. 587 f.   The same author
assures us that it was the duty of the podestà himself to receive the
envoys of the Pope.   *Ib.,* c. 16 f., p. 602 f.

[3] *Cf.* ep. Inn. IV., ap. Rod., iii, p. 108.

[4] *Ep. Inn. III.*, vii, 83, with special reference to Assisi.

[5] *Cf.* examples of the use of this veto in Theiner, *l.c.*, i, nn.
139, 308.

they had to acquire papal permission.[1]   Sometimes, also,
as a punishment, the Popes curtailed the jurisdiction
of a commune, or forbade it to elect municipal officers.[2]
As a rule, too, in the States of the Church, the rector or
podestà of a city, who was elected annually,[3] had, except
with express pontifical leave to the contrary, to be elected
from among the citizens of the place.[4]   However, this
rule was often broken, and it is not rare to see the Popes
themselves elected podestàs for life.[5]

In some of the provinces, as in those of Campania
and the March, nobles or bishops held the supreme
civil and criminal jurisdiction in different places.[6]   Thus
we see Honorius himself writing that with a banner he
had invested Rainald, bishop of Fermo, who had belonged
to his court (de familia nostra) with the county of
Fermo.[7]   As the towns grew in power they were not
content to have their affairs managed for them from
without, and by one way or another, sometimes by
payment of money to the Pope, they acquired the right
of electing their own officials.[8]   With a central govern-

[1] Cf. Theiner, l.c., i, p. 106 ff., nn. 182-3 ; p. 129, n. 238 ; p. 265,
n. 423 ; Reg. Greg. IX., ii, pp. 277, 363, 667 ; Reg. Urb. IV., ii, 374,
384 ; Reg. Clement. IV., i, p. 2 ; Liber Censuum, i, p. 396, ed. Fabre.

[2] On Apr. 2, 1267, Clement IV. exempted the district of Pietralunga
from the jurisdiction of Città di Castello. Lib. Cens., i, 587 ; and
in 1281 Martin IV. forbade the people of Benevento to elect municipal
officials. Ib., p. 585 f.

[3] On the annual election of rectors, podestàs, or consuls, see Theiner,
l.c., i, p. 95, n. 161, and p. 165, n. 308. Cf. Latini, l.c., p. 576.

[4] Ib., p. 82, n. 137, and p. 264, n. 423. N. 113, p. 71, states that the
people of Porcena may elect their own consuls " ex hominibus Castri
vestri." N. 48, p. 40, shows Innocent III. forbidding the people of
Sutri "ut absque licentia . . . Rom. pontificis . . . numquam de
cetero assumatis extraneum ad vestre regimen civitatis."

[5] Cf. Reg. Honor. IV., pp. 584-5, and Theiner, i, p. 369, n. 544.

[6] Theiner, i, p. 48, n. 65 ; p. 305, n. 469.

[7] Cf. Regesta Firmana, p. 348, n. 75. Cf. nn. 74, 76-8.

[8] Ib., pp. 310-13, nn. 480, 482, 484, and Reg. Nich. IV., i, p. 550 f.
Cf. Liber Censuum, i, p. 594 f., ed. Fabre.

ment, like most of those in the Middle Ages, anything but strong, it is not hard to understand that there was a great deal of unrest at times in the states of the Church. Bishops and nobles were striving to retain their old privileges over growing towns now able to help themselves and eager for emancipation ; and in the towns themselves the mass of the people were battling for political freedom with the knightly class above them,[1] whilst their Podestàs or other chief magistrates were ever aiming at increasing their power at the expense of the central government.[2]

In the cities which had won the right of self-government the administration was usually in the hands of the Podestà, who was assisted by a body of *consiliarii* forming the *consilium*.[3] Hence the letters of the Popes are very frequently addressed to the " Podestà, consilium, and commune " of a city. On important matters the whole body of the citizens (universitas hominum) was summoned by the voice of heralds and by the sound of bells to deliberate together in the Palace of the commune.[4] To assist the Podestà in criminal cases were the judges (judices), who were either chosen by the people of the cities which had acquired that right,[5] or were nominated and paid by the Pope.[6] The account

[1] *Cf.* e. g. *Reg. Greg. IX.*, i, p. 438, and Theiner, *l.c.*, i, p. 76, n. 127.

[2] Hence we find Urban IV. threatening magistrates with deprivation of office and other penalties who should attempt to stop appeals either to the Roman Curia or to the rectors of the Provinces. *Cf. Liber Censuum*, i, p. 568.

[3] *Cf.* Theiner, *ib.*, " Consiliarii civitatis."

[4] " Congregata Universitate hominum Castri Radicofani in palatio Communitatis." *Ib.*, n. 434, p. 275. *Cf.* n. 451, p. 289.

[5] They had to be approved by the Pope, who refused to recognize them if he did not consider them suitable. *Cf. Epp. Innocent III.*, x, 161.

[6] *Cf.* a bull of Alexander IV. (March 19, 1257) conferring the office of judge and recorder (tam judicatus quam tabellionatus officia) on

book of Nicholas III. contains many entries of payments made to ordinary judges or to the supreme judge of a province ; [1] and other papal documents show the judges receiving instructions from Rome.[2]

The making of a papal Commune, 1252.

Before leaving this subject of the Popes' methods of ruling their States, we may notice one of the miscellaneous documents preserved by certain editions of the *Liber Censuum*.[3] It enables us to see the formation of a commune, and under what democratic conditions it took place.

On a certain Thursday in August, 1252, there met together in the hill town of Penna San Giovanni not far from Fermo all its people, its nobles and its commoners "in public parliament," under the presidency of the Rector of the March of Ancona, Walter, Archdeacon of Luni and papal chaplain. Thereupon the Rector asked that the fortified citadel of the place should be handed over to representatives of the Pope, as he wished to have it in his own hands, as the people had been in rebellion. Replying for the nobles, Monalducius, the lord of Paganelli, said that the request was reasonable, and proposed that the fortress should be given up.

a Roman citizen. The fitness of the candidate was certified in the Pope's presence, and then his various powers were confirmed to him by the bull. These powers of issuing decisions, examining witnesses, expounding the law, freeing serfs, etc., are thus expressed : " cum potestate dandi tutores et curatores, decretum interponendi, decernendi alimenta, testes recipiendi et publicanda acta, protocolla et instrumenta, exemplandi, nec non auctoritatem præstandi, emancipare, manumittere et adoptare volentibus." *Cf. Reg. Alex. II.*, vol. ii, n. 1815, p. 560, and see n. 2079.

[1] *Cf.* a payment of 53 pounds, 3 solidi, and 7 denarii to messer Giovanni d'Ascesi, " giudice generale ne la Marca : i quali denari sono per suo salario da dì xiii d'aprile infino a calen di luglio." *Introiti ed esiti di P. Niccolò III.*, p. 87, ed. Palmieri. *Cf. supra*, vol. ix, p. 72 n.

[2] *Reg. Greg. IX.*, i, p. 479, n. 756.

[3] i, p. 563 f., ed. Fabre.

He was followed by the notary, Master James Munaldi, who, speaking in behalf of the people in general, supported the motion of the lord of Paganelli, and when the motion was put by the Rector it was carried without a dissentient voice.[1] The fortress was to be used for the advantage of the Roman Church and the defence of the people of the locality. In turn the Pope permitted the people to form a commune, with such privileges as were generally possessed by the other communes of the March.[2]

The recent mention of Fermo serves to remind one, by means of a rescript addressed to it by Honorius in 1220, that the larger communes were sometimes called upon to see that justice was done by the smaller ones.[3]

As governments cannot exist without money, one of the most important duties of the papal officials, or of the locally elected rulers of the cities that were subject to the Pope, was to raise taxes both for local and general necessities. By the usual direct and indirect methods of taxation the local officials collected money, some of which they used for the purposes of local government. The rest they transmitted to the papal treasury for the general purposes of the government of the papal states. Unfortunately the sources of information on this subject at our command are as meagre as those on the other questions of papal government during this period. It is certain, however, that the papal revenues arising from the Church at large, in the

Papal Revenues.

[1] "Omnibus de parlamento nemine contra dicente predicta et ea approbaverunt." *Ib.*

[2] "Concedendo eisdem hominibus quod de cetero possint communantiam constituere, . . . et habeant jus et approbatas consuetudines quas habent communiter alie communancie que sunt in Anconitana Marchia." *Ib.*

[3] *Regesta Firmana*, n. 66, p. 344, annexed to the ed. of De Minicis of the *Cronache di Fermo*, Florence, 1870.

shape of charges for the issue of *bulls*, for exemptions, etc., or from special countries in the shape of Peter's Pence or feudal dues, were supplemented by the taxes paid by the states of the Church. For instance, in the year 1291 the city of Reate paid the papal treasury as its annual tax the sum of thirty gold florins ;[1] and about the same time the whole revenue of the Duchy of Spoleto, the County of Sabina, and three other places of smaller importance was 7,760 pounds, 41 solidi, and 4 denarii. After the salaries of the " Rector, judges, and officials, and the other necessary expenses " of the province had been met, there was left a sum of 2,611 pounds, 13 solidi, and 4 denarii to be handed over to the papal treasury for the general purposes of government.[2]

The nobles also who held portions of the papal states as fiefs [3] had also to contribute to the revenue of the Pope by payments for their fiefs.[4] Moreover, in further

---

[1] Theiner, *l.c.*, i, p. 321. " *Solutio census Communis Reatini.*" Then follows the receipt from the papal treasurer. Terni paid 100 pounds (*ib.*, p. 283). Fano and Camerino, 50 pounds each. *Cf. epp. Innocent III.*, iii, 52–3 ; or, in the case of Fano, 9 denarii from every hearth. *Cf.* ep. Inn. IV., Dec. 18, 1251, ap. Rod., iii, p. 107.

[2] Among other purposes to which these receipts were applied was that of making good deficiencies from other quarters of the papal States. The receipt (Theiner, *ib.*, p. 321) affirms this in so many words. The money helped " pro diminuendis debitis in quibus dicta Camera et Cardinales communiter tenentur occasione pecuniarum terrarum Ecclesie, in quibus plus expensuum extitit quam receptum." These particular monetary transactions were conducted through six firms of bankers. *Cf.* other documents, ap. *ib.*, pp. 268 ff. and 360 ff.

[3] They took the usual feudal oath to the Pope, and sometimes at least were invested with their fiefs by means of a silver cup. Cf. *Lib. Censuum*, i, p. 458, n. 206, ann. 1225.

[4] E.g., " Item a Ricardo de Anibaldis pro censu Castri Petre Porci quod tenet in feudum ab ecclesia Rom. 2 sol. proven." Theiner, p. 360. In 1267 Peter de Vico paid the Holy See annually 10 bysants for Città-Vecchia and Bieda. *Cf. Liber Censuum*, i, p. 452, ed. Fabre. Cities, too, were invested with fiefs and had to pay an acknowledgment

connexion with the feudal system, it may be added that the papal curia naturally drew revenue from the ordinary feudal dues such as *aids* at Christmas and Easter.[1]

As the thirteenth century advanced, moneys due to and by the Apostolic See on these various counts were paid over less and less directly. Debtors and creditors settled their business transactions through a third party. The Templars or civil bankers (cambiatores, campsores, and finally, most commonly, mercatores) were increasingly employed as the medium for the transmission of moneys by rulers and by all who had large pecuniary transactions. For a long period these bankers were known as *Lombards*, as it was in Lombardy and the adjacent provinces that a rapid development of commerce led in the twelfth century to the rise of the system of banking. Papal documents of this period show constant transactions between the Popes and banking companies in Pistoia, Piacenza, Florence, Lucca, Siena, etc. For instance, a letter of Cardinal Ugolino Conti cites a declaration of Sinibaldus,[2] the *camerarius* of Honorius III., to the effect that " Aeringerius, the son of Foresi, the Florentine banker," had paid to him " sixty pounds of the provinois of the Senate in behalf of the commune of Modena in payment of the tax due by it for two *castra*." [3] Moreover,

Money transactions through bankers (mercatores).

for them. Ferrara had to pay the Pope an annual tax " of 30 marks of legal silver " for Massa Fiscalia, with which it was invested. *Lib. C.,* i, p. 479, ann. 1221.

[1] *Cf.*, e.g., " Castrum Roscianum (Castel Rosciano on the left bank of the Chiaggio between Bettona and Tergiano) solvit . . . pro *adjutorio* Nativitatis vi libras, pro *adjutorio* Pasce resurrectionis iii libras." See a document concerning the papal revenue drawn from the Duchy of Spoleto, ap. *Liber C.,* i, p. 450 ff.

[2] Both these men were afterwards Popes, Gregory IX. and Innocent IV.

[3] G. Levi, *Documenti ad illustraz. del Regist. del card. Ugolino,* ap. *Archiv. della Soc. Rom. di storia,* 1889, p. 312. This document is

a letter of Honorius himself shows that moneys were paid by his order to Sienese bankers in order that they might be at the disposition of the bishop of Siena.[1]

These *campsores*, whom Matthew Paris calls *Caursini* as well as mercatores,[2] and who found their way all over Europe, were largely employed by the Popes to collect the Peter's Pence and the other revenues due to them. Even when these merchant-bankers did not directly charge interest, they of course made profit out of their work. The taxes were paid them in the money, not unfrequently depreciated, of the country whence they were collected, and sometimes even in kind. It was, therefore, in exchanging such receipts into the currency of Rome that the bankers made their money. They gave acknowledgments to the papal officials for the amounts they had received in the different countries, and then settled the sum payable in Rome " in provinois of the Senate." Not always were the merchant-bankers content with the profit which they made by exchange.

further interesting as giving a description of the chamberlain's seal : Round it ran the words : " Me cum prole pia custodi Virgo Maria," and within the circle of this invocation were three images with two stars above them.

[1] " Cum Egidius . . . capellanus noster mercatoribus Senensibus quamdam concesserit pecunie quantitatem ad certos terminos nostre camere persolvendam, cujus summam, nomina mercatorum et terminos quibus ipsa pecunia solvi debet, per transcriptum litterarum ejusdem capellani, quod tibi hiis presentibus mittimus interclusum, perpendere poteris." Levi, *Regist. dei Card. Ugolino*, p. 152 f. " Bobo Johannis Bobonis " seems to be the first papal banker (campsor cameræ) whose name is known to us. *Cf.* Jordan, *Le Saint Siège et les banquiers italiens*, Brussels, 1895, and his *De mercatoribus cameræ Apost.*, Condate Rhedonum (Rennes), 1909, from whom, after verification, these references have been taken. *Cf. supra*, vol. ix, p. lvii ; and W. E. Rhodes, " The Italian bankers in England," ap. *Hist. Essays by members of Owen's College*, London, 1902 ; and R. J. Whitwell, " Italian Bankers and the English Crown," ap. *Transactions of the Roy. Hist. Soc.*, 1903, p. 175 ff.

[2] *Chron. maj.*, iii, 188 f., and 328 f.

Despite the laws against usury, they contrived under
one term or another to charge interest, " pretending,"
says Matthew Paris, who denounces them most cordially,
" not to know that whatever is added to the principle
(accrescit sorti) is usury under whatever name it may
be called." [1] No doubt with the growth of the banking
system it came to be recognized at Rome that, at least
in certain cases, some interest could be charged on
loans. At any rate, in practice the Popes would appear
to have tolerated the addition as interest of an eighth,
or even of a quarter, to the sum originally borrowed.

[1] *Ib.*, p. 328.

CHAPTER V.

THE BRITISH ISLES. ACTION OF HONORIUS IN VARIOUS COUNTRIES.

Sources.—In addition to those cited in previous volumes we have only to add *Royal and other historical letters illustrative of the reign of Henry III.*, 2 vols., London, 1862, ed. W. W. Shirley, *R.S.* Various English Monastic Annals, such as those of Dunstable, are now useful. Ed Luard, *R.S.*

Modern Works.—The first place must be given to that excellent and painstaking work of Miss Kate Norgate, *The Minority of Henry the Third*, London, 1912, of which free use has been made in the following pages. The little book of H. R. Luard, *On the relations between England and Rome*, Cambridge, 1877, is of no little utility as a catalogue as far as it goes, viz., to the end of the year 1235. Letters printed in full from the MS. register of Honorius give special value to the short work of N. Mengozzi, *P. Onorio III e le sue relazioni col regno di Inghilterra*, Siena, 1911.

Honorius and King John.

To Englishmen, Honorius III. ought to be a person of special interest for, through his legates,[1] he was the effective ruler of our country during the minority of Henry III. His rule ought, moreover, to be viewed by them with gratitude, as it is agreed by historians who have made a special study of this period that his rule was distinctly beneficial.[2]

Up to the time of his death, Innocent III. was engaged in supporting King John against the citizens of London, and a large number of his barons, who, in conjunction with his rival, Prince Louis of France, were in possession

[1] The legate Pandulf was "practically the ruler of the country." Luard, *England and Rome*, p. 67 n.

[2] "That, on the whole, the powers of the Papacy were judiciously exercised, cannot, I think, be denied ; and that the object of the Popes, at least at this time, was to do right seems to me equally clear." *Ib.*, p. 68. Miss Norgate's testimony is to the same effect.

of his capital and nearly half of his kingdom. In this, as in other matters, Honorius continued the policy of his predecessor, and a few days after his election dispatched a letter (July 25) to Gualo, cardinal-priest of St. Martin. Consoling him for the difficulties he had met with in the performance of his duty, he confirmed his appointment as legate, and bade him encourage " our most beloved son John, King of the English, our vassal and illustrious crusader." [1] Again, about two months later (September 20), after he had received from the legate a letter which had been addressed to Pope Innocent, he wrote to sympathize once more with his trouble, and gave him " full power to help the King and Kingdom in every way that he thought to be expedient," whilst warning him to be careful " not to do anything in an over-bold manner (insolenter) " which might bring disgrace upon the Church.[2]

The advice was in season, for Gualo had a most delicate task to perform. In October, King John, realizing that his last hour was drawing nigh, wrote to tell this to Honorius, and to assure him that, whilst he was earnestly deliberating how he might best provide for the honour of God and the Roman Church, as well as for the succession of his son, he called to mind that " our kingdom is the patrimony of Blessed Peter and the Roman Church, and is under the divine apostolic protection." [3] Accordingly in the presence of our nobles we entrusted " our kingdom, which is yours," and our heir to your protection. " If

---

[1] Ep. i, 4, ed. Horoy.

[2] i, 29. *Ib.* He also wrote in John's behalf to the archbishops of Bordeaux (Sept. 16), Rheims, Rouen, etc. (Oct. 26), bidding them take strong action in John's behalf. Potthast, 5333 and 5348.

[3] " Ad memoriam reducentes quod regnum nostrum esset patrimonium b. Petri et S. Romane ecclesie et divina et apostolica protectione munitum." Ep. of John, ap. Mengozzi, p. 88, or Raynaldus, *Hist. Eccles.*, 1216, n. 31 f.

you will stretch out to him your fatherly hand, his succession is assured, and if you will grant us the absolution of our sins we may enjoy the benefits of God's mercy."

The acces-
sion of
Henry, 1216. A few days after the dispatch of this pitiful letter, King John went to face his Maker (October 18), after having named Cardinal Gualo, William the Marshal, earl of Pembroke (to whom he had specially commended his youthful son), and others the executors of his will.[1]

John's death and the papal protection procured the crown for Henry, and saved the country from the rule of France. Gualo and the Pope at once took up the cause of the young prince. Under the presidency of the former, a council held at Gloucester (October 27) decided that Henry should be crowned on the following day.[2] Accordingly, on the feast of SS. Simon and Jude, the youthful prince was crowned King of England by the bishop of Winchester acting under the orders of the legate, inasmuch as the Archbishop of Canterbury, Stephen Langton, was absent from the realm.[3] During the ceremony the young monarch swore to honour God and his Church, to do justice to his people, and to abolish all evil customs. "He then did homage to the holy Roman Church and to the

[1] Rymer, *Fœdera*, i, pt. i, p. 144, ap. Norgate, *John Lackland*, p. 285. *Cf.* ep. Hon., i, 149, Jan. 17, 1217, ed. Horoy.

[2] Roger of Wendover, vol. iv, p. 1 f., ed. Coxe.

[3] Henry himself, in a letter to the Justiciar of Iréland, says he was crowned "by the hands of Gualo . . . and the bishops then present." See the Close Rolls ap. *Foed.*, i, pt. i, p. 145. This is explained by William of Coventry (*Mem.*, ii, p. 233, R. S.), the *Annals of Merton* (ap. Petit-Dutaillis, *Louis VIII.*, p. 512), and others to mean that he was actually crowned by the Bishop of Winchester by order of the legate : "ex jussu legati." According to the Chronicle of Melrose, an. 1216, the abbot of Westminster and the prior of Canterbury appealed to Rome against the action of Gualo—the first because the coronation had not taken place at Westminster, and the second because it ought to have been performed by the Archbishop of Canterbury. Under the circumstances, it is not to be supposed that these "touchy" persons got much satisfaction from Rome.

Pope for the kingdoms of England and Ireland, and he swore that he would faithfully pay the thousand marks promised by his father to the Roman Church." [1]   The next care of the legate was to secure the services of the best man in the realm, Pembroke the Marshal, to be the guardian of the King and the country.   Gualo, so we are told by William's biographer, " prayed the Marshal in God's name to take the regency (la baillie) for the remission of his sins . . ." [2]   Thus adjured, the Marshal accepted the charge, and at the further request of the legate, he named the Bishop of Winchester guardian of the young King's person.[3]   Hence, says William of Coventry, " by common consent the care of the King and the kingdom was entrusted to the legate, to the Bishop of Winchester, and to the Marshal, William earl of Pembroke." [4]

While, on the one hand, the prompt action of the legate and the tender youthfulness of the King appealed to many of his father's enemies, and induced them to come over to his side in order not to visit the sins of the father on his child, there were on the other hand others who declared

The action of the Pope and the legate in Henry's behalf.

---

[1] R. of W., *l.c.*, p. 2.

[2] No decision could at first be arrived at :—

> " Mès que li legaz tote veie
> Les mena a la dreit veie (way),
> Tant preia por Dieu e requist
> Le Mar que il preïst
> La baillie en remission
> De ses pecchiez en en perdon."

L'hist. de Guillaume le Maréchal, vol. ii, v. 15547 ff.   *Cf.* the words of the Marshal on his death-bed :—

> " E li legaz grant peine i mist
> Et tant me preia et requist
> Que, por vos toz oveques lui,
> Le rei et le reigne rechui."
> > *Ib.*, v. 18009 ff.

[3] *Ib.*, l. 15597 ff.

[4] *L.c.*, ii, p. 233.

that they would never have any of John's offspring to
rule over them.   Against these, Gualo, acting on his
instructions, exerted himself to the utmost.   He argued,
he entreated, and he threatened.   Against the wilful, he
even " drew the sword of Peter." [1]   This last act of
rigour he exercised at the council of Bristol (November 11),
to which he summoned the bishops and the loyal nobles.
After the cardinal had compelled all present to swear
fealty to the young king, he put the whole of Wales under
an interdict " because it held with the barons," and he
repeated his excommunication of the King's enemies,
including Louis of France.[2]

Honorius
supports
Gualo.

The able and prudent measures taken by Gualo to
secure the succession of Henry and the expulsion of the
French from England were backed up by energetic
action on the part of Honorius.   One letter followed
another in quick succession.   On December 1, the rebellious
barons of England were reminded that they could no
longer plead " the intolerable yoke " of King John.   They
should now give their allegiance to his son, who certainly
had not offended them.   We in whose hands the King
left his children and his kingdom will take steps to remove
the abuses of which you complain.   If the barons do not
listen to him, who is the special guardian of the orphan
as well as the suzerain of the kingdom, he will invoke
heaven and earth against them.[3]   On the other hand, the

[1] " At legatus pro viribus partes regis fovebat mandans et monens
. . . arguens et increpans in contradicentes vel inobedientes gladium
Petri exserens ; acceperat etenim hoc in mandatis."   Will of C., *ib.*
[2] Rymer, *ib.*, and the Waverley Annals ap. *Annal. Monast.*, ii,
286 R. S.   The Chronicle of Melrose, an. 1216, says that the legate
included in his sentence : " Our Lord the King of the Scots and all
his nobility," and that he did not " hesitate to place the lands of all
of them under interdict."
[3] Ep. i, 74, ed. Horoy.   "Nos, enim, in cujus manibus et tutela
idem rex (John) et eosdem pupillos reliquit et regnum, de . . .
gravaminibus quæ per abusum ab eodem rege vobis dicebatis inferri

earl of Pembroke, the justiciar Hubert de Burgh and the
other faithful nobles are exhorted to be constant in their
fidelity (December 3),[1] and his legate Gualo and other
ecclesiastics are exhorted to firmness in Henry's behalf,
and instructed to proclaim that the oaths taken by the
barons to Louis were unlawful (December 3).[2]

To bring direct pressure on Louis, Honorius bade the
abbots of Cîteaux and Clairvaux go to Philip of France
and urge him [3] to restrain his son, and at the same time
to remind the Prince himself that the Pope's hand will
be raised against him if he does not cease to persecute
the royal orphans.[4] Probably about this same time he
wrote to Henry himself, exhorting him to cling to virtue
from his youth, and to reverence God in his ministers, in
order that he might hereafter be able to govern his people
" in sweet peace, and rich rest." Moreover, " because
character is wont to be formed by those with whom we
live, do you strive," he wrote, at the close of his letter, " to
have prudent and honourable friends who, with true
zeal for your advantage and honour, may in your interest
endeavour to bring about what may please God and man."[5]

Honorius writes to the young King.

. . . sic vobis curabimus providere, quod a cordibus vestris cujuslibet
. . . rancoris scrupulus . . . merito poterit amoveri."

[1] Ep. i, 81. *Cf.* also a similar letter of Jan. 19, 1217, printed in
full ap. Mengozzi, p. 89. In it he says that although he had full
confidence in the Marshal, " Licet de tua constantia geramus spem
certam . . . te tamen apostolicis exhortationibus confortandum
duximus."

[2] i, 79, to Gualo, to whom the Pope gives full power to do all that
he shall think to be expedient for the advantage of Henry and his
Kingdom and for the honour of the Holy See.

[3] " Quem adhuc in minori officio constituti sincera dileximus . . .
caritate." Ep. i, 85, Dec. 6, 1216.

[4] *Ib.*

[5] Mat. Par., who alone has preserved this document. *Chron. maj.*,
an. 1218, iii, p. 34, R. S. *Cf.* Ep., i, 162, Jan. 20, 1217, of the Pope
to Henry. In this letter the Pope says he is glad to hear that Henry
has taken the cross (" suscepto crucis signaculo ") in order in due

Fresh action
of Honorius
in Henry's
behalf, 1217. With the new year Honorius renewed his exertions in Henry's behalf. The archbishop of Dublin was exhoited to ensure the loyalty of the Irish (January 17, 1217).[1] The Scotch, too, and the Welsh were urged by him to return to the fealty of the young king.[2] Writing to the Scottish monarch (Alexander II.), Honorius upbraided him with having departed from his loyalty to his natural lord, and to his mother the Roman Church. He exhorted the King to have regard to the tender age of Henry, and to the Church of Rome : and, on condition of his disregarding his disloyal oaths to Louis, he promised him the favour of the Apostolic See, and help to recover his own rights.[3] On the same day that he wrote to the archbishop of Dublin, he gave Gualo a more detailed account of the powers with which he was entrusted in England, Scotland, and Wales. He may proceed in every way against all—whether prelates or others—who adhere to Louis, and he may dispense with oaths which have been taken to that prince, or with vows taken by would-be crusaders. He can, moreover, supply vacant cathedrals and abbeys with such as are faithful to the King and to Rome ; and he may devote attention to finding a suitable wife for the young King, since such was the will of the late king.[4]

course to fulfil the vow taken by his father. True to his rôle of protector of the widow and orphan, Honorius, like Innocent, worked to secure Berengaria's dowry for her. Potthast, 5753–4 ; 25718–19 ; 25744, and Shirley, *Royal Letters*, i, pp. 6 f. and 70. He also took John's widow, Isabella, under his protection. Potthast, 25759–60 and 25990.

[1] Theiner, *Vet. mon. Hib.*, p. 2, n. 5. The Pope says he must work for Henry because he is a vassal of the Roman Church, a ward, and a crusader, and because King John, in his last agony, commended him to the care of the Apostolic See. *Cf. ib.*, n. 7.

[2] Ep. i, 141, Jan. 17. *Cf.* also 142 to the archbishop of Bordeaux.

[3] See the document in Norman French, ap. *Calendar of Docs : relating to Scotland*, ii, p. 117, R. S.

[4] Ep. of Jan. 17, in full ap. Shirley, i, 527. The letter opens with great praise for Gualo for the way in which he is fulfilling his arduous duties.

Then to show that he was in earnest, he directed the legate a few months later to remove the lax canons of Carlisle, and replace them with those who would be loyal to Henry and the Pope.[1] About the same time, too, he told the prelates of England that they must grant to the legate such an "aid" as he might fix for the needs of the King and kingdom.[2]

In his zeal for the interests of Henry, the legate did not allow the powers granted him to lie dormant. Relying on their privileges, the Cistercians who had taken part with the barons under King John thought they could continue to do so. But Gualo took strong measures against them. He placed their monasteries under interdict, suspended or excommunicated their abbots, and, says one of their own historians with great indignation, " he caused discipline to be publicly inflicted upon their bare flesh before the church-doors, because they had communicated with the rebels."[3] An appeal to Rome did not benefit the refractory monks, " for our lord the Pope had granted to this legate a degree of authority hitherto unknown and unprecedented ; for he had the power, so to speak, of doing to the clergy throughout England, Scotland, and Wales whatever entered his mind. He might translate bishops and abbots, and other prelates of churches, and clerks, or depose them and

Vigorous action of Gualo against the Cistercians, 1217.

---

[1] Ep. i, 357, July 13, 1217.

[2] Ep. to Gualo, of July 8, 1217. In the same letter he says that he has been advised to name the earl of Chester as colleague to William the Marshal, seeing that he is getting old. But he is aware that " power loves not partners," and therefore he leaves the whole matter to the discretion of the legate.

[3] One of the anonymous contributors to the Chronicle of the Cistercian house of Melrose, an. 1217, p. 194, ed. Fulman, ap. *Rer. Anglic. SS.*, Oxford, 1684. The best ed. of the *Chronica de Mailros* is that published by Stevenson for the Bannatyne Club in 1835. But that edition is rare, and we have had to use that by Fulman, and Stevenson's own translation of the Chronicle, London, 1856.

substitute others, and suspend and excommunicate them and absolve them. And," so concludes the Cistercian historian's tirade against the legate, " what was more important still, he might deprive of their privileges even the monks of the Cistercian order." [1]

Honorius acts in concert with Gualo.

Whilst cardinal Gualo was working in England with such vigour and prudent skill for the cause of the young king, the Pope was seconding his efforts abroad. Especially did he strive to induce Philip of France to recall his son. He reminded that monarch that, whilst there was war even in lands that bordered on his, the realm of France was enjoying peace and prosperity. He then assured him that he was grieved at the way in which his son Louis was opposing the designs of God, seeing that he was in arms against the " Roman Church, the mother of all the faithful," and that he was striving to disinherit " a coheir of Christ " by his efforts to drive from his own " an orphan, a ward of the apostolic see, and one who has taken the Cross." Finally, he implored him " to fulfil the duties of a father towards Louis ; and, in order to induce him (to return to France) either by soft words or by threats, to put before him that he was incurring the divine condemnation and that he was scandalizing the church, and earning the maledictions of the people, as he was preventing them from carrying out their duty and their wish to free the land of the Lord." [2]

Gualo working with William the Marshal, 1218.

Meanwhile if the Pope's appeal to Philip did not meet with much success, the same cannot be said of the action of Gualo. Not content with using his legatine power

---

[1] That Gualo was not treating the monks too harshly would seem to be proved by the fact that, in the general chapter of their order, " two abbots and five priors of Wales were removed from their offices . . . on account of the excesses which they had committed against the said cardinal." *Chron. de M.*, an. 1217, p. 167, of Stevenson's translation.

[2] Ep. i, 304, ed. Horoy, or ed. Shirley, i, p. 529 ff., Apr. 21.

against such of the clergy as were slow to return to their allegiance to the English crown, he was ably co-operating as the principal member of the council of regency, with that " verray perfight gentil knight," the regent, William the Marshal, against the barons who adhered to the cause of Louis. On the day after the council of Bristol, he, together with the earl, " governor of ourself and of our realm," issued in the King's stead a new charter in order to satisfy the just demands of those who felt the need of reform, and were not unnaturally distressed at the condemnation of the Magna Carta by the Pope. This first charter of Henry III., in the main the same as that signed by King John, concluded by setting forth that certain contentious clauses in the former charter had been omitted in the present one, and left over for further discussion.[1] " The form of the document," notes a modern writer,[2] " must have been determined by Gualo and William conjointly, and it reflects the utmost credit upon the wisdom, tact, and moderation of both."

The indefatigible legate next turned his attention to the best way of dealing with Louis and his French and English followers, who were still in possession of a goodly portion of the country. To dignify the boy-King's cause, he bade his followers assume the cross, the badge of the Crusaders, as a sign that their enemies were infidels.[3]

[1] C. 42. The charter is stated to have been issued " Per consilium venerabilium patrum nostrorum d. Gualonis, tituli S. Martini presbiteri cardinalis apostolicæ sedis legati, Petri Wintoniensis, etc." It concludes by stating that " as at present we have not a seal, we have caused the present charter to be sealed with the seals of our venerable father the lord Gualo . . . and of William the marshal, earl of Pembroke, the ruler of ourself and of our kingdom." Ap. Stubbs, Select Charters, p. 337 ff. Cf. his Constitutional Hist., ii, p. 21. The Annals of Waverley, an. 1218, note that the new charter was " secundum cartam regis Johannis."

[2] Norgate, The Minority, p. 14.

[3] Will. of C., Mem., ii, p. 235, and Ann. de Waverl., an. 1216, ap, Ann. Monast,, ii, 287, R. S.

Louis leaves
England,
Sept., 1217.
The party of Louis steadily decreased, and after his
defeat at Lincoln (May, 1217),[1] and the refusal of his
father to intervene actively in his behalf, the French
Prince was ready to make peace. With the terms of the
treaty which he thereupon concluded at Kingston-on-
Thames in September with the English regency, we have
no concern. Suffice it to note here that, on the one hand,
he had to promise to obtain the confirmation of the treaty
by the Pope and the legate, and that, on the other, he
secured an indemnity of ten thousand marks.[2]

There was some little difficulty at first about the absolution of Louis from the sentence of excommunication
under which he had been placed by Gualo. The legate
insisted that he should present himself for absolution in
the usual garb of a penitent, " barefooted and shirtless,
wearing a woollen gown," like Henry IV. at Canossa.
However, at the request of the Prince's followers, Gualo
consented that the penitential garment should be covered
by his robe.[3] After having been duly absolved by the
scarlet-clad cardinal,[4] Louis was escorted by him and by
others to Dover, whence he sailed to France (September).[5]

[1] The victory is attributed in the first place to Gualo by the *Annals
of Merton*, of which Petit-Dutaillis, *Louis VIII.*, p. 513 ff., prints a
fragment : " Hoc anno destructi sunt barones apud Lincolniam . . .
per d. Gualonem . . . et per Petrum Wintoniensem, etc."

[2] See the letter of Henry to the Pope of Nov. 6, 1217, ap. Shirley,
i, 6 ff. ; Rymer, *Foedera*, i, pt. i, p. 148 ; Rog. of W., an. 1217, iv,
p. 30 ff.   Peace was made, says the *Liber de Antiquis Legibus*, p. 203,
ed. Stapleton, " per d. Gallonem legatum." *Cf. Contin. Chron. Wil.
de Novoburg.*, p. 525, ap. vol. ii of the *Chronicles of Stephen*, etc., R. S. ;
Chron. de Mailros, etc.

[3] *Hist. de G. le Mar.*, ll. 17704 ff.   "Nuz piez, en lanjes, sanz
chemise." *Cf. Chron. de Mailros*, an. 1217.   "Discinctus et discal-
ceatus." *Cf. Annals of Merton, l.c.*

[4] " Le legant tout vermel viestu " is a description of Gualo given
in *Hist. des ducs de Normandie*, p. 204.

[5] *Ib.* ; Roger of W., iv, p. 32, Louis departed "cum opprobrio
sempiterno."   For the conditions on which Louis and his followers
were absolved, see Lingard, *Hist. of Eng.*, c. 6.

The crown was now safe on the head of the boy-king, The Pope is thanked for his help, 1217. and all fear of French domination was at an end. That this was due in the first instance to Honorius and his able legate Gualo, was well understood by the leaders of the royal party. They accordingly inspired a letter of thanks which was sent to the Pope in the King's name (November 6).[1] Henry is made to thank the Pope, by whose aid his sorrow was turned into joy, and through whom he had passed from darkness into light, and from a narrow crib to a great kingdom. He would, moreover, never cease to thank him for all his favours, and especially for having sent him such a capable guardian as cardinal Gualo. Seeing his indebtedness to the Pope, " his most dear Lord," he was the more sorry that he could not at present pay him the thousand marks which were yearly due to him. The envoys he was sending to the Pope would explain to him that war had so impoverished the people that he could not raise money enough for the needs of his treasury, that he had to pay Louis ten thousand marks for the peace, and that, by the Pope's own command, he had also to pay " the illustrious Queen Berengaria " the sum of five thousand marks. He therefore begged the Pope to grant him time, assuring him that meanwhile the condition of the country was improving.

Abundantly satisfied with this explanation, Honorius, at the request of Louis, confirmed the peace of Kingston-on-Thames,[2] and, moreover, agreed that his letters against

[1] Shirley, i, p. 6 ff. " Quarum (the money) solutio non maturata tempore nostro juxta quod expediret, satis est nobis molestiæ materia, simul et doloris." Cf. also a letter of July 24, 1219, in which the King is made to repeat his gratitude to the Apostolic See. Ap. Rymer, Foedera, i, p. 229, ed. 1727. See also the letter that follows. Later on in life (in 1245) he told bishop Grosseteste that he was ever going to show obedience to the Pope and the Roman Church, for, through cardinal Gualo, "it peacefully subjugated our country to us, consecrated and crowned us King, and raised us to the throne of our country." Ep. 117 of Gross., p. 338 f., R. S.

[2] Ep. ii, 186, Jan. 13, 1218.

Louis should be considered null as long as he observed the said peace.[1]

Gualo works for the good order of the land, 1217–18.

The first part of the task of the Pope[2] and his agent had now been safely accomplished. The foreigner had been driven from the land. It now remained to reintroduce law and order which had naturally suffered greatly during the war, and to this further task Gualo and the Marshal now devoted their attention. Assemblies of the magnates were held, and while the Great charter was reissued, a Forest charter was issued for the first time (1217). Both were sealed with the seals of the legate and the Marshal, as they were both framed by their advice,[3] and while no doubt the Marshal saw to the destruction of the illegal castles (omnia castra adulterina) which had sprung up during the war, the legate took in hand the punishing of those among the clergy who had favoured Louis.

One of those who were specially punished by Gualo was Simon Langton, the brother of Stephen, who was accused of having caused religious services to be performed for Louis and the excommunicated barons by excommunicated priests. The legate insisted that Simon should go to Rome to plead his cause before the Pope (Feb., 1218).[4]

[1] ii, 105, of the same date.

[2] Seeing the paramount share taken by the Pope's legate in the expulsion of Louis, it is not surprising that certain continental chroniclers affirm that Louis left England at the Pope's bidding. *Cf. Ann. Acquicinct.*, an. 1216, ap. *M. G. SS.*, xvi, p. 505, and Andrew Marchianensis, *Hist. reg. Franc. contin.*, an. 1218, ap. *M. G. SS.*, xxvi, pp. 213 and 470. Will. of Coventry expresses his profound astonishment at the way in which the hosts of Louis were dispersed. But, he says, the reason is plain : he came over against the prohibition of the Roman Church, and remained here under its anathema. *Mem.*, ii, 239.

[3] *Cf.* Stubbs, *Select charters*, p. 344 ff., and *Lib. de antiq. leg.*, p. 203, and *Ann. Waverl.*, an. 1218.

[4] Roger of W., an. 1217, iv, p. 33. For the action of Gualo in Scotland, see the *Chron. de Mailros*, ann. 1217–18 ; and for that in London, see *Hist. des Ducs*, p. 206, and *Ann. Dunst.*, p. 52.

Moreover, in the language of Roger of Wendover, " immediately after Louis's departure from England, the legate sent inquisitors through all the counties of England to find out all of the clergy, of whatever rank they might be, who were guilty of the slightest implication in the rebellion; and, after suspending them and depriving them of their benefices, to send them to him. He then distributed all the said benefices amongst his own clerks, and from the losses of others enriched all his own followers.   Hugh, bishop of Lincoln, too, came to England ; and, in order to regain his bishopric, paid down a thousand marks sterling for the use of the Pope and a hundred for the legate.   Many, both bishops and religious, followed his example, and at ruinous expense won the legate's favour." [1]

How much truth there is in this tirade it is hard to say.   The firmness, or perhaps we ought rather to say the autocratic methods, of Gualo undoubtedly made him many enemies, who never ceased accusing him to the Pope ; [2] and it is quite possible that their machinations may have produced ill-feeling against him in some quarters at Rome.   But, if he was recalled by the Pope, it is certain that it was because he had frequently asked to be recalled.   He had assured the Pope that he was worn out by his arduous labours.[3]   And if he left England, according to Walter of Coventry, " with an infinite amount of money got together in some way

Gualo leaves England, Nov., 1218.

[1] *Ib.   Cf.* Walter of C., *l.c.*, p. 240.

[2] *Ib.*, pp. 235–6.   The Cistercians never forgave Gualo for his action against them both in England and Scotland, and they never rested till at Rome " they fully obtained their object against the said cardinal."   *Chron. de Mailros*, an. 1218.

[3] See the letter of Honorius appointing his successor Pandulf. Ep. iii, 20, Sept. 12, 1218.   " Cum . . . (Gualo) . . . nobis *frequenter* supplicaverit . . . ac etiam per fratres nostros fecerit supplicari, ut ipsi, continuis fatigato laboribus, redeundi licentiam concedere dignaremur," etc.

or other," he left[1] it, even so, with the country very
greatly indebted to him; but, in all probability, he left
it with only a part of the arrears due to the Pope from
England and Ireland.[2] King Henry himself is a witness
to the work done for him and the kingdom by the legate.
"When, whilst still under age," as he wrote to Bishop
Grosseteste, "we were deprived of our father, with our
kingdom not only alienated from us, but actively opposed
to us, our Mother the Roman Church, through the Lord
cardinal Gualo, at that time legate in England, brought
back the realm to subjection to us and to peace, consecrated and crowned us King, and placed us on the
throne."[3]

One of the last acts of Gualo was to attest the King's
seal. We have seen that hitherto the acts of the realm
have been sealed with the seals of Gualo and the regent
Pembroke. But the Marshal was growing old, and Gualo
was about to leave the country, and so a seal was ordered
to be made for the King. A week or two after he had
joined in attesting the new seal, Gualo returned to Rome
(c. Nov. 30, 1218),[4] where Honorius was eagerly awaiting
his coming, seeing that he was a man well able to give
advice.[5] "His work in England was done, and well done."[6]

[1] *L.c.*, p. 241.
[2] *Cf.* the *Close Rolls*, i, pp. 376b, 377, ap. Norgate, and *Ann. Winton.*,
an. 1219. The insinuation of Walter, "and the charges of avarice
and extortion brought against Gualo by some modern writers, are
groundless," avers Miss Norgate, *Minority*, p. 103 n. Gasquet, *Henry
the Third*, trusts rather too much to Matthew Paris.
[3] See his letter of 1245, quoted by Grosseteste. Ap. *Epp. Gross.*,
n. 117, p. 339, R. S.
[4] He left England "about the feast of St. Andrew" (Nov. 30),
according to Coggeshall, p. 186, who has been followed by the continuator of Will. of Newburgh, an. 1218, ap. vol. ii of the *Chronicles
of Stephen*, etc., R. S.
[5] Ep. iii, 20. "Præsentiam ejus Apostolicæ Sedi, cum sit vir
magni consilii, necessariam affectantes."
[6] Norgate, *l.c.* Gualo always retained his interest in England (*cf. Royal*

On the Monday following the feast of St. Andrew, The arrival of Pandulf, 1218. there arrived in London another legate, Pandulf, bishop-elect of Norwich, who had already been employed in the capacity of a papal commissioner by Innocent III. He was sent by Honorius because he was convinced (imo scimus) that there was need of one " de latere nostro " to keep " the king and the kingdom itself " at peace, and because he had full trust in his prudence and loyalty.[1]

Pandulf had not been in the country many months The young King entrusted to the care of the Legate, May, 1219. before he was called upon to assist at the death-bed of the faithful regent, William the Marshal. The old earl, knowing well the turbulence and ambition of many of the nobles, felt that the King would only be safe under the closest papal protection. Accordingly, in the presence of his youthful monarch and of the magnates who were gathered round his bed, he told the Legate : " I will commit my lord into the Hand of God, and into that of the Pope, and into yours, as you are here in the Pope's stead." [2]   The dying act of the regent was, despite the efforts of Peter, bishop of Winchester, confirmed by common consent after his death, and the Legate became " the first chief minister (consiliarius) of the whole realm of England." [3]

In his capacity as prime minister of the country, Pandulf's legation, 1218–21. Letters, i, pp. 228, 241) and came to be known in it as a man " of venerable memory."   See Archbishop Gray's Register, p. 80, ed. Surtees Soc.

[1] Ep. iii, 20.

[2] Hist. de Guill., v, 18074 ff.

" Jo vuil mon seignor ci baillier
En la main Deu, en l'apostoire,
E en la vostre, c'est la voire,
Qui en son liu estes ici."

[3] Mat. Par., Chron. maj., an. 1239, vi, 64. Pandulf, it may be noted, is often wrongly called a cardinal. He appears to be confused with cardinal Pandulf Masca of Pisa, who died in 1201.

Pandulf displayed the same courage as he had done when he was Innocent's envoy to King John.[1] He strove, moreover, to inspire the other ministers with a like determination, and so we find him urging the justiciar, Hubert de Burgh, not to be frightened into being guilty of injustice, " for we ourselves will fear nothing whatever any man may urge against us." [2] Throughout the whole of his successful term of office he worked hard for the interests of the King and country. Perhaps because he was himself attached to the papal *camera*,[3] he watched very carefully over the royal treasury, as the King was burdened with debts, and the revenue was small.[4] In general he was kind to the submissive and firm towards the recalcitrant. He showed all the favour it was possible to those ecclesiastics who had been treated with severity by Gualo,[5] but he set himself to work with vigour to tame the unruly barons and to recover the royal castles. Hence, it is said of him that " he manfully suppressed many bellicose disturbances which had not been previously quelled." [6] With his co-operation, also, great councils were called together in 1219 and 1220 to take measures for the pacification of the realm;[7] and Henry was solemnly

---

[1] *Cf.* Norgate, p. 109, and Gasquet, p. 41 ff. Maurice, *Stephen Langton*, p. 241, regards him as " probably the wisest and most moderate " of the King's counsellors.

[2] *Royal Letters*, i, p. 78 f.

[3] He always signs himself and is always addressed as " D. Papæ camerarius."

[4] *Royal Letters*, i, 27, 35, 112 ff.　*Cf.* Norgate, p. 113 f. ; Gasquet, 46 ff.

[5] *Ann. Dunstaplia*, ap. *Ann. Monast.*, iii, 53.

[6] *Flores Hist.*, an. 1221. This work is the Westminster version of Matthew Paris which used to be assigned to a supposed Matthew of Westminster.

[7] *Contin. Chron. Will. de Novob.*, an. 1219, " mediante legato Pandulfo, de reformatione regni et pace." *Ib.*, an. 1220.

crowned at Westminster (1220) in order to strengthen his position.[1]

Throughout the entire period of his legation Pandulf's action was largely directed by the Pope. No doubt with a view to leaving him a freer hand, Honorius postponed his consecration as bishop of Norwich, so that he might be more independent of the Archbishop of Canterbury.[2] Letters of the Pope to Pandulf are extant giving him instructions and commands on all manner of subjects concerning both temporal and spiritual affairs. At one moment he is giving him directions how to deal with treaties between England and Scotland;[3] at another bidding him see that the lay and clerical magnates of Ireland render their dues to their King;[4] and again, at another, commanding him not to suffer the great ones of the land to retain possession of the royal domains, seeing that the King is suffering from poverty, whereas the Kings of England were wont to be conspicuous for their wealth.[5] Seeing that the King "has assumed the cross (crucesignatus), is a ward and an orphan, and under the special protection of the Apostolic See," his cause, said the Pope, is ours.[6]

Papal direction of Pandulf.

[1] *Ib. Cf. Flores Hist.*, an. 1220. In this instance the legate acted in response to a direct command from Rome, as the first coronation was not solemn enough, nor performed in the place "required by the custom of the land." *Walt. of Cov.*, ii, p. 244.

[2] Ep. of Sept. 5, 1218, ap. Shirley, *Royal Letters*, i, 533.

[3] *Ib.*, p. 16.

[4] Theiner, *Mon. Hibern.*, nn. 23 and 24.

[5] Shirley, i, 535, May 26, 1220, and p. 121, May 28, 1220.

[6] *L.c.*, i, 535. See also (ap. *ib.*, p. 174) the Pope's letter of Apr. 29, 1221, to the Archbishop of York and his suffragans in which he tells him that he has heard with great grief that a serious conflict is beginning to break out in England, which if not suppressed will be calamitous to the whole kingdom. "Hence we bid each of you act as though the affair was his own personal concern, and use all earnestness and diligence to stamp out the incentives to war, and to arrange terms of peace . . . so that the people may enjoy the blessings of peace and prosperous repose."

In purely ecclesiastical matters also, Pandulf was under the guidance of the Pope. He is directed to see to the consecration of the lawfully elected Gilbert to the see of Ardfert, and to cause the Bishops of Waterford, Emly and Limerick to be sent to Rome if it be a fact that they have consecrated the intruder John.[1] A little later he was commissioned to report on certain acts of injustice said to have been perpetrated by the bishop of Glasgow.[2]

Pandulf
leaves
England,
1221.

The paramount position in England thus occupied by the legate was not to the taste of cardinal Stephen Langton, Archbishop of Canterbury, who had meanwhile returned to England, May, 1218. His power in the country was reduced almost to nothing; and this he felt was good neither for the credit of the archdiocese nor for the country.[3] At any rate, whatever may have been his views on the situation, he went to Rome in the autumn of 1220, and obtained from the Pope an undertaking that during his lifetime no other legate should be sent to reside in England.[4] There do not, unfortunately, seem to be any papal letters extant in connexion with the departure of Pandulf. Consequently all we know about it is that, in July, 1221, he publicly, " at the command of the Lord Pope," resigned his legation,[5] and left the country "after the feast of

---

[1] Theiner, *l.c.*, n. 25, July 16, 1219.

[2] *Ib.*, n. 29, Dec. 7, 1219.

[3] At any rate, Giraldus Cambrensis in writing to the cardinal at this time to dissuade him from resigning and joining a religious order, assures him that the troubles which have fallen on clergy or people have not come from him, but " from the incompetence of the King and from the chief curia which did not refuse the honour offered to it—principis ignaviæ et principali curiæ oblatum honorem non recusanti, est imputandum." Ep. ap. *Opera*, i, p. 401 ff., R. S.

[4] *Ann. Dunst.*, vol. iii, pp. 62 and 74, Ann. Monast.

[5] Walt. of Cov., ii, p. 250, and *Flores Hist.*, ii, 172.

St. Michael." [1] Leaving England itself at peace, he went on the King's behalf to Poitou in order to maintain peace in that province, and to promote its good government.[2]

When he had successfully fulfilled his difficult mission in that country,[3] he went to Rome and there received episcopal consecration as bishop of Norwich (May 29, 1222).[4]

Pandulf
bishop of
Norwich,
1222.

As bishop of an English see, Pandulf's interest in our country did not lessen ; and on the death of Philip of France (July 14, 1223) he strove to induce the Pope not to allow Louis to be crowned King of France till, as he had sworn to do at the peace of Kingston,[5] he had restored Normandy to Henry.[6] But Louis was crowned (Aug. 6) before the Pope could interfere, even if he could have been induced to move in the matter. Moreover, when Pandulf, along with other English envoys,

---

[1] *Flores, ib.* ; W. of C., says "soon after his resignation." *The Annals of Dunstable* : "statim pro d. rege profectus in Pictaviam treugas inter nos et Pictavenses prorogari impetravit." *L.c.*, p. 75. Of course, Matthew Paris, *Hist. Anglor.*, iii, p. 245, R. S., adds "non vacuis clitellis."

[2] See the preceding note, and the *Patent Rolls*, i, p. 303 f., and the Close Rolls, i, p. 477b. *Cf.* Norgate, *l.c.*, p. 175 ff., who justly notes that the entrusting of this commission to Pandulf by the King's ministers "is a strong testimony to the estimation in which their previous relations with him had led them to hold his character, his abilities, and his devotion to the welfare of the King and kingdom " (p. 178).

[3] Honorius also worked in Henry's behalf in Aquitaine. *Cf.* epp. v, 144–5, of Sept. 25, 1220 ; ap. Shirley, *Royal Letters*, i, p. 536 f. ; *cf. ib.*, p. 157 f. ; *Patent Rolls*, i, p. 389. On June 25, 1222, he, for the second time, threatened to excommunicate Hugh of Lusignan, count de La Marche, and his wife Isabel of Angonlême, the widow of King John and mother of Henry, for the trouble they were causing in Aquitaine. *Cf.* Rymer, *Fœdera*, i, pt. i, p. 169 ; Norgate, pp. 145, 187 f.

[4] *Ann. de Waverl.*, ap. *Ann. Monast.*, ii, p. 296.

[5] Roger of W., an. 1217, iv, 31 ; *Liber de antiq. legibus*, p. 204.

[6] *Ann. de Dunstap.*, an. 1223, p. 81, R. S.

interviewed the French king a few months later (Oct.),
he was curtly told by that monarch, not only that
Normandy had, through the murder of Prince Arthur,
been legally adjudged to the crown of France, but that
he himself intended to prosecute his claim to the crown
of England.[1]

The departure of the resident legate from the country
was a decided loss to it. As soon as the recognized
supreme authority of Pandulf was removed, the chief
magnates of the royal Council began to intrigue against
each other both at home and at Rome. Especially
were Peter des Roches (De Rupibus), bishop of Winchester,
and Hubert de Burgh, the justiciar, bitter rivals. Whether
then, in consequence of the suggestion of one of these
statesmen,[2] or because the Pope himself in his care of
the realm thought it the best way of checkmating the
intrigues, at any rate, in April (13), 1223, he addressed
a series of letters to Peter and Hubert and others in
which he declared the young King of age, although
he had not attained his sixteenth year. He knew,
he wrote, that in years his very dear son Henry was only
a youth ; but, as he had heard with pleasure, he made
up for his lack of years by a superior intelligence. He
should, therefore, not be prevented from regulating
the business of the realm. The bishop of Winchester,
the Justiciar, and William Brewer, a baron of the
exchequer, were accordingly instructed to give Henry
the " free and unfettered disposal of his kingdom ",
and to cause the resignation into his hands of any royal

---

[1] Cf. ib., p. 85 ; Coggeshall, p. 197, and Roger of W., an. 1223,
iv, 86.

[2] Years later Hubert maintained that Peter had striven to induce
the Pope to antidate the King's coming of age, and then that Honorius
finally consented to do so "at the suggestion of the archbishops,
bishops, earls, and barons." Cf. his Responsiones ap. Mat. Par.,
Chron. Maj., vi, p. 69.

castles held by him or others.[1] Ralph Neville, bishop
elect of Chichester and vice-chancellor, was commissioned
to use the royal seal henceforth only in accordance with
the King's pleasure.[2] Two other letters ordered the
barons, under pain of excommunication, to obey their
sovereign.

In connexion with the execution of the papal mandate, Fresh man-
it is certain that trouble arose, and that some of the dates from
the Pope
barons broke out into open rebellion against the King, regarding the
surrender of
i.e., particularly against Hubert de Burgh. But, owing the castles,
to the intrigues that were then going on, it is very 1223.
difficult now to unravel the complicated events which
followed the publication of the Pope's decision. It is,
however, possible that this outbreak of the barons may
have been caused by the Justiciar's continuing himself
to hold certain lands and castles belonging to the King,
and at the same time endeavouring to force others to
surrender the royal property held by them.[3] This
conjecture would appear to be borne out by the fact
that the King himself privately requested the Pope
to order the Bishop of Winchester, the Justiciar Hubert,
and others by name to give up to him the bailiwicks
and royal castles in their possession.[4] Then, fearing,

[1] The second of a group of four letters in the *Red Book of the Exchequer*, f. 171. *Cf.* Norgate, pp. 202 and 286 ff.
[2] The last of the group just mentioned. It is also printed in Shirley,
R. L., i, 430 f. *Cf.* Roger of W., an. 1223, iv, 88 f. ; and *Ann. de
Dunstap.*, p. 83. " De mandato d. Papæ et assensu baronum provisum
est . . . quod ipse rex haberet legitimam ætatem." *Cf.* also *Queri-
monia Falcasii* (Falkes or Fawkes of Bréauté, an unprincipled soldier
of fortune), ap. *Walt. of Cov.*, ii, pp. 261–2.
[3] Hence, we find Falkes and his party insisting that if he and his
party surrendered their castles, so also should the Justiciar and his
party : " protestantes . . . quod, sicut aperte fiebat eorum restitutio,
et aperte justiciarii et suorum similiter esset restitutio facienda."
Querem. Falc., p. 262.
[4] The letters both of the King and of the Pope on this subject are
lost ; but we know of them by a letter of the Pope (Nov. 20, 1223, ap.

or being made to fear, that he had gone too far, at least as far as the Justiciar was concerned, if not also as far as some of the other more powerful nobles were concerned, he begged the Pope to annul his orders. Honorius, however, lest, as he said, he should be accused of levity, refused to recall his mandate, but left the time of its being put into execution to the King's discretion.[1]

Submission of the barons, 1223-4. Still the rebellion of the barons remained to be put down, and on November 19 the King wrote both to the Pope and the late legate Gualo, begging them to urge the barons to due submission.[2] However, through the support of Stephen Langton and the bishops, the King found most of the magnates around him in arms, when he kept Christmas at Northampton.[3] And, as the rebellious barons still refused to obey the behests of the Pope and the King and to surrender the royal property, " the archbishop and his suffragan bishops," in accordance with their instructions from Rome,[4] " clad in white vestments, and with lighted candles, excommunicated all disturbers of the peace of the kingdom." Stephen then sent word to the disaffected barons that unless

Shirley, i, 539, or Mengozzi, p. 90) in which he says that he issued the said injunction in consequence of representations on the King's behalf : " quia literæ hujusmodi ex parte tua et ob tui causam a nobis petitæ ac concessæ fuerunt." Cf. Rog. of Wend., l.c. In this matter of the resumption of his castles, Walter of Coventry distinctly states that the King acted very diplomatically, "consilio fretus subtiliori." L.c., p. 252.

[1] Ep. just cited.

[2] These two letters may be read ap. Rymer, Fœdera, i, pt. i, p. 171. At the same time Hubert de Burgh wrote to Honorius to ask him not to allow certain mischief makers then in Rome to return to England. Ap. ib.

[3] Ann. de Dunstap., p. 84.

[4] According to Roger of Wend., iv, p. 88, the Pope sent a "bull" to the bishops bidding them compel the barons to give up the King's castles under pain of ecclesiastical censure. No doubt this "bull," of which Roger alone seems to make mention, was issued with the other letters to Hubert de Burgh, etc., on Apr. 13, 1223.

" by the following day they resigned into the King's hands all the castles and honours pertaining to the crown, he and all the bishops would assuredly excommunicate them by name." This had the desired effect ; and all the hitherto refractory barons submitted to the King (end of 1223 and the beginning of 1224).[1] Even Falkes himself was at length compelled by force to submit (Aug., 1224).

Meanwhile, though cowed for the time, the disaffected parties were not satisfied. When they found that while they had given up such royal castles as they possessed, the Justiciar had contrived to keep possession of some at least of those which he had held, they were very indignant both with him and with the Archbishop for supporting him.[2] They appealed to Rome (early in 1224), but the archbishop and some of his suffragans would only allow their envoys to leave the country after they had sworn not to attempt anything in Rome " to the prejudice of the King and country," by which the bishops specially understood that no legate was to be asked for.[3]

No sooner, however, did the envoys reach Rome than they earnestly begged the Pope to send a legate

Appeals to Rome, 1224.

---

[1] *Ib.*, pp. 92, 94 ff., 103, 107 f. *Cf. Quer. Falcas.*, p. 262 ; Coggeshall, p. 203 ff. (from whom it appears that the barons were tricked by Hubert ; for when they gave up the castles which they held, on condition that he gave up those he held, he received them back from the King as soon as he had surrendered them) ; *Ann. de Dunstap.*, p. 84.

[2] " Archiepiscopus . . . omnes barones æqualiter possessione castrorum privavit. In hoc tamen dolus non defuit, quod comite Cestrensi et suis corporaliter castra restituentibus, justitiarius cum suis castra quæ tenebant sicut antea tenuerunt." Though this comes from the memorial of Falkes de B. to the Pope, there is no reason to doubt the accuracy of this statement as it is substantiated by Coggeshall as we have seen. *Quer. Falcas. coram d. papa*, ap. *l.c.*, p. 262.

[3] *Ib.*, pp. 262–3 ; *Ann. de Dunst.*, 89.

to England.[1] But, constantly assured by the archbishop's letters and by his commissioners that the
country was at peace, Honorius would not even send
the nuncios he had at first thought of sending.[2] He
contented himself with writing to urge the King "not
to incline to one side or the other, but to show himself
equally impartial to all parties." He further advised
him not to exact any accounts from his vassals for the
moment, but to put off the exaction of his dues to a more
favourable opportunity.[3]

There is no doubt that what the archbishop had said
was substantially true. Before the end of April nearly
all the barons who had been in opposition to the Justiciar
and the Archbishop had submitted to them in presence
of the King.[4]

Falkes in
Rome, 1224.

An exception to the general rule was Falkes de
Bréauté. He resorted to force in order to maintain what he
held to be his right, but was at length compelled by force to
submit (Aug., 1224). But submission was alien to the nature
of Falkes.   He betook himself to Rome, presented
a memorial to the Pope containing a judicious blend
of truth and falsehood,[5] and succeeded in impressing
upon the Pope that the archbishop had been deceiving
him, and that he, Falkes de Bréauté, was an injured man.
Force had been used against him though he was a

---

[1] *Ann. de D., ib.   Cf.* ep. of Aug. 17, 1224, of Honorius to archbp.
Stephen Langton, ap. *Royal Letters*, i, p. 543.

[2] *Ib.*

[3] Ep. of March 14, 1224, ap. *Royal Letters*, i, p. 540 f. *Cf.* the King's
reply to this letter and to one of Jan. 18, 1224 (ap. *ib.*, p. 218), in behalf
of the bishop of Winchester, ap. *ib.*, p. 224. This letter of the King
was written "shortly after June 22," and aimed at showing that he
was forced to take up arms by the unruly conduct of Falkes.

[4] See the King's letter to Honorius of June, 1224, ap. *Royal Let.*,
i, p. 224 f.

[5] See his *Queremonia.*

Crusader, and before the affair could be judged by the Pope.[1]

Even before Falkes himself reached Rome, the Pope had so far embraced his cause as to blame the King for not attending to his previous advice, and for making war inopportunely upon Falkes. He pointed out to Henry that it was preposterous to turn against his own subjects arms that were needed for his enemies abroad.[2] He reminded him of all that Falkes had done for himself and his father, and bade him for the moment cease his attacks on him, putting off the consideration of any grievance against him till a more suitable time.[3]

At the same time no doubt, he wrote in a very strong manner to Cardinal Langton. " We have not yet been able," he said, " to force our mind to credit what has been suggested to us about you by many . . . We thought of that eminent knowledge of Divine Scripture which you possess, of that uprightness which you should have put on with the bishop's office and dignity, and of that abundance of love which has been shown to you by the Apostolic See . . . Thinking of all these points we could not bring ourselves to think anything evil or unworthy of you " . . . But, he continued, whilst some were assuring us that England was in a turmoil, and were earnestly begging us to send over a legate, " your messengers were asserting that all was at peace, and were exerting themselves to prevent the dispatch of a legate." Though somewhat suspicious, " for why do you fear the eyes of the Apostolic See," we trusted you, and gave up the idea first of sending a legate and then of sending nuncios, because your letters assured us " that peace was fully established in England."

[1] *Ib.*, p. 265.
[2] At this very time Henry was losing Poitou.
[3] Ep. of Aug. 17, 1224, ap. *R. Letters*, i, 544 f.

Thereupon we were informed that the King was in arms
against Falkes, and that you were supporting him . . .
If, urged the Pontiff, you say that discord broke out
after the dispatch of your letters, and that justice
required proceedings to be taken against Falkes, you
should have notified the facts to us at once ; and, at a
crisis like the present, should have preferred prudence
to justice. "Where is the abundance of your wisdom
if your advice causes the King to make war on his own
people with the enemy at his gates." [1] The letter
concluded by ordering the archbishop to cause the King
to give up his attack on Falkes, and to take off the
excommunication which he had pronounced against
him.[2]

The Pope
continues to
intercede for
Falkes,
1224–6.

Before these letters could reach England, the castle
of Falkes had been taken, and he himself was a prisoner
in the King's hands (Aug., 1224).[3] Moved, however, no
doubt, by the Pope's representations, the King did not
behead Falkes, but banished him from the country, after
he had been made by the Archbishop to swear not to
complain to the Pope.[4] But by Easter (1225) Falkes had

[1] "Ubi est enim tuæ abundantia sapientiæ, si tui consilii est, ut
rex cum suis guerram incipiat, dum videt externos sibi querram
inferre." Ep. of Aug. 17 (?), 1224. Gasquet's translation of this letter
is followed for the most part. Maurice, *S. Langton*, p. 264, appears to
have lost sight of chronology in his arrangement of these letters. He
makes a letter of June in which the King expresses his intention of
going to attack Falkes' castle of Bedford (ap. *Royal Let.*, i, 224), an
answer to this letter of Aug. 17, from which it appears that Falkes
had been attacked.

[2] Ep. ap. *Royal Let.*, i, p. 543. Llewellyn, "Prince of North Wales,"
and Ranulf of Chester (ap. *ib.*, pp. 229 f. and 233 ff.) wrote to Henry
about the same time in the same strain as the Pope.

[3] According to Coggeshall, Falkes was at first imprisoned till
the judgment of the Pope and of the King could be known.
Chron., p. 208.

[4] "Juramento exacto quod nihil apud vos (the Pope) de illatis
injuriis impetrare deberem." *Querm. Falcas.*, p. 270. It must be borne

found his way to Rome,[1] had presented his case, his *Queremonia*, to the Pope, and had implored his assistance.

What with the stories told them by the agents of the King and bishops of England on the one hand, and by those of Falkes and of the King of France on the other, the Pope and cardinals, including even Gualo, were quite at a loss what to believe or what to do. They confessed they were in despair about the whole situation,[2] and naturally thought of sending someone over to England to find out the truth. But the visit of a papal official was not desired by the party in power in England,[3] and their agents were instructed to block such an undertaking if they could. For a time they succeeded, and before Christmas were able to report that all the talk in the Roman Curia was about the approaching feast, and not at all about a legate.[4] The words of the King's agents were helped no doubt by two strong letters from the papal legate in France, Cardinal Romanus. In one to the Pope himself he declared that Henry " and almost the whole of England " was very much put about by his taking up the cause of Falkes, and that his patronage of the man was hindering his (the legate's) endeavours to make peace between England and France, and to

in mind that this assertion is only made by Falkes, who also assures us that he had occasion to remind the archbishop : " ab antiquis patribus sit statutum ut ab ecclesia Romana tam Cantuariensis quam ceteræ per orbem ecclesiæ regerentur." *Ib.*

[1] He required the help of the Pope to reach Rome, as he was imprisoned on his way by the King of France. A papal mandate secured his release. Walter of Cov., an. 1224, ii, p. 254.

[2] See the letter of Geoffrey Craucumb, etc., ap. *Roy. Let.*, i, 240 f. Dec. 22, 1224.

[3] See two letters of the legate Romanus, one to the Pope, the other to a certain Master T., written naturally in a stronger style ; ap. Rymer, *Fœdera*, i, p. 274 f., ed. 1727.

[4] " Scituri quod quantumcumque curiam in adventu nostro turbatam invenissemus, in recessu tamen hujus totum erat de festo et nihil de legato." *Ib.*

settle the Albigensian affair.[1] In another letter to
a simple member of the papal curia, a certain Magister T.,
the legate said the same, but in much more forcible
language. He insisted that the times were evil, much
more so than was understood by such as his correspondent, who, sitting in their rooms in ignorance of what
was going on, were provoking kings and kingdoms
to the ruin of the Church by interfering in matters that
concerned them not.[2]

But Falkes was insistent. His *Queremonia*, as we have
said, was laid before the Pope at Easter (1225). Influenced
no doubt by that specious document, Honorius displayed
renewed interest in its author. He instructed his legate
in France, the cardinal-deacon Romanus, to induce
King Louis to protect Falkes in the meantime till he
could bring about his reconciliation with Henry, or arrange
for his fulfilling his vow as a Crusader.[3] Furthermore,
at the request of Falkes, he decided to send an envoy
(nuncius), Master Otho, to England.[4]

In apprising the King of this intention, Honorius
again reminded him of all that Falkes had done for his
father and himself ; described Otho as a man of remarkable uprightness of character, and, owing to his merits,
as beloved by all ; and begged him to grant a favourable

---

[1] Ap. Rymer, *l.c.*, p. 274.
[2] *Ib.*, p. 275. Both these letters were written towards the close of
the year 1224.
[3] Ep. ix, 170, of June 4, 1225, ed. Horoy, or ap. *R. F. SS.*, xix, p. 767.
[4] See a letter of the King's agents to Henry of *c.* end of Aug., 1225,
ap. *Royal Let.*, i, 264 ff. Maurice, *l.c.*, p. 265, is mistaken with regard
to Otho. He was merely a nuncio not a legate. A legate a *latere*
represented the Pope himself. Hence, when he appeared in a country,
the ordinary ecclesiastical jurisdiction was superseded ; but a nuncio
was merely an envoy sent for a particular object, and he had no
authority over ecclesiastical persons or things generally. It was not
till 1237 that Otho came to England as *legate*.

hearing to the other matters which Otho would propound to him, but especially to his request in behalf of Falkes.[1]

If the Pope's general patronage of Falkes was very little to the taste of the Justiciar's party,[2] still less was the news of the dispatch of a nuncio in his interests. The King's agents were at once told to do all they could to render his mission abortive. As will readily be believed, they had no difficulty in winning over to their master's views the legate Romanus, who in their behalf strove to hinder Otho from proceeding to their country, and showed them how, by artfully causing delays, to prevent Otho from doing anything should he arrive in England.[3] But though Otho expressed his surprise that Henry should be angry at his coming, seeing that he was coming for the good and not for the harm of the country,[4] he did not allow himself to be prevented from fulfilling his mission. He landed in England seemingly towards the close of the year 1225, and at once appealed to the King on Falkes' behalf. Henry, however, would not hearken to him, but declared that " for his open treachery " Falkes had been duly tried and condemned, and that, although the care of the Kingdom belonged to him as King, still he ought himself to abide by the laws of the realm. " When Otho heard this he ceased to ask anything further of the King on behalf of Falkes." [5] But, if the servant ceased to work for the unfortunate man, the master did not. Honorius, believing, no doubt, that whatever might be his crimes, Falkes was being as much sacrificed to party vengeance as punished by strict justice, again turned specially to the archbishop

[1] This letter has been preserved by Walt. of Cov., ii, 274.
[2] See the letter of Romanus to the Pope, ap. Rymer, i, pt. i, p. 94.
[3] Ib., and the following letter, ap. R. Let.
[4] Cf. his letter, ap. Roy. Let., i, 270.
[5] Roger of Wend., an. 1225, iv, pp. 107 f. and 117 f.

of Canterbury, and bade him beware of attaching himself to men who were committing an injustice. The greater the wisdom and knowledge which had been given him by God, the stricter would be the account he would have to render of the manner in which he had administered justice.[1] Whether this appeal would have been more successful than its predecessor can but be matter for conjecture, as Falkes died soon after on his way back from another visit to Rome, 1226.[2]

The envoy Otho puts forward a scheme for helping papal finance, 1225-6. The envoy Otho had, however, another commission to perform besides that of interceding for Falkes de Bréauté. He had to put forward once more the scheme for relieving the pressure on papal finance which, originally suggested by the emperor Henry VI., had been propounded by Innocent III. at the Lateran council, and then dropped by him owing to strong opposition.[3] To remove all ground for bringing accusations of avarice against the Roman Church, and yet at the same time to enable it to deal with the countless matters which were brought before it for settlement without cost to the appellants, and to meet the many calls upon its treasury,[4] Honorius proposed that in each cathedral and collegiate church a prebend should be set aside for the use of the Apostolic See, and also a certain proportion of monastic and episcopal revenues.[5]

As the money raised by this means would have enabled

[1] Ep. of July 11, 1226, ap. *R. Let.*, i, 547.

[2] *Ann. de Dunst.*, p. 89 ; Rog. of Wend., iv, 137.

[3] *Cf. supra*, vol. xii, p. 294 ff.

[4] For instance, in asking Pandulf to forward Peter's Pence, Honorius says that he has many debts due to his having sent so much money to the Holy Land (*Calendar of Pap. Let.*, i, p. 75), and to fraud having been practised against him by some unknown merchants of Bologna. *Ib.*, p. 76.

[5] *Cf.* the Pope's letter of Jan. 28, 1225, to the hierarchy of England, ap. Walt. of Cov., an. 1225, ii, p. 274 ff., or *Reg. S. Osmundi*, i, 366 ff. *Cf.* ii, 51-4.

the Pope adequately to remunerate his officials, and
hence to free him from the necessity of appointing them
to livings in different countries, Honorius concluded
his letter by arranging about the beneficed Roman
clerics in England. After the adoption of his scheme,
the prebends were to return to their original churches
" lest if they are given to successive foreigners, as has
sometimes happened, they should cease to be available
for the normal dependants of the Churches, or at least
to be generally useful." [1]

Brought before the King by Otho, the scheme was
referred by him " to the clergy and laity of the kingdom." [2]

Before discussion on the matter was terminated,[3] Assembly at
Otho, at the request of the archbishop, was recalled by St. Paul's,
the Pope (1226).[4] After the departure of the nuncio, 1226.
Stephen Langton himself, in accordance with the papal
instructions, convoked the King and all the prelates
and nobles of the country to meet at St. Paul's on
May 4, in order to send their reply to the proposal of
Honorius.

Meanwhile, the papal legate in France, Cardinal (Council of
Romanus, had held a council at Bourges on the same Bourges,
1225.)

---

[1] He had already (Feb. 1221) ordered " the archbishop of York
to publish throughout England that on the death of clerks of the
Roman Church or other Italians holding benefices in England, the
Pope will not for that turn appoint thereto." *Calendar*, i, p. 79.

[2] Rog. of Wend., an. 1225, iv, p. 107.

[3] It was first discussed and postponed at Westminster, Jan. 13, 1226.
Cf. Rog. of Wend., an. 1226 *init.*

[4] Walt. of Cov. "Litteris d. Papæ acceptis, repatriavit." These
are the last words in Walter's *Memoriale*, ii, 279. *Cf.* Rog. of
Wendover, iv, 123, who adds details of his own, some of which are
certainly not accurate : He tells us how Otho, after looking askance
(obliquo occulo) at the letters, with downcast mien threw them into
the fire, and left England with " empty money bags—clitellis vacuis."
As a matter of fact, the *Close Rolls* (ii, p. 149 f.) and the *Patent Rolls*
(ii, pp. 24, 27 f.) show that he took to Rome 1,500 marks of the tribute
money due from England. *Cf.* Norgate, p. 263 f.

subject (Nov. 30, 1225).[1]   The cardinal-deacon of
St. Angelo, who is described by the Pope as "distinguished
by birth and character, as well as by constancy and
industry,"[2] and who was in fact one of the Frangipani,
and related to Louis himself,[3] had come to France to
promote not only the war against the Albigensians,
but also the scheme to improve the condition of the papal
finances.   The assembled Fathers, including seven
archbishops and one hundred suffragan bishops from the
nine provinces, showed themselves unfavourable to the
scheme.   According to Roger of Wendover, who gives the
fullest account of this gathering, some of them even said
that they did not wish to be without friends in the
Roman Curia, or to cease giving presents.   Others expressed the fear that the Roman Procurator who would
have to collect the revenues from the prebends assigned
to the Pope would prove an extortioner and an oppressor ;
that the officials of the Church of Rome would become too
rich, and that the more they had, the more they would
want ;   that wealth would only increase the seditions
among the Roman families and parties (parentelæ), and
so add to the existing danger of the destruction of the
entire City by them ;[4] that they could not bind their
successors to accept to what they themselves might agree

---

[1] *Chron. Turon.*, ap. *R. F. SS.*, xviii, p. 310. *Cf.* n. 285 of the
Actes de Louis VIII., ap. Petit-Dutaillis, *Louis VIII.*, p. 488.

[2] Ep. ix, 78, Feb. 15, 1225.

[3]   " Del linage des Froiepains.
                        S'iert parens le roi d'auques loing."

Phil. Mouskes, *Chron.*, v. 25378-9. The poetical chronicle of this cleric,
which brings the history of the Kings of France down to 1241, is contemporary at least from 1213. We have used the ed. of Reiffenberg,
Brussels, 1836 f.

[4] " Item, multæ divitiæ facerent cives Romanos insanire, et sic
inter diversas parentelas tantæ orientur seditiones, quod posset timeri
totius excidium civitatis, cujus etiam nec modo est expers omnino."
Chron., an. 1226, iv, p. 122.

to ; and lastly some hinted that an attempt to enforce such a measure might even end in a general secession from the Church of Rome.

Seeing the strength of the opposition to his proposal, the legate declared that the scheme was contingent on its being accepted by the empire and the other nations, and that he would not move further in the matter till it was accepted by the other nations.[1]

It may be easily conjectured how this action of the French episcopate affected the decision of the English bishops at St. Paul's. They declared, according to Roger, that the grant asked for concerned the whole of Christendom, and that, when they had before them the example of the other kingdoms, the Pope would find them even more ready than the other kingdoms to fall in with his wishes.[2] According, however, to Walter of Coventry, they held that even if the other nations granted the required prebends, the English nation ought to be exempted, seeing that in virtue of the action of King John, it paid a regular tribute to Rome.[3]

The assembly rejects the papal scheme.

Considering the enormous amount of work the Popes were called upon to perform in the interests of the various countries of Christendom, and considering how their revenues were being constantly seized by the emperors and the powerful, during their struggles for the necessary rights of the Church, we may safely assert that the nations behaved neither generously nor wisely in not adopting this or some other similar scheme which, without throwing all the burden on the clergy, would have made the Roman Church more independent and less open to

[1] Walter of C., *l.c.*   According to the *Annals of Dunstable* (p. 100) Romanus also made a vain attempt to induce Louis to restore to Henry Normandy, Anjou, and Aquitaine.

[2] Roger, *l.c.*

[3] Ann. 1226, ii, p. 279. With this the *Memoriale* of Walter unfortunately comes to a close.

the charge of avarice. As it was, the Roman Pontiffs had to go on endeavouring to do the work expected of them as best they could, and in order to raise the necessary money, they had to have recourse to methods which proved hurtful both to their temporal and spiritual authority, and more financially detrimental to the nations than the scheme proposed.

Honorius
works for
peace,
1225–6.

It is out of the question for us to attempt to relate all that Honorius did in Henry's behalf, or to enumerate all his relations with the clergy and people of England. In the interests of his ward, and in those of the Crusades on the one hand, and on the other in the interests of the campaign against the Albigensians, which he was anxious for Louis VIII. to prosecute, Honorius strove to make peace between England and France. We have seen how the legates whom he sent to England endeavoured to induce Louis to restore what his father had taken from the English crown. And, at Henry's request, he strove to effect the same, or at least to make peace between the two kingdoms by the legates whom he sent to France. His legate in that kingdom, cardinal Romanus, negotiated between the two courts (1225).[1] But Henry was not really anxious for peace, as he was desirous of recovering Poitou ; and, whilst treating for a truce with Louis, was forming alliances against him. The French king, however, had at last been induced by the Pope to undertake an expedition against the Albigensians on condition that the Pope would take his kingdom under his protection whilst the expedition lasted.[2] Accordingly, on April 27,

---

[1] " Misit rex (Henry in 1225) Romam nuntios elegantes de rege Franciæ conquerentes quod Pictaviam et alias terras regis Angliæ, vassalli ecclesiæ Romanæ, temere præsumpsit invadere." *Ann. de Dunstap.*, p. 93. For the action of Romanus see various letters in the *Patent* (i, 579, etc.) and *Close* (ii, p. 43) *Rolls*.

[2] Roger of Wend., *Chron.*, an. 1226, iv, p. 125 f. Cf. *Actes de Louis VIII.*, n. 317, Jan. 1226, ap. Petit-Dutaillis, p. 492.

1226, Honorius addressed a letter to Henry in which he declared that if the King's counsellors had followed his advice, there would have been peace long ago between the two countries. As it is, however, Louis has taken up arms against the Albigensians, and Henry must not interfere with him in the meanwhile.[1]

Bitterly disappointed, Henry brought the Pope's letter before his counsellors. "But," says Roger of Wendover, "all the prelates and nobles gave it as their opinion that the desired expedition should be put off until the result of the difficult and expensive expedition of the French king should be seen"; and one among them who professed to be an astrologer boldly declared that the result would be fatal to the King, as he would either not return alive or would suffer great loss in his goods and followers.[2] Overjoyed at this prediction, concludes the chronicler, Henry agreed to postpone his undertaking.

But whilst thus blocking schemes which were calculated to bring greater trouble than glory on his vassal, Honorius helped him in his real needs. He had been much impressed with the young King's need of money, and resolved to help him in his need. On condition that Henry would confirm the Great Charter, it was agreed by the clergy, nobility, and people, at a large assembly in London (Christmas, 1224), to give the King a fifteenth on all movable property. This at any rate is the statement of Roger of Wendover,[3] but there seems to have been some difficulty as far as the clergy were concerned. According to the *Annals of Dunstable* the secular clergy would not agree to pay the tax;[4] and consequently, after Henry had agreed to confirm the Charter, the

Honorius helps Henry in the matter of money, 1225.

---

[1] Ep. ap. *Royal Let.*, i, p. 545 f.
[2] Roger, *l.c.*
[3] *Ib.*, an. 1225, *init.*
[4] An. 1225, p. 93.

fifteenth was formerly granted (February 2nd, 1225) on all movable property, "except the churches."[1] But Henry had meanwhile appealed for the support of the Pope. This he secured, and on February 3rd a letter left the Lateran addressed to the clergy of England. Honorius pointed out to them that when the Church of its own accord (*sponte*) helped secular princes in their needs, there was no sacrifice of ecclesiastical liberty, but there was the performance of a duty of charity. He accordingly bade them help Henry in his necessities, but urged them to see to it that the money collected was not wasted on what was "superfluous and useless," but was carefully expended on what "was necessary and useful." On the other hand he consented to the proposition that this subsidy granted by the Church should not constitute a precedent.[2] On the receipt of this letter the archbishop of Canterbury addressed another to his suffragans. "As it is necessary to obey the commands of the lord Pope, and as it is fitting generously to help the lord King in his needs, we bid your Fraternity" cause all the clergy, regular and secular, of your diocese, to give a suitable aid to the King from the sources on which the fifteenth has not been paid, "in accordance with the instructions of the Pope."[3] The letter of Honorius clinched the matter; and, to the great regret of some at least of the religious, the subsidy was paid. Roger of Wendover bewails the fact that "an appeal to the Pope was of no use; for, the order of things being changed, archbishop and bishops, by the

---

[1] "Præterquam de ecclesiis." Walt. of Cov., ii, 256. The reissue of the Charter of Liberties and of the Forest was not made till Feb. 11, 1225.

[2] Ep. ap. W. of C., ii, 256.

[3] Ep. ap. Walt. of Cov., an. 1225, ii, p. 257. On Jan. 29, 1226, the Pope wrote a similar letter to the hierarchy of Ireland, ap. Rymer, *Fœdera*, i, p. 285, ed. 1727 ; or ap. *Patent Rolls*, Henry III., vol. ii, p. 80. *Cf.* pp. 101–2, 138, 152. It is not given so well ap. Theiner, *Mon. Hibern.*, p. 25.

authority of the Pope and the church's censure, compelled those to pay whom the lay power could not, and they were thus deprived of all relief." [1]

After this wail, Roger tells us that, in February at a council at Oxford, Henry declared himself to be fully of age, and so released altogether from wardship, and fit to take the chief management of all kingly duties. "As the honoured Honorius, the soul of all honour," [2] died in the following month, the relation of guardian and ward which had existed between the Pope and the King came to an abrupt termination. Whatever else Honorius may have had to answer for at the great judgment seat, there would seemingly have been no room for a charge against him on account of the "ward and orphan" whom he had striven, he wrote, to place under "prudent and honest men who were without suspicion in their country, and who might teach him to fear God and love his subjects," [3] and whose interests he had regarded as his own. [4]

Henry of full age and the death of Honorius.

If only because it concerns one of our cathedrals, justly said to have the most graceful spire in Europe, we must not pass over the bull of Honorius regarding that of Salisbury. In the year 1218, Richard Poore, translated from Chichester to the See of Salisbury " by the authority of the lord Pope," wished to remove his cathedral from

Change of site of Salisbury cathedral, 1218-19.

---

[1] An. 1227 *init.* Writing to bishop R. Poore, Henry promised that the fifteenth granted to him at the instance of the Pope should not be turned by him into a precedent. *Cf. Sarum Charters*, p. 170 *R. S.*, or *Reg. S. Osmund*, ii, 67. *Cf. ib.*, pp. 55-76.

[2] So was he described by the Senator of Rome in a letter to Innocent IV., ap. Höfler, *Albert v. Beham*, p. 138.

[3] *Reg.*, n. 2429, Pressutti, or *Brit. Mus. Addit. MS.*, 15, 352, f. 74, quoted by Gasquet, p. 48 f. *Cf.* ep. i, 350.

[4] *MS., ib.,* f. 32, quoted *ib.*, p. 50. Whoever desires a fuller account of the multifarious relations of Honorius with England than we have been able to give must consult the *Calendar of Papal Registers*, and Gasquet's *Henry III. and the Church.*

Old to New Sarum. Accordingly, he applied "to that supreme city of refuge, which is mother and mistress of all the cities of God in the world, i.e., to the most holy Roman See." [1] In accordance with the wishes of the Pope, Richard submitted the reasons for his wish to the legate Gualo. Among the inconveniences of the old site, he called attention to the high winds that blew there, and to the scarcity of water. On the strength of the recommendation of the legate, Honorius gave full permission for the removal of the cathedral, but insisted that it was not to cause any person to lose any of his rights. [2]

SCOTLAND, IRELAND, AND THE ISLE OF MAN.

The legate James.

While the Registers of Honorius show that very many communications passed between him and the clergy and people of Scotland and Ireland, they also show that they concerned for the most part only the ordinary topics of Church government, the election of bishops, dispensations, and the like. We may, however, take a brief notice of some of his relations with those countries.

His work in Scotland.

In renewing for the benefit of King Alexander II. the decision of Celestine III. that the Church of Scotland was to be dependent only on the Holy See, Honorius laid it down that "no one but a Scotchman, unless specially sent by the Pope, shall exercise the office of legate in that realm." [3] Hence, when in 1220, Master James, papal chaplain and penitentiary (*pœnitentiarius*), [4] appeared as legate in Scotland under the protection of the King of England, it was because he had been " speci-

---

[1] *Regist. S. Osmund*, ii, p. 5, *R. S.*

[2] Bull of March 29, 1219, ap. *ib.*, pp. 5-7.

[3] Ep. of Nov. 21, 1218, ap. *Calendar of P. L.*, or Theiner, *Mon. Hib.*, p. 8.

[4] This title appears as *Pœnitentialis* in the *Chron. of Melrose*, an. 1221.

ally sent by the Pope." [1] Among other exercises of his
power, the legate assembled the bishops of Scotland to
meet at Perth (February, 1221). Except that the provincial council thus summoned lasted for four days,[2]
nothing for certain is known about it. It is possible,
however, that the question of the solemn coronation of
the Scottish king by the legate may have been brought
before it. Giraldus Cambrensis in his *De instructione
Principum*,[3] when treating of the rulers of Scotland,
remarked that " the Princes of the Scotch, who are called
kings, just like the Princes of Spain are not wont to be
crowned nor anointed." But Alexander II., like Pedro II.
of Aragon in the days of Innocent III.,[4] was anxious to
add dignity to his position by a solemn coronation, and
he induced the legate to request permission of the Pope
to perform this function. But Master James had for some
reason lost caste in Rome, and no doubt the influence of
the English was strong there. At any rate, in reply to
his request, Honorius told him that he wished " he had
chosen, as ordered, such companions as would not, either
by word or deed, have injured his good fame ; but, as
he had not, it is his own doing that many speak ill of
him." The Pope went on to express a hope that he would
" so act as to show his detractors to be false, and to reduce

[1] *Patent Rolls*, Henry III., vol. i, p. 271, *R. S.* See also the letters of
July 31, 1220, recommending Master James to the kings of Ireland and
Scotland, ap. *Calendar*, i, p. 74. *Cf. Regist. Episcop. Morav.*, p. 16. In
the early part of the same year Ægidius de Torres, cardinal-deacon of
SS. Cosmas and Damian, had been sent to Scotland to collect the taxes
for the Crusade. Fordun, *Scotichronicon*, l. ix, c. 36.

[2] *Chron. of Melrose, ib.* This council may have dealt with some of
the questions discussed by the provincial synod which Honorius
authorized (May 19, 1225, Potthast, n. 7412) the Scotch bishops to
hold. For its work, see Bellesheim, *Hist. of the Church of Scotland*, i,
341 ff., and Dowden, *The Mediæval Church in Scotland*, p. 229 f.

[3] P. 201, ed. 1846.

[4] *Cf. supra*, vol. xii, p. 170.

them to silence. As to the demand made by the king of
the Scots to be crowned by the legate, it is no affair of
his, since that king is said to be subject to the King of
England. The Pope, therefore, wished the legate to have
nothing to do with the coronation, unless the King of
England and his councillors should consent, in which
case he can proceed to it, taking counsel of the prelates
of England." [1]

The legate
James in
Ireland,
1221.

From Scotland Master James passed over to Ireland
" to regulate and constitute ecclesiastical discipline," [2]
as Honorius considered that there were many abuses
which needed correction.[3] He entered the country with
the best of recommendations. King Henry, addressing
the Justiciar and the magnates of Ireland, declared that
the Pope had sent as his legate thither Master James, his
chaplain and penitentiary, a man of learning and virtue
(*religione probatum*), and he bade them pay him all
honour and reverence as the legate of the Pope, and give

[1] *Calendar of P. L.*, i, 83. The letter is undated, but was probably
dispatched in the early summer of 1221. The influence of England is
plainly seen in the refusal of Gregory IX. in 1233 to a similar request
of the same king. *Cf.* Rymer, *Fœdera*, i, 328. True to his character
as a peacemaker, Honorius constantly urged Pandulf, his legate in
England, to foster peace between England and Scotland. *Cf.*
Calendar, i, pp. 73, 75.

[2] *Cf.* the *Annals of Loch Cé*, i, p. 263, *R. S.*, and the *Annals of Ulster*,
ii, p. 269, *R. S.* Both these documents assign 1221 as the year of the
visit of the legate to Ireland, and the former states that he left Ireland
in the same year in which he came to it. See also the *Annals of the
Kingdom of Ireland*, by the Four Masters, ed. J. O'Donovan, i, p. 199,
Dublin, 1848. The *Annals of Clonmacnoise*, cited *ib.*, say " James the
Pope's legate came to Ireland this year, went about all the kingdom for
the reformation of the inhabitants, and constituted many wholesome
rules for their salvation." *Cf.* ep. Greg. IX., Jan. 4, 1235, ap. Theiner,
Mon. Hib., p. 30.

[3] See the Pope's letter of Nov. 19, 1219, to the Irish Hierarchy,
ap. Potthast, 6163. Malone, *Church Hist. of Ireland*, p. 136 f., is of
opinion that the picture here given of the abuses in the Irish church is
overdrawn.

him all needful assistance. They were, moreover, to seek
his guidance if anything fresh should arise which touched
the King or his kingdom of Ireland.[1] On the legate's
arrival we may presume that he took steps to carry out
the mandates which the Pope had addressed to him with
a view to improving church discipline, and to checking
acts of injustice and oppression which were being exercised
by the English. Among other things which the legate
was ordered to amend, was " a corrupt custom " which
had been brought to the notice of the Holy See by the
archbishop of Cashel. By this custom, if an Englishman
lost anything, and swore that it had been stolen by an
Irishman, and if his oath was supported by six Englishmen, then, even if the Irishman was able to prove his
innocence by the testimony of thirty or more witnesses,
he was compelled to make restitution. Master James
was ordered to see that equal justice was meted out to
all without respect of persons.[2] He was also commissioned
to revoke alienations of property unjustly made, and
to declare void the statute by which some English
prevented Irish clerics, however learned and fit, from
obtaining ecclesiastical dignities.[3]

Whether or not, with regard to this last point the
action of the legate was unsatisfactory, a few years later
Honorius addressed a letter to the clergy of Ireland,
annulling the iniquitous decree made by some Englishmen that no Irish cleric, however good and learned he
might be, should be promoted to any ecclesiastical dignity.[4]

[1] *Patent Rolls*, Henry III., vol. i, p. 271, *R. S.*

[2] *Calendar*, p. 75, or Theiner, *Mon. Hib.*, p. 16. *Cf.* ep. Greg. IX. just
cited.

[3] *Calendar, ib.*

[4] *Cal.*, p. 97 ; Theiner, p. 23 ; Shirley, *Royal Let.*, i, 541. From letters
of King Henry III. to the archbishop of Dublin (Jan. 7, 1222, in *Doc.
relating to Ireland*, i, 1026) and to Geoffrey de Marisco (June 26, 1222,
ap. *ib.*, 1037) we learn that James deposed the bishops of Killaloe and
Ardfert.

" Unwilling," wrote the indignant Pontiff, " to overlook such a presumptuous and wicked abuse, we, by the authority of these presents, declare null and void this decree wanting as it is in any semblance of justice or decency." [1]

Privilege for the See of Dublin.

We may conclude our account of the relations of Honorius with Ireland by telling of the *privilege* which he issued in favour of the archbishop of Dublin. In Ireland, as in so many other countries in the Middle Ages, there was an endless dispute for supremacy between the chief ecclesiastics in the country. No doubt because favoured by the English, the archbishop of Dublin very often succeeded in pushing his claims for primacy as against those of Armagh. Following up privileges granted by Lucius III. (1182) and Innocent III. (1216), Honorius issued a bull which prohibited " any archbishop or bishop of Ireland, except the suffragans of Dublin or apostolic legates, to carry the cross erect without the consent of the archbishop of Dublin, or to hold assemblies (*celebrare conventus*) except those of religious or to hear ecclesiastical causes unless delegated by the Pope in the province of Dublin." [2]

The Isle of Man, 1219–23.

Before leaving these islands, we must record the action of Reginald, King of the Isles. To preserve his independence, he imitated the example of so many other of the less powerful rulers in the Middle Ages, and submitted the Isle of Man to the suzerainty of the Pope. On September 22, 1219, he wrote to tell Honorius that, at the suggestion of the legate Pandulf, he had made over to

---

[1] Of all this valuable work in the interests of Ireland, such a writer as Killen, *Eccles. Hist. of Ireland*, takes no notice, but contents himself with observing that the legate " collected horse-loads of gold and silver from the clergy of Ireland by simony," quoting (i, p. 264) as his authority the *Annals of Clonmacnois* in those of the *Four Masters*, iii, 199 n. The reference is careless. It should have been to the *Annals of Kilronan*, where the legate is called " James Penciail."

[2] *Calendar*, i, p. 83. *Cf. A Church Hist. of Ireland*, by Malone, p. 224.

St. Francis preaching before Pope Honorius III. (Giotto di Bondone).
From the upper church of St. Francis at Assisi.

(*Photo.*)

him the Isle of Man to be held in future by him and his
heirs in fee from the Roman Church. He and his heirs
would offer homage to the Pope for it, and in sign of their
subjection would each year deposit for his use twelve marks
sterling in the Abbey of Furness. He concluded by saying
that the legate had invested him with the island by means
of a gold ring, and that he had sealed his letter with his
seal and " made it patent " in order that there might be
no doubts in connexion with it.[1] Reginald's offer was
duly accepted, and a papal letter of May 23, 1223, added
another realm to the vassal kingdoms subject to the
temporal jurisdiction of the Holy See.[2]

Various Deeds of Honorius.

The other actions of Pope Honorius, though well Confirms
deserving of elaboration, cannot here receive more than orders.
a mere mention. It has already been told how he gave
formal confirmation to the Order of St. Francis and that of
St. Dominic,[3] and it may be added that now he did all that
he could to favour their spread. He recognized in them
the salt that was to preserve the masses, especially in the

---

[1] *Calendar*, i, p. 69 ; or Rymer, i, 234, ed. 1727 ; or Fabre, *Liber
Censuum*, i, 260. In Rymer the letter ends : " Et ne super his aliquando
possit dubitari, has literas fieri fecimus patentes et sigillo nostro
muniri." On *patent* and *close* letters, see *supra*, vol. x, pp. 2, 234.

[2] *Calendar*, i, p. 91, or Theiner, *Mon. Hib.*, p. 21. The Registers of
Honorius show that he took under his protection kings, nn. 19 (Thessalonica), 330 (Hungary), 399 (Norway), 504 and 612 (Aragon), 990
(Portugal) ; queens, nn. 80 (Portugal), 82 (Castile), etc. ; nobles, nn.
30, 103, 281, 324 ; peoples, n. 439 ; monasteries, nn. 21, 60, etc. ;
hospitals and lepers, nn. 128, 161, 599 ; and treaties and agreements,
nn. 94, 298, 312, 321, 330, 1782.

[3] *Supra*, vol. xii, pp. 281 and 284 ; and on the relations of Honorius with
the Dominicans, *cf.* Vincent of Beauvais, n. 123, ap. *M. G. SS.*, xxiv,
p. 166, and the *Regest. Hon.*, nn. 193, 269, 313, 1082, 1255, etc. He
commends St. Francis, *ib.*, n. 2461, and confirms his Order, n. 4582.

towns, for whom little enough was being done by the clergy.[1]

The Franciscans, especially, stood in need of the help of the Pope. From the narrative of the " Three Companions," [2] we learn that eleven years after the founding of their Order, a number of them were " sent forth throughout all the provinces as it were, of the whole world wherein the Catholic faith is held, and observed." But from some provinces, from Germany and Hungary, for instance, they were expelled in case they might be infidels ; for although Innocent III. had given a verbal approval of their Order, it had never been formally approved. As Innocent was dead when the Friars returned, cardinal Ugolino took St. Francis to Honorius, who solemnly confirmed the rule which the saint had presented to him. On June, 11, 1219, he issued an encyclical to the bishops of the Catholic world, and exhorted them to receive the Franciscans as " faithful Catholics." [3] The rough ways were now made more or less plane, and the poor Friars were able to perform their glorious mission in peace.

Poland.

In our biography of Innocent III.,[4] we have spoken of the anarchical conditions which troubled the Grand Duchy of Poland after the death of Boleslas III., Wry-mouthed. Like Innocent, his successor worked hard to restore a little peace to that distracted country. We find

[1] The Dominicans or Friars Preachers came into England in 1221, and the Franciscans or Friars Minor in 1224. *Cf. Ann. Angliæ*, ap. *M. G. SS.*, xvi, p. 484, and Thos. de Eccleston, *De advent. FF. Min.*, c. 1, Eng. trans., p. 132. For a most charming account of their early work in England see Jessopp's essay " The coming of the Friars," London, 1889.

[2] C. 16. *Cf.* Salter's trans. *Cf.* Jordanus, *Chron.*, cc. 3, 6, 18, ed. Boehmer.

[3] Ap. Wadding, *Ann.*, i, p. 301 ; or Horoy, iii, p. 246, n. 233. *Cf.* Glassberger, *Chron.*, pp. 11–12. *Cf.* the letter of Honorius to the French bishops of May 20, 1220, ap. Wadding, i, 360.

[4] Vol. xii, p. 50 ff.

him confirming the peace which had been made between Wladislaus, duke of Kalisch, and Ladislaus III., grand duke of Poland (February 9, 1217),[1] and taking under his protection Wladislaus himself, the possessions which he held at the moment, and all such as by *righteous means* he might obtain in the future.[2] Honorius, no doubt, added the words " by righteous means," because, at the very time, he was striving to make him restore to Henry, Duke of Silesia, the castle of Kalisch.[3]

Somewhat later, Honorius received a letter from the grand duke himself. After due profession of his submission to the Pope,[4] he said that, since his Holiness was the divinely constituted Vicar of Him who strengthens the strong, and remakes what is broken, he believed that he should seek for the support of his authority especially in what concerned peace. Accordingly he has sent to him the treaty which he has made with his nephew, Henry, Duke of Silesia, in order that it may, by the plenitude of the Pope's authority, be made lasting.[5] Honorius accordingly duly confirmed the treaty and ordered the bishops of Poland to enforce its observance by canonical censure.[6]

Finally we find the Pope confirming various liberties which Wladislaus of Kalisch and three other local dukes had granted to the Polish Church.[7]

Like his predecessors, he favoured the development of the Universities by supporting the students in Paris

Protects university students.

---

[1] *Cod. Diplom. maj. Polon.*, i, nn. 89, 90.

[2] *Ib.*, n. 91. These documents are also in Theiner, *Mon. Polon.*, i.

[3] *Ib.*, nn. 93, 94, of Feb. 22, 1217, and 99.

[4] " Paratum ad omnia sue subjectionis obsequium." *Ib.*, n. 95.

[5] *Ib.*, n. 95.

[6] *Ib.*, nn. 96, 98, May 9, 1218.

[7] *Ib.*, n. 114. *Cf.* n. 68. *Cf. The Hist. of Poland*, by J. B. Ostrowski, 3 vols., London, 1841 ; see vol. i, p. 147. We have followed such documents as we could find, and not the modern historian.

and in Bologna against the efforts that were being made, whether by ecclesiastical or civil authorities or by masters, to use the students for their own ends and purposes. Though indeed in the case of Paris, whilst endeavouring to make peace between the ecclesiastical authorities and the students, he ordered the seal of the latter to be broken,[1] and it was not till the year 1246 that " the right of common seal " was granted them.

Peter of Courtenay whom Honorius, as we have seen,[2] crowned emperor of Constantinople, was captured on his way to that city by Theodore Angelus, then Despot of Epirus, and afterwards *Emperor* of Thessalonica. The Pope's efforts to obtain the release of Peter were in vain ;[3] but time brought its revenge, and the despot at length became glad of the Pope's protection.[4] Others also in those parts turned to him for help, and he found it necessary to write severe letters to the patriarch Gervase letting him know that he would not suffer his disobedience.[5]

Moreover, by supporting the new emperor Robert, and in many other ways, Honorius did much towards

Protects the oppressed in the Latin Empire of Constantinople.

---

[1] *Cf.* his letter of May 31, 1222, ap. Denifle, *Chartul. Univ. Par.*, i, p. 102. According to the *Annals of Dunstable*, p. 98, the seal was broken by order of the legate Romanus in 1225. *Cf.* Rashdall, *The Universities of Europe*, i, pp. 161, 173, 223-5. Other letters of Honorius regarding the Universities are *Regest.*, nn. 597-8, 1880, 1976, 2058, 3192. Besides protecting students, he followed, as he said, the example of Popes " Callistus II., Eugenius III., Alexander III., Clement III., Celestine III., and Innocent III.," and, in a letter addressed to all " faithful Christians," forbade the molestation of the Jews. *Reg.*, n. 866. He also endeavoured to secure the throne of Sweden to the son of Eric II., also named Eric, who ultimately became king (Eric III., the Lisper). *Reg.*, n. 2170, Aug. 7, 1219.

[2] *Supra*, p. 44.

[3] *Reg.*, nn. 684-5, 687-91.

[4] *Ib.*, nn. 1023-4, 1029-31, 4121. Still later letters, however, 5132-3, Oct. 21, 1224, show Theodore once more " accursed and excommunicated."

[5] *Ib.*, 332, 340 ff., 1206, 1585.

putting on a satisfactory footing the organization of the new Latin Empire both in Church and in State.[1]

Animated with a great zeal for the propagation of the faith, he addressed a circular letter to all the metropolitans of Europe, begging each of them to pick out at the very least two religious, Cistercians by preference, good and learned men, ready if necessary to face martyrdom, and to send them to him in order that he might send them forth to the ends of the earth.[2] His correspondence " with all the Kings of Russia," [3] and his numerous letters regarding Prussia and Livonia [4] show his eagerness to withdraw men from schism and from paganism, and to protect such pagans as had embraced the faith from molestation.[5]

To secure fair treatment for the Christians living in Mohammedan Spain, Honorius wrote to the Almohad caliph of Cordova, the worthless Yusuf abou Yacoub (1214–1224), or, as he calls him, " Albujacob Miramomelinus." [6] He put before the Caliph the fact, that he to whom Christ had entrusted the whole flock suffered a vast multitude of men who live under the law of Mahomet,

Propagates the faith.

---

[1] *Ib.*, 3856, 3863, 3869, 3904, 3914, 4059–60.

[2] *Reg.*, 3209 ; printed in full in Raynaldus, *Annal. Eccles.*, 1221, n. 47.

[3] *Reg.*, 6180.   The Russians had professed their desire to abjure their errors.

[4] *Reg.*, 389, 816, 1274, 1281–4, 2223, 3787 ff., etc.   *Cf.* Henricus, *Chron. Livon.*, c. 29, etc., ap. *M. G. SS.*, xxiii.

[5] *Reg.*, 6181, and ep. i, n. 220, ed. Horoy.   " Sub interminatione autem anathematis districtius inhibemus ne quisquam terram baptizatorum de Prussia . . . cum exercitu intrare præsumat."   We are writing this at a time (Dec., 1914) when the barbarous methods with which the Prussians are waging war in Belgium and France served forcibly to remind us that they did not embrace the saving faith of Christ till the thirteenth century, and that, as soon as they dared, they, or their leaders at least, proceeded gradually to give up every fragment of it.

[6] On the title " Miramomelinus " see *supra*, xii, p. 178 n.

but reside in Christian lands freely to practise their rites, and so enjoy " the consolation of humanity " ; and he hence took occasion to urge him in turn to allow the Christians in his territories to practise their religion in peace.[1]

He pursues the Albigensians.
But if Honorius had no objections to Moslems openly practising the observances of their belief in the midst of a Christian people, he could not tolerate the extravagant doctrines of those apostate Christians, the Albigensians.

Through the intercession of Innocent III. himself, the Lateran Council left part of his father's lands to the young count Raymond VII. It was not long before he recovered most of the rest by force of arms.[2] Then, says one of our annalists, he begged Pope Honorius to put an end to the attacks on his territory, and to send good and wise men to preach to the people, while he engaged, on his side, utterly to root out from his dominions all the obstinate heretics whom these men should discover.[3] Honorius endeavoured indeed to provide the preachers, and begged the University of Paris to send some of its members to preach " in the parts of Toulouse."[4] He also sent thither to combat the " heretical depravity," Bertram, cardinal-priest of SS. John and Paul, " a man of approved virtue and distinguished learning, a man mighty in word and work." [5] But, at the same time, he thought it right to support Simon de Montfort;[6] and he did all he could by grants of taxes on ecclesiastical property to induce the

[1] *Reg.*, n. 2190, or iv, 17, Horoy. " Ut in hoc (the exercise of faith) nostræ ac tuæ gentis non sit dispar conditio, sed æquum hinc inde humanitatis solatium." *Cf.* 'Abd-el-Wahid, *Hist. des Almohades*, p. 281 ff., ed. Fagnan.

[2] *Cf. supra*, xii, p. 259.

[3] R. Coggeshall, an. 1222, p. 192 *R. S.*

[4] Ep. i, 156, ed. Horoy, Jan. 19, 1217.

[5] Ib., i, 153.

[6] *Reg.*, nn. 940–1, 943–6, 949, 1005–6.

King of France, Philip Augustus, to help him.[1] After
the death of Simon (June, 1218),[2] the Pope stood by his
eldest son Amaury de Montfort.[3] But the young count
Raymond VII. was irresistible; and the new legate
Conrad, cardinal-bishop of Porto, was as powerless against
him as Prince Louis of France who for a time assisted
Amaury.

Not long after the death of Philip Augustus,[4] Amaury
was compelled (January, 1224) to abandon Languedoc
altogether. Raymond VII., to whom the Lateran
Council of 1215 had left Provence, now master of the
adjoining territory on the right bank of the Rhone, was
in possession of all his father's territory. To obtain the
assistance of the new King of France, Amaury ceded to
him the rights over Languedoc which he had inherited
from his father. He also succeeded in keeping Honorius
on his side. A new legate Romanus, cardinal-deacon of
St. Angelo, was accordingly sent into France (c. February,

----

[1] *Reg.*, nn. 1615–17, Sept. 5, 1218.

[2] Our annalists have a high opinion of Simon de Montfort. One
speaks of him as " militia, pulchritudine, et sapientia commendabilis."
Ann. de Waverl., an. 1218, ap. *Annal. Monast.*, ii, 290 *R. S.*, and the
Annals of Dunstable, ap. *ib.*, iii, 54 : " Genere nobilis, sed fidei fervore
nobilior."

[3] *Ib.*, nn. 1582–3, Aug. 1218, and 1918, March 8, 1219, 2511–12,
June, 1220.

[4] William the Breton in his *Philippidos*, l. xii, v. 716 ff., tells us that
Pope Honorius straightway learnt of the King's death by a miracle,
i.e., through the agency of a dying man who saw a vision of Philip with
St. Denis, and told it to Thomas, the papal penitentiary, " Qui summi
vice pontificis peccamina punit." The sick man was instructed to
tell the Pope to absolve the late King, and to say Mass for him so that
his venial sins might be cancelled. The papal penitentiary is now
frequently mentioned in documents. We have just given one description of his office from William, and we will now give another from the
same writer, *ib.*, v. 736 ff.

> . . . " Pape vice qui delicta reorum
> Audit, et absolvit confessos rite reatus,
> Congrua diversis adhibens medicamina moibis."

1225)[1] and Louis was induced by the hope of acquiring Languedoc to undertake a new Crusade against the heretics,[2] with whom real patriots, who were sick of the cruelties and plunderings of the de Montforts' followers, had long been identified.[3] The death of Louis in the midst of the campaign (November, 1226) did not end the war, which Gregory IX., the successor of Honorius, did not allow to drop. At length in April, 1229, by the treaty of Meaux or Paris, Raymond had to agree to conditions of peace which gave the death blow at once to the heresy of the Albigensians, and to the independence of the South.[4]

---

[1] *Reg.*, nn. 5313–5, Feb. 15, 1225. A contemporary has left us a very pleasing picture of the legate. The Cistercian preacher Elinand (†1237) was at Toulouse when cardinal Romanus came to preside at the synod of 1229. In preaching to the assembly, he said : " Behold the representative of the Pope, behold the man who has brought us new rules of discipline, and who has given so many just sentences. To induce us to render homage to his person, and submission to his will, what stronger motive can we have than his own modesty. He journeys without pomp, shuns avarice, and does not run after presents. He seeks not our goods, but our hearts. I beg you to listen with humility to the precepts which for the common good he is about to give us." *Serm.* ap. Tissier, *Bibl. pat. Cisterc.*, vii, 306, Bonnefontaine, 1660.

[2] There was no longer much concern about the Albigensians as heretics ; most of the Crusaders were more concerned about seizing their lands. " Cura illis nulla vel modica investigandis erat hereticis aut tenendis," says Will. of Puylaurens, *Chron.*, c. 25, al. 27. Roger of Wendover, says *Chron.*, an. 1226, iv, p. 135, that this campaign of Louis was undertaken rather by "covetousness" than by "any wish to exterminate heresy."

[3] As Innocent III. had to condemn Simon de Montfort and his followers for not being too particular whose lands they seized, so Honorius had to tell Romanus to urge King Louis and his magnates "to lay aside all cupidity" and to refrain from seizing the territories of Catholics, and especially any lands belonging to the empire, England, or Aragon. *Reg.*, n. 5848, 28 Feb.–March, 1226.

[4] *Cf.* Schmidt, *Hist. des Cathares*, i, 268–284, for the history of the Albigensian wars during the reign of Honorius III., though it must be noted that he relies too much on the impassioned continuation of the poet William of Tudela. See also Petit-Dutaillis, *Louis VIII.*, 2nd part, cc. 4, 5, and *supra*, vol. xii, p. 259. When at this time Raymond

He undertook to be faithful to the Church, and to the King, to labour in every way for the extirpation of the heretics, to pay tithes to compensate the churches and churchmen for damage inflicted on them during the wars, to take the Cross as a penance, and, with the exception of certain domains for which he agreed to do homage to the King of France, to resign to him and to his heirs for ever the territories on this side of the Rhone, i.e., those on its right bank, and the territory " which is in the Empire on the other side of the Rhone, to the Church." [1]

Unhappily, and in this matter, too, Honorius followed Provisions. his great predecessor, he continued the system of Provisions.[2] As the episcopate of Europe would not adopt any scheme for relieving the financial strain experienced by Rome in its efforts to execute the judicial work thrust upon it, the Pope concluded that the Holy See had no other convenient way of rewarding devoted service than by ordering the ecclesiastical authorities in the different countries to appoint his nominees to vacant benefices. This system of Provisions as it was called, inaugurated, so it is now said, in 1137, under Innocent II.,[3] and developed under Hadrian IV., was strikingly furthered by Honorius III. After the pontificate of Honorius, we are told by Dr. Baier that the number of these papal nominations varied till about the middle of the pontificate of

VII. was absolved from excommunication, the historian speaks of him as " naked . . . nudum *in camisia et braccis.*" Will. of P., *l.c.*, c. 37.

[1] " Terram autem quæ est in Imperio ultra Rhodanum . . . præcise et absolute quitavimus dicto legato (cardinal Romanus) nomine ecclesiæ in perpetuum." Treaty of peace ap. Vaissette, *Hist. de Languedoc*, Preuves, No. 184, p. 332. *Cf. ib.*, n. 183 ff., p. 326 ff., for the various documents connected with the treaty.

[2] *Cf. supra*, x, 52 f., and xii, 289.

[3] *Cf.* Dr. H. Baier, *Päpstliche Provisionem*, Munster, 1911. According to this author France provided most of the benefices, nearly half under Honorius III., Alexander IV., and Boniface VIII. Germany and Italy came next, and far below these countries, England and Spain.

Urban IV. Then it remained much as it had been under Honorius, save for a very exceptional rise in the time of Benedict XI. The Provisions were mostly in favour of Italians—of poor clerks in the twelfth century, and of the personnel of the curia in the thirteenth. In granting a Provision, Honorius generally advances some sound reason. He asks the Archbishop of Bourges to give a prebend to a "scriptor of the Apostolic See who had worked long and faithfully in the service of the church of Bourges,"[1] and he asks for another for a faithful servant who is devoted to study.[2] The famous scholar, Michael Scott, often experienced the help of the Pope in this way,[3] and if a relative occasionally experienced the same assistance, it was given, as Honorius explained, because men accused him of having no natural love.[4] If then the practice of Provisions grew considerably under Honorius, he could say something in defence of his action, as indeed he once did, whilst at the same time remedying an abuse in connexion with them. Writing to his "venerable brother the Archbishop of Canterbury," he said : "Since those who faithfully serve the Apostolic See, the head of the Universal Church, are proved to be of great service to its various members, it is right that they should be honoured with suitable benefices, lest, undergoing so arduous a service at their own cost, they should grow remiss. Hence it is that clergy of the Apostolic See, residing not without great labour and expense in England and other parts of the world, have obtained ecclesiastical benefices for a period, to the profit oftentimes of the patrons of the livings themselves. But it has sometimes happened that on the departure of these beneficed clergy,

---

[1] *Reg.*, n. 29. *Cf.* nn. 106 and 640.
[2] *Ib.*, n. 84. *Cf.* nn. 343, 1348.
[3] *Ib.*, nn. 4682, 4871, 5025, and 5470.
[4] *Ib.*, n. 1015. *Cf.* n. 5333.

they have, without consulting the patrons, left successors
. . . We, wishing to remedy this, and to prevent the
patrons' generosity from causing them a loss . . . decree
that, when such Roman or Italian clerics are leaving the
country, the livings which they have held shall not for
that time be conferred by us on any other person, but they
shall return to their patrons to be conferred by them on a
suitable candidate." [1]

Honorius was an old man when he ascended the chair Death of
of Peter, and the strenuous efforts which he made to III., 1227.
Honorius
follow in the energetic footsteps of Innocent III. did not
allow him to enjoy that dignified ease which is rightly
regarded as the reward of a well-spent life. He worked
hard to the very end, and died (March 18, 1227),[2] leaving
behind him a deserved reputation, if not for great genius,[3]
at any rate for holiness and generosity, and for being an
ardent lover of peace,[4] and that, too, not merely among the
Cistercians, who naturally praised him as he had been a

---

[1] Ep., v, 273, of Feb. 26, 1221, ed. Horoy.

[2] For the date see all the authorities in Pressutti, *Reg.* ii, p. 487 f.
Matthew Paris, while himself calling Honorius "a gentle old man,"
has a story about his death which furnishes another illustration of the
gibing tongues of the Romans who in their pasquinades never spared
even the sacred person of the Popes. On the tenth day before his
death, says Paris, when the Roman people, believing that he was dead,
had begun to plunder his property (in res papales debacchanti), he was
shown to them in his dying state from a high window. Hereupon "a
certain verse-maker" exclaimed :

> " Honorius, to many a grief this day,
> 'Tis shame for thee to live, make haste away.
> O pater Honori, multorum nate dolori
> Est tibi dedecori vivere, vade mori."

Hist. Anglorum, an. 1227, ii, p. 294 f., *R. S.*

[3] The *Annales Stadenses* say with justice, "Hic non erat multum
perspicacis ingenii, nec eminentis litterature, sed ecclesia Dei sub ipso
in competenter bono statu stetit." An. 1227, ap. *M. G. SS.*, xvi, p. 299.

[4] "Sanctitate et virtutibus plenus." *Chron. minor Erphord*, ap.
M. G. SS., xxiv, p. 197, "Etate senior, pietatis et misericordiæ singularis." *Chron. Turon.*, ap. *ib.*, xxvi, p. 476.

great admirer and benefactor of their order,[1] but even among such censors as Giles of Corbeil and Jacques de Vitry.[2] So dear was he to the Cistercians that they decreed that his anniversary had to be observed by them for ever.[3]

He was buried in St. Mary Major's in a tomb of porphyry resting on four little pyramids, made for him by his successor,[4] and, as we are assured, held in due reverence.[5] What Vasari in his biography of Arnolfo di Cambio says of the tomb of Honorius III. should be assigned to that of Honorius IV.,[6] but Canon Biasiotti has succeeded in finding out exactly where the tomb originally stood in front of the present chapel of the Manger.

[1] The *Chronicle of Melrose*, an. 1227, calls him "the father and protector of the Cistercian Order : may his soul live in glory." *Cf.* *Chron. Ign. Mon. Cist.*, p. 38.

[2] Jacques in his letter of Oct., 1216, ap. Boehmer, *Analekten zur Geschicte des Francis von A.*, n. 4, p. 96, calls Honorius " a good and religious old man, very simple and kind, who gave nearly all he had to the poor," and Giles, *Hierapigra*, i, v. 487 ff., ap. Vieillard, in his *Gilles de C.*, p. 360 ff., calls him the light of the Church, the mirror of virtue, the rule of wisdom, the tribunal of justice, the sun of eloquence, the moral antidote of vice, the asylum and refuge of the wretched.

[3] *Chron. pontif. Amiatinum*, ap. *M. G. SS.*, xxiv, p. 836.

[4] *Chron. min. Erphord.*, ap. *ib.*, p. 197.

[5] *Catal. Rom. pont. Viterb.*, ap. *ib.*, xxii, p. 352.

[6] *Cf.* the ed. of K. Frey, Munich, 1911, p. 476, etc. *Cf.* Venturi, *L'Arte*, iv, p. 121 ; Clausse, *Les Marbriers Romains*, pp. 320–1.

Leaden bulla of Honorius III. showing the heads of
SS. Peter and Paul on the reverse.

Gregory IX.

From a copy made by Grimaldi from the mosaic of
the facade of old St. Peter's.

GREGORY IX.

A.D. 1227–1241.

Sources.—Since the publication of the important modern biographies of Gregory IX. by Balan and Felten, there has become readily available the most authentic source for the *Life* of this Pope, namely his Register.[1] It has been edited by L. Auvray in three volumes, Paris, 1896–1910. This edition gives an analysis of 6,183 documents which varies in fullness according to the importance of the document or to the fact of its having been published in its entirety elsewhere. Unfortunately the index to the work is not yet ready, and the war which is now[2] falling so heavily on France will no doubt still further retard its appearance. B. Hauréau, ap. *Notices et extraits des MSS.*, t. xxi, pt. ii, p. 203 ff., published (Paris, 1865) in full with valuable notes a number of the letters of Gregory IX. till then inedited.

Fortunately, also, there has come down to us a contemporary biography of Gregory. It is the work of one of the Pope's ardent admirers, who, while he sometimes forgets his dates, never forgets to say hard things about the Emperor Frederick II., though he says nothing against his character, which is not corroborated by independent evidence. The author would appear to have died before the Pope, as his biography ends a few months before Gregory's death. It is not known for certain who the biographer was, but J. Marx, who has written a short treatise on the sources of Gregory's life (*Die Vita Gregor IX. quellenkritisch untersucht,*

---

[1] The *Annales S. Nicasii Remensis*, an. 1237, ap. *M. G. SS.*, xiii, p. 85, state that a record of a dispute between the canons and citizens of Rheims before the Pope was kept in the Cathedral treasury, and "in registro ejusdem Gregorii." Frederick II. also alludes to "regestorum vestrorum . . . archivium." Ep. Sept. 20, 1236, ap. H.-B., *Hist. Dip.*, iv, p. 906.

[2] Jan. 1915. Reference is made to the most dreadful war known to history—the European war which broke out in August, 1914.

Berlin, 1889), thinks it highly probable that he was a papal notary, John of Ferentino. Written in a more pretentious style than is usual with papal biographies, this *Life* has been already often printed (e.g., rather inaccurately by Muratori, *R. I. SS.*, iii, pt. i, p. 575 ff.), but only recently (ap. *Liber Censuum*, ii, p. 18 ff., ed. Fabre-Duchesne) in a satisfactory manner. The *Life* in *R. I. SS.*, iii, of Bernard Guidonis (see *supra*, x, 284), is, as we might expect from what we know of its author, mostly concerned with affairs in Languedoc.

In the *Fonti per la storia d'Italia*, G. Levi has published (Rome, 1890) *Registri dei Cardinali Ugolino d'Ostia et Ottaviano* ; and in *Archivio della Soc. Rom. di storia patria*, vol. xii (1889), p. 241 ff., *Documenti ad illustrazione del Registro del Card. Ugolino*. Ugolino's register is almost wholly taken up with documents concerning his legation in Lombardy in 1221.

Nearly all the chronicles of his time are useful as sources for the *Life* of Gregory. Of these many have already been noticed, as, for instance, those of the imperialists, Conrad of Lichtenau (*supra*, vol. ix, p. 298 n.) ; Richard of San Germano (x, p. 359 n.) ; Nicholas of Jamsilla (xi, 158) ; Gerard Maurisius (*ib.*, p. 203 n.) ; and the author of the *Chron. de rebus in Italia gestis* (ix, p. 308 n.) ; and those of others, whether papalists or not, Codagnellus (*ib.*) ; the unknown Cistercian author from the abbey of S. Maria de Ferraria (xi, p. 7) ; [1] Albert von Behaim or Beham (xi, 211 n.) ; Ricobaldi of Ferrara (*ib.*, p. 159), etc. In previous pages there has often appeared the name of the Franciscan Salimbene. Born in the year 1222, he compiled at different times a gossiping rambling chronicle from what he saw and heard as he wandered up and down northern Italy and France, and also from what he gathered in conversation with all sorts of people. This record of gossip, largely mixed with quotations from the Bible and with shrewd and moral reflections, is concerned with events between the years 1212 and 1288, which was a year or two before he died († c. 1290). Its interest arises from the fact that he came in contact with many remarkable persons, and that he touches in a light, pleasant way on all manner of topics that are not usually noticed by more serious historians ; whilst its credibility, resting, as it does, at times rather on chatter than on research, is often of no high order. Brother Salimbene's chronicle

---

[1] Unfortunately his valuable Chronicle finishes with the year 1227.

has, of recent years, attracted a great deal of attention.[1] The best edition of it is by Holder-Egger, *M. G. SS.*, xxxii. C. Cantarelli has given us an Italian translation of it, Parma, 1882, and G. G. Coulton in his *From St Francis to Dante*, London, 1906, professes to give in our own language "A translation of all that is of primary interest " in it.[2] By some modern critics Salimbene is also thought to have written the *Memoriale Potestatum Regiensium* (1154–1290), ap. *R. I. SS.*, viii, and also the *Liber de Temporibus* and the *Cronica imperatorum*, which Holder-Egger, their latest editor (ap. *M. G. SS.*, xxxi), ascribed to Albert Millioli.[3] Emo and Menko, the first two abbots of Bloemhof (Floridus Hortus), near Wittewierum in Frisia, drew up successively a reliable chronicle extending from 1204 to 1273. With a later continuation it extends to 1296, ap. *M. G. SS.*, xxiii.

About the year 1279 Thomas of Tuscany wrote in Florence the *Gesta Imperatorum et pontificum*, ap. *M. G. SS.*, xxii. His account of Gregory IX. is, however, very confused. Of local annals many Austrian annals (ap. *M.G. SS.*, ix) are useful, as is also the work of Rolandinus of Padua who wrote a reliable account of his native city from 1200–1260. Under the title of *De factis in Marchia Tarvisina* it may be read in either the old (vol. viii) or new edition of the *R. I. SS.* The Paduan Chronicle, which in the same volume Muratori printed under the name of *Monachi Patavini*, is in *M. G. SS.*, vol. xix, described as *Annales S. Justini Patavini*. As nearly all the great cities of northern Italy began to have their annals during this century, it is out of the question to enumerate them all here. We shall mention no more but the well-written continuation (1225–48) of the *official* annals of Genoa (ap. *M. G. SS.*, xviii, or less well-edited ap. *R. I. SS.*, xi) by " Magister Bartholomæus, who was constituted the scribe of the Commune of Genoa " in August, 1225, and the continuation of the Pisan Annals of Marango from 1175–1296 by Michael de Vico, a canon of Pisa in 1371, ap. *R. I. SS.*, vi. Inasmuch as the Florentine annals written in Italian and wont to be ascribed to

---

[1] *Cf.* on him Gebhart, *Les origines de la renaissance en Italie* ; and *L'Italie mystique*, Paris, **1890** ; and Taylor, *The Medieval Mind*, vol. i ; T. L. Kington Oliphant, *The Life of Fra Salimbene*, ap. *Transactions of the Royal Historical Soc.*, vol. i, 1872, p. 249 ff.

[2] On this work see a criticism of the *Saturday Review*, quoted vol. x, p. 63.

[3] *Cf.* Cerlini in the *Archiv. Muratorianum*, n. 8, 1910.

Riccordano and Giacotto Malaspini, uncle and nephew (ap. *R. I. SS.*, viii), and the *Diurnali* (ap. *R. I. SS.*, vii) in the Apulian dialect, put down to a Matteo Spinelli,[1] appear to be now generally recognized as forgeries, no further notice need be taken of them.

The Arabian chroniclers who treat of the Crusade of Frederick II. are summarized ap. Michaud, *Bibliothèque des Croisades*, iv, p. 426 ff. In poor verse, but in a trustworthy style, the clerk, Philippe Mouskes († 1244), in over 31,000 verses furnishes us with much valuable material for the history of France from about the end of the twelfth century to 1243. What he has to say of the years before the period named is of no importance. The whole poem was edited in two vols., Brussels, 1836, by Baron de Reiffenberg, but extracts from it may be read in *R. F. SS.*, xxii, and *M. G. SS.*, xxvi.

Modern Works.—The *Storia di Gregorio IX.* (Modena, 1872), by Professor D. Pietro Balan, is a voluminous production in three volumes of about 500 pages each. It is a reliable work containing a considerable number of important documents printed in full ; but its arrangement—more or less chronological—is not good, and it lacks an index and head-lines or side-notes or any other accompanying guide to the contents of its chapters. The important work of Dr. J. Felten, *Papst Gregor IX.*, Freiburg in Breisgau, 1886, with all the advantages of Balan's work, is less diffuse, and only suffers from following the chronological order. E. Brem (Heidelberg, 1911) treats of Gregory before he became Pope, *P. Greg. IX. als Kardinal bis zur Kaiserkrönung Freiderichs II.*; and G. Falco in *Archivio della Soc. Rom. di storia pat.*, vol. xxiii, 1910, of " I preliminari della pace di S. Germano." There are also to be taken into account various monographs on different episodes in connexion with Gregory's pontificate, e.g., Balan's *La prima lotta di Gregorio IX. con Federigo II.* (1227-30), Modena, 1871. This dissertation is included in his subsequent *Storia*. Balan defends the action of Gregory towards Frederick in the matter of the Crusade, whereas R. Honig, *Rapporti tra Federico II. e Gregorio IX. rispetto alla spedizione in Palestina*, Bologna, 1896, opposes it. Biographies of the principal men of his age also serve to throw light on that of Gregory. Such, for instance,

---

[1] Otherwise known as Matteo di Giovenazzo (Matthæus Spinelli de Juvenatio).

as those of G. del Giudice, *Riccardo Filangieri*, Naples, 1893 ; of H. Wallon, *St. Louis*, Tours, 1878 ;[1] of N. Valois, *Guillaume d'Auvergne*, Paris, 1880, etc.

[1] The biographies of St. Louis are numerous ; we may add those of F. Perry, *St. Louis*, London, 1901 ; M. Sepet, 1900 ; and A. Lecoy de la Marche, Tours, 1894.

CONTEMPORARY SOVEREIGNS.

EMPEROR OF THE ROMANS.	LATIN EMPERORS OF CONSTANTINOPLE.	EMPEROR OF NICÆA.
Frederick II., 1212–50.	Robert, 1219–28. Baldwin II., 1228–61.	John III., Ducas, Vatatzes, 1222–54.

KING OF FRANCE.	KING OF ENGLAND.
St. Louis IX., 1226–70.	Henry III., 1216–72.

ARMS OF GREGORY IX.

Gules an eagle displayed chequy or & sable crowned of the first.

CHAPTER I.

GREGORY BEFORE HE BECAME POPE. HIS ELECTION
AS POPE. HIS DECRETALS.

Another
member of
the Conti
family,
Hugo or
Ugolino.

FORTUNATELY for the independence of the Church and
the freedom of Europe, the reign of the aged, gentle,
excessively peace-loving Honorius was not commensurate
with that of Frederick II. As tyrannical as he was clever,
it was the aim of that most brilliant scion of the race of
the Hohenstaufen to bend all men to do his will, whether
in the domain of the soul or of the body. But in Gregory
IX. he encountered the first of those spiritual rulers whose
opposition was to prove fatal not only to his personal
ambitions but to his race. The domineering tendencies
of the Hohenstaufen dynasty were to receive no little
check from those distinguished members of the Conti
family, Gregory IX. and Alexander IV.

Ugolino's
(or Hugo's)
birth and
character.

The former of these, a grand-nephew of Innocent III.,[1]
whose greatness of soul he largely inherited, was the son
of the count of Segni, and was born (perhaps about 1170)
at Anagni, to one of the noble families of which his mother
belonged.[2] As we are expressly told by Honorius III.[3]

---

[1] At any rate related to Innocent in the third degree. "Innocentium
P. III. tertio gradu consanguinitatis attingens." *Vita.*, c. 2. Giraldus
Camb., *De jure Menev. eccles.*, Dis. II., calls him "consobrinus papæ."
Op., iii, 181 *R. S.*

[2] *Ib.* "De civitate Anagnia ortum trahimus," says Gregory himself,
ap. Ughelli, *Italia Sacra*, vol. ii, p. 310, cited by Brem. If Matthew Paris
were to be trusted, Gregory must have been born about 1140, because
according to him he was about 100 years old when he died in 1241
(*Chron. Maj.*, iv, 162 *R. S.*). But with good reason, Kington, Felten,
and Brem are agreed that no reliance can be placed on the statement.
In connexion with it we would call attention to the fact that very
many contemporaries tell us that Innocent III. was "young" and
Honorius III. "old," but Matthew Paris stands alone in his assertion
of the supposed remarkable old age of Gregory IX.

[3] See his *Register*, n. 5870, ii, p. 411, ed. Pressutti.

that a certain Adenulf " de Mathia " was Ugolino's brother, it is clear that " Matthew," [1] and not the Tristan of later authors, was the father of the future Pope. We may add here that the register of Giffard, archbishop of York,[2] shows that Ugolino had a nephew of the same name Adinulf, and that the said nephew drew a revenue of fifty marks a year from a Yorkshire prebend. According to his biographer, Ugolino grew up to be a man of fine form and feature, and was possessed of a clear understanding and of a retentive memory. His eloquence was quite Ciceronian, and his love of music considerable,[3] and he was a keen student of the Bible, which he loved to explain. Full of zeal for the faith, and for discipline, and eager to spread the blessings of Christianity, he proved a lover of chastity,[4] and a model of virtue. He was " as the noonday sun," even among the luminaries of the Church. As he was good in himself, so also was he good to others. He was, we are told, the consolation of those in distress by

[1] Various documents addressed to him or naming him as " citizen of Anagni " are extant. *Cf.* the *Registro del card. Ottaviano*, n. 30, ad an. 1252–3, " Nobili viro mathie civi Anagnino," and Theiner, *Cod. Diplom.*, i, p. 285, n. 446, ad an. 1285. " Adinulpho Mathie, civi Anagnino." If Gregory IX. died in 1241, at the age of 100 years, and his father was still alive in 1252, what must have been the age of the father ? What, too, must have been the age of one of his masters ? *Cf. infra*, p. 175.

[2] P. 84.

[3] Salimbene, p. 184.

[4] Salimbene, *Chron.*, p. 385, speaking of cardinal Octavian, says that there was a report (dictum fuit) that he was the son of Pope Gregory IX., and then immediately proceeds to give a probable origin of the report : " perchance because he had loved him with a special love. Forte quia dilexerat eum speciali amore." Mr. Coulton, who is fond of making such extravagant professions of fairness that one cannot help suspecting that he " doth protest over much," sees in this obvious expression of Salimbene's disbelief in the idle tale which he reports " a special accusation " of unchastity made by that author against the man for whom he always expresses respect. *Cf.*, e.g., p. 88, " Erat enim homo (Gregory IX.) multum compassivus habens viscera pietatis." See *From St. Francis to Dante*, p. 252.

his alms [1] and good counsel, and by the same means was a great supporter of the new religious Orders of SS. Francis and Dominic which in his days were doing so much for man's advancement in decency, virtue, and learning. Learned himself, Gregory not only professed himself enamoured of wisdom,[2] but proved himself a patron of learned men,[3] and one of the best friends that studies [4] and students [5] especially have ever had. His Privilege, *Parens scientiarum*, of April 13, 1231, addressed to the masters and scholars of Paris, " is justly regarded as the *Magna Charta* of its University."

---

[1] *Cf. Regist. Honor. III.*, n. 73, vol. i, 13, for a notice of his endowing a hospital when cardinal. See also his *Life*, c. 3, for the same, and for his generosity to religious orders.

[2] He speaks " sapientiæ, qua plurimum nos delectat." Ep. of May 10, 1231, ap. Denifle, *Chartularium Univer. Paris*, i, p. 147.

[3] He insists on Michael Scott, who is learned even in Hebrew and Arabic, being furnished with a proper benefice. Ep. Apr. 28, 1227, ap. *ib.*, p. 110.

[4] With the aid of masters sent from Paris he worked himself for the reform of the studies at home: "hiidem pro reformatione studii . . . laborantes." Ep. May 6, 1231, ap. *ib.*, p. 145, *cf. ib.*, n. 75. He erected a University (studium generale) at Toulouse, ep. Apr. 27, 1233, ap. *ib.*, p. 151. *Cf. Regest. G. IX.*, n. 1267 ; *ib.*, nn. 1388–9 *re* Cambridge.

[5] In their interests he compelled certain regular and secular clergy who had houses in Paris to have them properly assessed, like the ordinary citizens' houses, so that the students could not be overcharged for lodgings. Ep. June 15, 1237, ap. *ib.*, p. 160. It was through his exertions that Paris was saved as a University centre of theological, literary, and scientific learning. Owing to a quarrel between the University and the civil authorities, the former resolved to put an end to the *studium generale* at Paris, and our King Henry III. (see ep. of July 16, 1229, ap. *ib.*, p. 119) tried to capture it for England. But realizing what a blow it would be for learning if the University were permanently broken up, Gregory did not rest till the danger was averted. Epp. Nov. 23, 1229, *ib.*, p. 125 ; Nov. 24, p. 127 ; Nov. 26, 128, etc. *Cf.* on " The Great Dispersion and the Papal Privileges," Rashdall, *Universities of Europe in the Middle Ages*, i, p. 335 ff. See ep. Greg. of May 5, 1231, ap. *Chart.*, i, 144, for the study of arts and science at Paris. See also Crevier, *Hist. de l'Univ. de Paris*, i, p. 337 ff.

In this document [1] Gregory, besides making regulations for the external government of the University and authorizing the suspension of lectures as a means of safeguarding its liberties, took an important step towards extending its intellectual liberty. A council of Paris in 1210 had forbidden the reading in the Schools of " the books of Aristotle on natural philosophy," [2] and in the document referred to, Gregory renewed this prohibition. But, in renewing it, he gave a guarantee that the question of the books should be considered. Accordingly, on April 23, 1231, he issued a commission to William, archdeacon of Beauvais, and other distinguished masters of the University to examine the said books and to purge them of whatever might be dangerous to their readers. " As it is the end of the other sciences," he wrote, " to minister to the science of the Sacred Scriptures, the faithful should devote themselves to them in so far as they serve the will of Him who gave them to us. If then there be aught in them which is of a nature to injure the purity of the faith, it must be cast out, just as of old a captive woman of great beauty was not permitted to be brought into the home till she had been shorn of her flowing locks, and her sharp nails had been cut, and just as the Jews that they might be enriched with the spoils of the Egyptians, were commanded to take, not the poor vessels of bronze or clay, but the splendid ones of gold and silver. Inasmuch as, then, we understand that the books of natural philosophy, which were prohibited by the provincial council of Paris, contain much that is useful and much that is detrimental, we commission your discretion in which we have full

---

[1] A translation of it may be read, p. 7 ff., in *The Medieval Student*, by D. C. Munro, Philadelphia, 1899. See Gregory's *Regesta*, n. 203, July 7, 1228, blaming the " masters of theology " in Paris for adulterating the word of God with natural doctrine.

[2] See the decree, ap. *Chart. U. P.*, i, p. 70, n. 11.

confidence, by virtue of this apostolic rescript, and in view of the divine judgment to examine these books with all skill and care in order that what is useful may not suffer from what is hurtful, and so that the books may be forthwith studied without danger, when all that is erroneous or calculated to scandalize their readers has been removed." [1] Granted that Hauréau is correct in asserting that many letters have come from Rome in which philosophy has not been treated with equal honour, we must with him praise at least this Pope to whom the monuments of learning are vessels of gold, and who cites the Bible with such skill and grace in order to recommend the books of the philosophers. [2]

It would appear that the commissioners did not do much in the way of correcting the text of Aristotle ; but their work, no doubt, prepared the way for the abrogation of a detrimental decree. [3]

That Gregory possessed the great qualities of mind and heart which we have just enumerated is asserted not merely by his biographer but by general testimony. [4]

The early career of Ugolino.

Beginning his ecclesiastical career as a member of the church of Anagni, [5] he became later on one of the chaplains

[1] Ib., p. 143, n. 87. Cf. Roger Bacon, Opus Tertium, c. 8 f.

[2] Cf. his Grégoire IX. et la Philosophie d'Aristotle, p. 7, an extract from the Académie des inscriptions, Paris, 1872. We may note that it was the bad translations of Aristotle then in use which led to the condemnation of Paris. Cf. ch. vii, "Aristotle and the Church," in Aristotle and the Christian Church, by Brother Azarias. R. Bacon is always denouncing the bad translations of Aristotle, l.c., pp. 24, 32, 75, 469, 471 ff., etc.

[3] Hauréau on MS. 8299 of the Bib. Nat., ap. Notices et extraits, vol. xxxi, pt. ii, p. 288 f.

[4] " Religiosus et acutissime literatus." Albericus Trium. Font., Chron., ap. M. G. SS., xxiii, p. 919. See also Chronicles, ap. ib., xxiv, p. 141 ; xxxi, 506 ; Menko, ap. ib., xxiii, p. 536 ; Chron. mon. Cisterc., an. 1227.

[5] " Anagnia ecclesia, cujus olim in tenera ætate fuimus filius," says Gregory himself, ap. Ughelli, Italia Sacra, i, 312 ; cf. p. 310, cited by Brem, p. 2.

of Innocent III., and was by that pontiff soon made cardinal-deacon of St. Eustachius (1198), and then cardinal-bishop of Ostia, between the May of 1205 and that of 1206, seemingly in April, 1206.

Whether before or after he became attached to the church of Anagni, he is said by Boulay to have studied with distinction at the University of Paris,[1] and he is thought to allude to his studies there in a privilege which he subsequently granted to the University.[2]

However this may be, one of Ugolino's letters shows that he was far from unmindful of the days of his youth, and of those who had trained him in the ways of virtue and learning. When he was legate in Germany during the years 1207–9, he heard of the death of " the holy and moderate " Cistercian brother Rainer, with whom the biography of Innocent III. has made us familiar, and who had been Ugolino's master. Writing to some of the Cistercian abbots in south Italy to sympathize with them on the loss of so eminent a subject, he tells them that " every day he feels grief and is afflicted at the thought of Rainer's death, and can find no consolation." For it was Rainer who had striven " that Christ might be born in him." " I," he avers, " have no words of consolation by which I can soothe your grief inasmuch as I am over-whelmed by a like grief myself." [3] After speaking of the brother's gift of prophecy, his " unexampled knowledge of the Bible," and his eloquence, he assures us that even distant Spain knew of his virtues, and that " Pope Innocent (III.), whose innocence he commended to God with prayers and tears, knew of them even more fully."

His regard for an old master.

---

[1] *Hist. Universitatis Pari.*, iii, 680, ap. Balan, *Greg. IX.*

[2] Ep. of May 10, 1231, ap. *Chart. Univer. Par.*, ed. Denifle.

[3] " Ego quidem verba consolationis non habeo, quibus tuum possim delinire dolorem, qui simili dolore confodior." This letter is to be found ap. *Archivio Rom. di stor. patria*, vol. ii, 1879, p. 363 ff.

He concludes by telling the abbots that he has written " this in Germany, whilst much preoccupied in mind."

His great knowledge of Canon Law caused him to be very frequently employed by Popes Innocent and Honorius as an *auditor* or judge of appeal.[1] He is also said, by mistake, to have been archpriest of St. Peter's,[2] which basilica he, at any rate, did not forget to favour when he became Pope.[3]

Ugolino's legatine commissions.
As cardinal of St. Eustachius, the most important negotiations were promptly put into his hands. His conduct of some of them showed him a man of principle and high moral courage. He could not be frightened even by Markwald of Anweiler, the most unscrupulous minister of the fierce Henry VI.[4] His elevation to the see of Ostia (1206) added indeed to his dignity, but did not lessen the work he was called upon to do. This was only to be expected, seeing that in one capacity or another he was ever at the right hand of the untiring Innocent. In the year following his elevation to the see of Ostia, he was sent along with cardinal Leo as a legate into Germany to promote peace between the rival imperial candidates, Otho of Brunswick and Philip of Suabia. To those to whom he was accredited Innocent described him as an honourable and prudent man, and one for whom he had

[1] *Gesta Innocent III.*, c. 147. *Cf. Reg. Inn. III.*, v, 29 ; vii, 102 ; viii, 19 and 29. In the great struggle between the monks of Canterbury and its archbishops he favoured the monks. *Cf. Epp. Cantar.*, pp. 471 and 476. He also favoured, or seemed to favour, and certainly chaffed, Giraldus Cambrensis. *Cf. De jure et statu eccles. men.*, dist. ii, ap. iii, p. 181 f. But *cf. ib.*, d. iv, iii, p. 265.

[2] E.g., by Felten, relying on the document cited by Potthast, n. 939, Jan. 18, 1200. But Brem has shown that the Ugolino there mentioned was the cardinal of SS. Silvestro e Martino ai Monti who died March 9, c. 1206.

[3] *Ib.*, nn. 8213–14.

[4] *Cf. Gesta I. III.*, c. 23, which tells of Ugolino " resumpto spiritu fortitudinis." *Cf. supra*, vol. xi, p. 143.

a very special regard.[1] The negotiations in connexion
with the peace, and with the subsequent election of Otho,
caused Ugolino to go backwards and forwards between
Germany and Rome, and kept him engaged till the middle
of the year 1209.

Ugolino's second legatine commission was to Lombardy   His second
and Tuscany. He was sent thither by Honorius III. in commission,
                                                       1217–19.
the year 1217, to forward the interests of the Crusade
which that Pope had so much at heart. In recommending
him to the people of Pisa (March 6, 1217), Honorius
assures them that he is " the angel of the Lòrd of Hosts
whose lips guard wisdom and from whose mouth the law
may indeed be sought." He is a man who is ever pro-
claiming the glory of God, and whose character is as
bright as the stars of heaven.[2] On the success of the
cardinal's mission as far as the promotion of peace among
the warring cities of North Italy, and the successful
preaching of the Crusade during the the years 1217 and
1219 were concerned, we have already touched.[3] We may
add here that the energetic cardinal also strove to guard
the privileges of the clergy against the encroachments of

---

[1] *Cf. supra*, vol. xi, pp. 190–9 ; vol. xii, p. 48, and *Reg. Inn. III., reg.
de neg. imp.*, epp. 180–1 and 184. When we find it stated in the *Cron.
S. Petri Erford.*, an. 1207, p. 204, ed. Holder-Egger, that during their
sojourn in Germany the two cardinals collected a large sum of money
from the clergy, we may with Brem, p. 14, conclude that there is here
really question of nothing more than of the large sums which the
ecclesiastical establishments had to pay for the maintenance of the
cardinals and their naturally large suites, as they passed from one
religious house to another.

[2] Ap. Raynaldus, *Annales Eccles.*, 1217, n. 88. He was sent to Pisa
to protect the Pope's rights in Sardinia. *Cf. Reg. Honor. III.*, vol. i,
p. 71, n. 398, and p. 72, n. 407.

[3] *Cf. supra*, p. 15 ; and for one result of his peace efforts : " Pax facta
est (1218) inter Mediolanenses et Placentinos et suam partem et
Cremonenses et Parmenses et suam partem per Ugonem Ostiensem
episcopum, etc." *Ann. Cremon.*, an. 1218, ap. *M. G. SS.*, xxxi, p. 18.

the civil authorities in various cities,[1] and on the other
hand to promote clerical reform.[2]   In the February of
1219 he found his way to Venice,[3] and, among other works
accomplished in the interests of the Crusade, induced the
Doge, Pietro Zeno, to lessen the price for which he had
agreed to transport over a thousand knights to the Holy
Land.[4]

Ugolino and St. Francis.

Ugolino remained in North Italy till the end of July,
1219, as we learn from a letter of Honorius III. That
pontiff had already (August 27, 1218) instructed his
legate to take under the special protection of the Holy
See the houses of those women who had fled from the
world, the houses " of the Lord's poor ones in Tuscany or
in Spoleto." [5]   And on December 9, 1219, he wrote to
the abbess and nuns of the convent of Our Lady at
" S. Sepolcro a Monticelli " to express his satisfaction
that cardinal Ugolino, when legate in those parts, had
taken over their house in the name of the Holy See, and
had given its inmates certain rules, as he had informed the
Pope by a letter dated July 27, 1219.[6]   These " poor ones
of the Lord " were " poor Clares," the companions of
Agnes, the sister of St. Clare, the well-beloved disciple of
Ugolino's friend St. Francis.

It was in the first year of his legation to north Italy
(1217) that Ugolino met St. Francis,[7] and they immediately

---

[1] E.g., in Volterra. Cf. the documents ap. Levi, *Regist. del card. Ugo.
in Archivio*, p. 296.   Other documents concerning this commission of
Ugolino will be found in the same place.

[2] *Reg. Hon. III.*, n. 1687, i, p. 281, Nov. 17, 1218.

[3] Dandolo, *Chron.*, x, c. 4, n. 40, " Hugolinus . . . in Lombardiam
veniens ut seditiones securius removeret, Venetias venit."

[4] Levi, *l.c.*, p. 244.

[5] *Bullar. Francis. epit.*, ed. Eubel, n. 1.

[6] *Ib.*, n. 3. *Cf.* Levi, p. 245.   A little earlier we find him taking to
task " the podestà and the *consilium* " of Ferrara for intrenching on
the papal patrimony of Massa Fiscaglia. *Cf. Regist. del card.*, n. 3, p. 6.

[7] On the authorities for the *Life* of St. Francis, see *supra*, vol. xii,
262 f. There is reason also for believing that when Pope Gregory came

made a profound impression upon each other. The Saint recognized in the cardinal not merely the capable man of affairs, but a man also of sterling moral worth, " one who far outshone the rest (of the cardinals) in virtuous behaviour and holiness of life." [1] He " submitted himself to him in all ways, and revered him with wondrous and respectful affection." [2] He predicted his elevation to the Papacy, and when writing to him would not address him as " Bishop of Ostia," but as " the right reverend father (or lord) Hugo, bishop of the whole world." [3] He would, moreover, " greet him with unheard of blessings, and though he was a son in devout submission, yet at the Spirit's prompting he would sometimes comfort him with fatherly intercourse." [4] On his side, the cardinal soon " burned with exceeding love toward the holy man," and declared that " however disturbed or

in contact with St. Anthony of Padua, after hearing his eloquent and learned discourse, he is said to have addressed him as " the Ark of the Covenant." *Cf.* Alb. Lepitre, *St. Anthony of Padua*, p. 103, Eng. trans., London, 1913, quoting the *Life* of the Saint by a contemporary ap. *Portugalliæ Mon. Hist.*, i, Lisbon, 1856. Lepitre's is the standard work on St. Anthony.

[1] Thos. of Celano, *Vit. I.*, c. 5, n. 99. *Cf.* c. 27, nn. 74, 75.

[2] *Ib.*, c. 5, n. 100.

[3] *Ib. Cf. The Three Companions*, c. 16, n. 67.

[4] *Celano, ib.* The high opinion of Ugolino entertained by St. Francis was also entertained by his followers. Thomas of Celano whom we are here quoting says, *ib.*, c. 5, that " poverty was very pleasing to him, and he held holy simplicity in the greatest reverence . . . How often would he put off his costly garments, and arrayed in mean ones, going barefoot like one of the bretheren, would he entreat for the things that make for peace. The Lord gave him a learned tongue whereby he confounded the adversaries of the truth, refuted the enemies of the Cross of Christ, brought back wanderers to the way, made peace between those who were in discord, and bound together those who were in concord by a stronger bond of charity " (Howell's translation). The author of the *Life of St. Clare* calls Ugolino " A man most worthy of the Chair, as he was most venerable in merits," p. 26 ; *cf.* Robinson's translation. The *Legend of the Three Companions*, c. 15, tells of Ugolino's " glorious fame " among the other cardinals.

vexed he might be, on seeing St. Francis and talking with him, all mental clouds were dispersed, and serenity returned . . . He ministered to St. Francis as a servant to his lord . . . would often kiss his hands with his consecrated mouth," [1] and at the sight of the contrast between the poor man of Assisi with his poor companions, and his own fine escort of clergy and soldiers, would exclaim : " How will it fare with us who live so luxuriously day after day in superfluous delights ? " [2]

One result of this first meeting of St. Francis and the cardinal-bishop of Ostia (May, 1217) was that the latter persuaded the Saint not to go to France. " Brother, I do not want you to go beyond the Mountains, as there are many prelates who would gladly hinder the good of thy *religion* in the Roman Court. But I and the other cardinals who love this *religion* of thine could more readily help and protect it if you abide within this province." [3]

Ugolino and St. Francis in Rome, 1217–18.

Ugolino soon showed that he was not using idle words. About this time seemingly Francis had a vision of a little black hen vainly trying to gather a countless number of chicks beneath her wings. " I," he reflected, " am this hen, small in stature and black by nature . . . the chicks are the brethren multiplied in number and in grace, whom Francis' strength suffices not to defend . . . I will therefore go to Rome, that by the rod of her power the ill-disposed may be smitten, and the children of God enjoy full freedom . . . With her to protect it, no evil shall befall the Order." [4]

---

[1] *Ib.*, n. 101.

[2] *Spec. perfect.*, c. 21.

[3] *Spec. perfect.*, c. 65. *Cf.* Celano, c. 27, nn. 74–5. Celano gives as the reason for Ugolino's kind reception of Francis that " he was ever forward to supply the needs of poor men, and to handle their business with special care." See also *The Three Companions*, c. 15, n. 61.

[4] Celano, *Vit. II.*, c. 16, nn. 23, 24 ; *The Three Companions*, c. 16, n. 63.

Accordingly, whether at the instigation of Ugolino or not, Francis went to Rome, apparently during the winter of 1217–18, when the cardinal is known to have been there.[1] When he appeared to speak before the Pope " the venerable lord bishop of Ostia was in an agony of suspense, praying to God with all his might that the simplicity of the blessed man might not be despised " ; [2] for, as he had undertaken to watch over the interests of the new Order, he felt that " the Saint's glory or disgrace would rebound on him." [3] But Ugolino need not have had any anxiety. Francis spoke boldly before the Pope and the assembled cardinals, " and such was the fervour of his spirit as he spoke that, unable to contain himself for joy, as he uttered the words with his mouth he moved his feet as if dancing, not as in wantonness, but as glowing with the fire of Divine love, not provoking laughter, but extorting tears of grief. For many of them were pricked at the heart as they wondered at God's grace and the steadfastness of the man." [4]

The Saint's pleadings and Ugolino's influence [5] sufficed to silence those who were opposed to the establishment of new Orders, and those who feared that Francis' worship of Poverty savoured rather of fanaticism than true piety.[6]

Ugolino made official protector of the Franciscans, 1220–1.

[1] His signature is to be found in a document issued by Honorius III. from the Lateran on March 30, 1218, and in another of April 7, 1218, ap. *Epp. Hon.*, ed. Horoy, ii, pp. 687, 696. See also Potthast, *Reg.*, i, p. 678, whence it appears he was in Rome on Dec. 5, 1217. See also *ib.*, n. 5626.

[2] Celano, *Vit. I.*, c. 27, n. 73.

[3] *Ib.*

[4] *Ib. Cf. The Three Companions*, c. 16, n. 64.

[5] " For he was a stream of eloquence, a wall of the Church, a champion of the truth, and a lover of the humble." *Ib.*, from Celano.

[6] *Cf. St. Francis and Poverty*, by Fr. Cuthbert, ap. *Franciscan Essays* in the *British Soc. of Francis. Studies*, extra series, vol. i. In this essay the learned friar lays down that " The whole scheme of original Franciscan life was formed upon the acceptance (of individual and) of corporate poverty." P. 24. Still, as he insisted on the Friars working and giving

This discourse of Francis went a long way towards obtaining from Honorius the recognition of his Order. The next step taken by the Saint was in 1220-1, and he was moved to take it especially because many of the brethren were getting beyond his control. The astounding growth in the number of his followers had rendered the continuation of the original poverty and simplicity of Francis and his first few followers perhaps practically impossible. At any rate many wished in some particulars to break away from it, and showed themselves intractable in the gentle hands of Francis. In the midst of his difficulties he once more turned to Ugolino and to Rome.

The energetic cardinal had meanwhile returned to Rome to take part in the coronation of Frederick II. (November, 1220), and once more to give him the cross.[1] He had no difficulty in securing for his beloved Francis an interview with Honorius. "My lord," began the Saint, "I have pity for you, by reason of the anxiety and perpetual toil wherewith you must needs keep watch on behalf of the Church of God, and sore ashamed am I that you should have such care and anxiety for us, Brothers Minor. For while many nobles . . . and very many religions cannot enter into your presence, great . . . shamefacedness ought there to be in us in entering into your presence . . . and daring to knock at the door of the Tabernacle of Christendom. Wherefore I do humbly beseech your Holiness that you will deign to grant the lord Bishop of Ostia to be our Father, that in time of need the brethren may resort unto him saving always the dignity of your

alms themselves, "his social economy was the apotheosis, not of justice but of mutual charity." P. 29. "Freely give and freely receive, was his accepted law." P. 30.

[1] Ric. of San. Germ., *Chron.*, an. 1220, "Tunc imperator per manus Ostiensis episcopus . . . resumpsit crucem."

pre-eminence." [1] The Pope hearkened to the prayer of the Saint, and appointed Ugolino " the most worshipful Protector of his *religion*." [2]

Thus recognized by the Pope as the official protector of the new Order, Ugolino exerted himself in its behalf more than ever. To strengthen it, he introduced St. Francis to St. Dominic on one occasion, in order that it might be supported by the Dominicans. " I would, brother Francis," said the latter, " that thy Religion and mine might be one, and that we might live in the Church after the like pattern." [3] The cardinal himself, moreover, wrote to many prelates, who, under the impression that the new poor barefooted religious were heretics of some kind, had persecuted them, urging them to " oppose them no longer, but rather to give unto them counsel and help for preaching, and for dwelling in their provinces, as unto good men and holy religious approved by the Apostolic See." [4]

Formal confirmation of the Franciscan Order, 1223.

Hitherto, however, only a general approval of the Order had been granted by Rome. Innocent III. had merely given a verbal assent to the new Order,[5] and up to this Honorius had contented himself with referring to the

[1] *The Three Companions*, c. 16, n. 65.

[2] *Ib. Cf.* Celano, *Vit. I.*, c. 5, nn. 99, 100, and *Vit. II.*, c. 17, n. 25 ; and Jordan, *Chron.*, an. 1220, p. 14, ed. Böhmer ; Salimbene, p. 383, " Hugolinus qui fuit cardinalis ordinis fratrum Minorum, i.e., gubernator et protector et corrector fraternitatis et regule b. Francisci." *Cf.* p. 498, and the letter of Philip of Perugia on the cardinal-protectors of the Friars Minor, ap. *M. G. SS.*, xxxii, p. 680.

[3] Celano, *Vit. II.*, cc. 109–10, nn. 148–50 ; *Spec. Perfect.*, c. 43. On the frequent intercourse at this time between St. Dominic and Ugolino, see Guiraud, *St. Dominic*, p. 83.

[4] *The Three Companions*, c. 16, n. 66. Miss Salter's translation is used. *Cf.* Celano, *Vit. II.*, c. 109, nn. 148–50.

[5] *The Three Companions*, *ib.*, n. 62, state that Innocent sanctioned their Order and their rule, but " yet had he not confirmed it by his letters." *Cf. supra*, vol. xii, pp. 280, 283.

action of his predecessor.[1] Something more was desirable
and indeed necessary. Many things had happened to the
Order since Innocent III. gave his verbal approval to
its primitive rule presented to him by St. Francis.[2]
Regulations which might be sufficient for a few saintly
heroes would neither be numerous enough nor practical
enough for great numbers of men who, if good, were by
the very nature of things not heroes. It went to the
heart of Francis to have to modify his original rule ; but
modification was absolutely essential and relaxation
practically necessary. Even the first Rule of 1221
was not one which could receive the formal sanction of
the Holy See. It consisted of the Primitive Rule with
additions from papal decrees, capitular ordinances, and
decisions arrived at by the Saint himself to meet emer-
gencies. As a document it was an illogical patchwork,
and for that cause alone unsuitable to be erected by
papal decree into a legal constitution for the regulation
of the lives of a very large body of men of all sorts and
conditions.

Ugolino and
the Rule of
St. Francis.

It was to help Francis to draw up a Rule which would
be at once orderly and practical that Ugolino now devoted
himself. However, although such an ardent Franciscan as
Thomas of Celano declared " blessed and memorable " the
day " whereon God's Saint committed himself to so
venerable a lord," [3] some modern writers, theoretical
admirers of the Saint's wonderful life, regard him as the
evil genius of the Order which he founded. They brand
Ugolino and Rome for having dragged down the Francis-

[1] Ep. of June 11, 1219, ap. Eubel, or Potthast, 6081. Cf. ep. May 29,
1220.

[2] This rule is now lost. Fr. Cuthbert (Life of St. Francis, p. 87 ff.)
has extracted its chief clauses from what is known as the First Rule of
1221, which Francis drew up with the aid of Brother Cesar of Speyer,
and which may be read ib., p. 393 ff.

[3] Vit. I., c. 27, n. 74.

can ideal. But Ugolino and Rome knew that heroes were
not the order of the day, and that if the work of Francis
were not to die with him, his ideals must be presented in
such a way that they could be embraced by men who were
indeed aiming high, but were not all cast in an heroic mould.
Besides, to quote the words of a recent earnest Franciscan
writer, " to him the ideas of Francis were never merely
unpractical ideas, but the inspiration which he sought to
bring within the bounds of the practicable, and with
infinite patience to set himself to bridge over the gulf which
was widening between the mind of the founder and many
of the new leaders of the brethren. Let justice be done
to his memory. Not always did he see as Francis saw,
yet he never deliberately offended against the trust
Francis put in him." [1] Ugolino, too, knew well the mind
not only of Francis, but also of his brethren. According
to Celano he was " a brother among the brethren,"
among whom he would often go dressed in their mean
habit.[2] Moreover, he was wont " every year " to be
present at the Whitsuntide chapter of the brethren ;
and *The Three Companions* tells us that " when he came

[1] Fr. Cuthbert, *Life of St. Francis*, p. 254.
[2] *Vit. I.*, c. 5, n. 99. Even as Pope (as we learn from Philip of
Perugia, who wrote at the beginning of the fourteenth century on
the cardinal protectors of the Friars Minor), he sometimes wore the
Franciscan habit when he visited or washed the feet of the poor.
Philip's little work is printed by Holder-Egger at the end of his ed.
of Salimbene. *Cf.* p. 680. Philip drew his information on this
subject from " one of the brethren who was once a member of
Gregory's household." He also tells us that on one occasion when
Pope, and thus clad, he was washing the feet of a poor man, the
fellow not knowing who was before him, bade him begone and give
place to another brother who was better qualified for the task. He
adds, too, that " he had heard " that in Rome Pope Gregory was
wont to go about visiting the poor along with some Franciscans,
and in their habit. When Ugolino became Pope, he made his
nephew, who afterwards became Pope Alexander IV., protector of
the Friars Minor. *Ib.*

unto the Chapter, all the brethren assembled for the Chapter did go forth in procession to meet him. But he, as the brethren came up, dismounted from his horse, and went on foot with them unto the Church of St. Mary (of the Porziuncula), and afterward did preach unto them and sing Mass, wherein the man of God, Francis (as a deacon), chanted the Gospel." [1]

Therefore with his respect and love for Francis on the one hand, and his knowledge of the brethren, of the needs of the Church, and of human nature on the other, cardinal Ugolino was the very man to help Francis to draw up the definite rule of the Order.[2] That he actually did co-operate with him in its preparation, and not merely in that of the Third Order and in that of St. Clare, we know from his own words.[3] In fact " the blessed father provided what was needful, but that happy lord (Ugolino) carried the provisions into effect,"[4] or, to use the more definite language of a sixteenth century chronicler,[5] " St. Francis told the cardinal what the inspiration of the spirit had put into his mind, and the cardinal wrote it down with his own hand, and then added some things of his own."

How Ugolino modified the ideas of St. Francis.

A compilation of material regarding St. Francis, known as the *Legenda Antiqua,* and put together between 1318 and 1328 by a Franciscan who hailed from the Baltic provinces, gives us a story which may be authentic

---

[1] C. 15, n. 61.

[2] When Pope, Ugolino expressly declared that his long friendship with Francis enabled him to know his mind. " Cum ex longa familiaritate quam idem Confessor (Francis) nobiscum habuit, plenius noverimus intentionem ipsius." Ep. (Quo elongati) Sept. 28, 1230, printed in full, ap. Eubel, *Bullar. Francisc.,* p. 229 ff.

[3] " In condendo prædictam regulam (ac) obtinendo confirmationem ipsius per sedem Apostolicam sibi astiterimus dum adhuc essemus in minori officio constituti." *Ib.*

[4] Celano, *Vit. I.,* c. 27, n. 74.

[5] Mariano of Florence, cited by Jörgensen, *St. Francis,* p. 247.

enough to show at least the way in which Ugolino modified
the ideas of Francis. Especially with a view to safeguarding his regulations regarding the absolute poverty
to be practised by the brethren, the Saint wished to
introduce a clause into his rule whereby the brethren
might follow it even against their superiors, if the latter
did not interpret the rule strictly literally.[1] But the
cardinal, who knew that the introduction of such a clause
would mean the end of all discipline in any body of men,
assured the Saint that he would embody his wishes in
the new rule, but in terms other than those proposed by
him. Other terms were indeed used by the cardinal,
but they set forth the idea that the brothers were, when
all was said and done, always to follow the lead of their
superiors, and never to initiate a move on their own
account.[2] At any rate in the end Francis accepted the Rule
in the form in which it left the revising hand of Ugolino,
" for that he was sore afeared of scandal . . . and was
unwilling to contend with the brethren, but did against
his will condescend to their wishes, and did excuse himself thereof before the Lord." [3] Still, however much or
little Ugolino modified the ideals of St. Francis, it must be
understood, as the Saint's latest biographers are at pains
to attest,[4] that he did not destroy them. The second or
final rule contains " the essential principles " and
" essential maxims characteristic of St. Francis."

---

[1] Hence in his Testament which Francis ordered to be read along
with the rule he " strictly enjoined on all his brothers, clerics and
laics, not to put glosses on the rule." The rule and his Testament
were to be understood " simply and purely—simpliciter et sine
glosa." Cf. the Testament ap. Sabatier, *Spec. Perfect.*, p. 309 ff., or
in English, ap. Robinson, *The Writings of St. Francis*, p. 81 ff.

[2] This story is given by Jörgensen, p. 247. A translation of the
second rule, i.e., the rule now followed by the Franciscans, may be
read in Robinson, *l.c.*, p. 64 ff. Cf. Fr. Cuthbert, p. 322 f.

[3] *Spec. Perfect.*, c. 2.

[4] Jörgensen and Cuthbert, pp. 254 f. and 323 f., respectively.

Satisfied with the rule which was presented to him, Honorius III. on November 29, 1223, issued his formal approval of the Franciscan rule which he embodied in his brief.[1]

Elias of Cortona. Unfortunately, however, even this rule did not satisfy all the ministers of Francis. It was still too unworldly, too ethereal for some of them, especially for the ablest of them all, the despotic Elias of Cortona.[2] He never really accepted the rule sanctioned by Honorius,[3] and so readily put himself at the head of the party of relaxation; and, owing to the manner in which the single-minded Francis had trusted his forceful personality, got himself made, or at any rate was made, Minister-General of the Order, in succession to Francis (1221). There is no doubt that the saint himself had great confidence in his administrative ability, and that cardinal Ugolino on his side looked to him as the practical man through whom he meant to work his ideas for the future development of the Order.[4]

After the expiration of his term of office, Elias, so it is said, endeavoured to oust his successor John Parenti (1230).[5] Though he failed in this attempt, and incurred

---

[1] Ap. Eubel in full, p. 225 ff. *Cf. The Three Companions*, c. 62.

[2] The English friar, Thomas of Eccleston, who *c.* 1260 wrote an account of the coming of the Franciscans to England in 1224, more than once denounces the worldliness and cruelty of Elias. *De advent. frat.*, cc. 5, 12 ; or in ed. Little, pp. 36, 82. On Elias read Fr. Cuthbert, *St. Francis*, p. 257 ff., and Ed. Lempp., *Elie de Cortone*, Paris, 1901. The latter writer especially strongly sympathizes with Elias, but he takes an unnatural view of the relations between Gregory and the Franciscans, pretending that he organized them in order to prevent them from reforming the Church, instead of in order to secure the continuity of the Saint's work in reforming the Church.

[3] Eccleston, *l.c.*, c. 12, al. 13.

[4] *Cf.* their joint action in erecting the great church to St. Francis (†1226) which is the wonder and delight of every visitor to Assisi. *Cf.* Lempp., p. 80 ff.

[5] Eccleston, *ib.*

much enmity thereby, he contrived to regain the good-will of all by retiring to a hermitage, and practising or feigning to practise special holiness of life. But if he retired into a cell, his ideas did not retire with him. As far at least as modification of St. Francis' ideal of poverty, and of his views on study and learning was concerned, the great body of the friars, who came to be called Conventuals, embraced the views of Elias.[1] So strongly did they give expression to them, that the Zealots [2] or Spirituals, as the more heroic friars were named, had to agree that the questions regarding property especially should be referred to the Holy See. This had to be done despite the fact that in his Testament Francis had strictly forbidden the brethren to ask for any letters from the Roman curia—a prohibition which Rome might well declare to be " of very difficult observance." [3]

Cardinal Ugolino was now Pope Gregory IX., and, with Franciscans around him " as his secretaries and special chaplains," [4] was as interested in their welfare as ever. To deal with the question referred to him he promptly issued a decree (*Quo elongati*) in order to establish a *modus vivendi*. He declared that the *Testament* of Francis was not binding, seeing that though it was meant to bind all, it had not been agreed to by all. Further, though he reaffirmed the principle that the friars might not be the absolute owners of anything either as a community or as individuals, he sanctioned the first of a

---

[1] His zeal for the promotion of learning among the Franciscans is the only good thing for which Salimbene gives Elias credit : " Hoc solum habuit bonum frater Helyas, quia ordinem fratrum Minorum ad studium theologie promovit." *Chron.*, p. 104.

[2] Eccleston, c. 5, al. 6, where we are told that Elias " tyrannidem . . . in *zelatores ordinis* exercuerat." The *Conventuals* were so called because, in opposition to the Zealots, who often retired to hermitages, they lived in large convents in towns.

[3] *Cf.* Gregory's letter of Sept. 20, 1220.

[4] *Chron. Erphord. min.*, an. 1241, ap. *M. G. SS.*, xxiv, p. 199.

series of relaxations granted by the Holy See by means of which the friars could enter into those business transactions which large communities rendered necessary.[1]

But the difference between the ideals of the Zealots and those of the Conventuals, especially upon the vexed question of absolute poverty, was so deep that it was not easy to find a *via media* which would satisfy the extremists of the two parties. Hence, as a matter of fact, the schism in the Order, inaugurated by Elias of Cortona and those who sympathized with him, has to a greater or less degree, even up to the present day, never been wholly healed.[2] Sometimes, indeed, the schism between the two parties was wide and deep, and more than once has the Church of Christ been grievously disedified and injured by the acrimonious bickerings of the two parties. But it is ever so in the domains both of grace and of nature. Where the greatest good is done, there also, when at length inevitable natural weakness comes in, is the greatest mischief wrought.

Unfortunately, Gregory did not lessen the existing

Brother Elias passes over to the party of Frederick II.

[1] See the brief of Sept. 28, 1230, ap. Eubel, p. 229 ff., or Sabatier, *Spec. Perfect.*, p. 314 ff. *Cf.* the bull of Innocent IV., *Ordinem vestrum*, Nov. 14, 1245 (Eubel, p. 238) ; of Matin IV., *Exultantes Domino*, Jan. 18, 1283, in Eubel, p. 301. How far Francis carried his idea of poverty may be easily gathered from what Celano tells us in his *Vit. II.*, c. 29, n. 59. " He would not let the brethren live in any dwelling, even a small one, unless it were sure that there was some owner to whom the property belonged." One difficulty arising from his wholly impractical idea (impractical, that is, where there is question of thousands of men) was only got over in the lifetime of Francis by cardinal Ugolino's declaration that " a house of the brethren which had just been built at Bologna was his property." *Cf. ib.*, c. 28, n. 58. To simplify matters, Innocent IV., in the bull just cited, went further, and where the donors had not reserved any rights, declared all the property held by the friars to be vested in the Holy See.

[2] To-day there are three great divisions of the Franciscan Order. *Cf.* W. W. Seton, *Some New Sources for the Life of Blessed Agnes of Bohemia*, p. 6 ff., London, 1915.

friction in the Franciscan Order by tolerating the re-election of Elias. At first when he had heard of his attempt against John Parenti, he had been very indignant with him; but after he had been told of the penitential life he was leading in the hermitage, and after he had reflected on his intimacy with St. Francis, his indignation cooled down, and " he permitted Brother Elias again to be appointed Minister-General " (1233).[1] But the friar's domineering disposition and worldly views again guided his conduct towards each of his brethren and his policy towards the development of the Order as a whole. At length, under the influence of Brother Haymo, an Englishman, an appeal was lodged against him in a General Chapter in presence of Gregory and seven cardinals. After the Pope himself had preached, Elias set forth his defence so ably that Haymo would not have been allowed to reply but for the intervention of another Englishman, cardinal Robert de Sumercote. " My lord Pope," he said, " this old man is a good man, and it is well that you should hear him, especially as he is sparing of words." [2]

In his reply Haymo declared that, if it was true, as Brother Elias had alleged, that on his election the brethren had agreed that, if his health required it, he might even eat gold and ride on horseback, they had not given him permission to amass gold and to keep horses. " At this," says Eccleston,[3] " Brother Elias, unable to contain his rage," cried out that Haymo lied, and the partisans of both men raised a tumult. " Greatly moved," Gregory commanded silence, exclaiming, " ' These are not the manners of religious,' and for a long time he sat silent and pondering, till they were all filled with

Deposition of Brother Elias.

[1] Eccleston, c. 12, al. 13.

[2] Eccleston, *l.c.*

[3] On the *style* maintained by Elias, and his other shortcomings as a friar, see Salimbene, *Chron.*, p. 157, and the other pages before and after it.

shame." [1]   Meanwhile, cardinal Rainald (or Reginald),[2] "Protector of the Order," openly urged Elias to place his resignation in the Pope's hands, and Elias, as openly, refused. "Thereupon the Pope, having commended the personal character of Brother Elias, and spoken of his intimacy with St. Francis, concluded by saying that he had indeed believed his ministry to be acceptable to the brethren, but that now, since it had been shown to be no longer acceptable, his decree was that Brother Elias should be dismissed." [3]   He then summoned the Ministers-Provincial and the *Custodes* (Guardians) for a new election, and, we are told, "heard them orally before they gave their votes in writing." [4]   The new election resulted in the Minister of the province of England, Brother Albert of Pisa, being made Minister-General (May, 1239).

Excommunication of Elias.

But if Elias had been humiliated, he had not been reformed. From being a tyrannical superior, he became a disobedient subject, and, against the orders of Albert, "visited the houses of the Poor Ladies without leave," thereby incurring excommunication. As he refused to make amends, the matter was brought to the notice of Gregory ; and when, says Eccleston, he heard that the Pope desired him to obey the Minister-General in the same manner as any other brothers had to obey him, he would not brook the humiliation (for indeed he had never learnt to obey) but went over to the party of the emperor

---

[1] Eccleston, *ib.*

[2] Rinaldo Conti of Segni, cardinal bishop of Ostia, afterwards Alexander IV., and nephew of Gregory, who had appointed him protector of the Order in his own place. Acc. Salimbene, *Chron.*, p. 383, Gregory made him cardinal of St. Eustachius (Sept., 1227) "at the entreaty of the Friars Minor." He became bishop of Ostia in 1231.

[3] Jordan, *Chron.*, an. 1239, nn. 65–6 ;   Eccleston, *l.c.*

[4] Eccleston, *ib.*

Frederick. Wherefore, not without just cause, was he publicly excommunicated by the Pope." [1]

After his canonization of St. Francis,[2] and his declaration to the world of the reality of his stigmata,[3] the last important connexion which Gregory had with the Franciscans was his share in the election of another Minister-General. An early death prevented Albert de Pisa from holding his office for more than a few months. Accordingly, Gregory, " anxious," as he said, " that the Order should not be long without a Minister, summoned a general chapter to appear before him " [4] in Rome (November 1, 1240). Whether it was because Albert was always " commending the English above all other nations in that they were zealous for the Order," [5] or because the man himself was " the mirror of all that was honourable,"[6] at any rate, the Englishman, Brother Haymo, was chosen to succeed Albert. Gregory, we are told, himself received the votes of the electors, and then confirmed their choice.[7] A succession of such men as Haymo, whose learning and gentleness made him very successful " in maintaining the brethren in charity and peace," [8] might have been able to keep the Order together. The legislation of Gregory, at any rate, was unable to do so. Still, if it is true that his bull *Quo elongati* did put in great

Gregory confirms the election of Haymo, 1240.

---

[1] *Ib. Cf.* Salimbene, *Chron.*, pp. 110 f. and 159 f. ; *Catal. gen. minist. ord. frat. min.*, p. 659, ap. *M. G. SS.*, xxxii ; Ric. of S. German., *Chron.*, 1239, Elias " in odium pape imperatori adhesit." Gregory had at one time used him as an envoy to the emperor. *Cf.* Salimbene, *ib.*, pp. 36, 96, 99.

[2] An. 1228. *Cf.* Salimbene, p. 36 ; and *The Three Companions*, c. 18, nn. 71–2.

[3] Ep. of Philip of Perugia, ap. *M. G. SS.*, xxxii, p. 681, and ep. Greg. of March 31, 1237, Eubel, p. 22.

[4] *Catal. gen. minist.*, p. 660.

[5] Eccleston, *l.c.*

[6] *Catal.*, *l.c.*

[7] *Catal.*, and Eccleston.

[8] *Cf.* the latter, c. 13, al. 14.

distress " those friars who clung to the life of absolute poverty which St. Francis had lived," and if consequently " he aimed lower than the Saint," "his reasoning was sounder," and alone afforded sufficiently firm ground for the erection of an Order.[1] As his biographer says, " he gave form to a shapeless mass." [2]

Gregory and St. Clare. To know Francis was, of course, to know Clare ; and it was impossible for Ugolino to be interested in the one without being interested in the other. In fact, Clare's biographer states that " he loved the Saint most dearly with a paternal affection." [3] With all that, however, he could not induce her to alter her determination to abide by the ideas of St. Francis regarding the observance of strict poverty. " As he was seeking to persuade her that, on account of the condition of the times and the dangers of the age, she should consent to have some possessions which he himself liberally offered, she resisted with an unyielding resolve . . . To whom the Pontiff answered, ' If thou fearest thy vow, we release thee from thy vow.' ' Holy Father,' she said, ' never do I wish to be released in anywise from following Christ for ever ' " (1228).[4] The heroic constancy of the Saint did but deepen the admiration for her which he had conceived before he became Pope, and we are assured that it was " not without reason that the lord Pope Gregory placed very great

[1] *Cf.* the excellent first chapter (" From St. Francis to St. Bernadino of Siena ") of A. S. Ferrers Howell, *S. Bernadino,* London, 1913.

[2] *Vit.,* c. 3. "Minorum etiam ordinem, intra initia sub limite incerto vagantem, nova regule traditione direxit et informavit informem."

[3] *Vit. S. Clar.,* p. 26, of Robinson's trans. *Cf. supra,* vol. xii, p. 282 f. ; and the modern biography of *St. Clare of Assisi* by E. Gilliat-Smith, London, 1914, and that by Mrs. Balfour, *Life and Legend of the Lady Saint Clare,* 1910.

[4] *Vit., l.c.* In his notes Robinson cites two such offers contained in letters of 1219 and 1227, ap. L. Wadding, *Annales Minorum,* ad an. 1221, t. ii, p. 16, n. 20, and t. iii, p. 239, n. 17.

faith in the prayers of this Saint, for he had experienced their marvellous virtue and efficacy. Often indeed, when some new difficulty would arise . . . both when he was bishop of Ostia and after he had been raised to the Apostolic See, he would call upon the same virgin by letter to ask her assistance and he received help." [1]

When bishop of Ostia he drew up a rule, based on that of St. Benedict for some of the " Poor Clares," and we know that it was adopted by those at Monticelli near Florence, and we have noted that it was confirmed by Honorius III. [2] Seeing, however, that in 1228 Gregory himself granted Clare and her nuns of S. Damiano at Assisi the unique privilege of complete poverty, [3] it is not unnaturally taken for granted that at least St. Clare herself and her subjects had always remained true to the ideas of St. Francis. But it was not till August 9, 1253, that, at the instance of cardinal Rainald, a rule after Clare's own heart was finally approved by Innocent IV. and incorporated in his bull. [4] The rule had been compiled by the cardinal with the assistance of Clare herself (1252). It is described as a " truly Franciscan rule," [5] and begins

His privilegium paupertatis.

[1] *Vit.*, p. 44.

[2] *Supra*, p. 178.

[3] See *supra*, vol. xii, p. 287. " Sicut igitur supplicastis altissimæ paupertatis propositum vestrum favore apostolico roboramus." Ap. Robinson, p. 143, who gives the bull in full. Nevertheless on May 24, 1239, Gregory confirmed his rule of 1219 for some Poor Clares at least, Eubel, p. 26.

[4] Eubel, pp. 66 and 251 ff. In addressing Clare and " the other sisters of St. Damiano," Innocent declared that he approved " vitæ formulam juxta quam communiter in spirituum unitate ac voto altissimæ paupertatis vivere debetis vobis a beato Francisco traditam et a vobis sponte susceptam."

[5] Robinson, p. 96. He gives, p. 99, a translation of the Rule. *Cf.* Philip of Perugia, ap. *M. G. SS.*, xxxii, p. 680. " Hoc tantum audivi ab antiquis fratribus, quod ipse (Ugolino) cum b. Francisco patre nostro ordinaverunt et scripserunt regulam sororum ordinis S. Damiani, qui nunc vocatur ordo S. Claræ . . . Propter cujus

" The form of life of the Order of the Poor Sisters, which the Blessed Francis founded is this : to observe the holy Gospel of our Lord Jesus Christ by living in obedience, with poverty and in chastity. Clare, unworthy handmaid of Christ, and little flower of the most Blessed Father Francis, promises obedience and reverence to the lord Pope Innocent (IV.) and his successors canonically elected, and to the Roman Church. And as, in the beginning of her conversion, she with her Sisters promised obedience to the Blessed Francis, so does she promise to observe the same inviolably to his successors." [1] The rule ends as it had begun with a declaration of loyalty to the Church. " In fine, the Sisters are strictly obliged always to have that particular one of the Cardinals of the Holy Roman Church as their Governor, Protector and Corrector who has been appointed by the lord Pope for the Friars Minor, to the end that, ever submissive and subject at the feet of the same Holy Church, and steadfast in the Catholic faith, we may observe perpetually the poverty and humility of our Lord Jesus Christ and of his most holy Mother and the holy Gospel which we have solemnly promised. Amen." [2]

Blessed Agnes of Bohemia.

Still keeping to the charming circle in which moved Francis and Clare, we encounter the sweet figure of Agnes, " the light of all Bohemia," [3] the contemporary

regule artitudinem partim devotione, partim compassione cardinalis ipse perfundebatur multis lacrimis in scribendo."

[1] Robinson's translation, p. 99. The obligation of poverty was, of course, strongly insisted upon, and words of St. Francis were quoted to impress upon the Sisters the vow they had taken. " I, little brother Francis . . . beseech you all, my Ladies, and counsel you always to live in this highest life and poverty (i.e., that of Jesus Christ). And watch yourselves well, lest through the teaching or advice of anybody you ever depart from it in anywise." N. 6.

[2] *Ib.*, p. 123.

[3] Cf. her *Life*, ap. Seton, *Some new sources for the life of Bl. A. of Bohemia*, p. 64.

of both of them and the correspondent of the latter.
The daughter of Premysl Ottocar I. (1197–1230), first
Duke and then King of Bohemia, twice betrothed in
her childhood to distinguished men, and later on vainly
sought in marriage by our own King Henry III., and
by the Emperor Frederick II., Agnes refused to hearken
to the call of the glory of this world, and resolved to
embrace the poverty of Christ in the Order of St. Clare.
To ensure the accomplishment of her desire she sent
" honourable and discreet envoys to the noble Vicar
of Christ the lord Pope Gregory IX., to make known
to him her intention which she had so far kept secret."
" By gracious letters " Gregory approved of her design,
adopted her as his spiritual daughter, and throughout
all his life treated her with the greatest affection (c. 1234).[1]

The letters of Gregory support this assertion of Agnes'
biographer,[2] and show him at once taking under his
protection the convent and hospital which her brother
King Wenceslas had founded for her at Prague.[3]

Having entered the Order of St. Clare, she was, like
her holy model, not content with half measures, and
like her struggled hard to secure from the Holy
See the same full " privilege of poverty " as had
been granted by Gregory to St. Clare and her Sisters
at San Damiano. At length after some years of effort
on her own part, she secured the intercession of her
brother, King Wenceslas III. Assuring the Pope
that he loved his sister better than any being on
earth,[4] and promising to be more ready than ever to assist

---

[1] Ib., p. 74 f. "Adoptatamque in filiam multis spiritualibus donis
invisit, cunctis diebus suis eam prosequens pii patris affectu."

[2] He wrote about the beginning of the fourteenth century, when there
were people living who had known Agnes.

[3] Ep. Aug. 30, 1235, ap. Eubel, Bullar. Francisc., n. 140. Cf. ib.,
n. 141, and epp. of May 18, ap. Potthast, i, nn. 913–14.

[4] " Eam, ut verum fatear, sicut conjugem, et liberos, et universa
bona diligo, cunctisque mortalibus præfero in affectu." Ep. of 1237,

him and the Holy See in any public or private need, he begged him to grant her petition. Gregory, thereupon, conceded that the Abbess and her Poor Ladies should be permitted to renounce the revenues he had confirmed to them, and should not in future be compelled to accept possessions against their will.[1] Further than this, however, Gregory would not go. He regarded the idea of absolute poverty as impractical for any except perhaps for a few extraordinarily detached souls, and so would not confirm a rule which would have enabled other convents also to embrace the privilege of absolute poverty, conceded to Agnes and her nuns personally.[2] Still, however, both Clare and Agnes continued to press the Holy See for a general approval of the desired privilege. But, though in 1247 Clare obtained from Innocent IV. that she and her sisters might live " according to the rule of St. Francis in so far as it related to obedience, surrender of private property and chastity," [3] it was only in 1253 (Aug. 9) that he gave way, and finally granted them the privilege of not possessing anything in any way.[4] This privilege " the lamb of Christ (Agnes) induced Pope Alexander IV. to confirm to her and the sisters of her convent for ever " [5]; and then later on she assured Cardinal John of Gaeta (Orsini, afterwards Nicholas III.) that she would rather endure the last extremity of want than renounce it (1274).[6] In gratitude for this favour, for which she

cited by Seton, p. 175, from Erben, *Regesta Bohemiæ*, pars. i, p. 429, Prag, 1855.

[1] Ep. of Apr. 15, 1238, ap. Eubel, n. 238. *Cf.* n. 242.

[2] Ep. of May 9, 1238, n. 244. *Cf.* nn. 243 and 245.

[3] *Ib.*, Aug. 6, n. 474.

[4] *Ib.*, n. 678.

[5] *Vita. Ag.*, p. 84.

[6] *Ib.*, p. 88. The cardinal had desired her to accept certain possessions for herself and her sisters " propter maliciam dierum et instancia tempora periculosa."

strove as others do for wealth, she did not forget in the
hour of death (†1282) to exhort her Sisters ever " to
subject themselves to the Roman Church after the example
of the most blessed father Francis, and the dear maiden
Clare who had given them their rule of life." [1]

With these facts before us, and bearing in mind
Gregory's generosity to the Poor Clares,[2] we can now
realize in what sense we are to understand the words
of his biographer when he says that " he instituted
and highly (ad summum) developed the new order of
the enclosed Ladies." [3]

In the fascinating circle in which moved Francis, Ugolino and
Clare, and Ugolino was another saintly figure, that of St. Dominic.
Dominic Guzman, linked, equally with Clare and Francis,
in the sacred bonds of friendship with the cardinal-bishop
of Ostia, afterwards Gregory IX. As it was with the
Umbrian Saints so it was with the noble Spaniard.
The same natural instinct of holiness which attracted
Clare and Francis to Ugolino drew Dominic also to him ;
and the same sympathetic insight which led the cardinal
to encourage the yearnings of his friends of Assisi for
poverty and lowliness, induced him to befriend the
aspirations of the canon of Osma towards learning and
the glorious fruits of the intellect. Under the influence
of Ugolino, Honorius III. was not content merely with
giving the necessary formal sanction to the new Order

[1] *Ib.*, p. 116.
[2] He gave them the monastery of S. Cosimato in the Trastevere
in 1234. *Cf. Vit.*, c. 3, and nn. 219 j and k, ap. *Lib. Cens.*, i, p. 478,
which show Gregory's purchase of the monastery. His *Life, ib.*, tells
how " he gathered them together as daughters, revered them as
mothers, and abundantly helped them in their needs."
[3] C. 3. On St. Clare read a most sympathetic essay (" St. Clare ")
by Fr. Paschal Robinson in vol. i of the *British Society of Franciscan
Studies*, Extra Series.

of Friars Preachers which had been founded by Dominic,[1] but, by presenting the Saint with the Church of St. Sixtus on the Appian Way (1218), he gave the Order a permanent centre in Rome, and he entrusted Dominic with the reform of the congregations of religious women which in Rome had fallen into decay. To carry out this difficult, because most delicate, task, Dominic asked for suitable help, and among the three cardinals whom the Pope bade " stand by him, should he need their aid," was, of course, " Cardinal Ugolino, bishop of Ostia, who later on became Pope."[2] In this, as in all his enterprises, Dominic could always count upon the support of Ugolino, who on his side never lost an opportunity of advancing the interests of his saintly friend. Even after Dominic's death Ugolino was not unmindful of him, and on July 13, 1234, solemnly gave his personal testimony to his sanctity, and enjoined the universal Church to honour him as a saint.[3] After praising his sanctity, the Pope tells how " by his merits he founded the new Order of Preachers, edified it by his example, and confirmed it by evident miracles." Accordingly, continued Gregory, when to the proofs of his holiness which he gave us " during the long friendship which we had with him when we were in a lower station,"[4] was added the testimony of miracles,

---

[1] *Supra*, vol. xii, p. 284. A translation of the bull of confirmation may be read, ap. *The Lives of the Brethren*, by Fr. Conway, p. 297 ff.

[2] *The legend of St. Dom.*, by sister Cecilia, c. 2.

[3] Potthast, n. 9489 ; *Vita.*, c. 16.

[4] See the document almost *in extenso* in Raynaldus, *Ann. Eccles.*, 1234, n. 24. Gregory also canonized St. Anthony of Padua (*Vit.*, c. 17), St. Elizabeth of Hungary, and bishop Virgil of Salzburg, as may be seen by his bulls collected by J. Fontaninus, *Codex constit. in canoniz. SS.*, p. 60 ff. With regard to St. Elizabeth he had taken an affectionate interest in her during her lifetime, and had even induced her other most famous friend St. Francis to send her his poor cloak " as a tribute to her humility." *Vit. Greg.*, c. 22. *Cf.* Montalembert, *Hist. de S. Elisabeth*, vol. i, c. 10.

we determined to add him to the number of the saints, in the hope that we may experience the patronage in heaven of him whose friendship we enjoyed on earth.

Before speaking of Ugolino's last legatine commission to northern Italy, we may pause for a moment to note that he may be said still to be exerting a beneficent influence on the world. The good that men do is not always interred with their bones. By his intelligent and fostering care of the forces which Francis and Dominic brought into being, Ugolino Conti has continued up to this very day to bring hope to the hearts of men in pain and trouble, and light to their minds in doubts and difficulties. If one reads Carmichael's *In Tuscany*, or Jörgensen's *Pilgrimsbogen*,[1] one cannot fail to see that the sacred simplicity with which the rule of St. Francis inspired Brother Leo and Brother Giles still lives among his brethren; and the annals of the Franciscan Order of to-day proclaim that the sweet joy and hope of the faith of Christ which the Brothers Minor brought to the hovels of the poor in the thirteenth century [2] is at this hour being carried by them to many a squalid slum in our large towns. And if the light of faith was made to blaze more brightly and steadily by the intellectual toil of Albertus Magnus and St. Thomas

Present influence of Gregory.

[1] Selections of this beautiful work of the Danish convert have been translated into English ; but I am pleased to say that Miss Lund, who has already translated his *Lourdes*, is now engaged upon a complete translation of his *Pilgrimsbogen*.

[2] " Those masses, those dreadful masses, crawling, sweltering in the foul hovels, in many a southern town with never a roof to cover them, huddling in groups under a dry arch, alive with vermin, gibbering *cretins* with the ghastly wens ; lepers by the hundred, too shocking for mothers to gaze at, and therefore driven forth to curse and howl in the lazar-house outside the walls, there stretching out their bony hands to clutch the frightened almsgiver's dole, or, failing that, to pick up shreds of offal from the heaps of garbage—to these St. Francis came." A. Jessopp, in his fine essay on *The Coming of the Friars*, p. 20 f., London, 1899.

Aquinas in the early days of the Dominican Order, the voices of the Friars Preachers are not silent in our midst to-day. By such men as Lacordaire and Monsabré, the Dominicans still enkindle the bright flame of faith in the restless minds of men; and the renewed study of the philosophy of their great teacher, St. Thomas, is once more dissipating the thick mist of doubt which has fallen on the minds of so many in these our days. That the earth is still refreshed by these blessings is due in no small measure to the sympathetic and intelligent action of Ugolino Conti, first exerted seven hundred years ago.

Ugolino again in Lombardy, 1221.

The representations which reached Italy of the danger in which the Crusaders were of losing Damietta, caused Frederick to express renewed interest in the cause of the Cross. As a consequence, Cardinal Ugolino was for the second time sent to Lombardy with the main object of preaching a Crusade (March, 1221).[1] Again, too, did he go loaded with the eulogies both of the Pope and of the Emperor,[2] and this time with power from the latter to remove the ban of the Empire.[3] It is for this commission that the cardinal's register is so useful. It shows the varied work which often fell to the lot of a legate. Ugolino carried out the task assigned to him with his usual energy, firmness,[4] and tact. He made peace between hostile cities,[5] and from all sides received promises of men and money [6] for the Crusade and

---

[1] *Reg. Hon. III.*, n. 3178, i, 519, March 14, 1221.

[2] *Cf. supra*, p. 69.

[3] Ep. Fred., Feb. 10, 1221, ap. Ugolino, *Reg.*, p. 150 ff.

[4] *Reg. U.*, ep. 42. "Heretici et tyranni suis oppressionibus et erroribus infestant subditos et residentes in culmine dignitatum"— but still the cardinal was not daunted. *Cf.* ep. 46.

[5] Ep. 53, p. 70.

[6] Epp. 4–6, 8, 10, in which he notes that the men of Florence, though in great straits for many reasons, "concesserunt mihi per militem

regulated its interests generally.[1] He protected the clergy
in different cities from the oppression of the podestàs,[2]
and also the simple people (the popolo minuto) from
that of the knights.[3] In a word he so conducted his
mission as to win the warmest thanks from his master,
Pope Honorius III. He declared that the success of
his work was phenomenal, and seemed unable to praise
him enough for the peace he had brought about and the
sinners he had converted.[4]

On his return from this Lombard legation, Ugolino
seems to have passed most of his time in immediate
attendance on the Pope as one of his chief advisers.
He did not, however, cease to devote great attention
to the new Orders of Friars and to the needs of his
diocese of Ostia-Velletri. In this latter connexion we
have in his Register a number of documents by which
his episcopal city was entrusted to his relative Richard
Conti, count of Sora, on condition of his guarding it
against the Bovazzani, who had made preparations to
attack it.[5] Later on (1226), when it may be presumed the
danger had passed, and Ugolino wished to retake possession
of his city and property, he induced the Pope to pay
Richard all the expenses which he had incurred meanwhile
in the interests of the see.[6] He then thoroughly fortified

Ugolino from 1222-7.

viginti solidos illius monete et decem soldos per quodlibet foculare
peditis ad subsidium Terre Sancte."

[1] Ep. 77.
[2] Epp. 51, 72, 82.
[3] Epp. 38, 73.
[4] Ep. 107, June 7, 1221. "Optatum semper consequimur de
tua legatione profectum, et laboris tui fructus opinionem humanam
dignoscitur superare." Cf. ep. 109.
[5] Documents 103–4 and 115–20 of May 7, 1222. They were drawn
up for the most part at Anagni "in camera" of Ugolino, "with the
Pope's permission" as his letters "sua bulla bullatas" showed.
Document 121 shows Ugolino the successful peacemaker between
Velletri with other towns and Ninfa with others.
[6] Reg. Hon. III., n. 5886, Apr. 5, 1226. Cf. Felten, p. 18.

Ostia with walls and towers,[1] in order that it might be well able to hold its own against the Bovazzani in the neighbouring Tor Bovacciana.

On the day after the death of Honorius, when his body had been duly buried, the cardinals assembled in the monastery of St. Gregory on the Coelian, opposite to and under the protection of the Septizonium,[2] one of the many ruins about the Palatine which the Frangipani had turned into fortresses. After a devout celebration of the mass of the Holy Ghost, the cardinals, so at least says the author of the chronicle of the monastery of Villers, unable to agree on a successor to Honorius, entrusted their powers to three of their number. One of these plenipotentiaries was the Cistercian of Urach, Conrad, cardinal-bishop of Porto, a man of experience who had fulfilled important commissions in France [3] and Germany. The remaining two chose Conrad. But he firmly refused the proffered honour, exclaiming : " Never shall it be said that I had any hand in electing myself." Hence, concludes the chronicler, another was chosen.[4] But this author is the only one who appears to know anything about a disputed election. Accordingly, as it is certain that a successor to Honorius was elected on the morrow of that Pope's death, modern authors do not accept the account told by the monastic chronicle. It will be safer then to tell the story of Gregory's election in his own words. " As though divinely inspired all

---

[1] *Vit.*, c. 3.

[2] *Ib.*, c. 4. *Cf. supra*, vol. x, p. 27 n., whence it would appear that Innocent III. and Gregory IX. were elected in the same place.

[3] In France he had to deal with the Albigensians. A letter of his concerning them is quoted *supra*, vol. xii, p. 40.

[4] *Chron. Villariensis monast.*, ap. *M. G. SS.*, xxv, p. 198. *Cf.* " Conrad d'Urach," by D. Ambroise Clément, ap. *Revue Bénédictine*, vols. xxii–xxiii, 1905-6, Maredsous. On Conrad, German authors cite Roth v. Schreckenstein, *Forschungen zur deutschen Gesch.*, vii, p. 321 ff.

turned their eyes on our insignificant person. And although we were unwilling to bear the burden which they desired to place upon us, they greatly urged us, and even used violence (to place the papal mantle upon our shoulders). Despite, therefore, our reluctance, we at length submitted fearing to resist the will of heaven," March 19, 1227.[1]

When, therefore, the tearful resistance of Ugolino had been overcome " by the pious tearing of his clothes," as his biographer puts it, he was temporarily enthroned to receive the homage of the cardinals in the Septizonium. Clad in his full pontifical attire, he was then escorted by crowds of exultant people to the Lateran, and there enthroned with full solemnity.[2]

On the following Sunday (March 21), accompanied by " an innumerable multitude of the Romans," and resplendent " with gold and gems," he went to St. Peter's not to be consecrated, as he was already a bishop, but, according to custom, to receive " the pallium, the mark of the fulness of power." [3]   When Lent was over he was crowned on Easter Sunday in St. Mary Major's (Apr. 11), and on Low Monday (Apr. 19) went to St. Peter's thence to take formal possession of the Lateran.   Crowned with a double diadem,[4] and in golden glory " like unto one of the Cherubim," mounted on a richly caparisoned

Coronation of Gregory.

---

[1] Reg. ep. 1, of March 23, 1227, to the archbishop of Lyons. The words of the Pope have been interpreted by the statement of his biographer, c. 4, where it is said " lacrimabili et clamosa contradictione recusans, inter votivas eligentium manus pia vestium laceratione quassatus, etc."

[2] *Vit.*, c. 4. " Pontificali decoratus infula in Lateranensi palatio magnifice cathedratur."

[3] *Ib.*

[4] *Ib.* " *Duplici diademate coronatus.*" These words would seem to prove that, contrary to the common opinion (*cf. supra*, vol. iii, p. 17 n.), a tiara with a double crown was worn by the Popes before the fourteenth century.

steed, with the papal insignia borne in front of him,
" the Father of the City and of the World " was led
through the streets of Rome, escorted by a great number
of cardinals and prelates all clad in purple. On all
sides were heard the joyous acclamations of the people,
and the strains of the Kyrie Eleison. The streets,
gay with coloured carpets shot with gold and silver from
the looms of Egypt, and hangings from the dye-works
of India and Gaul, were fragrant with divers kinds of
incense. The resonant clangour of the trumpets as
they answered one another thrilled the crowd through
and through ; and while the judges and the notaries
were bright in their robes of silk, the great mass of the
nobles gleamed in cloth of gold. A crowd of Greeks
and a crowd of Jews offered their homage " to the Vicar
of Christ," each in their own way and in their own
language, while gangs of youths sang festive songs.
With his horse held by the Senator and Prefect of the
City walking by his side, the Pope passed before the
masses of the people who held in their hands flowers
and palm branches; and, riding beneath arches that
represented the heavens with their shining stars, he
finally reached the Lateran.[1]

The
Decretals of
Gregory,
1234.

In order to clear the way for an uninterrupted narrative
of the important political relations of Gregory with the
Empire as represented by Frederick II., we will here deal
with the great literary event of his pontificate, and state
his share in the construction of the great body of Canon
Law. His studies and his experience in dealing with
cases which had come before him as *auditor* and legate
had taught him that Gratian's Decretum was antiquated,
and that there was great need of simplifying and unifying
the existing mass of ecclesiastical laws. He had found

[1] With this brief description of the " possesso " given by Gregory's
biographer, *cf.* the full one given *supra*, vol. xi, pp. 31–2 and 40–3.

the decretals of his predecessors scattered in different
volumes, and moreover causing confusion by their close
resemblance, or by their contradictions, or by their
prolixity. He had, therefore, as he explained to the
University of Bologna,[1] commissioned the Dominican
Brother Raymund of Pennafort, his chaplain and
penitentiary, to omit superfluities and to collect into one
volume the said decretals, together with those of his
own, which in some cases cleared up what was doubtful
before.[2] Finally, in sending the work of Raymund to
Bologna, he ordered that it should be the one to be
used both in the courts and in the schools, and that no
one should presume to compile another " without the
special permission of the Apostolic See." [3] Raymund's
compilation in five books " of some two thousand
sections," though only an " inartistic and inorganic "
collection of papal decisions issued at different times,
was yet accounted the most finished portion of the
Canon Law, and was accordingly generally employed
by the commentators. Its appearance made quite a
sensation, and was noted by the chroniclers of the
different countries.[4] It has been published over and over
again, and has exerted the greatest influence on the law
of Europe, especially on the Teutonic portion of it.
" The decrees of the Popes," writes Janssen, " had been
from the earliest times the original source of Christian
German law, its first public official code being the

[1] See his letter (Sept. 5, 1234) prefixed to his collection of Decretals.
(*Corpus juris canonici*), vol. ii, p. 2 f., ed. Friedberg, Leipzig, 1881.

[2] *Ib.*

[3] *Ib.* A similar letter was sent to the University of Paris (ap.
Denifle, *Chart. U. Par.*, i, 154) and other places.

[4] *Cf.* the Chronicles of Emo, *M. G. SS.*, xxiii, p. 515 ; Menko,
ib., p. 536 ; Godfrey, of Viterbo, *ib.*, xxii, 363 ; Erphord., *ib.*, xxiv,
198–9, etc. Maitland, *ubi infra*, p. 131, notes that " the issue of the
papal law-books is singularly well attested by English chroniclers,"
and then gives examples. On St. Raymund of Pennafort, *cf.* Butler's
Lives of the Saints, i, p. 218 ff., Jan. 23.

collection of the edicts of Gregory IX. To this papal law book we owe the preservation, side by side with the growing recognition of Roman law, of a large number of German institutions and principles which, by incorporation with the papal decrees, obtained permanent legal form." [1] " To this day," we are assured, " the Decretals of Gregory the Ninth are quoted under the roof of Westminster Hall." [2]

As the Decretals of the Popes were perhaps in most cases replies to questions which had been put to them by different bishops, it is interesting to know that, as a very large number of those questions were asked by the bishops of our own country, England has to a very large extent been responsible for the growth of the Canon Law.[3] Of course, too, as the English Church, " as is just," followed the Roman Church,[4] and believed that the Pope " was the vicegerent on earth of no mere man, but of God Himself," [5] it, in common with all the nations of Christendom, at once received the new Decretals, and they immediately became the ecclesiastical law of the land.

[1] *Hist. of the German People at the close of the Middle Ages*, ii, p. 168, 2nd ed., London, 1905.

[2] Kington, *Fred. II.*, i, 360.

[3] " If the Pope acquired an almost unlimited power of declaring law, if all the important spiritual causes passed out of the hands of the ' ordinary ' judges into the hands of papal delegates, the bishops of England were more responsible for this good or bad result than were the bishops of any other country." F. W. Maitland, *Roman Canon Law in the Church of England*, p. 126. *Cf.* p. 130.

[4] So speaks John of Salisbury, ep. 17, ap. *P.L.*, t. 199.

[5] " Non enim puri hominis, sed veri Dei vices gerit in terris." Ayton's commentaries on the Constitutions of Otho and Ottoboni, p. 76, printed at the end of Lyndwood's *Provinciale*, Oxford, 1679. John of Ayton or Acton wrote between 1333 and 1348. Though a later writer, John is cited here because he is one of the most important of medieval English canonists, and because he wrote on the *Constitutions* of cardinal Otho who was sent by Gregory IX. as his legate into England.

CHAPTER II.

GREGORY AND FREDERICK II. FROM THE POPE'S ACCESSION
TO THE PEACE OF SAN GERMANO IN 1230.

No sooner was Gregory elected than, in accordance with The new custom, he notified his accession to the emperor and to the "Prepare Christian world.[1] All are urged, moreover, to get ready for the Crusade." for the Crusade, which is to be undertaken forthwith, and Frederick is exhorted " to fight the battles of the Lord with real earnestness (fide non ficta)," or else, however much he may love him, and wish to defer to him, he will not be able to pass over his conduct, especially seeing that at the emperor's own request, " we, when in a less exalted office, underwent many toils " to further the interests of the Crusade. Hearken, concluded the Pontiff, to our prayers, " lest you bring us and yourself into such straits that, however much we may wish it, we may not be easily able to extricate you." [2]

This last remark emphasizes the difference between the character of Honorius and that of Gregory. The former began his pontificate by stating that " he wished to proceed by clemency rather than by vigour " ; [3] but Gregory begins his by stating in fact if not in words that he must insist at all costs on justice.

He next dispatched letters to Lombardy. In the life of He makes efforts to Honorius, to which attention must constantly be given conclude if the attitude of Gregory towards Frederick is to be peace between properly estimated, it has been told how in the year 1226 Frederick and the Lombard League.

[1] *Regest.* (*R.*), nn. 1–3, March 23, 1227. " Per universum orbem de sua promotione et obitu predecessoris sui mittit litteras generales." Ric. of S. Germ., an. 1227.
[2] Ep. n. 343, ap. Rodenberg (Rod.), *Epistolæ selectæ*, i, p. 261 f.
[3] Ep. Hon., i, 30.

the Lombards, with good reason suspicious of Frederick, renewed their League, and how, not content with this, they had actively opposed him. In the strife that followed, both parties agreed to refer their differences to Honorius. The emperor at once accepted the Pope's award.[1] But the Lombards found excuses for not doing so, and Honorius died before they had signed the agreement which he had sent them.[2] Following in the wake of his predecessor, Gregory urged the Rectors of Lombardy quickly to accept the settlement of Honorius in order that the emperor might not be able to find an excuse for delaying the Crusade.[3] The exhortations of the two Pontiffs had their effect,[4] and Gregory was soon able to announce to Frederick and to the Princes of Germany that the Lombards had finally accepted the award of the Holy See. He at the same time urged them all to hasten their preparations for the Crusade.[5] A month or two later, aware of Frederick's sensual weaknesses, and perhaps learning that his preparations for the Crusade were not as forward as they ought to have been, he wrote, in virtue of his long-standing affection for him, to beg him to develop that part of his nature which he had in common with angelic natures, and to repress that which he had in common with the beasts of the field. Then, in order to impress upon his mind that his elevated position required him, for example's sake, to restrain his baser appetites, he made use of the symbolic meanings of the five imperial insignia, the cross, the lance, the crown, the sceptre, and the orb.[6]

[1] Ep. 340 of Feb. 1, 1227, ap. Rod., i, p. 258.
[2] Supra, p. 79 ff.
[3] Reg., n. 4, March 27, 1227 ; and nn. 28-9 of Apr. 16, 1227 : " Ne illorum dilatio more occasionem imperatori ipsi tribuere videatur, ac Terre Sancte subsidium retardare."
[4] See the letters of the League of March 26, ap. Reg., n. 12.
[5] Reg., nn. 30-3.
[6] Ep. of July 22, 1227, ap. Huillard-Bréholles (H.-B.), Hist. diplom.

Meanwhile, the cause of the Cross had been preached with great success throughout the different countries. " Forty thousand tried men were said to have marched from the kingdom of England." [1] Among those who went from England was the Bishop of Winchester, Peter des Roches, to whose counsels Matthew Paris attributes any honour or advantage which came to the Church during this crusade of Frederick II. [2]

Success of the preaching of the Crusade.

Accordingly, to be ready for the appointed time in August, thousands and tens of thousands of men from all parts began during the months of May, June, and July to assemble at Brindisi. But despite the earnest exhortations which Frederick had received from Rome, and despite, too, the warning note of the troubadour, reminding him that a vassal is busy with his own hurt who does not keep a promise which he has made to his lord, and impressing upon him that he ought to " cross there where Jesus willed to die," [3] the emperor was not ready. [4] The natural consequence was that in an unhealthy district, under the burning heat of the August sun, which

Crusaders assemble at Brindisi, May–July, but Frederick not ready, 1227.

Fred., iii, p. 6 ff. He writes, he says, in this strain " ex prerogativa dilectionis qua in minori officio sumus imperialem celsitudinem amplexati."

[1] Roger of Wendover, *Chron.*, an. 1227. Roger adds that Master Humbert, one of the preachers of the Crusade in England, declared that he had set down that number on his roll. The " tried men," however, were encumbered by "women and old men." *Ib.*

[2] *Chron. maj.*, an. 1238, iii, 490 R. S. Ernoul also, c. 40, p. 459, tells us of the number of English who went on the expedition, and of the great good effected by Peter des R. and another English bishop. " En cel ost ot moult d'Englès. Et s'i ot 2 evesques d'Engletiere qui moult fisent de bien en l'ost."

[3] See the poem of Elias Cairel quoted by Sedgwick, *Italy in the Thirteenth Century*, i, p. 107.

[4] Gerold, the patriarch of Jerusalem, in a letter which, forwarded " to all Christians " (Dec. 23, 1227), informed the Pope that he had to report " with distress of mind and many tears " that the emperor had not set out for Syria, " as we had all hoped he would." Ap. Rog. of Wend., *Chron.*, 1227, iv, p. 146, ed. Coxe.

Gregory's biographer [1] says was almost enough to melt solid metal, disease broke out among the loitering troops, and it would seem that thousands of them perished.[2] Meanwhile, some of the Crusaders, finding that the emperor was not ready to lead them, returned home,[3] and some sailed to the East without waiting for him.[4] At length, on the 8th of September, the Emperor put to sea along with Louis, Landgrave of Thuringia, the husband of St. Elizabeth of Hungary, and along with a large number of crusaders.[5] Instead, however, of proceeding to Palestine, he, according to one who was with the expedition, sneaked [6] back to Italy, and disembarked at Otranto two days after he had left Brindisi. Certain it is, at any rate, that he did not proceed to Syria, and that he himself declared that the reason of his abrupt return was ill-health on the part of himself and the Landgrave.[7] Certain it is also that the Landgrave died so suddenly

[1] C. 7.

[2] "The greater part," says the same authority, "ut major pars exercitus aeris et aque corruptione periret." "Pars cruce signatorum non modica in Apulia superveniente infirmitate cecidit per mortis occasum," says the imperialist Ric. of S. Germ., an. 1227. *Cf.* Conrad, *Urspergens. Chron.*, an. 1227, p. 115 ; and *Chron. de rebus in Ital. gest.*, an. 1227, ed. H.-B., p. 149. The last-named authority says that of the "maxima multitudo" who had come to Brindisi "innumerabiles" died.

[3] *Chron. de rebus.*, *l.c.*

[4] The letter of Gerold, *l.c.*; *Mon. Cisterc.*, an. 1227, p. 39 ; Ric. of S. G., *l.c.* ; Roger of W.

[5] "Li emperere entra en une galie et mut tout avant et tot li autre vaissiel aprés." Ernoul, *Chron.*, c. 40, p. 457. Ric. of S. G., *l.c.*

[6] "Quand ce vint le viesprée et il fu anuitie (night had come on), li emperere fist retorner se galye tot coiement c'onques *nus* ne le sot fors cil de la galye." Ernoul, *l.c.* *Cf.* Will. of Nangis, *Chron.*, an. 1229.

[7] See his letter of Dec. 6, 1227, "to all crusaders," ap. H.-B., iii, p. 36 ff. Frederick's partisans made the same excuse for his conduct, though Richard of San Germano admits that he had landed at Otranto "for some (unassigned if) necessary cause—ex causa necessaria "— before the Landgrave died, and he himself fell ill.

after his arrival at Otranto as to give rise to the usual
baseless suspicion of the administration of poison, and
that the return of Frederick ruined the Crusade. Those
who had gone to Palestine, when they heard that he was
not coming to lead them, at once left the Holy Land,[1]
and it was the general belief that he had once more
betrayed the cause. Our countryman, Roger of Wendover,
states that he " pretended to make for the Holy Land ; "
that " he said he was seized with a sudden illness ; "
and that his conduct " redounded greatly to his disgrace
and to the injury of the whole affair of the crusade." [2]

Many of the men on their return, so Gregory was Public feel-
informed, railed against Pope and Emperor alike for ing against the Pope and
sending them, as they said, to be laughed at by the Emperor.
Saracens, and to do nothing but see their comrades die.
Never again, so they declared, would they listen to either
Pope or Emperor on the subject of a Crusade.[3] Public
opinion such as this could not but powerfully affect

[1] According to Gerold's letter "more than forty thousand " left
Syria. *Cf. Mon. Cisterc., l.c.*, and Roger of W.

[2] " Tendere videretur ad terram promissionis, etc." An. 1227,
iv, p. 149. Alberic "of the Three Fountains " speaks with contempt
of the illness " vera vel simulata." The *Chron. Erphord.* "*Dolo
Friderici, ut fertur, interveniente.*" Ap. *M. G. SS.*, xxiv, p. 198.
Will of Andres, *Chron.*, says that he put off the Crusade " in enormem
lesionem Terre Sancte," ap. *ib.*, p. 767. Baldwin Ninoviensis (Ninove),
Chron., speaks of the Crusaders " impii imperatoris vanis promissionibus
defraudati," ap. *ib.*, xxv, 542. *Ann. de Dunstap.*, an. 1227, p. 107
R. S. " Cum Phedericus . . . simulasset se velle transire in Terram
Sanctam, etc." The Annals of Waverley, p. 303, R. S., add that he
was said to have been won over by Saracenic gold, " corruptus, ut
fertur, muneribus et xeniis paganorum " ; while the continuator of
Gervase of Canterbury boldly declares that " corrupted by the presents
of the pagans he only made a pretence of sailing." Mat. Paris, *Hist.
Anglorum*, " fingens se ægrotum," ii, 298, R. S. ; the *Chron. reg. Colon.*,
Contin. IV., an. 1227, p. 260, tells how a "picked expedition of Crusaders
from all parts of the world—cassatur et dissipatur, Friderico . . . sicut
dudum promiserat, non transfretante."

[3] *Mon. Cisterc., l.c.*

Gregory, and he felt, moreover, that the facts themselves
spoke the same language as the people. Had Frederick
been really sincere, had he been really ill, or, at any rate,
had he had any care for the interests of any but himself,
he would have immediately issued an explanation of his
conduct to the world. No such apology, however, was
forthcoming. He displayed on this occasion the same
cynical contempt for others as he had done throughout,
and, as a natural consequence, he bred disloyalty in his
subjects [1] and just indignation in the Pope.

He had denounced excommunication against himself
if he failed again to carry out his promise to sail to the
Holy Land,[2] and public opinion compelled Gregory to
proclaim the excommunication. Accordingly he assembled
a number of bishops and declared the Emperor excommunicated, 29th September.[3] Begging the princes of
Germany not to abandon the cause of the cross for
which the Church and the whole Christian people had
toiled so long and so hard, because it had been abandoned
by Frederick,[4] he made the excommunication known to the

[1] The death of many of the German princes at Brindisi, and the
report that the emperor had poisoned them, caused Louis of Bavaria
and others to waver in their loyalty to him—" videbantur aliquantulum
in fide regni claudicare." Ann. Scheftlarienses majores, ap. M. G. SS.,
x, p. 338. Cf. Mat. Par., Hist. Angl., l.c.

[2] Supra, p. 33.

[3] The anonymous Cistercian monk says he so acted because he was
affected by the complaints of the Crusaders against him and the
emperor. Chron., l.c. Cf. Chron. Siculum, ap. H.-B., i, 897, Ric. of
S. G.; Vit. Greg., c. 5. Even Frederick himself acknowledged that " to
avoid the blasphemies of men " the Pope could not have acted otherwise. The Pope " non poterat aliter apud homines blasphemias et
infamiam evitare." Ap. Böhmer, Regest. imp., v, part ii, p. 1176.
After this testimony what are we to think of authors who write about
Gregory's hatred of Frederick and his angrily excommunicating him
(cf. Hill, A Hist. of European Diplomacy, i, p. 338) ? One can only
conclude that they have not sufficiently studied the contemporary
authorities for themselves.

[4] Ep. Oct. 8, 1227, ap. Rod., i, 280.

Christian world.[1] In writing to our own Stephen Langton on the subject, he reminded him of the care the Church had taken of Frederick in his youth, and of the way in which, over and over again, he had broken the vow he had freely taken upon himself of sailing to the Holy Land under penalty of excommunication. Accordingly, "that we may not be like dumb dogs unable to bark, and that we may not seem to defer to man in disregard of God, by not punishing him who has brought such injury on the people of God, we, although unwillingly, have publicly declared the said Emperor Frederic to be excommunicated, inasmuch as he did not cross the sea at the appointed time, nor did he send thither the pre-arranged sum of money,[2] neither did he dispatch the thousand soldiers to be kept for two years at his expense for the assistance of the Holy Land." The Pope, after commanding Stephen to publish the excommunication, concluded his long telling letter by expressing the hope that Frederick would be moved to make atonement, " for we formerly loved him sincerely when we were in an inferior station." [3]

Unmoved either by adverse public opinion or by the action of Gregory, Frederick, so far from endeavouring to placate the Pope, affected to ignore the excommunication. It was accordingly more solemnly proclaimed

Solemn proclamation of the excommunication.

[1] Baldwin Ninov., *Chron.*, 1227, ap. *M. G. SS.*, xxv, p. 542 and the notes thereto. Ernoul denounces the emperor very bitterly " as a traitor to the pilgrims." Hence the Pope excommunicated him, and caused the excommunication to be proclaimed against him, " comme laron et traïtor et deloial qu'il estoit." C. 40, pp. 457-8.

[2] Promised by the emperor at San Germano. See the earlier part of this letter.

[3] Ep. of Oct. 10, 1227, ap. *Reg.* i, p. 101, n. 178, and iii, p. 565, or ap. H.-B., iii, p. 23 ff. " Qui (Gregory) ejus (Frederick) patronus fuerat spiritualis cum adhuc esset in minori officio constitutus." Thos. of Tuscany, *Gesta imp.*, ap. *M. G. SS.*, xxii, p. 511. On Gregory's action in this matter of Frederick's excommunication, see Blondel, *Fréd. en Allemagne*, p. 380 ff.

in St. Peter's on the octave of St. Martin (Nov. 18) ;[1] but, as the Pope soon after made known to Frederick, he was not anxious to go to extremities against him. He reminded him " that, perchance not without reason, we are accused as it were of cooking the kid in its mother's milk, and, to the prejudice of many and to the scandal of the whole church, of seeming to encourage you in your noxious doings." Certain it is that " we have observed towards you all the moderation we could, and have only published that sentence which you freely invoked upon yourself, and have kept back the others which you agreed should be passed upon you, if you did not fulfil the other conditions which you had undertaken to perform." [2] He assured Frederick that his goodwill towards him was unimpaired, and begged him to receive the punishment which had been inflicted upon him in good part, and to return to the bosom of the Church, by offering satisfaction to God who had done so much for him, and by being just towards men. He concluded by calling Frederick's attention to the fact that he was meanwhile bringing obloquy upon himself—" as we believe that you are fully aware "—by passing over the many acts of oppression and injustice of which the emperor was guilty in the kingdom of Sicily which, " by full right of propriety, belongs to the Roman

---

[1] Ric. of S. G., and *Chron. Sic.*, ll. cc. ; *Vit. Greg.*, c. 6. Archbishop Christian (†1251), *Chron. Mogunt.*, ap. Böhmer, *Fontes*, ii, 269, tells us that the emperor's excommunication caused great rejoicing among evilly disposed persons who hoped to fish in troubled waters. " Plough-shares were turned into swords and scythes into spears ; nor is there a man who does not carry flint and steel by his side in preparation for incendiarism."

[2] " Omne tamen quod potuimus erga te servavimus mansuetudinis moderamen, illam tantum sententiam publicando, quam ipse in te voluntarius feceras promulgari." Ep. ap. Rod., i, 32, or ap. H.-B., iii, 32 f. This letter is not dated, but was probably written after Nov. 18.

Church." [1] Further, to try the effect of verbal persuasion, the Pope sent to Frederick (Dec., 1227) Thomas, cardinal-priest of St. Sabina, and Nicholas, cardinal-deacon of St. Nicholas " in carcere Tulliano." [2] But the efforts of Gregory to induce the emperor to ask pardon of the Church, or to apologize to the outraged Crusaders were useless. Frederick had resolved to be absolute, and cared not that his excommunication had served as a signal for an outbreak of lawlessness, that men turned their ploughshares into swords, and that every man carried flint and steel always ready to burn and to destroy.[3]

After his solemn excommunication the emperor held a Diet at Capua (Nov.) in which he imposed fresh taxes for the Crusade that he was going to undertake next May (1228),[4] and he ordered a Diet of the whole empire to meet in March at Ravenna.[5] Moreover, besides insisting that, under pain of confiscation of their property, the clerics of the kingdom should, despite the interdict, continue to hold divine services,[6] he caused excuses of his conduct to be read in Rome to the people assembled on the Capitol,[7] and dispatched letters to peoples and kings in the hope of securing public sympathy. Utterly unable to justify in accurate detail his action in the matter of

Frederick's reaction against the Pope, 1227.

[1] " Sicut enim scire te credimus, contra nos mumuratur immo clamatur, quod prelatorum exilium, ecclesiarum, hospitalium, orphanorum et viduarum nec non aliorum religiosorum spoliationes et alias atroces injurias visi sumus hactenus sub dissimulatione transire." *Ib.*

[2] *Ric. of S. G.*, an. 1227 ; *cf.* ep. Greg. of the end of March, 1228, ap. Rod., i, p. 288, or H.-B., iii, p. 52.

[3] Christian, archbp. of Maintz, writing about 1250, *Liber de calam. eccles. Mogunt.*, also called *Chron. Moguntinum*, c. 22, ap. *M. G. SS.*, xxv, p. 247. *Cf.* note above.

[4] He had already taxed his kingdom for the expedition of 1227. Ric. of S. Germ., 1227.

[5] *Ib.*

[6] Ep. ap. H.-B., iii, 50 f.

[7] Ric. of S. G., *l.c.*

the Crusade, he told the whole story of his connexion with it in his own way, and finally insisted that he could not set out in August because he was really ill. But while his letter to the world at large was apologetic in tone, in that to our King he wantonly attacked the Roman Church.

His letter "to all Crusaders."
If an enemy from without, he wrote " to all the Crusaders," had attacked him and his people, he would have known how to deal with him. " But, when the Universal Father, the Vicar of Christ, the successor of Blessed Peter . . . devotes himself to stirring up hatred against us, who would not be disturbed and astounded ? Against our innocence such grievous troubles (bella) were prepared, that only grim necessity could have moved us to oppose them—seeing that we have believed that deference should humbly be paid to Blessed Peter on account of reverence for the Lord who when on earth conferred upon him the power of binding and loosing." [1] In glaring contradiction to all his previous utterances, he next declared that in his defenceless youth the Roman Church had behaved like a stepmother to him, especially in preferring Otho to him. He then proceeded to give his own version of his connexion with the Crusade from the days when at Aix-la-Chapelle, in order to make some return to God for what He had done for us, " we decorated our shoulders with the emblem of the Cross." He enlarged on the money he had expended in inducing some of his great vassals to take the Cross, and upon his own serious illness which prevented him from setting out in August. He assured the world that all was for the best, as he would set out next May with increased resources and at a season of the year better fitted for military operations.

[1] These words are part of the preamble of the very long apology which, on Dec. 6, he addressed " to all crusaders." Ap. H.-B., iii, 36 ff.

It is true the Pope had condemned him, but he had
not been allowed a proper hearing. His illness had not
been properly weighed, nor what he had actually done
for the Crusade duly considered. He assured the world
that he was innocent, and that he would not abandon
the cause of the Crucified. He accordingly begged
all to whom he wrote not to slacken their zeal in the
great cause, but to come next Lent to Ravenna where
the final arrangements for the Crusade would be made.
" We trust that the supreme Pontiff, mindful of our
devotion and not forgetful of the needs of the Holy
Land, will not suffer his devoted son to be kept long
away from the wonted tender love of Mother Church,
since, before he was called to his high place (ad altioris
loci speculam), we loved him sincerely." [1]

Such was the letter that Frederick addressed to those
who had a real interest in the Crusade, and who knew
something of his share in it and of that of the Pope.
His hypocrisy is, however, clearly shown by the letter
which he sent, " amongst other Catholic kings," to our
King Henry. In it there is no mention of the Vicar of
Christ " whom we once loved," and little attempt is made
to justify his conduct. He simply denounced the Roman
Church as a compound of avarice and pride which sought
the property of other churches and the subjection of
all kings, as it had sought that of King John of England.
It was for princes to combine against it, as they must
remember that " when a neighbour's house was on fire,
theirs was then in danger." [2]

Frederick's letter to the princes of the world.

In England we have evidence that the circular letters
of the Pope and the Emperor met with very different

King Henry's reply to the Pope, Feb. 20, 1228.

[1] *Ib.*
[2] Ap. H.-B., iii, p. 50, or Roger of Wendover, iv, 165, or Mat. Par.,
Chron. maj., iii, 152 R. S.
" Tunc sua res agitur, paries cum proximus ardet." Hor., ep. i,
18, 84.

receptions. Neither the artfulness nor the abuse of Frederick made any impression upon the rulers of the land, however they may have imposed upon the unwary.[1] In his reply to Gregory's encyclical, King Henry said that he had heard with grief of the Pope's sorrow regarding the failure of the relief of the Holy Land through the conduct of the emperor, " since on your safety and on the peaceful condition of the Church, depends the peace of Kings and Kingdoms." He added that he had also received letters from the Emperor setting forth that he had been treated hardly by the Pope, but that he would proceed to the Holy Land in May. He had, he continued, written back to the emperor urging him " not to dare (nullius temeritatis ausu) to withdraw from the devotion he owed to you and the Church, but humbly to follow your behests (humiliter obediat et obsequatur)."

In turn the King urged the Pope, " as Father and Lord to whom we are bound in full loyalty (cui in totius fidelitatis et obsequii plenitudine adesse volumus et tenemur)," for the sake of the Holy Land, the liberation of which " the world must ardently desire, to admit the Emperor to reconciliation," if, with fitting humility, "he would obey your directions (mandatis)." [2]

Henry's reply to Frederick.

Our King's reply to Frederick's violent attack on Rome was polite, but anything but encouraging. He was ready, he wrote, to help the Emperor " on condition that the fullness of the honour of the Church be respected." He informed him that he had asked the Pope on this occasion for the benefit of the Holy Land, " which the world knows

---

[1] According to Roger of Wendover, iv, p. 166, they caused no little hurt to the Church, at least in Italy, at the hands of such as were always ready for an excuse for plundering.

[2] Ap. Rymer, *Fœdera*, i, p. 299, Feb. 22, 1228, ed. 1727 ; or ap. *Close Rolls, Henry III.*, i, p. 93, R. S.

cannot be liberated without the imperial help," to pass over injuries which, under the circumstances, justice might compel him to punish, and to receive the Emperor into favour.

Our king concluded by exhorting the Emperor in whose hands God has placed the power of the world (vires mundi) at once to ask for the relaxation of the sentence passed against him, and to abide by his long-standing undertaking to liberate the Holy Land.[1]

But the exhortations of Henry were lost upon Frederick as completely as were the entreaties of the Pope. He continued his headstrong career of absolutism—not, however, unchecked. As he did not make the smallest advances towards " obeying the directions of the Pope," but added to his previous delinquencies by preventing the Archbishop of Taranto from visiting his people, plundering the Templars and Hospitallers and others, etc., Gregory, on Holy Thursday (23rd March) not only renewed the excommunication against Frederick (as he declared in a letter to the bishops of Apulia),[2] but also put under an interdict every place at which he should sojourn. Moreover, he threatened, if he did not observe the interdict, to proceed against him " as a heretic and a despiser of the keys of the Church," to absolve his subjects from their

Further decrees against Frederick, 1228.

---

[1] *Ib.* This letter was of the same date. A few months later (July 15, 1228) Henry again wrote on the same lines. He said he rejoiced if, as the emperor's letters declared, he had already set out "to serve the Crucified." He exhorted him to work for the honour of God and the Church, and to be reconciled to God and the Church, and concluded by hoping that, if he persevered in his intentions "according to the will of God and the honour of the Church" many would be induced to follow his example, and aid the Holy Land. Ep. ap. *Royal Letters*, i, p. 331, R. S. It will be seen that throughout his letter Henry insists that the emperor must consult "the honour of the Church." It was the one thing which Frederick failed to do.

[2] I.e., of the mainland of the kingdom of the two Sicilies.

allegiance to him, and to deprive him of his Sicilian fief as a disobedient vassal.[1]

Frederick rouses the Romans against the Pope, 1228.

Still Frederick paid no heed to the Pope, but retorted by persecuting the clergy of the kingdom for obeying him, and by imposing on them excessive taxes which Gregory forbade them to pay.[2] These taxes were said to be for the Crusade which the Emperor still declared he was going to undertake in May for the purpose " of *exterminating* the perfidious nation." [3] The Emperor further retorted by creating a party against the Pope in Rome.[4] He accomplished his purpose by means which can only be described as cunning.[5] He called to him a number of Roman nobles,

[1] Ep. *c.* the close of March, 1228, ap. Rod., iii, 288 f., or H.-B., iii, p. 52 ff. A little later (Apr. 7) a similar letter was sent to the king of England. In the register of Perugia, Apr. 7, it also appears, addressed "to all prelates." With reference to this sentence of Holy Thursday, Frederick himself acknowledged that, if the Pope had been able to prove him guilty of any fault with regard to his failure to start in August, he would have been within his rights in condemning him. " Sane si pro defectu quolibet negotii terre sancte quem serio fecissemus apostolica contra nos incanduisset auctoritas, foret utique patientius perferendum." Ep. of April, 1228, ap. H.-B., iii, 59. But, of course, he was innocent on that count, and the Pope on Holy Thursday had been guilty of encouraging against him Milanese rebels.

[2] Ep. Greg., May 7, ap. R. iii, 289 f. *Cf.* Ric. of S. Ger., 1228.

[3] *Cf.* his letter of April to the Podestà, consilium and commune of Cesena. " Nos etiam ad iter incepte transfretationis insistimus circa medietatem proximi mensis maii feliciter transituri . . . ad exterminium perfide nationis." This letter, like all his others at this time, shows that Frederick intended, or at least led the world to suppose that he intended, to try to crush the Moslems by force of arms. He was no doubt compelled to fall back upon negotiation because Europe would no longer trust him and follow him.

[4] " Romani *precepto imperatoris*, Gregorium P. . . invadunt et fugant." *Ann. Zwifaltenses*, x, 59. " Imperator . . . quosdam Romanorum pretio et mentita promissione corrupit." *Vit. Greg.*, c. 6.

[5] Whilst writing this at the close of the winter of 1914–15, and comparing the action of the present German emperor with the action of Frederick II., one cannot help but be struck with the remarkable similarity of the conduct of the Kaiser of the twentieth century with that of the thirteenth. With the treatment now being meted out to

chief of whom were the Frangipani, the lords of the region
about the Colosseum, who had hitherto for the most part
been staunch supporters of the Papacy. He bade them
estimate the value of their immovable property in Rome,
paid them the price they named, and then returned their
property to them as fiefs, so that they became his vassals,
his *men*. Accordingly, when Gregory was saying Mass
in St. Peter's as usual on the Monday (i.e., Easter Monday)
after his excommunication of Frederick on Holy Thursday,
they raised a disturbance against him even in the basilica
itself.[1] As the sedition did not die down, Gregory left the
city (Apr.), and retired first to Reati and then to Perugia.[2]

Meanwhile, events were not moving as Frederick would
have had them move. He had failed to impose upon the
mass of those who were really in earnest about the
Crusade. They did not present themselves for the great
diet which he had summoned to meet at Ravenna in the
early part of the year.[3] No meeting was held, and,
according to imperialist authors, the reason was that the
people of Verona and Milan, acting " as they said on the
authority of the Pope," prevented the envoys from
having access to Ravenna, and even plundered the
Crusaders.[4] As the Crusaders from without the kingdom

*Failure
of the
Ravenna
diet
and of the
Emperor to
sail in May,
1228.*

the priests of Belgium and its cardinal archbishop (Mercier) and the
bishop of Namur (Mgr. Heylen), compare Frederick's treatment of the
clergy who opposed him, and his action regarding the archbishop of
Taranto. Compare also the failure in both cases to gain over England,
and their attempts by gold to form parties in their interests in other
states. The same juggling with truth is, moreover, very conspicuous
in both.

[1] This we know even from the testimony of the imperialist Conrad of
Ursberg, *Chron.*, p. 115, ed. in usum schol.

[2] See also *Ann. Austriæ, cont. Scotorum*, ap. *M. G. SS.*, ix, p. 624 ;
other annals, *ib.*, p. 784 ; *Vit. Greg.*, c. 6 ; Ric. of S. Ger., an. 1228.

[3] *Supra*, p. 219.

[4] Conrad Ursberg, *Chron.*, *l.c.*, p. 116. There is no need to point
out the utter unlikelihood at least of the Pope's having ordered the
Lombards to plunder Crusaders. Even Frederick does not accuse
Gregory of having hindered the meeting of the diet.

of the Sicilies, made no attempt to send representatives
to Ravenna, so they made no effort to join the Emperor
in Apulia in May. From this or some other cause he once
more failed to set out at the time he had specified.

Frederick
sails for
Palestine,
June, 1228.

Utterly unable then to win the confidence of Europe
by promises, he devised a deeper scheme, by which he
hoped both to secure the sympathy of the world for himself and to bring discredit upon the Pope. He would
actually sail to the Holy Land, but not as he had given
Christendom to expect with a host in order " to
exterminate the perfidious nation " of the Saracens. He
would by treaty and concession gain what temporary
success he could from Melek el Kamil, the Sultan of Egypt,
with whom he had been in negotiation since the year
1227.[1] Accordingly, having arranged that in the event
of anything happening to himself, his eldest son Henry
should succeed him " in the Empire and in the Kingdom
of Sicily," [2] and having, equally against all his promises,
made Raynaldus, formerly Duke of Spoleto, not
merely regent of the Kingdom in his absence, but his
legate in the papal territory of the March of Ancona and

[1] Ric. of S. G., an. 1228. The Sultan of Egypt was ready to negotiate
with Frederick because at this time he was afraid of his brother, Melek
el Mu'azzam, who was Sultan of Damascus. *Cf.* Makrizi, *Hist. d' Égypte*,
an. 624 (A.D. 1226), pp. 356, 358, of Blochet's French trans. According
to Ibn-Wasil († 1297–8), quoted *ib.*, El Kamil offered " Vederik " the
city of Jerusalem. However, the Sultan of Damascus died in
1227. The Guelf Codagnellus plainly exposes Frederick's deceit in the
matter of his Jerusalem expedition. " Verum ut jussa summi pontificis
videretur velle observare, cum aliud haberet in corde quam perferret
ore cum aliqubus viris nobilibus, etc." P. 77, ed. H.-B., or p. 86, ed.
Holder-Egger. The Ghibelline *Chron. de rebus in Ital.*, p. 149, also
says he sailed " ut jussa d. Pape videretur observare."

[2] Ric. of S. Ger. In a diet at Baroli (Barletta) he decreed that
" si deficere imperatorem contingeret, sibi in imperio et regno
succederet Henricus."

in the lands of Matilda,[1] he sailed to the East with but few men in some fifty galleys (June).[2]

As he set out without informing the Pope, and as on his journey, over which he took two months, he behaved most treacherously to the regent of the kingdom of Cyprus where he remained for some weeks, the Paduan chronicler indignantly writes that " he crossed the sea like a pirate, so that the tremendous name of Roman Empire was lowered in the estimation of the barbarous nations." [3] When Frederick reached Acre (Sept. 7) the fact of his excommunication at once caused trouble. Before he set sail he had done his best to dissemble it.[4] It was, however, too well known; and so, although he was welcomed with no little pomp and outward show of honour, the leaders of the Crusaders would neither communicate with him *in sacris* nor even eat with him.[5]

Frederick's doings in the Holy Land, 1228-9.

---

[1] See his letters of appointment, etc., of June, 1228, ap. H.-B., iii, 65-8. He explained that he had been compelled to act in this way because "the rectors of the Church" were perpetually opposing his interests. Hence, "concessionem nostram predictam ipsi Romanæ ecclesiæ de vobis merito duximus revocandam." P. 68. This letter is addressed "toti communi Civitatis Novæ."

[2] *Cf.* ep. Greg. Aug. 5, ap. H.-B., iii, 73 ff. *Chron. Siculum*, i, p. 898. He went "quibusdam . . . regni sui." In almost the last words of his Chronicle, the anonymous Cistercian monk, we have so often quoted, says : " Ipse (Frederick) vero nichilominus (i.e. despite the prohibition of the Pope) ivit non cum multitudine pugnantium sed cum aliquantis de regno suo." According to Ernoul, *Chron.*, c. 40, p. 460, he did not even inform the Pope of his departure. Matthew Paris (*Hist. Anglorum*, ii, p. 303 R. S.) believed that Frederick sailed because he could no longer endure the gibes of men on account of his sloth.

[3] *Monach. Patav., Chron.*, an. 1227, ap. *R. I. SS.*, viii, p. 672 ; *Gesta Greg.*, c. 7. On Frederick's treachery in Cyprus, *cf.* Kingston, i, 308. Stevenson, *The Crusaders in the East*, p. 315, adds that " Frederick's interference in eastern affairs inaugurated a period of bitter strife in Cyprus and in Syria."

[4] " Prudenter excommunicationem Gregorii P. dissimulans." *Ann. Scheftlar.*, 1228, ap. *M. G. SS.*, xvii, p. 338.

[5] Roger of Wend., iv, p. 174.

Nor was the tension much lessened after he had declared that the Pope had excommunicated him unjustly, inasmuch as sickness alone had delayed his coming to Palestine,[1] for many began to entertain suspicions of him on account of his at once entering into negotiations with the Sultan of Egypt.[2] It became clear to them, especially in view of the insignificant force which he had brought with him, that he had not come " to exterminate " the enemy, as he had boasted, but to save his credit by a patched-up peace.

His negotiations with El Kamil.

If Frederick was disappointed at his reception by the leaders of the Crusaders, he was also doomed to some disappointment with regard to El Kamil. As we have already mentioned in a note, the rival of El Kamil, his brother the Sultan of Damascus, had died in 1227. This fact, combined with his knowledge of the discord between Frederick and the Pope and the Templars and the Christians in the East generally, rendered El Kamil less disposed to be accommodating.[3]

[1] *Ib.*

[2] He had no sooner landed than there came to him, from the Sultan of Egypt, presents not merely of gold and precious stuffs, but of "camels and elephants," and "other wonderful things which are not found in the regions of the West." *Ib.* This was one of the results of secret negotiations which the emperor had begun to carry on with the Sultan through his marshal. *Cf.* Ernoul, *Chronique*, c. 40, p. 460 f. See also the continuation of William of Tyre, l. 24, c. 87, ap. *Pat. Lat.*, t. 201, where it is distinctly stated that the marshal did not want the Christians of Palestine to know of his negotiations with the Sultan.

[3] " Li soudans sot le discorde qui estoit entre lui (Frederick) et l'apostole, and les Templiers et cels de le tiere." Ernoul, *ib.*, p. 463. *Cf.* also one of the many continuations of William of Tyre printed by H.-B., iii, p. 480 ff. " Quant li soudans qui estoit sages et soutis sot que li emperes estoit venus en la terre povrement et que li plus des pelerins s'en estoient ralez en lor pais, et que il estoit mal de l'iglise, et le mandement que li apostoiles avoit mande contre lui, si prisa moult pou son fait." L. 33, c. 6. How "povrement" Frederick was equipped in men and money we know also from the patriarch Gerold, May, 1229, ap. H.-B., iii, 135 ff.

He had only to fear that Frederick might throw in his lot with his brother's little heir who still held Damascus. Accordingly, five months elapsed before the Emperor could secure terms which would enable him to return to Europe with any prestige at all.[1] At length on February 18, 1229, a peace, for which Frederick alone on the Christian side was responsible,[2] was formally signed. It was to last for ten years.

By it, Jerusalem, the walls of which had been destroyed in 1219, was to be handed over to the emperor and his officials, except the mosque of Omar and the whole temple area generally, which was to be left in the sole control of the Saracens. Bethlehem and Nazareth and certain places on the road to them were also to be handed over to the Christians; but Frederick had to agree not to help " any Frank whatsoever " against the Saracens, and to do all in his power to prevent any one from undertaking any expedition against them.[3]

The treaty of Jaffa.

[1] A fourteenth century Arabic author Chems-eddin edh-Dhahabi, who wrote a history of Islam, has preserved a letter of Frederick to El Kamil in which he says : " It is you who have induced me to come here. The kings and the Pope know of my coming. If I were to return without having accomplished anything, I should lose all consideration in their eyes. After all, this Jerusalem, has it not given birth to the Christian religion ? Is it not you who have destroyed it ? It is now reduced to the last extremity of misery. Do you then give it to me in the condition in which it is now, in order that on my return I may be able to hold up my head among the kings ? I renounce beforehand all advantages I might draw from it." An extract in Michaud, *Bib. des Croisades*, iv, p. 429 f. *Cf.* what Gerold told the Pope, viz., that he had learned for certain that Frederick had said : " quod faceret (el Kamil) de ipso imperatore quidquid vellet quia nunquam contra eum de cætero se armaret." Ep. of March 26, 1229, ap. H.-B., iii, 103. See also Makrizi, *Hist. d'Égypte*, pp. 372–3, ed. Blochet.

[2] Frederick concluded the peace "sicuti ei visum est." Alberic of Trium. Font., ap. *M. G. SS.*, xxiii, p. 925.

[3] See the extracts from the treaty with his comments on them which the patriarch Gerold sent to the Pope, Feb. 18, 1229, ap. H.-B., iii, 86. See also the letters of Hermann von Salza, March, 1229, ap. *ib.*,

Frederick crowns himself in Jerusalem, March, 1229.

When the treaty had been duly concluded, Frederick marched to Jerusalem in order to be crowned its King, as he persisted in ignoring the rights of John of Brienne, although his wife Iolanthe through whom he claimed the kingdom had died (Apr., 1228) in giving birth to Conrad. The emperor reached the Holy City on March 17, and on the following day, which was the third Sunday in Lent, he went in state to the Church of the Holy Sepulchre and there placed on his head a crown of gold which had been laid upon the altar. But, as in accordance with the Pope's sentence,[1] wherever the emperor was, that place was under interdict, " he received no blessing from any prelate or ecclesiastic, nor was the ceremony accompanied by any religious function." [2] It was on

p. 90 ; of Frederick (*ib.*, p. 93) to the barons of the empire, March 18, 1229 (which was much the same as the one which he sent to our king Henry, March 17, ap. Rog. of Wend. iv., 189 ff.).   In neither letter does he tell the full truth about the privileges which the Saracens were to have in Jerusalem, nor about its walls.   In the letter to the barons he states that "we have given our attention to their rebuilding," and in that to Henry he asserted : " before we leave the city of Jerusalem, we have determined magnificently to rebuild it, etc."   Because the walls were not rebuilt, many authors, both ancient and modern, have stated that it was forbidden by the treaty to rebuild them.   But by the terms of the treaty, at least, Frederick could have rebuilt the walls. He did not, however, keep his promise.   Even such a reliable author as Bréhier, *Les Croisades*, p. 202, writes : " Il était interdit aux chrétiens d'en rebâtir les murs."   *Cf.* Gerold, March 26, ap. *ib.*, p. 102 ff., to the Pope, and p. 135, to all Christians ; and of the Pope to the King of France, July 18, ap. *ib.*, p. 147.   Ten years later, Frederick had the effrontery to pretend that Gregory had written to El Kamil to tell him not to give up Jerusalem to Frederick.   He "reserved " the Pope's letters which he pretended to have seized !   Ep. of Apr. 20, 1239, ap. H.-B., v, p. 296.

[1] The patriarch, indeed, renewed the sentence. *Ann. Stadenses*, ap. *M. G. SS.*, xvi, 360.

[2] The words of John of Ypres (†1383), who wrote a valuable *Chron. S. Bertini*, ap. *Biblio. des Croisades*, i, p. 415. *Cf.* l. 33, c. 8, of the French Chronicle, ap. H.-B., iii, 488.   " Onques ni ot prelat ne prestre ne clerc qui i chantast ne riens i deist."

this solemn occasion that the Grand Master of the
Teutonic Knights, in obedience to the emperor's instructions, explained to the assembled multitude both in
Latin and in German that the Pope had been compelled
to excommunicate Frederick as he could not otherwise
have avoided the ill-will of the world at large. Then,
with the object of winning, if he could, the support of
the Christians in the East, Hermann was further instructed
by his master to say that, if the Pope had known the
emperor's real mind in all that he had done, he would
have been displeased at the difficulties which certain
individuals in the East had put in his way, difficulties
which were injurious to the interests of Christendom.[1]

But his words were wasted. The simple soldiers,[2] The
indeed, and the pilgrims whose sole desire was to pray Crusaders on
where their Saviour had died for them, were carried away conduct.
with joy at the renewed possession of Jerusalem by
the Christians ; [3] but those who had any political fore-
sight, and those who were really responsible for the
maintenance of the Holy Land against the Saracen,

---

[1] Ep. c. 21, March, ap. H.-B., iii, 99 ff. H.-B., by mistake, has put
" incusavit " for " excusavit " in this passage. Hermann speaks as
though the patriarch had put Jerusalem under an interdict simply on
his own authority, and from personal motives. He forgets that the
Pope had already decreed that the interdict should follow Frederick.
The worthy Grand Master (who was in the main a very estimable
character) finishes his letter by declaring that he has not ordered his
writing merely to please the emperor. He wished simply to tell the
truth, and he believed that peace could not have been effected in any
other way : " pacem et treugas non potuit aliter stabilire." Perhaps
not, under the circumstances ; but it was Frederick's fault that the
circumstances were such. Besides, with all the favours which the
emperor showered on Hermann and his Teutonic knights, he could
scarcely be impartial.

[2] The "minutus populus " as Alberic calls them, *Chron.*, ap. *M. G. SS.*,
xxiii, p. 925.

[3] *Ib.* " Qualis autem letitia fuerit in introitu suo in Jerusalem vix
posset explicari sermone." *Cf.* a letter from Acre, Apr. 20, 1229, cited
in the *Annals of Waverley*, p. 305 R. S.

namely, the Patriarch and the Knights Templars and Hospitallers, knew that Frederick had ruined its interests by his delays, and since his arrival in it had worked merely for himself. On his outward journey they were aware that he had treacherously made himself master of Cyprus, and by his ignoring the patriarch,[1] humbling the old military Orders, and exalting the new German Order, they realized that he was aiming simply at increasing the extent of his own personal sway.

Apart, too, from the fact that their feelings were naturally outraged by the emperor's open indulgence in the less reputable ways of the Saracens,[2] and his equally openly expressed admiration for Mohammedanism at the expense of Christianity,[3] they thoroughly understood that a great opportunity had been thrown away by Frederick. On the one hand the heirs of the great Saladin were quarrelling among themselves, and

---

[1] See Gerold's letter to the Pope of March 26, 1229, where he tells how Frederick ignored all the responsible leaders of the Crusaders in Palestine, including the English bishops whose advice we know was so much regarded by them. " Postmodum vocati fuerunt magistri domorum (the grand masters of the Templars and Hospitallers) super hoc (the imperial financial position, etc.) requisiti qui una cum episcopis Anglie responderunt quod sine nostro consilio nihil penitus responderent, dicentes quod nostrum erat consilium potissimum requirendum, tunc propter dignitatem patriarchatus, tunc quia in illis partibus ac negocio precipue Jesu Christi legationis officio fungebamur. Ad hec imperator respondit quod nostrum super hoc consilium non requireret nec haberet."

[2] See ib., for his doings with "cantatrices . . . saltatrices . . . joculatores, personas . . . infames."

[3] We have Mohammedan evidence on this point in abundance. See § 78 of vol. iv of Michaud's Bib. des Crois. See also the narrative of the abbot Rothelinus, ap. ib., vol. i, p. 377. His work reaches to 1261 ; but does not appear to have been yet printed in full. If Frederick's words in Jerusalem in praise of Mahomet be compared with his letter to Richard earl of Cornwall (Mat. Par., an. 1244, iv, 302), his hypocrisy will be clear. In this letter he speaks of the Moslems' " superstitious rites, and secular pomps, with invocation of the name of Mahomet."

Christendom had on the other put substantial resources
at the disposal of the emperor. His selfishness had
thrown away the opportunity, and caused the dissipation
of the resources. It was true that the treaty agreed
to by one who was not even the *de jure* lord of the city,[1]
had put Jerusalem into Christian hands again. But,
inasmuch as the emperor did not fortify it, and the
Saracens, with their power not weakened, were allowed to
retain territory up to the very walls of the city, it was
obvious that, as El Kamil had himself declared, the
Christians were taking possession of nothing but ruins,[2]
and that, as soon as the truce was over, the Saracens
would again seize what they had ceded for the
moment.[3]

It is not indeed easy to pluck the brand of truth from
the burning words to which Frederick's action gave rise.
Still it would seem safe to argue from the writings of
English and French authors, who were not so directly
concerned in the struggle between the Empire and the
Papacy, that the just conclusion of the thoughtful
Crusader was that, in the affairs of the Holy Land,
the Emperor had made " confusion worse confounded." [4]

[1] The Sultan of Damascus, and not El Kamil, the sultan of Babylon
(Cairo), was at this time the *de jure* lord of Jerusalem, as Gerold pointed
out. *Cf.* his letters ap. H.-B., iii, pp. 87, 106, 137.

[2] Makrizi, p. 372, ed. Blochet.

[3] According to Ibn-Wasil, who had his information from one of El
Kamil's agents who was with the emperor in Jerusalem, Frederick
acknowledged himself the "mameluke" (slave or vassal) of the
Sultan, and declared that it was simply by his goodwill that the
Christians were in possession of the Holy City. Quoted *ib.*, p. 373.

[4] " Confundit etiam miserabiliter negotium Terræ Sanctæ." *Annals
of Waverley*, p. 304 R. S. *Cf.* Geoffrey de Courlon, *Cron. Senon.*,
who says that " Fredericus transivit ultra mare, relinquens xpistianis
Terre Sancte majorem desolationem quam consolationem." Will. of
Nangis, *Chron.*, 1232, says that Frederick's treaty was " Christianitati
damnosam " ; Brunetto Latini, *Li Tresors*, l. ii, pt. ii, c. 96. Fred. ;

Frederick
leaves
Palestine,
1229.

Meanwhile Frederick had heard that his schemes in Italy were not prospering.[1] Accordingly, ridiculed and despised by Moslems[2] and Christians[3] alike, he left Palestine secretly (May 1, 1229), and landed at Brindisi on June 10.

"il fist son traitement avoec le soudan ; et en somme il ordena plus de mal que de bien " ; and Phelippe de Nevaire, *Les gestes des Chiprois,* c. 139, " Ensi party d'Accre, l'emperor, heïs, et maudys, et vileynis." After noting that the patriarch, Templars, etc., had had no hand in Frederick's treaty, as they had been forbidden by the Pope to co-operate with him, Ernoul (c. 40, p. 465) adds that, if the Pope had not issued any such prohibition, they would not have had any part in it as it was altogether a disgraceful one : "car cele pais tint on à fausse et à malvaise." *Cf.* ep. Greg. of June 13, 1229, Rod., i, 309. A modern author has expressed himself very strongly but very properly on the view of Frederick's action in the East, which is put forward by many German and English authors without, as he says, consulting the original authorities. What Frederick effected in the Holy Land "deserves not even the name of success ; it was conceded by the policy of the Sultan . . . in fact it was asserted by contemporary writers that the emperor and the Sultan perfectly understood each other . . . that the articles of the treaty were purposely so loose as to be binding on neither, and that the Sultan of Damascus, nephew of the Egyptian potentate, was not included in it. To account for his precipitate departure, his partisans—such are nearly all the historians of Germany and France—report that it was caused by the unexpected invasion of Apulia by the papal troops. This is partially true, but they forget to inform us that Gregory did not resort to arms until Spoleto had been invaded by one of the imperial vassals, Raynaldo, duke of Spoleto, who doubtless acted from the orders of the emperor." S. A. Dunham, *The Germanic Empire,* i, p. 199 f.

[1] Epp. of Hermann, ap. H.-B., iii, 90, and of Thomas, count of Acerra, to Frederick, ap. *ib.,* p. 110 ff. *Cf.* the old French Chron., *ib.,* pp. 487–8.

[2] We have given above the contemptuous description left us by a contemporary Moslem. *Cf. supra,* p. 37. Another, Ibn-Wasil, cited by Blochet, *l.c.,* p. 375, set him down as cunning and as one who had no great scruple in violating his oaths. On the return of Frederick, *cf.* Döllinger, *Hist. of the Church,* iv, p. 39 ff., and p. 434.

[3] *Cf.* ep. Gerold, and the notes of H.-B., iii, p. 139 ; and Bréhier, *Les Croisades,* p. 204. Those who prefer to follow imperialist authors, whether historians (Ric. of S. G., the abbot of Ursberg, etc.) or poets (Freidank, who joined Frederick in Palestine), will form a different idea of Frederick's action in Palestine to the one given in the text.

We must now cast our eyes backwards to see what Gregory
had meanwhile taken place in Italy to cause Frederick opposes
force to
anxiety. He had learned that, as in the East so in the force.
West, his plans had not worked out as successfully as
he had hoped. He had not long left the shores of Italy
when the Pope had occasion to write that the emperor,
although he was reported to have put to sea with merely
a handful of men (cum paucis militibus), " had directed
a great army of Christians and Saracens [1] against the
patrimony of the Church." [2] The army was under the
leadership of Duke Raynaldus whom, as we have seen,
Frederick had, without any right whatever, set over the
March of Ancona.[3] The Duke had at once endeavoured
to corrupt the loyalty of its people to the Pope [4] and soon
after invaded it. It was in vain that Gregory remonstrated
with him [5] ; he even endeavoured to corrupt the loyalty

In the hope, however, of arriving at the truth, I have preferred to
follow, as far as possible, authors who were not directly connected with
the empire. The apology for the emperor is generally couched in some
such language as that of Freidank in his *Bescheidenheit*, ed. Bezzen-
berger, Halle, 1872.

> " O what in the world can a Kaiser do,
>   Since Christians and heathens, clergy too,
>   Are striving against him with might and main ?
>   'Tis enough to craze e'en Solomon's brain !
>   Since Frederick does the best he can
>   Upon us they needs must lay the ban ! "
>   Kingston's translation, i, p. 334.

[1] In 1221, Frederick had transported 20,000 of these cruel barbarians
from Sicily to Lucera in Apulia. They were fitting tools of a cruel and
sensual master.

[2] Ep. Aug. 5, 1228, ap. H.-B., iii, 75. *Cf.* ep. of Aug. 30 (?), ap. *Reg.*,
vol. iii, p. 568 ; of Aug. 6, *ib.*, p. 572 ; and of Dec. 20, ap. *Register of
St. Osmund*, ii, 144 R. S.

[3] *Supra*, p. 224.

[4] Ep. Sept. 23, to Azzo, marquis of Ancona, ap. Rod., i, p. 290 ;
Gesta, c. 8.

[5] " Ammonitus sepius," says Ric. of S. Ger., an. 1228, p. 129, ed.
Gaudenzi. *Cf.* ep. of Gregory to Raynaldus, Nov. 7, 1228, ap. H.-B.,
iii, 79, and ep. of Nov. 30 to the Genoese.

of the cities in the Patrimony itself, and in the Duchy of Spoleto, " with damnable avidity " sending them letters and presents, and striving by threats and promises to alienate the vassals of the Church.[1] Not content with this, the imperialists invaded the Patrimony, and also laid siege to Benevento " which is a special city of the Roman Church "—and that, too, by virtue of a special commission from the emperor.[2]

Feeling that it was time to act, Gregory excommunicated the savage Raynaldus[3] and his followers, and, as even Richard of San Germano puts it, " feeling that it was right to repel force by force," he commanded John of Brienne, Frederick's rival for the crown of Jerusalem, and cardinal John Colonna to take the field against him. Notwithstanding these measures, Raynaldus was able to continue his subjugation of the March, and had pushed on as far as Macerata when the Pope decided on an invasion of the kingdom to compel the duke to abandon the March in order to protect Sicily itself. He accordingly raised troops from Campania, gave them the badge of the cross keys,[4] and from Ceprano as a base sent them into the kingdom under the leadership of Thomas of Celano and others who had been exiled by the emperor.[5]

---

[1] Ep. of Aug. 30 just cited. *Gesta*, c. 8.

[2] So at least Gregory proclaimed to the whole Church. " In portu autem, paulo ante statuta edidit et litteras destinavit ad impugnandum et usurpandum patrimonium Apostolicæ Sedis, Beneventanam obsideri faciens civitatem, etc." Ep. *ib. Cf.* ep. of Aug. 6, 1228, ap. *ib.*, p. 573. *Cf.* the *Annals of Dunstable*, p. 114 R. S.

[3] The imperialist Ric. of San. Ger. tells us how he tortured the inhabitants of a rebellious city, "et Sarracenorum traditos potestati, quos secum de Apulia duxerat, in ipsis cruciatibus exalare coegit." *Chron.*, an. 1228, p. 129. *Cf. Gesta, l.c.,* and epp. Greg. of Nov. 7 and 30, ap. H.-B., iii, 79 ff., and Dec. 3, ap. Rod., i, 294.

[4] " Clave signati " . . . " qui clavium signa gerebat." *Ib.*, an. 1229.

[5] All this is from the imperialist Richard, and gives a very different version of the Pope's conduct to that which is given by many modern

We may pass over the details of the action of the papal troops, and the letters issued by Gregory at this period explaining his conduct towards the imperial party, and asking for aid.[1] We may also pass over the expulsion of the Franciscans from the kingdom on the ground of their carrying papal letters urging the bishops to recommend surrender to the Pope;[2] but we may note that, by the time that Frederick landed in Apulia, Raynaldus had been expelled from the March by John of Brienne aided by some Lombards,[3] and that the papal force, not without committing some atrocities,[4] had advanced in the kingdom as far as Capua.[5]

Meanwhile, Gregory was feeling acutely the financial strain caused by the upkeep of these forces. Apart from

Frederick returns to Apulia, 1229.

The Pope raises money, 1229.

authors. *Cf. Gesta*, cc. 8 and 10. According to the author of the *Gesta*, Gregory could draw both the spiritual and temporal sword against Raynald, "qui (the Pope) a Domino passuro querente de gladiis, recepit utriusque gladii potestatem." *Cf.* a letter of Gregory to the diocese of Salisbury of Dec. 20, 1228, already quoted from the Reg. of St. Osmund, ii, 144 ff. After telling of the invasion of the Patrimony, the Pope wrote : "Nos aperte videntes quod, nisi horum refrenetur audacia, non desinerent furere feritate, ad *recuperandas terras invasas*, et injurias propulsandas, quin potius ad . . . tuendam ecclesiasticam libertatem, excercere cepimus potentiam temporalem, pluribus ad hoc sub amplis stipendiis exercitibus congregatis."

[1] Epp. of Nov. and Dec. to Genoa, the bishops of Tuscany, the king of Sweden, etc., ap. *Reg.* i, p. 152 ff. ; and of May 15, 1229, to the Rectors of the Lombard League ; of June 4, to the Infante of Portugal ; and of June 26 (and July 13 and Oct. 9) also to the rectors of Lombardy in which he reminds them that he had taken steps against Frederick largely on their advice, as he "cum idem totis mentis affectibus aspiraret ad exterminium Lombardiæ," ap. Rod., i, 313. See also, epp. of Sept. 28 and 30, 1229, to bishops of France.

[2] Ric. of S. Ger., p. 131.

[3] *Ib.*, p. 132. See the Pope's letter to the archbishop of Milan, and his suffragans, asking for Lombard support. *Reg.*, n. 251, p. 153. He points out that he is fighting for ecclesiastical liberty, that the armies he is supporting must be paid, and that they must therefore contribute a tenth of their revenues. *Cf.* n. 6122, vol. iii, 577.

[4] See n. 1, p. 236.   [5] See n. 2, p. 236.

indirect expenses, the campaign is said to have cost him
one hundred and twenty thousand ounces.[3] He had to
write everywhere for money. It was, indeed, only fair
that the faithful should contribute their share towards
the expenses of the struggle in which the Pope was
engaged for the safeguarding of the proper liberty of the
Church, or for the maintenance not to say as yet of the
balance of power in Europe, but of that status of Europe
in which the Pope was recognized as the ultimate political
referee. This international position was especially
acknowledged to belong to the Pope in the matter of the
Crusades, and this position it was which had been so
flagrantly set at naught by Frederick. Still, when it
comes to taxation, nations which are at the moment
not affected by a breach of international law, are very
often not prepared to sacrifice much to prevent or punish

[1] The news of these atrocities grieved Gregory very much. In a
letter to cardinal Pelagius (May 19, 1229) he declared that the
" defender of ecclesiastical liberty " only " rarely and unwillingly "
drew the sword. When, however, the sword is drawn, it must be used
with all possible restraint, and under no circumstances must prisoners
be slain or mutilated. Ed. Rod., i, p. 305.

[2] *Chron. Siculum*, ap. H.-B., i, 902. Gregory is also credited on some
rather obscure evidence (which is not much elucidated either by the
Register of the Pope or by that of Frederick) with having endeavoured
to stir up trouble in Germany against Frederick by setting up a rival
to his son, Henry VII. This he is stated to have done through his
legate Otho, cardinal of St. Nicholas in *carcere Tulliano*, who had been
sent into Germany in 1228 "statum ecclesiarum Alemannie respecturus."
Cf. Chron. Ebersheimense, n. 41, ap. *M. G. SS.*, xxiii, p. 452 ; Alberic,
Chron., ap. *ib.*, an. 1230, p. 926 ; Conrad of Fabaria, ap. *ib.*, vol. ii,
p. 181. *Cf.* H.-B., iii, 115, 221, n. 399. Whatever efforts Gregory made
in this direction were a failure.

[3] " Preter illa (expenses) que memoriam extimantis effugiunt,
centum viginti millia unciarum (or denariorum) . . . tunc expendit."
Gesta, c. 10. The biographer adds that later on Frederick promised to
refund this money, but, as usual, did not keep his promise. Still the
Chron. de rebus in Ital., an. 1230, p. 150, ed. H.-B., says that, after
the peace of San Germano, Frederick gave the Pope " propter labores
et expensas Ecclesiæ 32 millia librarum privinisinorum (sic)."

breaches of that really all-important law.[1] When, therefore, a papal representative appeared in our island as in other countries, and demanded a tenth of all movable property in England, Ireland, and Wales, there was much discontent. The discontent was perhaps aggravated by untactful manner on the part of the envoy Master Stephen. At any rate, the laity flatly refused to pay the tithe ; but the clergy, under threat of ecclesiastical censures, finally, after much grumbling, consented to meet the demand. " However," says our historian, " in this tithing one circumstance gave some slight consolation and comfort to many, which was that continental kingdoms and those at a distance were not exempt from this taxation.[2] When at length," he continued, " the full amount of money collected in this way reached the supreme pontiff, he liberally distributed it to John of Brienne and to the other chiefs of his army." [3]

At length, in August, Frederick was ready to take the field. Fortunately for him he obtained the help of the German Crusaders. When with him they were leaving Palestine, they had refused to help him against the

Frederick takes the field, 1229.

---

[1] What has so far (March, 1915) happened in the present European war furnishes abundant proof of this.

[2] We are expressly told that the French Church granted the Pope a tithe of its revenues. *Cf. Annals of Dunstable,* p. 114 R. S.

[3] Roger of Wendover, *Chron.,* an. 1229, iv, p. 198 ff. The Pope, in pointing out that Frederick had acted " contra legem Christianam," was in effect stating that he had acted against the common law of Christendom. Though Gregory was therefore contending for the rights of the universal Church, i.e., as Europe was then constituted, for the international law of Europe, still his efforts were not sufficiently appreciated in England to make men ready to support them by their money. Hence, there is no doubt that this frequent demand for money, which was in many cases at least quite just, but never particularly easy to be comprehended adequately by the multitude, was the cause of much of the ill-feeling which gradually accumulated against the Holy See. *Cf.* Greg. ep. of Dec. 20, 1228, ap. *Register of St. Osmund,* ii, p. 144.

Church, but, when an adverse wind drove them to Apulia, they gave way.[1] With these, with levies from Apulia, with men and money from Theodore Angelus, despot of Epirus,[2] and especially with his ferocious Saracens, the emperor left Barletta to drive the " key-bearers " from his dominions. This he proceeded to do with success and excessive cruelty.[3]

Negotiations for peace, 1229–30.

Meanwhile, whether to gain time or because he did not feel sure of ultimate success (especially as he had reason to fear the setting up of a rival to his son in Germany),[4] or perchance for some more honourable cause, Frederick, more than once during the autumn of 1229, entered into peace negotiations with the Pope.[5] But as it is not known on what conditions he wished to come to terms,[6] it is no more possible to say whether he was in earnest on these occasions than he was in Palestine when he sent

[1] " Magnus exercitus militum Theotonicorum." *Chron. Sic.*, ap. H.-B., ii, pt. ii, p. 902 ; Ric. of S. Ger., an. 1229.

[2] Ric. of S. G., pp. 134 and 135 ; ep. Greg. of *c.* Aug. 20, 1229, Rod., i, 320.

[3] " Et facta interfectione civium maxima nimis crudeliter se vindicavit, et multa mala commisit." Alberic T. Font., *Chron.*, ap. *M. G. SS.*, xxiii, p. 925. *Cf.* Rog. of Wend., an. 1230.

[4] Ep. Greg., Oct. 23, 1229, ap. *Reg.*, iii, p. 592.

[5] Ric. of S. G. In almost the last words of his chronicle (p. 117, ed. in usum schol.) Conrad of Ursberg says : " Omni tempore, quamdiu denunciabat eum (Frederick) Papa excommunicatum, beneficium absolutionis humiliter cum omni obedientia et devotione et justitiæ exhibitione postulavit."

[6] It is true that on Nov. 10, 1229, Gregory forwarded to the Rectors of the Lombard League certain terms of peace which Frederick had offered, and asked for their advice upon them. But the " quoddam scriptum " does not appear to have reached us. Ep. ap. Rod. i, 327. No doubt a comparison between the various conditions of peace put forth by the Pope after Nov. 10, 1229 (when he granted his legate, Thomas, cardinal priest of St. Sabina, the necessary faculties for absolving Frederick, ap. *Reg.*, iii, p. 590), and the final terms of the peace of San Germano (July, 1230), might enable one to form a conjecture as to the proposals of the emperor. *Cf. Reg.*, iii, 593 ff.

an embassy to Gregory soon after his arrival there to ask for peace.[1]   At any rate, even after he had by November recovered most of his territory, dismissed the Germans, and returned to Apulia to avoid the winter,[2] the negotiations continued.

According to Conrad of Ursberg, Frederick begged Leopold Duke of Austria and other German princes to mediate between him and the Pope.[3]   Whether this is so, or whether they were influenced by what they had heard of the quarrel from the returning German Crusaders, it is certain that duke Leopold, " the only solace of the Clergy," [4] and other German princes came into Italy about the month of March.[5]   They at once interviewed the Pope who had returned to Rome after an absence of nearly two years.

The machinations of the imperial party in Rome had forced him to leave the city in April, 1228.[6]   But in February, 1230, occurred one of those terrible inundations of the Tiber which age after age have devastated Rome, and materially assisted in the destruction of its ancient

Intervention of Leopold of Austria, 1230.

Overflow of the Tiber, 1230.

---

[1] For notice of the fact of this attempt see Ernoul, c. 40, p. 462, and the *Annals of Dunstaple*, p. 114 R. S.   According to the latter authority Gregory refused the desired absolution until the emperor had made satisfaction for the wrongs he had inflicted on the Templars, etc.

[2] *Chron. Sic.*, ap. H.-B., i, p. 963.

[3] Already on July 18, Gregory had informed the Duke, along with the rest of the world, how Frederick had made peace with the one " whom he had been made emperor to attack—quem, ut impugnatorem fidei, fideliter impugnaret accuperat imperialis culminis dignitatem." Ap. Rod., i, 315.

[4] So he is called by the *Annales Gotwicenses*, an. 1230, ap. *M. G. SS.*, ix, p. 603.

[5] *Chron. Siculum*, ap. H.-B., *l.c.*, p. 903.

[6] Ric. of S. G., p. 128.   Discontent with the Pope's support of their enemy, Viterbo, also moved the Romans on this occasion.   *Cf.* the *Annals of Vendôme*, ap. *Eng. Hist. Rev.*, Oct., 1898, p. 698 ; the *Annales Stadenses*, an. 1228 ; and the *Vita* or *Gesta* of the Pope, c. 13 ; *cf.* c. 10.   The papal biographer gives a rather confused account of the events of this period.

monuments. According to Gregory's biographer, the
water rose to the level of the roofs of the houses in the
lower part of the city,[1] and caused a great destruction of
life in men and animals, as well as a great loss of food and
property of all kinds. Then, as in the case of the great
flood just before the election of the first Gregory, the
retiring waters left behind them a great quantity of dead
fish and various animals, which the biographer describes
" as a great mass of serpents." Their corruption, as
before, engendered a plague from which many more men
and cattle perished. Recognizing in these calamities the
hand of God punishing them for their treatment of the
Pope, a deputation left Rome for Perugia. It included
" the chancellor, Pandulf of the Subura, the proconsuls
of the city, and a number of deputies (legatos)."[2] Moved
by their entreaties, Gregory returned to Rome (c. February
24), where he was received with the greatest joy by its
fickle people.

The peace
negotiations
in the hands
of the Princes
of the Em-
pire, 1230.
When he had relieved the wants of the inhabitants by
the supplies which he caused to be brought into the city
from the neighbourhood, and when he had improved the
drainage of the city,[3] Gregory was free to attend to the
suggestions of the duke of Austria and his companions
from Germany. In reply to Leopold's request that peace
should be made, as the existing state of things was good
neither for the Pope himself nor for the emperor, Gregory
is reported to have asked what sort of peace could be
made, seeing that the emperor had deceived him so much
that he could not believe a word he said, nor trust any

[1] According to the *Annals of Austria, contin. Scotorum*, ap. *M. G. SS.*,
ix, p. 625, the waters rose to the steps of St. Peter's ; and Alberic,
Trium Font., says that 7,000 men were reported to have been drowned.
Ap. *ib.*, xxiii, p. 926.

[2] *Vita*, c. 13.

[3] *Ib.*, c. 14.

oath which he might take.[1] The duke, however, assured the Pope that, if terms of peace were agreed upon, the princes would guarantee their observance.[2]

Fresh terms were accordingly drawn up, and sent to the emperor by the princes. In a letter to the emperor which accompanied them, the Pope told Frederick that he had heard that it was his majesty's opinion that Gregory must be a different person from the bishop of Ostia, and did things that the bishop would never have thought of attempting. If that is so, added Gregory, addressing the emperor, then you are the sole cause of the change, and your own conscience will let you know that you are alone to blame. You have done to us what you would never have done to the " bishop of Ostia." [3]

Even the efforts of the princes of the empire could not easily bring Frederick to make the necessary submission. His violence,[4] and his desire for revenge [5] on those who had aided the Pope against him, caused the negotiations to drag on from month to month. In fact, the great difficulties in the way of peace lay in the Pope's resolve to stand by the Lombards and others who had stood by him, and in his determination not to give up without suitable safeguards the cities which had turned over to him during the course of the struggle.

[1] " Quel pais ferois je ? Il m'a tant menti, qu'à poines porroie je croire chose qu'l me deist, ne seirement q'il me feist." Ernoul, c. 40, p. 467.

[2] *Ib.*

[3] Ep. *c.* end of March, 1230, ap. *Reg.*, iii, 602. The reader will not have forgotten that Gregory was bishop of Ostia when he was elected Pope.

[4] See the ep. just quoted regarding his " aliquos Regni clericos et laicos in tractatu pacis ignominiose morti et horribili crudeliter exponendo."

[5] Hence the Princes were slow to furnish the necessary guarantees of safety for those " who had adhered to the Church." *Cf.* epp. of July 3, 1230, to the legates and to the Princes, ap. *ib.*, p. 605 ff.

At length, however, Gregory drew up a series of articles (July 12, 1270) [1] which Frederick, though he found them hard " to his highness," accepted in the hope that the Pope would treat him with his former love. [2] Accordingly, before the end of July, the papal legates John, cardinal bishop of Sabina, and Thomas, cardinal priest of Sta. Sabina, were able to report to the Pope that they had received at San Germano the emperor's oath to abide by the terms of the peace, and also the oaths of the princes to see to their observance (July 24). [3] During both July and August, a number of documents were issued either at San Germano or in the neighbourhood of Ceprano, setting forth the conditions of the peace. [4] In the first place Frederick agreed to stand by the decision of the Church with regard to the things on account of which he had been excommunicated ; [5] to pardon all who had adhered to the Church, whether Germans, Lombards, Tuscans, or French ; to respect the Duchy of Spoleto, the March and the Patrimony of the Church generally ; [6] to make good the damage done to the property of the Templars and others in the course of the quarrel ; to restore their sees and property to exiled bishops ; [7] to refrain from imposing any special taxes on the clergy, or from bringing them before civil tribunals

[1] Ep. ap. *Reg.*, iii, 607.

[2] Ep. of Fred., July 19, *ib.*, p. 609. *Cf.* the Pope's reply, *ib.*, p. 610.

[3] Ep. ap. *ib.*, p. 611. *Cf.* Ric. of S. Ger., and the documents ap. H.-B., iii, 207 ff. Leopold of Austria, to whom the peace was mainly due, was too ill to take the oath. He died soon after this. *Cf.* various annals of Austria, ap. *M. G. SS.*, ix, pp. 507, 603, 626, etc. *Cf.* Alberic T.F., *Chron.*, ap. *ib.*, xxiii, pp. 926–7 ; and Ric. of S. Ger.

[4] Ap. H.-B., iii, 207 ff.

[5] In a document (*ib.*) addressed " to all men " Frederick swore " quod nos pro omnibus pro quibus excommunicati sumus . . . stare precise mandatis Ecclesie."

[6] *Ib.*, pp. 208–9.

[7] *Ib.*, p. 213.

or from interfering with ecclesiastical elections,[1] and to give up for a time certain castles as a guarantee of his good faith.[2] On the other hand, means were to be found for restoring to the emperor without the loss of honour to the Church, the cities of Gaeta and Sant Agatha, which during the war had gone over to the Pope.[3]

At length, after months of wearisome negotiations, "the emperor and his followers were by the cardinal-bishop of Sabina absolved from the bond of excommunication on Wednesday the feast of St. Augustine (August 28) in the chapel of St. Justa in the camp before Ceprano." [4] A day or two after this (September 1) the emperor and the Pope met at the foot of the hill on which stands Anagni, entered that city in state, dined together in company with Hermann von Salza, and held long converse together. On the following day there was a public banquet in Gregory's paternal mansion, and then Pope and emperor parted, seemingly the best of friends.[5] Frederick himself a little later assured our king that in the interview which he had had with the Pope, Gregory had so judicially reviewed the whole of his action that he had removed all the rancour he had felt against him.[6]

The Emperor is absolved from excommunication, 1230.

[1] *Ib.*, pp. 217–19.

[2] *Ib.*, pp. 215–16.

[3] *Ib.*, p. 208. . The English reader will find translations of two or three of these documents in Thatcher, *A source book for Mediæval Hist.*, p. 240 ff., though by mistake " the Duchy " is described as " the Duchy of Rome " and not of Spoleto.

[4] Ric. of S. Ger. *Cf. Ann. Scheftlar. maj.*, an. 1230, ap. *M. G. SS.*, xvii, p. 339 ; and especially Frederick's letter "to the illustrious king his very dear friend "—probably our King, Henry III., ap. H.-B., iii, 227. See also Gregory's letter, *ib.*, p. 228.

[5] Ric. of S. Ger. ; Rog. of Wend., iv, p. 216, ed. Coxe, and *Vita Greg.*, c. 11.

[6] *Ep. cit.* " Tam benigne propositum nobis sue intentionis aperuit de ipsis que precesserant nil omittens et singula prosequens evidentis judicio rationis, quod etsi nos procedens causa commoverit . . . sic benivolentia quam persensimus in eodem omnem motum lenivit animi, etc."

Once again " the *Sacerdotium* and the *Imperium* were
bound together in the bond of charity." [1]

In considering the terms of the treaty which we have
just seen signed, one cannot fail to be astonished " that
the Pope, the weaker party, gains almost everything,
(and that) the emperor, fresh from his conquests, at the
head of a great army, can compass little more than his
absolution from the sentence of 1227," [2] and has to engage
to surrender claims which were so much the logical outcome of his absolutist ideas that in practice he never
abandoned them. This result has been ascribed to the
Pope's " obstinate firmness, to the precarious condition
of Italy and Germany, and to his still great authority in
Europe." [3] Somewhat broadened, the last-named cause
was the true one. It was the opinion of the Crusader, and
that still stood for the mass of European opinion, that
Frederick had betrayed the cause of the cross, and it was
the opinion of kings [4] and princes that he had not consulted " the honour of the Church." Frederick accepted
the peace of San Germano because the pressure exerted
upon him by the princes of the empire, acting in harmony
with the public opinion of Christendom, was more than he
could withstand.

[1] *Ib.*
[2] Kington, *Fred. II.*, vol. i, p. 359.
[3] Balzani, *The Popes and the Hohenstaufen*, p. 187.
[4] See above for the letters of Henry III. to the emperor, p. 219 ff.

CHAPTER III.

GREGORY AND FREDERICK II. YEARS OF PEACE,
1230–1236.

THE treaty of San Germano ushered in a few years of Harmony between the Pope and the Emperor. peace during which, in the main, the Pope and the emperor acted together; and, in accordance with the idea of the Holy Roman Empire,[1] mutually assisted one another. Frederick gave the Pope help against the Romans, supported his efforts to bring about a reconciliation between Rome and Viterbo, submitted Lombard difficulties to Gregory's arbitration,[2] co-operated with him against heretics, and even chose a wife in accordance with his suggestions. Gregory on his side pushed the emperor's claims in Palestine and in Lombardy, and stood by him against his rebellious son. His support enormously increased the imperial prestige. Writing to him in the last of these happy years of peace, Conrad bishop of Hildesheim averred : " The Apostolic See, looking not merely to its own interests, but to those of its friends (devotorum), raising on high the imperial dignity, has, through your favour and the divine providence, caused our glorious lord emperor so to prosper throughout Germany, that all yield to his will, all resistance has

---

[1] Cf. a remarkable letter of Frederick on the essential unity of the Empire and the Papacy. "Quamquam hec duo, sacerdotium et sacrum imperium, vocabulorum appareant nuncupatione discreta, significationis tamen effectu sunt eadem ejusdem originis, divine potentie silicet initiata principiis, ejusdem gratie favore fovenda, et quod abominamur exprimere, ejusdem nostre communis fidei subversione tollenda."

[2] Cf. H.-B., epp. of Aug., 1233, and Sept., 1234, ap. " Rouleaux de Cluny " in Notices des MSS., t. xxi, pt. ii, pp. 357-60.

vanished, and he has found both the greater and the lesser Princes well disposed, and ready to carry out his wishes." [1]

Even during these years of peace there was not perpetual sunshine ; and passing clouds, some of them no bigger than a man's hand, showed that a storm was brewing.

Gregory supports the Emperor's claims in Palestine.

In the course of his efforts to advance the interests of Frederick in Palestine, Gregory had no little difficulty in connexion with the Knights Templars and Hospitallers. Because these powerful bodies, as composed of Churchmen, were naturally disposed to stand by the Church in her difficulties, they were viewed with suspicion by the emperor, and even oppressed by him when he could. This increased the opposition of the Knights to him, and where they could, especially in Palestine, where the imperial power was of recent establishment and weak, they endeavoured to thwart his designs. In order, therefore, to promote harmony between the contending parties, Gregory begged the emperor to be guided by mercy rather than by justice, and to restore what he had taken from the Knights, reminding him that it was they who had preserved the Holy Land, and that it was the general belief that without them it could not be held.[2] On the other hand, he dispatched letter after letter to the Knights in Palestine urging them not to break the peace made by Frederick,[3] but to be loyal to his representative in Palestine and to oppose his enemies.[4] Moreover, after the election of John of Brienne as emperor of Constantinople

---

[1] Ep. of c. July 20, 1235, ap. H.-B., iv, pt. ii, p. 730.

[2] Ep. Feb. 26, 1231, ap. Rod., i, 346. Cf. ep. Jan. 19, 1231, ib., p. 343, ep. Apr. 29, 1231, ap. ib., p. 439, for a proposal to facilitate an understanding between the parties.

[3] Ep. ap. H.-B., iii, 266, of Feb. 26.

[4] Ep. July 28, 1235, ap. ib., iv, 736. Cf. epp. of July 26, ap. ib., iii, 376-9.

(1230),[1] Gregory,[2] who had hitherto recognized his claim
against that of Frederick to the kingdom of Jerusalem,
felt free to recognize Frederick as the *de jure* as well as
the *de facto* King of Jerusalem.[3] In the very letter in
which this title of King of Jerusalem is discussed and
conceded by the Pope, one of its sentences shows very
clearly on what different lines Gregory and Frederick
were working. The latter was striving to make the
empire hereditary in his family, and to include all countries
within that empire, whereas the former's aim was to
preserve the principle of free election to the empire and
keep the different countries distinct. Accordingly, he
informed Frederick that in accordance with his wishes
he had notified the prelates that the emperor was sending
to Syria as his representative his marshal Richard
Filangeri. " But," he added, " we have said that he is
to be called not the legate or bailiff of the empire, but your
legate or the emperor's legate, and it is our wish that
you also should carefully observe this distinction, lest
prejudice should thereby be begotten to your heirs,
as if the kingdom of Jerusalem were subject to the
empire." [4]

After this, Gregory worked harder than ever to ensure
a loyal obedience to the emperor, protesting to all in the
Holy Land that it was Frederick's intention to preserve

---

[1] Georges, *Jean de Brienne*, p. 58 ff.

[2] He strongly urged John to accept the offer made to him : " Li
apostoilles li dist ce c'om li avoit mandé de Constentinobie, et molt
li proia qu'il le feist, et qu'il s'en conseillast." Ernoul, *Chron.*, c. 41,
p. 470.

[3] Hence his letters are henceforth addressed " Friderico illustri
Romanorum imperatori, semper augusto, Hierusalem et Sicilie regi."
Ep. of Aug. 12, 1231, ap. H.-B., iii, p. 297. When in this letter Gregory
says that he has not hitherto given Frederick the title of King of
Jerusalem, he would appear to have forgotten his letter of March 23,
1227.

[4] " Quasi regnum Jerozolimitanum imperiali dicioni subesset." *Ib.*

each one's right intact,[1] and he strove to assure the emperor that he worked for him because he was convinced that " in the exaltation of the empire, which was the defensive arm of the Apostolic See, the Church was exalted, and that in the depression of the empire, which was the mirror of the Church, the Church was itself depressed." [2] With all the Pope's help, Frederick's schemes in the East were not very successful. His authority in Palestine was vested in his marshal, Richard Filangeri, whose haughty conduct was the cause of much of the turmoil in which the Holy Land was kept after Frederick's departure. The marshal, moreover, failed in his attempt to carry out his instructions to break the power of the house of Ibelin in Cyprus. Through that power, Henry of Lusignan became king of the island in 1232. It was consequently lost to the empire; [3] and, though the emperor kept a hold on Palestine for some time longer, Queen Alix or Alice of Cyprus and her second husband were in 1243 declared regents of the kingdom for her son king Henry of Cyprus, and Frederick's garrison was expelled. " Thus," says the Chronicle of Cyprus, "was plucked out the horrid nest of the Lombards, so that they had never any more power in Syria or in Cyprus." [4]

---

[1] Epp. of July 26 ff., 1232, ap. Rod., i, pp. 383 ff. He tells the patriarch of Jerusalem that his action against the emperor is getting the Pope into trouble, " as there is one who, drawing an argument for the past from the present troubles, contends that it was not devotion to the Apostolic See that caused you to oppose him, but hatred of his person—odium aliunde conceptum." P. 383. *Cf.* ep. March 22, 1234, *ib.*, p. 471 ; epp. Aug. 7 ff., 1234, *ib.*, pp. 480–3. *Cf.* epp. July 28, 1235, *ib.*, p. 548 f. ; of Sept. 22, 1235, *ib.*, 554 ff. ; of Feb. 23, 1236, *ib.*, p. 573.

[2] Ep. cit., p. 554.

[3] *Cf.* the French continuation of William of Tyre, l. xxv, c. 20 ff., ap. *P. L.*, t. 201, p. 1021 f.

[4] *Gestes des Chiprois*, p. 143, n. 243. "Adonc fu desraciné, et araché le pesme ni (for nid) des Longuebars, si qu'onques puis n'orent pooir en Surie ni en Chipre." Ed. G. Raynaud, Geneva, 1887.

The emperor also experienced the Pope's help during these years of peace in connexion with his son Henry VII., who was his representative in Germany. Frederick had reason to suspect his son's loyalty at least as early as the spring of 1232.[1] At that time father and son were reconciled through the mediation of the princes of the empire ;[2] but Frederick remained far away from Germany, and there seemed to Henry to be abundant opportunity for rendering himself independent. Accordingly, "led away by evil counsellors," he showed favour to his father's enemies, and did not hesitate steadily to thwart his wishes,[3] although he had sworn to the Pope not to be a party to any detrimental act to his father under penalty of excommunication.[4] He even entered into negotiations with the Lombard League.[5]

Now in real distress, Frederick sought out Gregory at Reate towards the end of May (1234). He brought with him his little son Conrad, and implored the help of the Pope against Henry.[6] He would leave his son in the

---

[1] See a document of Apr., 1232, ap. H.-B., iv, p. 325, in which some twelve princes state that they had been requested by Henry, King of the Romans, to mediate between him and his father, and to swear that, if the King did not abide by the promises he had made, they would support the emperor and abandon his son.

[2] *Ib.*

[3] See ep. Greg., July 5, 1234, ap. *ib.*, p. 473.

[4] Ep. of Henry, Apr. 10, 1233, ap. H.-B., " Rouleaux de Cluny " in *Notices des MSS.*, t. xxi, pt. ii, p. 356.

[5] *Chron. re reb. in Ital. gest.*, an. 1234, pp. 151–2, ed. H.-B. This Ghibelline author pretends that the Pope was privy to these schemes : " Et hæc de mandato P. Gregorii tractabantur." It must be borne in mind that this writer is not a contemporary. *Cf. supra*, vol. ix, p. 308 n. There is, however, no reason to doubt that Henry endeavoured to strengthen his position by an alliance with the League. *Cf. Annal. Marbac.*, an. 1235, p. 96, ed. Bloch, etc.

[6] *Vit. Greg.*, c. 20. " Contra Heinricum ejus filium, in ipsius juris invidiam sibi jura imperii vindicantem, ad Ecclesie patrocinium implorandum, Reate concitus nec invitatus advenit." *Cf.* Ric. of S. Ger., p. 146, ed. Gaudenzi, and *Chron. Sic.*, ap. H.-B., *Hist. dip.*, i, pt. ii, p. 905.

Pope's hands as a hostage, and he would help him against the Romans if only he would help him against his rebellious son.[1] Gregory received the emperor most kindly,[2] and promised to do all he could to bring the undutiful son back to the path of virtue.

But it was to no purpose that Gregory warned the youthful sovereign, that, as the emperor was the divinely appointed defender of the Church, any injury done to him was done to the Church.[3] The misguided youth continued in his evil course, and so the Pope sent instructions to the archbishop of Trier to the effect that, if Henry would not obey his father, he was to proclaim throughout Germany that the excommunication which Henry had invoked on himself, in the event of his disobedience, had now fallen upon him.[4] Then, following the example of Frederick,[5] Gregory supported this command by a letter to the princes (March 12, 1235) urging them to strive to bring back the king to his duty, and declaring null and void all oaths taken against the emperor.[6] On the same day he also bade the bishop of Ratisbon, the imperial chancellor, send to Rome certain ecclesiastics who had attached themselves to the king's party.[7]

Henry, however, continued to set both Pope and

---

[1] *Vita, ib.*

[2] " Post familiare convivium quod eadem mensa et scutella communis utrique principi ministrarat." *Ib.* Gregory's biographer believes that even on this occasion Frederick was playing a part ; and in later times Dante's famous commentator Benvenuto da Imola, *Coment. in Infern.* XIII., vol. i, p. 443, ed. Lacaita, asserted that Henry was completely innocent, but was suspected by Frederick of being in league with the Roman Church because he had urged him to cease injuring that Church to which he owed so much.

[3] *Ep. cit.*

[4] Ep. July 5, 1234, ap. H.-B., iv, p. 473.

[5] *Cf.* Frederick's letters of Feb. or March, 1235, to the Princes, and then to the people of Worms, *ib.*, p. 524 ff.

[6] *Ib.*, p. 530.

[7] *Ib.*, p. 532.

emperor at defiance till the latter appeared in Germany with a large army, and, adds Gregory's biographer, " furnished with papal letters like a new legate of the Roman Church (1235)." [1] Great must have been the astonishment of the less luxurious Germans when they beheld their emperor, whom they had not seen for some fifteen years, enter their cities " with numerous carriages profusely ornamented with gold and silver, with purple and fine linen, and with gems and precious fittings, with camels and mules and dromedaries, and bringing with him to guard his money and his treasures, crowds of Saracens and Ethiopians skilled in curious arts, and accompanied by apes and leopards." [2]

With so great a force did he come that he was able to lay siege to ten of his son's castles at once.[3] The king's supporters fell away from him rapidly, and he had to throw himself upon his father's mercy.[4] This he obtained (July),[5] and on August 1, Gregory commissioned the bishop of Ratisbon to remove from him the sentence of excommunication.[6] It would seem, however, that at any rate before this commission reached Germany, Henry had been cast into prison, from which death alone was to release him. He had refused to comply with some of the conditions of reconciliation, and had been at once committed to prison in Heidelberg. He was ultimately removed to Apulia, where he died in 1242.[7]

---

[1] *Vita*, c. 25.

[2] Godfrey of Viterbo, *Contin. Eberbac.*, ap. *M. G. SS.*, xxii, p. 348.

[3] Roger of Wendover, *Chron.*, sub fin.

[4] *Ib. Cf. Annal. Erphord.*, an. 1234 ; and *Chron. Sic.*, ap. H.-B., i, pt. ii, p. 905.

[5] *Cf.* ep. of Conrad, bp. of Hildesheim to the Pope, *c.* July 20, 1235, ap. H.-B., iv, p. 730.

[6] Ap. H.-B., *ib.*, pt. ii, p. 738.

[7] *Chron. Sic.*, ap. H.-B., i, p. 905 f. ; *Chron. de rebus in Ital.*, pp. 152, 187 ; *Annal. Wormat.*, an. 1233, ap. *M. G. SS.*, xvii ; *Chron. reg. Colon.*, *Contin. IV.*, an. 1235, p. 266 ; Tolosanus, *Chron.*, c. 202, p. 732 ; etc.

Frederick
marries an
English wife,
1235.

In the interval between the reconciliation and punishment of king Henry, his father married, as his third wife, Isabella, the sister of our king Henry III., and of Richard, duke of Cornwall, afterwards king of the Romans (July 15).[1] Now it appears, from various letters of Frederick, that this marriage was to a very large extent the work of Pope Gregory. The emperor often declared to his friends that " in accordance with the ideas (ad tractatum et ordinationem) of our most dear father, the lord Gregory, by the grace of God supreme pontiff of the Holy Roman Church, we have decided to take to wife Isabella the sister of our most dear friend the illustrious king of England." [2] Moreover, having " full confidence in the Pope's paternal interest in him," he entrusted to him all the arrangements connected with the dowry which his wife was to bring to him, both the amount of it and the time in which it was to be paid.[3] Gregory also took upon himself the task of assuring the king of France that the marriage did not portend any hostile movement against his territory.[4] Similarly, when Frederick himself gave the French king the same assurance, he told him that his marriage was the result of the action of the Pope. In the previous summer (1234), so he wrote to Louis, when he had an interview with the Pope, and the latter had urged him to marry for the good of his soul, in order that he might lead a more honourable life, he had entrusted the task of finding him a wife to the paternal solicitude of Gregory

---

[1] Cf. the letter of Conrad just cited ; the *Annals of Worms*, and the close of the *Chronicle* of Roger of Wendover.

[2] Ep. of Nov. 15, 1234, ap. H.-B., iv, p. 503 ff.

[3] Ep. of Dec. 9, 1234, ap. *ib.*, p. 515 f.

[4] Ep. Apr. 16, 1235, *ib.*, p. 537. " Pro constanti teneas quod a nobis et imperatore . . . nihil in hac parte geritur per quod vel in minimo statui tuo derogetur."

himself, and it was on his advice that he was taking the
sister of the king of England.[1]

But the most important matter concerning which Gregory and
Frederick sought the Pope's support was the question of the Lombards,
his relations to the great Communes of Lombardy. 1230-6.
Whether it was that they had seen enough of Frederick's
character to enable them to be sure that he was by heredity,
by his natural character, and by resolve a thoroughgoing despot, and that on the first opportunity he would
break them to his will, or whether it was that immunity
from control since the death of Henry VI. and continued prosperity had rendered them disinclined to submit
to any authority which would force them to follow any
particular regime other than their own ideas, even, e.g.,
to cease from fighting with each other—it is certain that
the majority of the greatest of the Lombard Communes
soon made it clear that they would not accord to
Frederick that measure of submission to which they were
bound by the Peace of Venice and Constance.[2] We have
seen that during the pontificate of Honorius III. they
had shown themselves hostile to Frederick, and that
Gregory had had to exert himself to induce them to accept
the decision of that Pontiff in the dispute between them.
When Gregory himself not long afterwards stood in need
of support to enable him to resist the aggression of

[1] Ep. Apr. 25, 1235, *ib.*, p. 539. " Idem venerabilis pater attente
nos monuit ut matrimonium . . . gratia sobolis et honestioris vite
contrahere deberemus . . . Cumque duxerimus idem negocium com-
mittendum provisioni et arbitrio tanti patris providit et . . . rogavit
ut sororem illustris regis Anglorum . . . ducere deberemus, etc."
Gregory's biographer, who never spares Frederick, after assuring us
(c. 25) that he would never have obtained Isabella but for the intervention of the Pope, says that the emperor's object in marrying Isabella
was to get possession of England, the King and kingdom of which are
subject to the Roman Church both by willing devotion and by feudal
law "de cujus arbitrio rex et regnum devotionis proposito, et subjectionis
conditione dependent."
[2] *Cf. supra*, vol. x, pp. 114 ff., 247 f.

Frederick's vicar in Apulia, the Lombards promptly embraced his cause, and as we have also seen, managed to spare from the men they needed for their own internal dissensions some hundreds of soldiers to help him.

The Emperor proposes to hold a Diet in Ravenna, 1231.

Soon after the peace of San Germano had been concluded, the Pope wrote to the heads of the Lombard League (Rectoribus Societatis Lombardiæ) to tell them that Frederick had submitted, and had promised not to take reprisals for the assistance which they had granted the Roman Church.[1] He therefore bade them take the oath of fealty to him as agreed upon,[2] and soon afterwards, in accordance with Frederick's request, urged the people of Pistoria to be duly obedient to him.[3] Moreover, influenced perhaps by the news of the renewal of the League of the great cities of the March of Verona,[4] and certainly by Frederick's arbitrary conduct towards the Lombards,[5] Gregory counselled him to hold a " general Diet " in Lombardy in order to facilitate a complete understanding as to the imperial and communal rights. Frederick accordingly summoned a Diet to meet at Ravenna on November 1,[6] and the Pope bade his epis-

[1] Ep. Oct. 10, 1230, ap. H.-B., iii, 243.

[2] *Cf.* ep. March 25, 1231, ap. Rod., i, 350, wherein Gregory sent to Lombardy the "formam cautionis" according to which they had to swear.

[3] Ep. May 13, 1231, ap. H.-B., iii, 282.

[4] See the document whereby Mantua, Brescia, Vicenza, Padua, Verona, and Ferrara renew their League, July 12, 1231, H.-B., iii, p. 200 ff.

[5] According to the Pope he was acting more by might than right. *Cf.* ep. of May 18, ap. Rod., i, p. 355, "non juris ordine sed virium potestate procedas."

[6] Ep. of Fred. to the Genoese (Sept., 1231) in which he bade them send representatives to the Diet (generalis Curia) which he had summoned in accordance with the Pope's advice. Ap. H.-B., iv, p. 266 f. The object of the Diet was "pacem universalem imperii reformare, disponere statum Italiæ prosperum et tranquillum, sedare discidia civitates inter et extra ferventia et inter vicinos populos omnem turbinem et odii fomitem amovere."

copal agents in Lombardy instruct the rectors of the
League to offer every facility for the meeting of the
Diet.[1]

But the members of the League mistrusted Frederick
even more now than they had done in 1226.[2] They
formally renewed their League at Bologna (October, 1231),
against " all men and persons who wished to enter their
territory with violence." [3] Further, " in the interests
of peace and concord and in order that not even a spark of
trouble (scintilla mali) might arise between them and the
emperor," they sent picked envoys " to the greatness of
the Supreme Pontiff," humbly and earnestly to beg " his
highness and excellence" to urge the emperor not to
come to Lombardy with an army, and to point out to the
Pope that if he did so come, there might follow loss to
the Roman Church.[4]

Realizing that, under the circumstances, there was no
chance of a successful Diet on the Feast of All Saints
(November 1), the emperor prorogued it to the middle of
March (1232), but nevertheless entered Ravenna in the
course of the month with an army.[5] Presuming, therefore,

The League prevents its being held.

[1] Ep. Sept. 27, 1231, ap. H.-B., *l.c.*, p. 267.

[2] *Cf.* a document of May 11, 1232, ap. H.-B., iv, p. 348, where we
read that the League declared " timere de ipso (the emp.) ne velit
malum et gravamen inducere super eos, et ideo si qua faciunt vel
fecerunt, pro defensione sua se facere asserunt et fecisse."

[3] Codagnellus, ad an., and a document ap. H.-B., iv, 937.

[4] *Ib.*

[5] " Imperator cum militum comitiva Ravenam accedens ibi
yemavit." *Chron. de reb. in Ital.*, an. 1231, p. 150. Years after
(June, 1236) Frederick boldly asserted to the King of France that he
had entered Lombardy with an unarmed escort " sub inermi tantum-
modo et domestico comitatu." Ap. H.-B., iv, pt. ii, p. 875. These
assertions of Frederick, made years after the events to which they
relate, have no value when they clash with the statements to the
contrary of reliable contemporary witnesses. In this case the assertion
of the *imperialist* chronicler just cited in connection with Frederick's
army is supported by that of another equally imperialist writer,
Richard of S. Germano. He tells us that on Christmas Day, 1231,

no doubt justly, that he had come with warlike intentions, the troops of the League took possession of the passes of the Alps, and thereby cut off communication between the emperor and Germany.[1]

Gregory
attempts to
mediate,
1232.
Distressed at this state of things, as most fatal to the interests of the Holy Land, to which his heart was still turned, Gregory dispatched to Lombardy (January, 1232) James Pecoraria, cardinal bishop elect of Preneste, and Otho, cardinal deacon of St. Nicholas *in carcere Tulliano*.[2] Straightway on their arrival they invited the League to send envoys to meet them at Bologna on March 1 to discuss the situation.[3]   After the meeting, they proceeded to Ravenna ; but, before they reached it, Frederick left it privately and made haste to Venice, and thence by sea to Aquileia.[4]   There in April he had an interview with his son Henry and many of the princes of the empire,[5] and commanded them to appear in arms in Lombardy by the following March, giving them money for the purpose.[6]   Meanwhile, disgusted at the conduct of the

the emperor permitted his Sicilian levies to return home. He had evidently come with his feudal host. " Et eo die licentiam dedit omnibus de regno qui secum iverant in propria revertendi."

[1] " Imperator apud Ravennam manens, bellum molitur contra Longobardos, sed non proficit, Longobardis viam precludentibus filio suo regi et milicie Germanorum." *Chron. reg. Colon., Cont.*, an. 1232, p. 263.   *Cf.* Corio (†1519), *Histor. di Milano*, p. 95 v., cited ap. H.-B., *Hist. dip.*, iv, p. 284 f. ; ep. Fred., *l.c.*, and a document of May 11, 1232, ap. H.-B., *ib.*, p. 348.

[2] Ric. of San. Ger., and Codagnellus, ad an. 1232.   On the distinguished card. James P., *cf.* a little pamphlet (estratto dall' *Archivio Storico per le Provincie Parmensi*, 1902) by Mons. P. Piacenza, *Cardinale Jacopo P.*, Parma, 1905, where various points (e.g., the date of his death, June 25, 1244) connected with his career are cleared up.

[3] Cod., *l.c.*

[4] *Ib.*, *Chron. de rebus in Ital.* ; Tolosanus, *Chron.*, c. 194.

[5] A document in H.-B., iv, p. 329, supplies us with the names of many of them, archbishops, bishops, abbots, dukes, etc.

[6] " Qui omnes (the Princes) . . . sua juraverunt precepta, dando eis in mandatis et districte precipiens ut quilibet eorum cum forcia

emperor, which they justly regarded as an insult to their
master, the cardinals returned to Bologna and dismissed
the envoys.[1]   However, before he returned to Apulia
(c. May 20) Frederick named Hermann von Salza his
plenipotentiary to treat with his " beloved friends " the
cardinals as arbitrators, and he promised to accept the
agreement to which with them the Grand Master might
give his consent.[2] On their side the rectors of the " League
of Lombardy, the March (of Verona) and Romania," also
agreed to accept the mediation of the cardinals, and to
discuss with them the alleged grievances of both parties.
These were mainly on the part of the emperor, that the
League had most seriously offended him in preventing
the holding of the Diet at Ravenna which he had summoned
in the interests of the Holy Land, of the empire, and of
other important matters.   This they had done by closing
the passes of the Alps.   On the part of the League, it
was contended that they were afraid that the emperor
intended to injure them, and that they were acting
throughout in self-defence.   Consequently a means had
to be sought of making satisfaction to the emperor, and
of guaranteeing the safety of the League, if king Henry
and the princes of Germany were to be allowed free access
to the emperor.   In all cases of doubt the legates and the
Pope were to be the ultimate referees.[3]

After what we have seen of the warlike arrangements The
made by Frederick at Aquileia, it is not surprising that Emperor not
the efforts of the cardinals to preserve peace were not in earnest.
successful.   The emperor's representative did not put in

militum ad partes Lombardiæ usque ad kalendas marcii accedere
deberet." *Chron. de reb.*, p. 151.

[1] Cod., p. 111.

[2] See the document of May 10, 1272, ap. H.-B., iv, p. 344 ff.

[3] See the documents of May 13, 1232, ap. H.-B., iv, p. 346 ff.
" Reservata eisdem legatis et d. Pape potestate interpretandi si aliquod
dubium fuerit super omnia supradicta."

an appearance at one conference, so that the Pope
decided to proceed with the negotiations himself on the
feast of All Saints (November 1).[1] Frederick was, however, bent on war, for a letter of November 15 shows
him calling upon the prelates and nobles of Burgundy to
join him with their armed contingents in the following
May.[2] He also took under his protection Ezzelino III. da
Romano [3] who was to earn a dreadful notoriety for his
infamous cruelties, and who, in opposition to the League,
had made himself master of Verona, the key to the passes
of the Alps in its vicinity.

Meanwhile, however, the negotiations went on. The
Lombard ambassadors reached Anagni in November, but
it was not till December that Peter della Vigna and the
other envoys of the emperor arrived.[4] The imperial
agents were the bearers of a most philosophically subtle
letter on " the two swords." Because two swords were
said to be *here*,[5] i.e., in the same sheath of the Church,
one cannot be drawn without the other. Hence the Pope
and the emperor, who are one with the union of Father
and Son, must draw this sword against " the perverters
of the faith, and those who rebel against the empire." [6]

---

[1] Ep. of July 12 to the Emperor, ap. *ib.*, p. 366.
[2] Ep. ap. H.-B., iv, 403. " Imperialis edicti auctoritate citamus
. . . quatenus in proximo futuro maio ad nos veniatis cum armatorum
laudabili comitiva." This attempt on the part of Frederick to convert
his nominal suzerainty in Burgundy (Arles) into a real one is curious.
It evidently seemed so to Frederick himself, as he notes that for a
long time past the Burgundians have not rendered any service to the
Emperor. This was no doubt due, he said, to the fact that they had
not been asked to do so.
[3] Epp. of Dec., 1232, ap. *ib.*, p. 406 ff.
[4] Ric. of S. Ger. *Cf.* ep. Fred. of Dec. 3, 1232, ap. *ib.*, p. 408 ff.
[5] " Lord, behold, here are two swords." St. Luke xxii, 38.
[6] *Ep. cit.* " Igitur, beatissime pater, nos duo qui unum dicimur
et idem pro certo sentimus, salutem communis fidei unanimiter
procuremus, relevemus ecclesiasticam libertatem oppressam, et tam
ecclesie jura quam imperii restaurantes, commissos nobis gladios in

But whilst his envoys were talking, Frederick was Rebellion in acting. His vassals of the kingdom were ordered to be ^{Sicily.} ready to join him with all their men on the first of February, 1233.[1] Once more, however, the emperor's schemes failed. Rebellion broke out in Sicily proper, and though it was stamped out with cruel treachery in April,[2] it delayed Frederick's march to the North. Besides, with Henry's plotting for a share of the empire,[3] and with the general neglect of the imperial call to arms on the part of the great ones of the kingdom of Arles,[4] he would not have found much support in the north. He accordingly temporized with the Pope, who urged him to make peace with the Lombards, and to agree to lay aside all enmity to the League if it guaranteed five hundred men to help him in the Holy Land for two years.[5] After expressing discontent at what he declared to be the inadequacy of the compensation offered him,[6] Frederick agreed to accept it,[7] and in April (1234) placed the whole question of his relations with " Lombardy, the March of Treviso (Verona) and Romaniola " in the hands of " our Mother the Holy Roman Church, which impartially preserves the rights of all." [8] He was in this submissive mood, seeing that he

perversores fidei et rebelles imperii acuamus." Altogether this is one of the most curious imperial letters ever written.

[1] Ric. of S. Ger.

[2] *Ib., contin. G. Malater.*, ap. *R. I. SS.*, v, 604 ; *Chron. Sic.*, ap. H.-B., iii, p. 905. Some of the rebels were burnt. *Cf.* ep. Greg. of Feb. 10, 1233, ap. H.-B., iv, 423.

[3] *Annal. Schefttar.*, an. 1233, ap. *M. G. SS.*, xvii, 340.

[4] *Cf.* Fournier, *Le Royaume d'Arles*, p. 133 ff.

[5] Ep. of Greg. to Fred., June 5–7, 1233, ap. H.-B., iv, 431.

[6] Ep. of July 12, 1233, ap. *ib.*, p. 442.

[7] Ep. Aug. 14, *ib.*, p. 451.

[8] Ep. of Apr., 1234, *ib.*, p. 465. " Nos attendentes qualiter S. R. Ecclesia mater nostra singulis, ex debito, quo tenetur indifferenter ad omnes, illibata jura conservet, etc." He professes that he ought to regulate his work for the honour of the Church and the reformation of the Empire according to the advice of the Roman Church. *Cf.*

needed the Pope's help, because, as we have said, his son Henry in Germany was in rebellion and was, moreover, making friends with the Lombards.[1]

Naturally pleased at this readiness on the part of the emperor to forward the cause of peace, Gregory, who was greatly in need of his aid against the Romans, endeavoured to uphold him against his rebellious son by exhorting the Lombards to allow troops to come from Germany to Frederick,[2] by receiving him most courteously at Reate, by supporting his interests in Palestine, and by ordering the German bishops to take steps against Henry.[3]

Frederick goes to Germany, 1235.

When he had secured the goodwill of the Pope, and had asked him to instruct the men of Spoleto and the March of Ancona to help him,[4] Frederick proceeded to Germany, and, as we have seen, soon broke the power of his rebellious son (1235). But then, feeling strong in the support of the German princes,[5] and trusting that by his marriage with Isabella of England he had secured the alliance of its king,[6] he was no longer disposed to stand by his engagements with Gregory regarding the Lombards. Their encouragement of the designs of king Henry renewed all his resentment against them. At a great Diet at Mainz

ep. of Sept., 1234, ap. *ib.*, p. 490, and a corresponding letter of Gregory, Oct. 27, ap. *ib.*, p. 491. Frederick explained that by the whole question (totum negotium) he understood both the past excesses of the Lombards, and their detention of the regalian and other rights of the Empire.

[1] " Fredericus intellexit Henricum . . . contra eum cum Lombardis conjurasse." Tolosanus, *Chron.*, c. 202. *Cf. Mon. Patav. Chron.*, ap. *R. I. SS.*, viii, p. 674, and *supra*, p. 330.

[2] Ep. May 20, 1234, ap. H.-B., iv, 470. These troops were summoned from Germany largely at least to help the Pope against the rebellious Romans. See *infra*, p. 286.

[3] *Cf.* ep. of July 6, 1234, ap. *ib.*, p. 473, and *supra*.

[4] Ap. H.-B., iv, p. 484.

[5] See the letter of bishop Conrad cited above, p. 251.

[6] Cf. Fournier, *Le Roy. d'Arles*, p. 138 ff., on the importance of the Emperor's change of policy about this time. He turned from France and Provence to England and Toulouse.

(August) he appealed to the German princes for aid against the Lombards, and found that they were not unwilling to grant it.[1] He thereupon resolved to crush the Lombards by force.

He did not, however, directly take out of Gregory's hands the task of settling the difficulties between himself and the League which he had so freely committed to him, but he did so in effect. He informed the Pope that, if he did not succeed in settling the differences between himself and the Lombards before Christmas, he and the German princes would invade Lombardy in the ensuing April (1236).[2] Gregory at once declared that the addition of such a condition rendered vain all hope of a settlement by negotiation, as the time allotted was all too short, and begged that the emperor would leave the matter in his hands absolutely, as he had done in the first instance (September 22).[3] Still, though he protested to Frederick that the time allowed for the transaction of such important business was " far too short," he called upon the rectors of the League to send plenipotentiaries to him by

Altered tone of Frederick to the Pope re the Lombards, 1235.

---

[1] Cf. Annal. Argent., ap. Boehmer, Fontes, iii, p. 109. Cf. a letter of Fred. (June, 1235) ap. Chron. de reb. in Ital., p. 153 ; and documents ap. H.-B., iv, pp. 759, 930. In the last letter addressed to his subjects of the kingdom of Sicily towards the end of the year 1236 Frederick boasted that he had Germany with him ready to crush " a certain factious section in Italy," " ad cujus expugnationem animosa Germania plene nostris exposita manibus se satis viriliter et potenter accingit . . . Multas nam nobis personas Germania germinat."

[2] Cf. the document just cited, from H.-B., iv, p. 759, and Frederick's long letter of June, 1236, ap. H.-B., iv, 872 ff. In this letter the emperor stated that through his agent Peter della Vigna he had held out hopes of the time allowed for the negotiations being prolonged to the feast of the Purification. See also a letter of Gregory to Fred. of March 21, 1236, ap. ib., p. 824.

[3] See Gregory's letter to Hermann von Salza, ap. Rod., i, p. 556. Cf. his letter to Fred. of March 21, 1236. " In eisdem litteris (of the emperor) talis extitit adjecta conditio per quam compromissum penitus tollebatur, et tantum non videbatur posse negotium terminari."

December 1, and asked the emperor to send Hermann von Salza to assist in the negotiations.[1]

War in sight. The Lombards renew their League, 1235.

Whatever hopes may have been entertained by Gregory of preventing hostilities between the emperor and the Lombards would appear not to have been shared by the latter. They, at least the Milanese and the inhabitants of some ten other great cities, renewed their League (November 5–7) and their resolve to prevent " the Teutons and their allies from coming to the detriment of the League of Lombardy." [2] As the Lombard envoys were really unable (so at least they said) to reach the Pope in time,[3] no conference was held by him in December on the matters in dispute between Frederick and the Lombard cities. The year 1235, therefore, came to an end with every prospect of war, and that not only between the emperor and the Lombards, but also between the emperor and the Pope. Gregory must have been profoundly disgusted at Frederick's mocking treatment of him in this question of his arbitrations in Lombardy, and must have felt that there was now no hope of his being able to restrain any longer the despotic nature of the emperor.

Gregory's difficulties with Frederick during the years of peace.

Even during these years of comparative peace, when Frederick made profession of acting in union with the Church,[4] the Pope had had no little difficulty in keeping

[1] Ep. of Sept. 23, 1235, ap. *ib.*, p. 557. *Cf.* ep. of Sept. 26, *ib.*, p. 560.

[2] See the documents regarding this renewal ap. H.-B., iv, p. 796 ff. The Lombards, fearing the emperor's power, wished to guard themselves against possible danger to their liberties : " tue metu potentie sibi a futuris student casibus precavere." Ep. of Greg. ap. *ib.*, p. 813. Feb. 28, 1236.

[3] See the last letter, and one of Apr. 1 to the Rectors of the League.

[4] Ep. Oct. 27, 1232, ap. H.-B., iv, 401 ff. From what Frederick's envoys had told the Pope of their master's intentions, Gregory in this letter expresses the hope that now the Church and the Empire are going to bear and to lighten one another's burdens.

him within bounds. He had had to urge him not to persecute the Church and not to be an enemy of public liberty,[1] not to turn on those who had once been his creatures,[2] and not to burn his enemies under the pretence of burning heretics.[3] He had, moreover, also been obliged, after he had had to find fault with some of the emperor's acts, to endeavour to soothe the imperial temper irritated at being even justly called to account.[4]

From the details which have been given so far in this chapter, it would be fair to conclude that all the favours during these years of peace between the empire and the Church were granted by the Pope to the emperor. That such, however, was not the case was stated at the beginning of the chapter, and will be established by details when, in treating of Gregory as a local sovereign, we shall have occasion to relate the aid given by Frederick to him against his rebellious subjects.

[1] Epp. of July 5, 1231, ap. H.-B., iii, p. 289 f.
[2] Ep. of June 7, 1231, in behalf of the son of the Duke of Spoleto, ap. ib., p. 286.
[3] Ep. of July 15, 1233, ap. ib., iv, p. 444.
[4] Ep. July 27, 1231, ap. ib., p. 498.

CHAPTER IV.

GREGORY AND FREDERICK II. RENEWED HOSTILITIES BETWEEN THEM. THE POPE RESISTS THE EMPEROR'S ATTEMPT AT GRASPING "WORLD-POWER" (1236–1241).[1]

Frederick and the Pope. Their changed relations.

DESPITE the ominous close of the year 1235, there was no overt hostility between the Pope and the emperor for a year or two, not even though Frederick's attack on the Lombard League had begun before the year 1236 had run its course. In fact, Frederick continued to try to secure the support of the Pope in his efforts against the Lombards, and begged our king to use his influence in his behalf. Accordingly, on June 3, Henry wrote to ask Gregory to assist the emperor against the rebellious Lombards, " as far as he could with justice." [2] Whatever answer the Pope returned to this communication, he continued for many more months his efforts to keep the peace between the Lombards and Frederick.

Frederick's resolve to crush Lombardy.

But the latter, feeling strong now that the rebellion of his son had been crushed, that he had an easy road into Italy, as Verona the key to the Brenner pass was in the

---

[1] His heart, says Brunetto Latini, *Li Livres dou Trésor*, L. i, pt. ii, c. 95, was set on being the lord of the world. " Ses cuers ne bavit à autre cose fors que a estre sires et souverains de tout le monde. . . . Il cuidoit bien par lui et par ses filz sousprendre tot l'empire et la terre toute, en tel maniere que ele n'issist jamais de leur subjection." P. 92, ed. Chabaille. This insatiate ambition of the Emperor of Germany was in the thirteenth century crushed principally by the influence of the Popes ; now (April, 1915) to do the same work it is requiring the united efforts of millions of men of several nationalities, and is costing millions of lives. B. Latini (†1294), born in Florence in 1230, took a distinguished part in the government of his native city, and suffered exile through his devotion to the Church party (that of the Guelfs). *Cf. supra*, vol. ix, pp. xxxviii and xliii

[2] Rymer, *Fœdera*, i, pp. 228–9.

hands of his partisan Ezzelino, that he had the men of Germany to fill the ranks of his armies, and that he had the wealth of Sicily to fill his treasury, was resolved to bend the Lombards to his will. " The splendour of our position urges us," so he proclaimed to his people, " to exact due subjection and obedience from those over whom the Roman empire holds sway." [1] " Why is it that the providence of God has so assisted us that the Eastern kingdom of Jerusalem . . . the kingdom of Sicily . . . and the most powerful kingdom of Germany . . . are living at peace and in loyalty to our name, except that in this way that section of Italy which our power encompasses on all sides may return to our obedience and to the unity of the empire ? " [2] For " some people in Italy would despise the imperial sceptre, and, forgetful even of their own advantage, would prefer the luxury of some shadowy liberty to peace and quiet, and to law and justice." [3] " Italy, as is well known to all the world, is my inheritance. It would be equally wrong and wicked to strive for what belongs to another, and to abandon what belongs to oneself, especially when insolent Italians, insolent Milanese especially, have loaded me with injuries and have shown me no manner of reverence." [4] Germany was ready to purge the granary of the cockle of Italian sedition. It would supply him with a numerous army to crush the Italian rebels and to bring peace to himself and the kingdom of Sicily which would furnish him with the

[1] Ep. May, 1236, ap. H.-B., iv, pt. ii, p. 848. " Nos excitat Cæsaree fortune fastigium, ut ab eis, quos Romane ditionis habet imperium, subjectionis et obedientie debitum exigamus."

[2] Ib.

[3] Ep. June, 1236, ap. ib., p. 873. " Quidam Italiæ populi sceptrum contemnere conantur imperii, ac etiam proprie commoditatis immemores, libertatis cujusdam vage luxuriam quieti pacis imponunt, et equitati justitie pretulerunt."

[4] Ep. end of June, 1236, ib., p. 881.

money for this great undertaking.[1]   It is true that there
is some trouble in Austria, but we have sent four armies
there, and will nevertheless enter Italy with a great army.
" Know," he wrote to his vicar in Italy, Gebhard von
Arnstein, " that the sending of the armies into Austria
has not lessened the army with which we intend with good
fortune to cross the Alps, but has rather increased it, so
that all may realize that so great is the power of the
empire that we can raise many different armies." [2]
When he had made up his mind to punish rebellious
subjects, it was intolerable that an outsider should step
in and thwart in any way the execution of his designs.[3]

Gregory fails
to make
peace, or to
obtain re-
dress of
grievances,
1236.

Such being the openly avowed ideas of Frederick, it is
clear that, despite his asserted wishes to the contrary,
" imperial prosperity had hurried him from humility to
virulent pride," [4] and that no man could have induced

[1] See Frederick's letters to the Sicilians of the close of the year
1236, ap. *ib.*, p. 932.   In place of demanding men which Germany
will supply he asks them to give him plenty of money : " In liberali
sustentatione rerum vestrarum gratie nostre premium hilariter
repensetis."

[2] " Scias insuper quod pro exercitibus missis in Austrian, nedum
quod minoratus sit numerus militum cum quibus Alpes disposuimus
prospera sorte transire immo pocius crevit, ut pateat universis tantam
imperii esse potentiam, quod diversos exercitus facere possumus et
habere."   Ep. July 11, 1236, ap. *ib.*, p. 889.   What Englishman in
1915, when he reads such utterances, would not think he was listening
to the Kaiser of his own days ?

[3] A letter of June, 1236, in which Frederick denounces the Lombards
to the King of France, concludes with this attack, seemingly on the
work of the Pope for peace.   He calls on all Princes to consider what
it means when, after they have to punish rebellious subjects, " vestris
negotiis extrinsecus aliquis se interponat, causamque aliquam . . .
afferat, per quam vestra precidat proposita."   Ap. *ib.*, p. 880.   He
induced Béla, King of Hungary, to write (July 5) to the Pope in the
same strain.   Ap. H.-B., " Rouleaux de Cluny," in *Notices des MSS.*,
t. xxi, pt. ii, p. 362.

[4] He expressed anxiety " ne imperialis prosperitatis eventibus de
humilitatis homine rapti in virus superbie subito videremur."   Ep.
March, 1237, ap. H.-B., v, 34.

him to grant peace to any but to such as were willing to
bend an abject knee before him. Gregory at any rate
failed to keep the peace between the Lombards and the
emperor, or to induce the latter to refrain from exercising
those ecclesiastical rights in Sicily which he had expressly
resigned.

At the beginning of this eventful year, 1236, which was
to see the commencement of a fourteen years' war between
Frederick and the Lombard League, Gregory, while
thanking the emperor for what he had done for the Church,
and while assuring him that both before and after he
became Pope he had, even unknown to him, worked in his
interests, complained to him that " in the kingdom," the
churches were plundered and their ministers exiled by the
imperial agents ; that the very stones of churches were
used to erect barracks for the Saracens at Lucera, and
that, against the terms of the treaty of San Germano,
certain nobles had been treated in the most shameful
manner. Should the emperor urge in excuse the renewal
of the Lombard League, the Pope averred that they
are liars who say that that was due to the Church, and he
urged that it ought not to be imputed to him " if the
Lombards or others, through fear of your power, strive to
guard themselves against future dangers, and, in accordance with the dictates of worldly wisdom, set afloat such
stories regarding the Church as they think will be for their
own advantage." [1] The actions of the Pope prove that
he had done nothing against the imperial interests in
Italy. But with regard to the abuses which continue to be
perpetrated in the kingdom (of Sicily) the emperor ought
to fulfil his promises as to their amendment, or otherwise

Gregory complains of abuses in the kingdom of the two Sicilies, 1236.

---

[1] Ep. Feb., 1236, ap. H.-B., iv, 813. "Nam si Lombardi vel alii
tue metu potentie sibi a futuris student casibus precavere . . . non
est quod nobis valeat imputari."

the claims of justice must be attended to without further delay.[1]

To these complaints Frederick at first returned an answer which, if not altogether in good taste, was not ill-natured. Consideration for " the rock of Peter," as he expressed it, compelled him to be mindful of the Pope's position. But he had not the eyes of a lynx that he could see from Germany what his officials were doing in the kingdom of Sicily, nor had he a voice of thunder so that he could make his wishes heard there, and he really did not know what his officials might be doing in his absence. Moreover, if it was merely that the rights in connexion with episcopal elections which had been held by his predecessors were being exercised, no wrong was being done to anyone.[2]

But, after he had entered Italy with an army, his tone with regard to the papal grievances in Sicily distinctly changed. Writing from his camp when he was besieging Mantua (September 20, 1236), he complained that the Pope had not supported him in Lombardy by excommunicating the Lombards, and asserted that what the Pope called abuse of ecclesiastical privilege was merely the preservation by him of rights held by his predecessors who had not equalled him in power or renown. Though he intended, he continued, to live and die in the Catholic faith, and was resolved to punish those who interfered with it or with the work of the Crusades which he considered to be his especial concern, he was nevertheless resolved to put down those who under cover of religion preached sedition, such as John of Vicenza, a Dominican whose remarkable spiritual and political career anticipated that of the Dominican Savanorola.[3] The churches of

[1] Ib.

[2] Ep. Apr. 16, 1236, ap. ib., 828 ff.

[3] Cf. Kington, Fred. II., i, p. 505 ff., for a notice of the wonderful work for internal peace among the Lombard cities wrought by friar

Sora he declared he would not restore, because that city had incurred his wrath and had been banned for ever ; nor would he readily order the repair of Monreale. Restitution in certain cases he had ordered to be made, but should anything be lacking in this matter, the Pope must remember that he himself would not restore Città di Castello to the empire.[1]

In his reply to this very assertive document, the Pope animadverted on its style, and on the style of other letters which he himself and the cardinals had lately received from " his imperial excellency." They were haughty and wholly wanting in " the manna of sweetness." Then, perhaps at necessary, certainly at great, length he replied to the emperor's allegations in order. With regard to his action concerning the Lombards the emperor's own agent, Hermann von Salza, would be able to enlighten him. Besides, the Lombard envoys could not get to him within the time prescribed by the emperor.[2] Even with regard to those promises of giving satisfaction which the emperor had made he could not trust them, as he had been deceived so often.[3] Concerning, therefore, the oppression of churches and individuals in the kingdom, " in which without your authority no man moves hand or foot, it is unworthy of you to oppose to our positive assertions the negative of imperial ignorance." It was preposterous to

Gregory's further protest.

John, especially during the year 1233.   He lost his influence by inter-fering too much in politics.

[1] Ep. of Sept. 20, 1236, ap. H.-B., iv, 905 ff.   This letter of Frederick, like so many others, is very long and very far from being readily intelligible in parts.

[2] Vide *supra*, p. 261.

[3] " Cujus (the emperor) pollicitus de satisfactione præstanda quibusdam ecclesiis et personis, sicut sic in principio, sic in fine non credimus, qui simili promissione delusos multoties nos dolemus." Ep. of Oct. 23, 1236, ap. H.-B., iv, p. 918.   The literary style of both the papal and imperial chancellaries is now becoming more ponderous, and hence the reading of their letters is becoming more onerous.

give as an excuse for not making restitution that we, against our conscience, would not give up Città di Castello. You knew that the rebellion of its inhabitants could not give you any right to a city of the Church. Moreover, it was not for the emperor to judge of the Pope's conscience. His conduct with regard to Sora and other persons and places showed that " against the peace made between you and the Church (the peace of San Germano), you are making yourself the judge of spiritual matters as well as secular." [1] Appealing then to the supposed Donation of Constantine, and to the generosity of Charlemagne, Gregory pointed out that Frederick was only concerned in injuring where they had been bountiful.[2] But, concluded the Pope, the worst thing about the emperor's conduct was that it was hindering " the recovery of the Holy Land, and the interests of the Cross." So act, then, " that God may never repent of having so greatly exalted you . . . and that we may, not without reason, rejoice in the Lord over the imperial prosperity."

War in Lombardy.

Whilst this correspondence, indicative of an approaching rupture between the Pope and the emperor, was going on, war had already broken out between Frederick and the Lombards, despite all the efforts of Gregory to stop it. He had assured the emperor that the Lombards were willing to come to terms, and that they had been unable to present themselves to him within the limited time finally fixed by Frederick. He had, moreover, begged the emperor to send back Hermann von Salza to continue the negotiations, and had sent envoys to the Lombard cities

---

[1] Ib. Cf. the detailed list of the Pope's grievances with regard to Sicily and that of the counter charges of the emperor, with the Pope's replies thereto. Ap. Rod., i, pp. 596–8.

[2] He speaks of " Urbem cum toto ducatu suo quam sparsis in ea pecuniis nobis turbare moliris." H.-B., ib., p. 921. Cf. Ric. of San Germano, who says that in this year (1236) Peter Frangipane made war on the Pope and the Senator in the emperor's interests.

to urge peace upon them.[1] While keeping up a show of negotiating with the Pope, Frederick began his preparations for war by sending into Verona before the end of April a body of five hundred mercenaries under the command of an experienced soldier, Gebhard of Arnstein.[2] At the same time he issued a proclamation in which he set forth that in crushing the Lombards he would be working for the benefit of " the Apostolic See, the head and Mother of all the churches . . . which derive their authority from it, and are instructed by its example," and for the good of the Crusades.[3] Accordingly, he intended, so he declared, to enter Italy in the summer " along with our princes," in order to eradicate heresy therefrom, to re-establish therein the rights of the Church and the empire, and to administer impartial justice. Moreover, as the peace which he had made with the Sultan was drawing to a close, he had decided to hold on the subject of the Crusade a great Diet at Piacenza, to which the envoys of all the cities of Italy were invited, and at which he expected to have the envoys " of all the kings of the West." [4]

The emperor was, however, not sure of the co-operation of his own princes. Frederick the Fighter, duke of Austria (1230–46), was aspiring to independence, and was conspiring with the Milanese.[5] Nevertheless, undeterred

Frederick enters Italy 1236.

[1] See his letters of March 21 ff., 1236, ap. Reg., vol. ii, pp. 333, 341 ff., 345, or ap. Rodenberg, i, pp. 576–83. On the " time limit," see also Gregory's letter of Oct. 23, 1236, ap. H.-B., iv, p. 917.

[2] *Chron. reg. Colon., Cont. IV.*, an. 1236, p. 268. " Imperator moturus bellum Longobardis sibi rebellibus," etc. *Cf. Annal. Argent.*, ap. Böhmer, *Fontes*, iii, 110.

[3] Ep. already cited of the beginning of May, 1236, ap. H.-B., iv, 847. " In hoc (i.e., in his subduing ' illius Italiæ medium ') crucis negotium directissime procuratur."

[4] *Ib.*

[5] Epp. Fred. ap. H.-B., iv, 852 and 883. *Cf. Chron. r. Col., ib.*, p. 269 ; and the *Annals* of the learned and diplomatic Benedictine abbot Hermann of Altaich (†1275) ap. Böhmer, *ib.*, ii, 504.

by the rebellion of the duke, he rejected the mediation of cardinal James Pecoraria, whom the Pope had, in accordance with the emperor's request for a legate, sent to Lombardy in June,[1] refused to consider the question of the Crusade until he had mastered Italy (Lombardy), the wealth of which was necessary for that purpose,[2] tried to win over the Romans,[3] dispatched four armies against Austria,[4] and at length descended into Italy (August, 1236).[5]

At once Lombardy was in a blaze, and " the Teutonic fury " proceeded to devastate the country.[6] Many of the cities made manly preparations to resist the Teuton,[7] but others, not from love of the emperor, but from hatred of

[1] June 10, 1236. *Vita Greg.*, c. 26. *Cf.* ep. Greg., ap. H.-B., iv, 870. Pecoraria was not of high enough birth for Frederick ! *Cf.* ep. Greg., Oct. 23, *ib.*, p. 916. See, however, *Chron. de reb. in Ital.*, an. 1236, p. 160. Frederick was enraged with him for making peace between the factions of Piacenza. *Cf. Vit. Greg.*, n. 26. *Cf.* also John de Mussis, *Chron. Placent.*, ap. *R. I. SS.*, xvi, p. 462. He notes that, after the peace, the people of Piacenza opposed the emperor. See also H.-B., iv, p. 904 n. ; v, 33.

[2] Ep. Fred., June, 1236, ap. ib., p. 880. The emperor declared to the Pope he was a Christian, ready to crush the enemies of the Cross, but he could not fight the Saracens when there were so many heretics to subdue in Italy. Besides, he needed money for the Crusade, and so "opes ejusdem terre in opem et ultionem Crucifixi convertere destinari. Abundat quidem Italia armis, equis et opibus."

[3] See his letter to them, ap. *ib.*, 901. *Cf.* ep. Greg. of Oct. 21, 1236, *ib.*, p. 921.

[4] Ep. Fred., July 11, 1236, *ib.*, p. 889.

[5] Parisius de Cereta (fl. 1279), one of the best of the Veronese chroniclers. *Ann. Veron.*, ap. *R. I. SS.*, viii, p. 629. *Cf.* on this expedition of Frederick a fragment, ap. H.-B., iv, p. 948 ff. ; Maurisius, *Cronica*, ap. *R. I. SS.*, viii, in the new ed., p. 37 ff. (on this time-server, see *supra*, Vol. xi, 203 n.) ; *Chron. de reb. in Ital.*, p. 161, which contains the fragment just mentioned ; etc.

[6] Rolandinus, one of our best guides in these affairs, *Cron.*, ap. *R. I. SS.*, viii, new ed., p. 47. " Theotonicus furor vastarit Gazum," etc.

[7] One of the last entries of Tolosanus records the sending by his City of soldiers to the service of the Lombard League at Mantua and Brescia. *Chron.*, c. 218, p. 742.

Milan, favoured his cause.[1] Acting " like a most savage dragon," [2] or " like a most benign lord," [3] according to points of view expressed by anti-imperialistic or imperialistic Italian writers, Frederick sacked Vicenza.[4] Then, with the aid of Ezzelino and Salinguerra, lord of Ferrara, who had been brought over by the tyrant of Verona to the side of the emperor, he was successfully subduing the March of Treviso (or Verona), when the rebellion of Austria forced him to return to Germany (November). His boasted four armies were unable to subdue the duke.

Meanwhile, whilst Frederick was forcing the duke of Austria [5] to temporary submission, or at least temporary helplessness, the Pope sent two fresh cardinals into Lombardy in the hope that they might succeed where Pecoraria had failed. They were his nephew Rainaldus, cardinal-bishop of Ostia, and Thomas of Capua, cardinal-priest of Sta. Sabina—both very distinguished men.[6] Moreover, in the spring of the year, he bade the Lombard cities send ambassadors to Mantua, there to meet the cardinals and to consult with them on making peace between themselves and with the emperor, and on the state of the Holy Land.[7]

Another embassy from the Pope, 1236.

[1] Maurisius, *ib.*, p. 37.

[2] Godi (†1313) of Vicenza, *Cron.*, ap. *R. I. SS.*, viii, p. 12 of the new ed.

[3] Maurisius, *l.c.*, p. 44. The unrestrained spirit of partisanship in which many Italian historians write makes the acquisition of truth from them by no means easy.

[4] Maurisius himself at first suffered in this dreadful sacking.

[5] That "furiosus ille juvenis " as the emperor called him. See his letter of Dec., 1237, ap. H.-B., v, 143.

[6] Ep. Greg., of Nov. 29, 1236, ap. Rod., i, p. 606. " Quorum publicis vacare laudibus superfluum reputamus . . . Sperantes ut quo plenius ipsos Dei sapientia virtutum insignibus dotasse dinoscitur, eo que sunt salutis et gratie facilius et felicius operentur." According to Gregory's biographer these legates also were sent at the emperor's request, " ad ipsius imperatoris instantiam." C. 26.

[7] Ep. of May 23, 1237, ap. *ib.*, p. 610. *Cf.* epp., *ib.*, pp. 609, 611.

Events were, however, steadily moving in the direction of continued war between Frederick and the Lombards, and towards an open quarrel between him and the Pope. Seemingly, without a word to Gregory, the emperor, whilst still in Austria, brought about the election of his son, the youthful Conrad, as king of the Romans, " by the archbishops of Maintz, Trier, and Salzburg, the bishops of Babenberg, Ratisbon, Frising, and Passau, the king of Bohemia, and the dukes of Bavaria and Carinthia, and the Landgrave of Thuringia," assembled at Vienna (February or March, 1237).[1] However, while ignoring the Pope in this important matter, Frederick, after leaving Austria (April), made some show of meeting his wishes by sending to him Hermann von Salza and Peter della Vigna to treat on the Lombard question.[2] But again it would seem that he was not very anxious for any peace which did not involve complete submission; for again did he limit the time for negotiations, and that, too, though the cardinals had had to put off the meeting at Mantua on account of a plague which they found raging there.[3] They received a very strong letter from Hermann von Salza who had returned from the Pope to the emperor, and who notified them (about the end of July) that he was coming to them. After telling them that the emperor was on the move " with a

---

[1] *Cf.* the election decree ap. H.-B., v, 29 ff., and *Chron. reg. Colon. Contin. IV.*, p. 270 f.   It is interesting to note this list of electors. The electors have not yet been reduced to seven.

[2] Ric. of S. Ger., an. 1237 ; Hermann of Altaich, *Annal.*, ap. Böhmer, *Fontes*, ii, p. 504.

[3] See their letter to the Pope of the beginning of July, 1237, ap. H.-B., v, 87.   They named Brescia as the new place of meeting and the feast of St. James, July 25, as the time ; they also informed the Pope that they had found all Lombardy torn with internal dissensions, and that prisoners were treated most inhumanely.   " Ecce mucro furit, ignis vorat, manus rapit, pupillo non parcitur, non excipitur vidua, et sacris reverentia non habetur."   However, by their exertions, prisoners, at any rate, were being better treated.

victorious army " to re-attack Lombardy, he impressed
upon them that at a recent meeting of the Chapter of the
Teutonic Knights, at which were present one hundred of
them, belonging to the noblest and most powerful families
of Germany (a fact he would like the cardinals and the
Apostolic See to grasp), all urged him to have nothing
more to do with the Lombard negotiations. " The
princes of Germany blamed him for negotiating, as they
wanted the Lombards to be brought into subjection to
the empire, and not by compromise but by the shedding of
blood, as a raging empire in arms requires." [1] He assured
the cardinals that it was only through deference to the
Pope's wishes that his Order allowed him to make a last
effort for peace. The " unconquerable " Cæsar is following
him, and if, when he arrives in Italy, a peace is not arranged,
he will at once let loose on the rebels the irresistible rush
of his Germans.[2]

There was, however, small chance of peace in Lombardy, with the local rivalries everywhere so strong.
Nevertheless, the cardinals, seemingly along with Thaddeus of Sessa and Peter della Vigna, " judges of the
emperor," [3] met the rectors of the Lombard League at
Fiorenzuola near Piacenza. As a basis for negotiation
the cardinals proposed that the Lombards should take
the oath of fealty to the Emperor, that they should
dissolve the League and not renew it, that they should
furnish the emperor with troops for the Crusade, that
they should give up all claims to the rights that belonged
to the empire, and that those who had been exiled from

War between members of the League, and supporters of the Emperor, 1237.

[1] The letter of Hermann, ap. *ib.*, p. 93. " Prout in arma furens
imperium exigit."

[2] " Incipiet contra rebelles vires suas strenue exercere, Theotonicorum
suorum furioso impetu dissoluto." *Ib.*

[3] At any rate, they are named as being with the cardinals soon after
their arrival in Lombardy. *Chron. de rebus in Ital.*, an. 1237, p. 164.

Piacenza should be restored.[1] The negotiations, however, came to nothing.[2] Whilst the Milanese and others were anxious to forward them, they were blocked by Zeno the Venetian podestà of Piacenza, who had been instructed not to agree to any concordat which did not include the Venetians. Seeing that there was no hope of peace, the cardinals withdrew from the assembly, observing that the Lombard was ready to accept terms of peace after he had inflicted the injury.[3]

It would seem that they did not meet Hermann von Salza at all.[4] However that may be, war between the emperor and the League was now inevitable, and it began by the people of Faenza, allies of Milan, attacking Ravenna which belonged to the imperial party. Frederick at once ordered assistance to be sent to his partisans, and amongst others who went to aid them, there came ten thousand Saracens from Lucera (August).[5]

The battle of Cortenuova, Nov., 1237. In the following month Frederick himself appeared in Italy at the head of a great army.[6] Success at first

---

[1] Ib., p. 166. "Dimittere et relaxare ei omnes rationes et jura imperii."

[2] Peter della Vigna would lead us to suppose that neither the cardinals nor the Lombards were in earnest. He tells the archbishop of Capua : "Labore tamen continuo laboro dum inter Charybdim et Scyllam, inter Cardinalium silicet et Lombardorum astutias, navicula filii tumidis fluctibus fatigatur." Ap. H.-B., Pierre de la Vigne, p. 306.

[3] Ib., p. 167. "Lombardus pactum post dampnum suscipit actum." I do not profess to know whether I have quite hit off the meaning of this dictum.

[4] As Frederick would not see them in October after his entry into Italy, they returned to Rome. Ric. of S. Ger., an. 1237. Cf. the letter (Oct. 18) of John of Colonna, cardinal of Sta. Prassede, to cardinal Otho, the legate in England, ap. H.-B., v, 124 f. He says the cardinals have returned from Lombardy : "sed pacis . . . vestigia non apparuerunt, quia non paruerunt pacis bajulis discordie sectatores."

[5] Ric. of S. Ger., an. 1337.

[6] Cf. epp. of Fred. ap. H.-B., v, 113 f., for Frederick's description of his army : "cum victorioso exercitu nostro " . . . " Ecce venimus, et cum tam honorabili militum comitiva, quam a longe retroactis

smiled upon him, and the League sustained a severe defeat at Cortenuova, half-way between Milan and Brescia. The *carroccio* of Milan fell into the hands of the victorious emperor, who promptly sent it to Rome in order that the sight of it might strengthen his party. When, drawn by mules and filled with standards and trumpets taken in the battle, it drew near the city, the Pope, according to an imperialistic chronicler,[1] was grieved to death, and forbade its being brought into the city. The imperial party, however, went out to meet it, brought it within the walls, and caused it to be placed solemnly in the Capitol by the cardinals of their party.[2]

Immense was the joy of the imperial party at this great victory. News of it was sent everywhere,[3] and " with filial devotion " Frederick begged the Pope and the cardinals to return thanks to our Lord, who had so " victoriously elevated the sacred empire." [4] The Milanese, who were recognized as the soul of the League,

The Emperor will have the unconditional surrender of Milan, 1238.

temporibus Romani principes non duxerunt." *Cf. Chron. de rebus in Ital.*, p. 167. " Imperator cum magno exercitu Veronam accessit." Despite these assertions, Tont, *The Empire and the Papacy*, p. 381, says : " But a small portion of his army came from Germany."

[1] The author of the *Chron. de rebus in Ital.*, p. 172.

[2] *Ib.* See Frederick's letter to the Romans, ap. H.-B., v, p. 161. Of these cardinals who favoured the Emperor we may presume that John of Colonna was one. He afterwards, in accordance with the spirit of opposition to the reigning Pope so often displayed by his family, openly went over to Frederick (Mat. Par., *Chron. maj.*, an. 1240, iv, p. 59 R. S., and Ric. of S. Ger., an. 1241, init.), and in his letter just quoted showed that he was opposed to the prevailing views in the Sacred College.

[3] *Cf.* letters of Dec. 4, 1237, of Frederick, etc., ap. H.-B., v, p. 132 ff. A letter was even sent to the archbishop of York. The letters of Peter della Vigna on the same subject are most exultant and poetical. " Tunc Theutonici suos gladios rubenti sanguine rubricaverunt . . . Fidelis Cremona cum sociis civitatibus secures sanguine saturabit, et suas evacuaverunt pharetras Sarraceni." Ap. *ib.*, p. 137 ff. *Cf.* p. 147.

[4] Ep. ap. *ib.*, p. 145.

were terrified and offered terms which Frederick would
have done well to accept. But, unduly elated at his
signal success, he listened to the counsels of him

> " who held
> Both keys to Frederick's heart, and turned the wards,
> Opening and shutting with a skill so sweet,
> That besides me, into his inmost breast
> Scarce any other could admittance find." [1]

Frederick listened, that is, to the counsels of Peter
della Vigna, whom Gregory's biographer calls " another
Achitophel by whose advice to the contempt of the princes,
the imperial majesty is directed." [2] He listened also, with
unwise elation, to the words of another evil counsellor,
to Ezzelino da Romano, telling him : " Now by God's
grace are nearly all Italy and the other kingdoms (provinciis) of the world well-nigh in complete subjection to
your most illustrious name." [3] Nothing, therefore, would
satisfy the emperor but the unconditional surrender of
Milan. This the Milanese, fired by the indefatigable legate
Montelongo, absolutely refused, and both parties girded
themselves for a war to the death. [4]

Further
negotiations
with Rome
about peace,
1238.

Thinking that he was now master of the situation, [5]
Frederick appears to have made no effort to prevent his
officials from usurping papal rights. Accordingly, whether

---

[1] The words of Peter della Vigna in Dante's *Inferno*, Canto xiii.
The poet, who is very free with his admissions into Hell, puts there
Frederick " the second of that name " (Canto x), Ezzelino da Romano
(Canto xii) and Peter della Vigna.

[2] C. 26.

[3] Rolandinus, ap. *R. I. SS.*, viii, p. 62, new ed. " Imperator . . .
sequens in omnibus consilium Ecelini." *Liber regim. Paduæ*, ap. *ib.*,
new ed., p. 314.

[4] *Chron. de reb.*, p. 171 ; *Mon. Patav. Chron.*, ap. *R. I. SS.*, viii,
678 ; Mat. Par., *Chron. maj.*, iii, 496. According to Paris, Frederick
was on this account regarded as an inexorable tyrant. " Ex tunc
igitur cœpit imperator favorem multorum amittere, quia factus est
tirannus inexorabilis."

[5] " Cuncta pro voto sibi mentiens successura." *Vita Greg.*, c. 26.

with or without his knowledge, his officials seized papal property in the March of Ancona, and acted therein as though they had full jurisdiction.[1] If Frederick paused to heed the Pope's complaints about this conduct of his officials, he did not pause in his endeavours to raise a great army to crush Milan,[2] nor to strengthen his party in Rome.[3] His son, Conrad, joined him in June with a large number of Germans, and Gebhard of Arnstein came from Tuscany which he had subdued with another army. When, then, in July (1238), Frederick began the siege of Brescia with an army of Germans, Italian allies from Rome, Tuscany, Lombardy, the March (of Verona), and Romagna, Saracens (milites soldani), and even soldiers from England, France, Spain, Provence, and from the Greek emperor Vatatzes,[4] he might well fancy himself the lord of the world. However, he kept up an appearance of being anxious to maintain peace " between the Church and the empire"; and Thaddeus of Sessa, the archbishop of Messina, the papal ambassador (responsalis), and others passed backwards and forwards between Anagni and Frederick's camp right on to the end of the year.[5]

[1] Ep. Greg. ad Fred., March 4, 1238, ap. Rod., i, 620.

[2] See his boastful letter to our King Henry, c. May, 1238. When he has raised a great host from Italy and Germany he intends: "imperialia castra movere et victricibus aquilis victricia signa ferentibus contra rebelles nostros prostratis hostibus victoriosis successibus triumphare." Ap. H.-B., v, 208. Cf. his letter to the people of Pavia, c. June, ib., p. 217, and Ric. of S. Ger., an. 1238.

[3] See the oath of Jacobus Girandi taken in the presence of Peter Frangipane to be loyal to Frederick (June, 1238), though on condition that he does not wage war with the Romans " in general "; ap. ib., p. 209.

[4] Chron. de rebus, an. 1238, pp. 173–4. The historian also notes with wonder the mules, camels, and dromedaries that carried his treasures.

[5] Ric. of S. Ger., l.c.

Four bishops, legates of the Pope, laid before the emperor Gregory's grievances. They mostly concerned " the kingdom," and, as they were largely those of which he had already complained in the beginning of 1236, and for which he was to excommunicate Frederick in the spring of 1239,[1] it may be assumed that his assertion that the emperor's replies to the delegates [2] were " vain quibbles . . . or fictions," was justified.[3]

Frederick usurps rights in Sardinia, 1238. In the very midst of these negotiations, Frederick showed how far he was anxious to remain at peace with the Church by another act of usurpation with regard to the rights of the Church of Rome. Without going into any elaborate discussion as to the origin of the Church's rights in Sardinia, it is quite certain that at this period the recognized suzerain of the island was the Pope.[4] Now in the beginning of this year (1238) there died the husband of Adelasia, *Queen* or *Lady* (donnicella) of part (Torres) of

---

[1] *Supra*, p. 267, and *infra*, p. 284 f.

[2] These replies may be read ap. H.-B., v, 249 ff. (they are dated Oct. 28, 1238), or Mat. Par., *Chron. maj.*, iii, 551 ff. R. S. Paris is hopelessly confused in his narrative of the relations between the Pope and the Emperor at this time. He assigns this document to the year 1239, and gives it after the document which sets forth the counts on which Frederick was excommunicated in March, 1239 ; and he also assigns to the same year (1239) a letter of Frederick (iii, 563) which belongs to June, 1236 (ap. H.-B., iv, p. 873), and another which clearly belongs to 1229 or 1230 (iii, 536). In many respects Paris is one of the most unsatisfactory of the mediæval historians which I have read. He is inaccurate, and an inveterate grumbler, and his reiterated allusions to money become positively nauseous. No doubt the Popes at this period had unsatisfactory money dealings ; but Paris cannot mention them or the see of Rome without dragging in " avarice and money " even on occasions when he obviously has not the slightest grounds for supposing that money entered into them in any unsatisfactory manner.

[3] Mat. Par., *l.c.*, p. 562.

[4] *Cf.* the acknowledgment of papal suzerainty by "the lady Benedicta, judicissa Kalaritana," ap. *Liber Censuum*, i, p. 542, ed. Fabre. *Cf. ib.*, pp. 573 ff., 578 ff.

the island of Sardinia.[1] In writing to console the widow [2] for the loss " of so noble a husband," Gregory reminds her that he died a good death, urges her to draw a lesson from his death as to the vanity of this world, and to devote herself rather to prayer for her dead husband than to tears. Then in virtue of his rights as feudal superior of the Lady [3] he pointed out that as it was expedient for herself and her country that she should have a husband to protect her, so it was proper that she should accept one who was loyal to the Apostolic See.[4] Accordingly, on the last day of May, he informed the Lady of Torres that he had provided a husband for her in the person of Guelf of Porcaria, an energetic and powerful man, and a devoted son of the Church. At the same time he warned her under pain of excommunication and " the privation of all her territories," [5] against marrying anyone "who might be able to injure the rights of the Church." [6] But the emperor saw in the state of things in Sardinia an opportunity of extending his power. Asserting that the island had originally belonged to the empire, and that "I have sworn, as all the world knows, to recover the scattered portions of the empire," [7] he dispatched to the island with an armed force his natural son, Enzio. Whether through fear, or because she was attracted by the idea of an imperial alliance, and by the handsome appearance of Enzio, the Lady "of the greatest and most important part"

[1] Cf. supra, vol. ix, 35 ff. ; vol. xi, 127 ff., etc.

[2] The Pope calls her Agnes, but in her charters she calls herself Adelasia.

[3] Gregory speaks of " terra sua. que est Romane ecclesie specialis." Ep. of May 4, 1238. Cf. ep. of Apr. 30, ap. Rod., i, p. 624 f.

[4] Ib.

[5] "Cum eadem terra specialiter b. Petri juris existat." Ep. of May 31, 1238, ap. ib., p. 629.

[6] Ib.

[7] Mat. Par., Chron. maj., an. 1239, iii, 527. Sardinia "cujus insulæ jus ad patrimonium b. Petri specialiter pertinere perhibetur."

of Sardinia set at naught the Pope's prohibitions and
the wishes of her people, to her own undoing, and married
the emperor's son.[1]   By this action of the emperor, the
loss to the Pope, as Matthew Paris takes notice, " was
great, but the manner in which the loss was inflicted made
it seem all the greater." [2]   In fact, this last act of aggression on the part of Frederick, which took place about the
time that the Pope's delegates were sending him the
imperial replies to his charges (Oct., 1238),[3] seems to have
exhausted Gregory's patience.   He found Frederick's
replies to his allegations thoroughly unsatisfactory.
They repeated, in reference to the same charges, the same
protestations of ignorance of the alleged grievances, or of
intention to amend them as were made in 1236.   Besides,
the Pope could not but ask himself the question as to what
Frederick's attitude towards the Church was likely to be,
should he become absolute master of all the territory
round Peter's patrimony, when he acted in so high-handed
a fashion whilst the power of the Lombard Communes
was still unbroken.   It behoved him, then, to try to curb
Frederick's arbitrary conduct before the Lombards were
crushed.[4]

[1] *Ib.* ; and *Chron. de reb.*, p. 176.   *Cf.* E. Besta, *La Sardegna
Medioevale*, p. 203 ff., Palermo, 1908.   Among other authorities he
cites the *Liber judicum turritanorum*, written towards the close of the
thirteenth century, and found by him in the state archives of Turin.
According to the authority just cited, Adelasia soon found that from
being " the Lady " she had become " the servant."   In 1243 she
repented of her action and was reconciled to Rome (*cf.* a letter of
Innocent IV., ap. H.-B., vi, p. 135 f.) after she had been abandoned
by "the King of Sardinia," as Enzio styled himself.   Frederick
afterwards pretended that the Pope had excommunicated him because
" our magnificence " would not condescend to ally this same Enzio
with a niece of the Pope.   See his letter of Apr. 20, 1239, to our
Richard of Cornwall.   Ap. H.-B., v, 305.

[2] *L.c.*

[3] The document of the four bishops of Oct. 28, ap. H.-B., v, 249 ff.

[4] A cleric residing at the Roman curia writes to a friend, " Scientes

It was with this end in view that he had already on August 6, 1238, sent as his legate into Lombardy his incorruptible, and very capable, distant relative, the notary, Gregory of Montelongo, in order that he might bring about peace and harmony among the Lombard Communes in the interests of the Church.[1] He now made it known to the emperor that unless substantial satisfaction were made to him, he would excommunicate him.[2] This Frederick had no thought of offering, but he tried to ward off the impending blow by an attempt to frighten the cardinals.   In a letter which he addressed to them (March 10, 1239) he reminded them that they, as ministers of Peter's successor, would be sharers in any precipitate action of the Pope, who, for the sake of rebellious Lombards, proposed to draw the spiritual sword against the Roman emperor, " the advocate of the Church, and the one appointed to assist the preaching of the Gospel." [3] This, he maintained, was the less excusable as proper inquiries

Excommunication of Frederick, 1239.

---

quod Ecclesia Romana totis viribus contra imperatoram et ad ejus destructionem laborat." *Ep. c.* June, 1239.

[1] Potthast, n. 26284, vol. ii, p. 2109.   The Chroniclers Pipino (ap. *R. I. SS.*, ix, p. 658) and Ricobaldo (ap. *ib.*, 129) note that Gregory was sent : " ut in omnibus conatibus Imperatoris obstiteret."   Frederick was very indignant at this nomination, for he chose to regard him, as he had regarded James Pecoraria, as his personal enemy.   See his letter of April 20, 1239, ap. H.-B., v, 301.   Salimbene, *Chron.*, ap. *M. G. SS.*, xxxii, 388, tells us of the great, but vain, efforts made by Frederick to win Montelongo to his side ; but he also says that the legate was neither chaste nor scrupulous.

[2] "Ammonicione premissa" (*Ann. Parmenses*, an. 1239, ap. *M. G. SS.*, xviii, p. 669) is asserted by several authors.   *Cf.* even Mat. Par., *Chron. Maj.*, iii, 532 f., who tells of the numerous letters which Gregory sent to the emperor before excommunicating him, and also the many envoys he dispatched " whose authority ought to have been regarded."   See also Monach. Pat. (*Chron.*, ap. *R. I. SS.*, viii, p. 678), who adds : " Summus Pontifex per experientiam cognoscebat, animum Imperatoris esse proclivem ad opprimendum ecclesiam, si posset sibi subjicere Lombardiam."

[3] Ep. ap. H.-B., v, 283.

were being made into all alleged grievances, which were
to be adequately dealt with. Should, however, " the
Apostolic Father " proceed against us, the enormity of
the act will prevent us from bearing it patiently, and force
us to take such vengeance as emperors are wont to exact.
We should be glad to confine our vengeance to the offender,
and to those of his flesh and blood, but to this the imperial
dignity could not condescend ; so that in defending ourself
from our persecutors we shall have to attack those who
resist us. He concluded by urging them to restrain the
unjust and gratuitous aggression of the Pope, otherwise
he will meet injuries with injuries.

The cardinals, however, were not overawed; and as
both they and their head had had enough of the emperor's
promises, and of his continued violation of the treaty
of San Germano, Gregory excommunicated him on Palm
Sunday (March 20), and solemnly proclaimed the excommunication on Holy Thursday (March 24). He declared
" Frederick called emperor " excommunicated for some
seventeen reasons, for creating sedition in Rome, and,
against his oaths, endeavouring to drive the Pope and
his cardinals from his See ; [1] for preventing the legate
cardinal James Pecoraria from proceeding to Provence to
deal with the Albigensian heresy ; [2] for refusing to allow
no less than twenty cathedral churches and two monas-

[1] Hence the *Chron. parva Ferrariensis* tells us that Salinguerra and
others of the imperial faction were aiming at the ruin of the Roman
Church. " Cum innotesceret (cunctis) prudentibus, salinguerram et
complices ejus odio esse usque ad perniciem Ecclesiæ Romanæ," etc.
Ap. *R. I. SS.*, viii, p. 484. Frederick's efforts to stir up sedition in
Rome will be brought out when Gregory's relations with the Romans
are dealt with.

[2] *Cf.* ep. Fred. of 1238, towards the end of the year. Ap. H.-B., v,
269. Frederick accused him of fomenting rebellion in Lombardy,
and hence " pes ejus de nostra licentia terram ipsarum partium non
calcabit." He calmly added that the Pope had others whom he might
send instead of James.

teries in the kingdom of Sicily to be filled up, for permitting in the said kingdom clerics to be seized, imprisoned, proscribed, and slain ; for seizing, contrary to his oaths, the lands of the Church, Ferrara, Sardinia,[1] etc., for despoiling Monreale, Cefalù, and other cathedrals and monasteries as well as the Templars and Hospitallers of their possessions ; for proscribing, contrary to the terms of the peace of San Germano, those who had supported the Church, and for impeding the Crusade and preventing the strengthening of the Latin empire of Constantinople, etc., etc.[2] Gregory further absolved all from the oaths of fealty they had taken to Frederick, and declared his intention of deposing him and of proceeding against him as the law required for heresy, of which he was generally accused.[3] Letters dispatched to the ruling clergy and laity of the East and West soon made known the excommunication and its chief grounds to the civilized world.[4]

Frederick, perhaps at this moment at the height of his power, was keeping Easter (March 27) at Padua, and was showing himself to the people in all his glory with the imperial crown upon his head, when it was whispered about that he had been excommunicated only a few

Frederick's fury at his excommunication.

---

[1] *Cf.* Mat. Par., *Chron. maj.*, iii, p. 532. It was found, he says, that in the Lent of this year : " quod, faventibus quibusdam magnatibus et judicibus Sardanicis, terram et castra episcopi Sardanici, sibi (the emperor) accepisset et tenuisset," etc.

[2] *Cf.* Mat. Par., *ib.*, iii, 518, tells of the vexation of Frederick because the Pope helped the emperor Baldwin whom he chose to regard as a rival. No word is said of Frederick's action in Lombardy, for which many reasons could have been given.

[3] This important document is given, ap. H.-B., v, p. 286 ff., and by Mat. Par., *ib.*, iii, 533 ff. " Multis clamantibus per universum quasi orbem quod de catholica fide recte non sentiat," almost the last words of the decree.

[4] Epp. of Apr. 7, ap. Rod. i, pp. 637–41. The grounds are declared to be " many and valid " by the *Chron. Reg. Colon. Contin. V.*, p. 272.

days before.[1] " The divine omnipotence," observes the historian we are quoting, " plays with the affairs of the world, and we know not what will happen even in the course of an hour." [2]

Furious at the action of the Pope, the emperor at once summoned a great assembly to meet in his palace at Padua, and, through Peter della Vigna, after setting forth his unique merits, he declared that, had the excommunication been just, he would have submitted to it, but as it was unjust, very different would be his action.[3]

Taking no notice of the excommunication and deposition,[4] and paying but little regard to the truth, he addressed a very long circular letter to Richard earl of Cornwall,

[1] Rolandinus, *Chron.*, cc. 9 and 10, p. 64.

[2] *Ib.* The excommunication of Frederick is mentioned by contemporaries all over Europe ; but apart from the *entourage* of the emperor himself, no one hints that it was unjust. *Cf.* e.g., *The Annals of Tewkesbury*, ad an. " Frethericus imperator excommunicatur ad. Papa, propter contumaciam," etc., p. 113 R. S., *Ann. de Waverleia*, an. 1239, p. 321 R. S. ; *Ann. de Dunstaplia*, an. 1239, p. 148 R. S. ; *Chron.*, Alberic Trium. Font., ap. *M. G. SS.*, xxiii, p. 944 ; Baldwin of Avenne, *Chron. Hanon.*, p. 453, ap. *ib.*, xxv, p. 453 ; *Ann. Stad.*, ap. *ib.*, xvi, p. 363 ; etc., etc. There was no general condemnation of Gregory's action because, as we have said before, it was known to be the law of Christendom that the emperor could be excommunicated by the Pope for " heresy and for divorcing his wife, or for destroying holy places." " Der keiser sol noch enmag niemant bannen want der bapst allein. Das sol er thun nit wann umb drei sach. Der ist eins, das erst ob er an dem glauben Zweivelt. Das ander ob er sein eeweib fären läst. Das dritt ob er gotsheüser erstöret—Imperatorem in bannum declarare nemo protest nisi Papa. Hoc tamen non facere debet nisi tres ob causas. Una est si Imperator de fide Orthodoxa dubitaret. Altera est si ab uxore diverterat. Tertia est si ecclesias (aut alia loca pia) destrueret." The Swabian Mirror, c. 29, in Senckenberg, *Corpus juris German*, ii, p. 39 f., ap. Balan, *Storia di Greg. IX.*, iii, p. 461. Whatever were his public declarations about his orthodoxy, Frederick's want of orthodoxy was well known, and there was equal knowledge of his treatment of " pious places."

[3] Roland., *l.c.* ; *cf. Liber regim. Paduæ*, ap. *R. I. SS.*, viii, new ed., pp. 313–14.

[4] *Gesta abbatum Horti S. Mariæ*, c. 41, ap. *M. G. SS.*, xxiii, p. 594.

and to the various princes of Europe against "the
calumnious lips of his detractors, and the poisonous
inventions of factions," and also against one (Pope
Gregory) who used to be "our especial friend when he
was in an inferior station." Premising that the Pope
had "an itching to cause public disturbance," he gave a
garbled version of the story of Gregory's relations
towards him up to the period of his second excommunication, even declaring that whilst he had found a true
mother in the Church, he had always found the father
false.[1] He insinuated that, whenever the Pope had acted
with him, he had always, in an underhand manner,
worked against him, and he appealed in proof of this
to certain papal letters which he said he had in his
possession.[2] He averred that the legates, James Pecoraria,
and then Gregory of Montelongo, whom the Pope had
sent into Lombardy to make peace, were wolves in sheeps'
clothing, and worked against his interests. For having
excommunicated him, Gregory was spoken of as "the
so-called vicar of Christ, the preacher of peace, but in
reality the author of schism, and the friend of error."
He was further declared to be unworthy of any pontifical
authority at all in that he favoured heretical Milan, and
sold dispensations. Hence "not in contempt of the papal
office or of the apostolic dignity to which all professors
of the orthodox faith, and we more especially, are bound
to submit,"[3] but on account of his unworthy person, he

[1] "Veram matrem nostram Ecclesiam ex agnitione catholice fidei
reperisse cognoscimus, sed patrem semper invenimus simulatum." Ep.
of Apr. 20, 1239, ap. H.-B., v, p. 295.

[2] It is to be noted that he does not cite a single word from these
alleged letters, and that no such letters are to be found in the papal
registers.

[3] "Non in contemptum papalis officii vel apostolicæ dignitatis, cui
omnes orthodoxe fidei professores, et nos specialiter pre ceteris fatemur
subesse, etc." Ib., p. 304. Frederick declared that the real cause of the
Pope's action was the Lombard affair, though he dared not mention
it openly.

called on the cardinals to summon a general council. In concluding his lengthy indictment of the Pope, he urged the other princes to assist him, " for the humiliation of all other kings and princes is believed to be an easy matter, if the power of the Roman Cesar . . . is broken."

On the same day (April 20) he wrote to upbraid the Senator of Rome, and the Roman people generally, for allowing their lord, who had done so much for the City, to be excommunicated. Unless they atoned for their conduct, he would withdraw his favour from them.[1]

Gregory replies to the Emperor's circular letter, May, 1239.

To these letters of Frederick, wanting at once in truth and in restraint, Gregory was not long in replying. After about a month, letters, couched in almost identical terms, began to pour from the pontifical chancery to the rulers, ecclesiastical and civil, of Christendom. Matthew Paris cites the one addressed to the archbishop of Canterbury and his suffragans, and dated May 21.[2] If the papal letters were wholly unlike the letters of Frederick in the matter of truth, they bore some resemblance to them in the vigour and directness of their language. Opening with a quotation from the Apocalypse,[3] Gregory compared the emperor to the beast which came up " out of the sea, having seven heads and ten horns . . . and upon his heads, names of blasphemy." With its claws and teeth of iron this beast, wrote the Pope, is striving to rend every-

---

[1] Ap. H.-B., v, 307. About the same time also Peter della Vigna, or one of Frederick's partisans, circulated a very abusive letter against the Pope, "the man of blood," who was engaged in nothing but hoarding up money, eating and drinking. " In cujus vasis et ciphis aureis scriptum est : ' Bibo, bibis.' " If the Pope does not receive the emperor back into the bosom of the Church, then he like a lion . . . " Plantando justitiam *Ecclesiam diriget* . . . destruens cornua superborum." Ap. *ib.*, p. 310.

[2] *Chron. maj.*, iii, 590 R. S. Rodenberg (i, p. 645 ff.) cites with greater accuracy the same letter as addressed to the archbishop of Rheims.

[3] xiii, v. 1 ff.

thing, to trample on the world, and to tear down the wall of the Catholic faith. Blustering in his greatness, and unbalanced by the power he has acquired, he has turned on his benefactress the Church, whilst striving to soothe her with his painted words.

Gregory then proceeded to give the lie to the emperor's statements in detail, pointing out, among other things, that the course of events was proving that Frederick would have done well to have followed his advice, and tried to have overcome the Lombards, strong in the number of their people and in the height and thickness of their walls, rather by diplomatic kindness than by military force.[1] But this " hammer of the world, eager to crush kingdoms, and to make the world a desert," had reduced the church in Sicily to servitude, and had tried to defame his lord's[2] personal character, accusing him, among other things, of wasting the patrimony of the Church—him " who, by God's grace, has increased the said patrimony to no small extent." The Pope's long indignant protest against Frederick's calumnies is brought to a conclusion by a strong charge of rationalism against him.[3]

This and the other letters issued by Gregory on Frederick's excommunication went far to counteract the ill-feeling against the Papacy which Frederick's letters had naturally aroused in the minds of men who were

The excommunication of Frederick is pronounced in different countries.

---

[1] Since his success at Cortenuova, Frederick, despite the means at his disposal, had effected little or nothing against the Lombard League. His failure to take Brescia, the siege of which he had to abandon (Oct. 1238), was " the turning point in Frederick's struggle with the Lombards. His failure encouraged his adversaries beyond measure." Butler, *The Lombard Communes*, p. 277.

[2] In other letters Gregory was not slow to remind Frederick that he was the Pope's vassal for the kingdom of Sicily. *Cf.* e.g., ep. of Apr. 11, 1239, ap. H.-B., v, 290.

[3] Ap. Rod., i, p. 645 ff. It is at the close of this letter that Gregory gives the story relative to Frederick and the three imposters.

ignorant of the facts of the case, or who, for any reason,
were ill-disposed to papal influence; and, although they
did not counteract the emperor's letters entirely,[1] they
prevented them from achieving their principal object.
Frederick had fondly hoped to prevent his excommunication from being published in England and other countries.
To his intense chagrin, however, he was disappointed.
Without any opposition the excommunication was proclaimed in the different countries of Christendom.[2]

Efforts to
make peace
between the
two powers,
1239.

Among the princes of Christendom at this epoch, the
most worthy in every way was St. Louis IX., of France.
Into the great contest between the emperor and the Pope
he would not, however, be drawn, although the action of
the former in cultivating alliances with his enemies
(England and Toulouse) might have naturally induced
him to take the part of the Pope. Still, he strove, unfortunately, however, to no purpose, to make peace
between the empire and the Papacy.[3] Another Saint also,
Ferdinand III. of Castile and Leon (1230–52), made a
forlorn effort to mediate between the Pope and the
emperor. Before this he had in vain tried to get justice
from the emperor,[4] and a favour from the Pope from whom
he had endeavoured to obtain the title of emperor.[5]

[1] Cf. Mat. Par., Chron. maj., iii, 608 f., though what he there says is
more the expression of his own views than those of the public at large.

[2] Ib., p. 545. "Denuntiatus est excommunicatus Frethericus dictus
imperator . . . per totum regnum (England). Nec erat qui contra-
diceret." Frederick's letter of Apr. 20, 1239, to the Romans, ap. H.-B.,
v, 307, shows his vexation that his excommunication was proclaimed
at Rome "without any resistance on the part of the Romans." Cf.
ib., pp. 464 and 467, for his annoyance with regard to England.

[3] Alberic Trium. Font., Chron., ap. M. G. SS., xxiii, p. 944 ; Ægidius
Aureæval., c. 133. Cf. St. Louis, by H. Wallon, p. 63, Tours, 1878.

[4] Cf. ep. of Ferdinand to the Pope, Dec. 4, 1239, ap. Rod., i, 661,
and see J. Laurentie, Saint Ferdinand III., p. 118 ff., Paris, 1910.

[5] Alberic Trium. Font., Chron., p. 936. "In curia Romana talem
petitionem proposuit rex Castelle Fernandus, quod nomen imperatoris

Professing, " after the manner of his ancestors," the greatest devotion and gratitude to the Pope, " the vicar of Christ and the vicegerent of the true God," who " gives abundantly the food of faith to all the faithful," he declared that he had heard of the manner in which the emperor, who had been so " wonderfully " exalted by the Holy See, had provoked it to anger, " to such an extent that it was necessary for him to be touched by the hand of the Lord." Seeing, therefore, that the members cannot be sound when the head is troubled, he was anxious, he continued, with the Pope's permission, to make an attempt at mediation in order that the Church might not be without its defender (athleta). He then brought his letter to a close by suggesting that the abbot of St. Facundus (Sahagun), in whose prudence and integrity he had the highest confidence, might act as his agent in the proposed mediation.[1]

Frederick was not, however, prepared to listen to any mediation which would have involved compromise. Acting, as his enemies said, like " a madman," [2] and setting at naught his excommunication,[3] which he chose to attribute, now to his refusal to accept the Pope's niece as a daughter-in-law,[4] and now to his success against the Lombards,[5] he took such steps as he hoped would injure

Frederick takes steps against the Pope, 1239.

et benedictionem volebat habere, sicut habuerunt quidam antecessores ejus." The fact is, however, that his namesake Ferdinand I. had been induced by Rome to give up the usurped title of emperor. *Cf. supra*, vol. vi, p. 195 f.

[1] Ep. of Dec. 4, 1239, ap. Rod., i, 659. *Cf.* the two following letters, and epp. of the emp. of May, 1240, ap. H.-B., v, 991, Sept., p. 1047. The emperor's letters contained nothing but promises.

[2] " Quasi rabidus," says the author of the *Vita Ricciardi* (Count of San Bonifazio), ap. *R. I. SS.*, viii, p. 130.

[3] Ep. Greg. of Sept. 24, 1239, ap. Albert v. Behaim, p. 7.

[4] Fred.'s letter of Apr. 20, 1239, ap. H.-B., v, 305.

[5] *Ib.* " Hec est causa . . . videlicet pro Lombardis, que cor pape pungebat . . . licet ipsam foras educere propter vestrum et audientium scandalum, non auderet," p. 306.

the papal cause. He ordered that all Dominicans and Franciscans of Lombard origin should be expelled from the kingdom of the two Sicilies,[1] and that from all religious who were left behind guarantees should be exacted that " they would not act against (offendant) the emperor." [2] Nobles who had favoured the papal party were to be dispatched to Lombardy with their vassals ; the churches were to be taxed for the emperor's service, and clerics of the kingdom—except suspects— were to return home on pain of the confiscation of their goods. The property in the Sicilies, of clerics who did not belong to the kingdom, was to be confiscated and no one was to be allowed to go " to the Roman Church " without the special permission of the Justiciary. Finally, any person who brought into the kingdom papal letters against the emperor was to be hanged.[3]

Frederick next tried to detach the cardinals from the Pope. Reminding them that God had appointed the Papacy and the empire to rule the world,[4] he averred that Gregory, who was no other than Antichrist, was endeavouring to pervert the established order, and had defamed him by telling the people that he had declared that the world had been deceived by three seducers. As a matter of fact, he believed that our Lord was coequal

Frederick tries to undermine the loyalty of the cardinals.

[1] They did not, however, leave the kingdom till November, 1240. *Cf.* Ric. of S. Ger., ad an.

[2] Pretending that his quarrel with the Pope was a personal affair, Frederick wrote "to the Masters of the Sacred Order of Friars Preachers," assembled in general chapter in Paris, and begged them not to allow their brethren to run up and down the world with letters and on embassies against us and the empire. Ep. of Feb. 27, 1241, ap. H.-B., v, 1098 ff.

[3] Ric. of S. Ger., June, an. 1239. Mat. Par., 1239, iii, 538, says that Frederick caused Monte Cassino to be seized and the monks expelled because they dared to proclaim his excommunication.

[4] " Sacerdotium scilicet et imperium unum ad cautelam reliquum ad tutelam." Ep. *c.* July, 1239, ap. H.-B., v, 348.

with the Father and the Holy Ghost, that Mahomet was in hell,[1] and that Moses was the friend of God. He was greatly distressed because the cardinals, "who were the foundation of the Church, and its columns, the assessors of rectitude, the senators of Peter's City, and the hinges of the world," had not opposed the violent actions of the Pope, "as the planets are set to retard by their opposite motion the velocity of a great body." The Pope was envious of the imperial successes. Simonides, when asked how it was that there was none who envied him, replied : " Because I have never had a success." But, continued Frederick in his usual boastful style, because, by the blessing of God, all things are succeeding with me, and "I am pursuing the rebellious Lombards even to the death," " the apostolic pontiff " is striving with your aid to thwart me. Therefore, in opposing him, I am only opposing a corrupt individual and not the Church itself, which I reverence and honour. You, then, must recall him from the evil path on which he has entered, or " all the world shall see how the Augustus will proceed against his persecutor and his chief supporters, and how the sword shall cut in deeply the vengeance of Cesar." [2]

Having thus striven to debauch the loyalty of the cardinals, Frederick next tried to do the same with the Pope's subjects. He informed the people of the March of Ancona and of the Duchy of Spoleto that he absolved them from the oath of allegiance which they had taken to the Roman Church, that they should never again be alienated from the empire, and that he was sending his

[1] He testified to the belief that the body of Mahomet was suspended in the air. " Mahometi vero corpus is ære pendere didicimus obsessum demonibus, animam Inferni cruciatibus deditam, cujus opera tenebrosa fuerunt." *Ib.*

[2] " Alioquin, utraque terra sentiet qualiter in persecutorem ac consequentes principes et fautores procedat Augustus, et qualiter ferro cesareas inferat ultiones." *Ib.*

son Enzio, "the illustrious King of Sardinia," to receive
their oaths of fidelity to himself.[1] He also drew tighter
the bonds which bound him to the count of Toulouse,
whom he thanked for his vigorous opposition to the
Pope and the count of Provence.[2] Then, to strengthen
his hands by clerical support, he accepted the service of
the notorious Brother Elias of Cortona, St. Francis'
successor as Minister-General of the Franciscans. He
went over to the emperor rather than obey Albert of
Pisa who had been elected minister after the deposition
of Elias himself.[3] Furthermore, all during the rest of the
year 1239, he ceased not to ravage as far as he could
the parts of Lombardy which were still quite unsubdued.
Nor, whilst striking with the sword, did he disdain to
strike with the pen. He wrote or caused to be written
and to be fixed up in the Pope's bedroom a lampoon to
the following effect :

" The stars and fates, and flight of birds decree
    Of all the world one hammer there shall be.[4]
    Rome totters, through a mass of errors led,
    And of the world shall cease to be the head."

In the matter of verse, however, Gregory was easily
equal to his opponent, and is said [5] to have retorted :

" Scripture and Fame, your sins, all loudly tell
    Your life but short, and then for ever hell."

[1] *Cf.* documents of August, 1239, ap. H.-B., v, 374 ff.

[2] Ep. of Sept., 1239, ap. *ib.*, 403.

[3] Thos. of Eccleston, *De adventu Frat. Min.*, coll. xiii, p. 86, ed.
Little. "Hence," adds Thomas, "he was, not without just cause,
publicly excommunicated by the Pope." *Cf.* Mat. Par., *Chron. maj.*,
1239, iii, 628 ; Ric. of S. Ger., an. 1239, and ep. Fred. ap. H.-B., v, 346.
In his opposition to Gregory, Elias anticipated the action of the famous
English Franciscan, Occam.

[4] Albert von Behaim or the author of a pamphlet against Frederick
in June, 1245, calls him "terræ malleus universæ." Ap. *A. v. B.*, p. 61,
ed. Höfler.

[5] By Mat. Par., 1239, iii, 551, who gives the verses. The Chronicle

Whether Gregory wrote this couplet or not, there is no Action of the Pope against the Emperor. doubt that he took much more effective measures against Frederick than writing a few verses against him. To make known the doings and excommunication of the emperor, or to organize opposition to him, he made use of his legates in the different countries, cardinal Otho in England, the notary Gregory ot Montelongo in Lombardy, cardinal James Pecoraria in France,[1] and especially the bold and energetic advocate Albert von Behaim in Germany. The last-named, who had been sent on a mission to Germany in 1238, had the hardest task to perform. It was in Germany that it would be necessary to bring about the election of another king of the Romans to replace the excommunicated Frederick, and yet the bishops there were unwilling to denounce him.[2] Getting, however, in touch with the Duke of Austria, still unsub-

---

of St. Pierre le Vif, by Geoffroy de Courlon, gives an account of a landslip and other phenomena which are supposed to have provoked the verses. P. 515 f., ed. Julliot. It may here be noted that not a few of the minnesingers, at one time enthusiastic supporters of Frederick, turned against him when his conduct brought upon him the condemnation of the Church. Among such was Reinmar of Zweter (between 1220–45) who, about the year 1239, reminded Frederick that the empire was not his, but that he was only its advocate, and called upon the princes to proclaim his guilt. Cf. F. H. von der Hogen, *Minnesinger Manessiche Sammlung*, ii, n. 113, ap. Merkel, *L'opinione*, p. 73. Another such was Wernher von Hornburg, ap. *ib.*, p. 75 ff., while Von Wengen, *ib.*, pp. 78–9, frankly espouses the cause of the Pope, declaring that such as have deprived him of his rights are lost.

[1] He had been sent into France in Oct., 1239. Cf. Ric. of S. Ger., an. 1239. Gregory of M. was of the family of Innocent III. Cf. ep. Inn. III. of June 15, 1213, ap. Potthast, n. 4760. Cf. "La legazione in Lombardia di Gregorio da Monte Longo negli anni, 1238–51," by G. Marchetti Longi, ap. *Archivio Rom. di storia pat.*, vol. xxxvi, pp. 225 ff., 585 ff., 1913. Salimbene, *Chron.*, ap. *M. G. SS.*, xxxii, p. 388, calls him "one of the seven notaries of the Roman Curia."

[2] "Papa sollicitavit . . . episcopos ut imperatorem denuntiarent. Sed episcopi Teutoniæ ne hoc fieret supplicabant." Albert. Stad., *Chron.*, 1239, ap. *M. G. SS.*, xvi, 365. On the defiant attitude of most of the German bishops, see Albert v. B., pp. 14 ff., 19, etc.

dued and still in arms against Frederick, with Wenceslas III., king of Bohemia, Otho I., duke of Bavaria, and others,[1] the legate brought it about that the dignity of king of the Romans was offered to Abel, king of Denmark.[2] On his declining the dangerous honour, it was offered with like result to Otho of Brunswick,[3] as he was terrified by the return of Wenceslas to the allegiance of Frederick [4] (summer, 1239).

Seeing that it was unlikely that any suitable German prince would accept the papal offer of the imperial title, Gregory resolved " to transfer it from the Germans to the Gauls," and for that purpose sent into France cardinal James Pecoraria, who was accompanied by Tedaldus or Theobald Visconti, afterwards the saintly Pope Gregory X.[5] As Frederick had caused the passes of the Alps to be watched in order to prevent any communication with the Pope,[6] the cardinal owed it to a disguise that he contrived to enter France. Informing the French on the part of the Pope that the empire was vacant, he offered it, if not to the king of France himself,[7] at any rate to his

---

[1] In one of his notes Albert v. B., p. 6, quotes a friend as saying that " all the Princes were on the Pope's side except the fools (Raspo) Landgrave of Thuringia and the Margrave of Meissen."

[2] *Ib.*, *cf. ib.*, p. 22, for the reasons of Abel's refusal. *Cf.* also Alberic Trium. Font., *Chron.*, an. 1241, ap. *M. G. SS.*, xxiii, p. 949.

[3] Alberic, *ib.* Albertus Stadensis, *Chron.*, ad an. 1240, declares that some of the princes told the Pope that it was not within his rights to change emperors, but to crown them when elected by the princes. Gregory writes, " I hear that Conrad bishop of Frising says that we have no (temporal) jurisdiction (nil juris) in Germany." Extract from ep. of Nov. 27, 1239, ap. Alb. v. B., p. 5.

[4] *Cf.* Alb. v. B., p. 14 f.

[5] See his contemporary biography, ap. *R. I. SS.*, iii, pt. i, p. 599, and ep. Greg. Oct. 21, 1239, ap. H.-B., v, 457.

[6] " Itinera obsidens Romipetis insidiatur." Vincent of Beauvais, *Spec. Hist.*, l. xxx, c. 138.

[7] The *Chron. reg. Colon., Contin. V.*, p. 273, says that the empire was first offered to Louis and then to others. " Proponit (James P.) ad

brother, Robert of Artois;[1] for, as it was said at the time, "the Church of Rome cannot long remain without a Catholic advocate, especially when it is attacked by heretics."[2] However, through the action of the queen-mother, Blanche of Castile,[3] this effort also failed. Either she did not consider that her son was seated sufficiently firmly on his throne to warrant his taking or supporting a step that might involve the country in a serious war,[4] or else she was resolved that France should remain neutral in the great struggle.

Undeterred by these failures, Gregory continued to encourage the Lombards,[5] and to bring about alliances among them [6] or with them.[7] Hence, Milan, Piacenza, and Genoa, agreed with the Pope that no terms should

mandatum Pape Romanum imperium, quod dicebatur vacare, a Germanis transferre in Gallos, ad hoc recipiendum sollicitando regem Francorum."

[1] Alberic, *l.c.* ; Mat. Par., *Chron. maj.*, iii, p. 624.

[2] Alb. v. B., in a report to the Pope, p. 16. *Cf.* p. 22. The report was sent about the middle of August, 1240.

[3] Alberic, *Chron.*, *l.c.* There is extant a letter of Frederick to Robert in which he appears to thank Robert for thus declining the proffered honour : "honoris augusti fastigium." Ep. ap. H.-B., v, p. 1086.

[4] Mat. Par., *Chron. maj.*, iii, p. 624 f., has embellished his account of this negotiation with a papal letter of which he gives what *is said* to have been its tenor ("cujus summa et tenor talis fuisse *perhibetur* "), and with "the considered reply of the French." "The details of the declamatory recital of Matthew Paris" are rejected by Huillard-Bréholles, *Introduction*, p. 300 ; and Lavisse, *Hist. de France*, ii, p. 82, notes that "most of the diplomatic documents of the time of Louis IX. which have not perished have been preserved by unreliable (peu sûrs) chroniclers like Matthew Paris, or have been mixed up with other documents."

[5] Ep. of August, 1239, to encourage the people of Bologna to help Paul Traversari to hold Ravenna against Frederick, ap. H.-B., v, 373.

[6] *Cf.* Caffaro, *Ann. Genuen*, an. 1238, ap. *R. I. SS.*, vi, p. 479, for an alliance between Genoa and Venice for nine years at the request of the Pope. See also the actual treaty of Nov. 30, 1238, ap. H.-B., v, 1223.

[7] For an alliance with Venice against Sicily, *cf.* ep. of Venetian envoys of Sept. 23, 1239, ap. H.-B., v, 390.

be made with Frederick without the consent of all the contracting parties.[1] Gregory strove also to get help from France,[2] and to prevent united hostile action by Germany.[3] Further, to oppose Enzio, " king of Gallura," in the March of Ancona, he dispatched the most warlike of the cardinals, John of Colonna,[4] and whilst excommunicating its invader, he renewed the excommunication of his father.[5]

Frederick marches south against the Pope.

Irritated by the Pope's activity against him, and allowing his irritation to outweigh the military necessities of the hour, Frederick, instead of first completing the subjugation of Lombardy,[6] vainly proclaimed that he had arranged everything in those parts,[7] and in January entered Tuscany with the intention of seizing the States of the Church of Rome (January, 1240).

Sending letters to the principal cities in the papal states,[8] he strove to win them over to his side by soft words. " Do you acknowledge us," he cried, " as your prince and gracious master (possessorem), prepare the way of (your) lord, make straight his paths, remove the bolts from your gates that your Cesar, terrible to rebels, may come to you in gentleness." [9] By joining material force to honied speech, Frederick succeeded in occupying many of the Papal cities; and where, as at Spoleto, resistance was made to him, he ordered the officials of his kingdom to seize the persons and property of such members of the

[1] *Chron. de rebus in Ital.*, p. 178.
[2] Ep. Oct. 23, 1239, ap. *ib.*, p. 457.
[3] Ep. Nov. 23, 1239, ap. *ib.*, p. 526.
[4] Ric. of S. Ger., 1239.
[5] *Ib.*
[6] *Cf.* Butler, *The Lombard Communes*, p. 281 f.
[7] " Dispositis enim nostris beneplacitis in partibus Lombardiæ." Ep. of Fred., Jan., 1240, ap. H.-B., v, pt. ii, p. 652.
[8] Ap. *ib.*, 662 ff.
[9] *Ib.*, p. 665. Folignio he tried to gain over " ex illa causa potissime quod in Fulgineo fulgere pueritia nostra cepit." P. 662.

recalcitrant city as happened to be in residence there at the moment.[1] Thinking that he had gained over the people of Rome itself, by offering their principal men, notably Napoleon Gaetani, John of Poli, Otho Frangipane, and Angelo Malabranca, important posts in the empire,[2] he would not listen to any suggestions of peace with " the improvident ruler, and useless pastor of God's flock." [3] It was, he said, " his fixed and irrevocable resolve " to reunite to the empire " the duchy (of Spoleto), the March (of Ancona) and other territories which had for a long time been separated from it " ; [4] and he announced " to his faithful subjects " with much boastfulness, but not as much truth, that, with the exception of a few places which had either put off their actual surrender to await his personal approach, or which a strong force was subduing, he was practically master of the states of the Church up to the very gates of Rome. Moreover, with the favour of the whole Roman people, " we are preparing to enter the City in state, in order to revive the ancient glories of the empire, and to crown our victorious eagles with the triumphant laurels which are their due." [5]

But Frederick had to deal with one who was at least as firm as himself, and much less of a braggart. Knowing that the Emperor had a strong party in Rome, and that

Solemn procession in Rome.

[1] Ep. of Feb. 1, 1240. ap. *ib.*, p. 702.

[2] Ep. of Feb., ap. *ib.*, p. 761.

[3] Ep. of Feb. 2, *ib.*, p. 707. With a knowledge of the intentions of the Almighty, which German emperors in our day also claim, Frederick continues : " Cum autem grave tulerit Dominus et indignum quod a sanctuario suo vel a Petri sede fuisset nostri juris invasor egressus, contra opinionem et votum illius ad propria nos reduxit."

[4] *Ib.* *Cf.* Ric. of S. Ger., 1240.

[5] " Restat igitur ut favente nobis universo populo Romano nostroque sicut cepit adventui acclamante, Urbem feliciter ingredi disponamus ut antiquos imperii fastos et triumphales lauros victricibus aquilis debitas reformemus." Ep. of Feb. 1240, ap. *ib.*, p. 762 f. " His calumniators " would be sorry when they beheld him "whom with wagging (dissolutis) tongues they had provoked."

many were calling on him to come to take possession of the city,[1] Gregory had recourse to prayer. In solemn procession he carried the great relic of the true Cross and the heads of the Apostles SS. Peter and Paul to the basilica of St. Peter, and there addressed the people on their duty to defend the Church and the relics of St. Peter (February 22). Moved by the words and actions of the Pope the people took the cross against the emperor and declared that they would defend their mother, the Roman Church, to death.[2]

With another of his many boasts rendered idle, Frederick retired into Apulia (March, 1240) to raise money by excessive taxation, especially of the clergy.[3]

Peace negotiations, 1240. Feeling no doubt that this Roman expedition with its successes and failures would probably render both the Pope and the Emperor more disposed towards peace, the German princes now (April, May, 1240) renewed the efforts in that direction made by the ecclesiastics among them in the September of 1239.[4] But though Gregory was disposed to treat for peace, Frederick, having wrung large sums of money from the kingdom,

[1] *Chron. de rebus.*, p. 182 ; *Vita*, Greg., c. 42.

[2] *Ibb.*, p. 182 and c. 46, and *Ann. de Dunstap.*, p. 153 f. *R. S. Cf.* Gregory's own account of the Romans' change of sentiment, ap. H.-B., v, 776, Feb. 1240, and also that of Frederick, ap. *ib.*, p. 840, March 16. Frederick's version only reflects upon himself. He declares that the Pope's action " induced some boys and old women and a very few hired troops to assume the cross against us." Were that the fact, then he was easily kept out of the city ! Clement IV. (ep. 627, ap. Mart. and Durand, *Thes. nov. anecdot.*, ii, p. 588) recalls Gregory's carrying the heads of the Apostles.

[3] Ric. of S. Ger., an. 1240. Frederick's letters are full of boastfulness. Here is another example : " Exurgat igitur invicta Germania . . . nostrum nobis defendatis imperium per quod invidiam omnium nationum, dignitatum omnium et mundi monarchiam obtinetis." Ap. H.-B., v, 846.

[4] Ep. ap. H.-B., v, 398, for the September effort ; *ib.*, p. 985 ff., for the letters of April and May, 1240.

was resolved, as he said, " in the strength of his arm to humble his enemy . . . and to prevent him from daring to raise his voice against our sacred empire and against our person." [1] But the fall of Ferrara and the capture of his powerful ally, the old warrior Salinguerra, through the energy and treachery of Gregory of Montelongo and the League (June, 1240),[2] made Frederick willing to listen to peace proposals. In fact he wrote to tell his friends that peace would soon be made between him and the Pope and he would then return to the North and crush the Lombards. He believed, he said, that the Pope " was really a lover of peace (pacis zelatorem)," and he himself " as a Catholic prince and a grateful son " had " a son's reverence " for the Church.[3] But the negotiations came to nothing. Peace, which Frederick declared had come to their very gates, fled far away again, because " Gregory called Pope " insisted that the Lombards should be included in the peace, whereas " it seemed intolerable to us to grant a truce to rebels worn out by long fighting and almost completely subdued." [4]

After the hopeless breakdown of the peace negotiations, Frederick returned to Lombardy, " powerfully to crush," as he expressed it, " all rebels beneath his feet." [5] In

Frederick returns to Lombardy, and the Pope calls a General Council, 1240.

[1] " Copiosis opibus de regno mostro assumpto." Ep. of Fred. to his son about the very beginning of June, ap. *ib.*, p. 1003.

[2] By the authority of the Pope, Azzo of Este was made the ruler of the captured city " quæ juris erat ecclesiæ." *Cf. Vita Ric. Comitis,* ap. *R. I. SS.,* viii, p. 130.

[3] Ep. of June, 1240, H.-B., v, 1004. *Cf.* the following letter to Frederick, duke of Austria.

[4] Ep. of Fred. to one of the princes, July 18, 1230, ap. *ib.*, p. 1014 f. He continues in his usual boastful style : " Ad quorum (the Lombards) persecutionem et vindictam accincti, vexilla victricia et prepotentia castra nostra triumphaliter duximus educenda."

[5] Ep. of F. to the people of Cremona, end of July, ap. *ib.*, p. 1017 f. " Quocunque rebelles occurrerint per nostram potentiam sub pedibus nostris oppressuri."

August, whilst he was lightly beginning the siege of
Faënza which was not destined to be successfully
terminated till the following April, Gregory, thereby
giving the Emperor his way,[1] called a General Council,
or really a Diet of Christendom (as he summoned all
its bishops and princes), in order to submit to it the merits
of his dispute with Frederick.[2]

No sooner, however, was the Council summoned than
Frederick protested against its meeting. He denounced
it to the cardinals and to the Kings of England and France.
It had been called, he declared, by one who was " the
most capital enemy " at once of the empire and of its
head, it had been summoned not for peace but for war ; [3]
and to it had been summoned even his most bitter
enemies. Therefore, as he plainly told the King of

---

[1] Frederick had more than once said that a General Council should be
called. *Cf.* his letters of Apr. 20, 1239, and March 16, 1240, ap. *ib.*,
pp. 304 and 843, " Generale petentes concilium convocari." Mr. G. C.
Macaulay in his excellent article in the *English Hist. Rev.*, vi, p. 1 ff.,
1891, " The capture of a General Council," thinks : " it is quite out of
place to charge the emperor with inconsistency because he endeavoured
to hinder the meeting of the council summoned by the Pope with whom
he was still at war," and not by the cardinals as he had suggested. But,
apart from the fact that he knew perfectly well that it was not within
the competence of the cardinals to summon a General Council, it was
matterless whether it was summoned by the Pope or by the cardinals—
as far at least as the hierarchy of Europe was concerned. In either case
all the bishops would have had to be summoned, and as a matter of fact
all were summoned by the Pope. Hence, if Frederick's cause had been
just, he could well have relied on the bishops of the Empire at any rate
to see that no injustice was done to him. Besides, such impartial
persons as the king of France and the kings of Christendom generally,
were all summoned. It was a Diet of Christendom that was called
together.

[2] *Cf.* the letters, ap. H.-B., v, 1020 ; or *Reg.* iii, 389 ff., Aug. 9, 1240,
for the first convocation of the Council, which summoned it to meet on
the following Easter Sunday (March 31, 1241), and *ib.*, p. 403, Oct. 15,
1240, for the second convocation, in which he bids all to carry out his
orders and to come, despite the threats of Frederick. *Cf.* Rodenberg,
i, p. 679 ff. *Cf.* Mat. Par., iv, 30.

[3] Ep. of the end of August to the Cardinals, ap. H.-B., v, 1027.

England, he " would not allow the council to be summoned
by the Pope." Then, " arrogating to himself the rights
of the priesthood," [1] he asked our king by means of the
bishops of his country to let it be known by all that
" no one should go to the council in the expectation
of receiving a safe conduct from him." Much as he loved
the English people, " he would not tolerate the presumptuous audacity of such as should set his prohibition
at naught, and go to the council at the summons of his
enemy." [2]

As far, however, as this country was concerned,
neither the entreaties nor the threats of Frederick were
able to effect their object. The king always declared
that it was his duty to obey the commands of the Pope,[3]
and the English bishops " in obedience to the Pope's
orders, boldly prepared, although with great risk, to
cross the Alps at Christmas." [4]

It must not, however, be supposed that the Emperor's
threats and actions were altogether without effect. Both
were partially successful. The prelates or their proxies
who attempted to reach the Pope through his territories
were " attacked, seized, imprisoned, tortured, or even

Effect of the Emperor's threats.

---

[1] " Vendicare sanctuarium indevotus intemptat "—a phrase used
by the Pope in his second letter of convocation to the Council, Oct. 15,
1240, ap. *Reg.*, iii, p. 404. Some wish to change the " Vendicare " of
the Register and Matthew Paris (iv, 97) into " venditare."

[2] Ep. of Sept. 13, 1241, ap. *ib.*, p. 1038 ff. *Cf.* his letter to St. Louis
of France, *ib.*, p. 1075, in which he upbraids the Pope especially for
favouring Milan "hereticorum nidus Mediolanensium mansio, viciorum
sentina notissima."

[3] Mat. Par., *Chron. maj.*, iv, 4. *Cf.* p. 10, " Nec volo nec audeo
d. Papæ in aliquibus contradicerĕ " ; and p. 19.

[4] *Ib.*, p. 74. Gregory had ordered the archbishop of York and the
bishop of Durham to come as soon as possible for consultation purposes,
and he asked them, in order to avoid vanity and expense, not to travel
with too many followers. Ep. to Archbishop Gray, ap. *Hists. of the
Church of York*, iii, p. 137 *R. S.*

in many cases (plures) punished by a dreadful death." [1]
Others were too frightened to think of obeying the
Pope's orders under the circumstances, and so to prevent
themselves from being too isolated in their disobedience,
they endeavoured to bring others to their point of view.
A letter, very interesting but very long, of one type
of cleric has come down to us. It would appear to have
been written by some French or, perhaps more likely,
by some English cleric, and it was sent round to a number
of those who had been convoked to the Council.[2] The
anonymous writer first of all points out the dangers
of the journey, and then the dangers from the unhealthy
climate of Rome, the " Urbis inurbana pericula." At
sea there was the indigestible biscuit, wine spoilt by the
perpetual motion of the sea, corrupted water alive with
worms which, with the greatest loathing, can only be
drunk with closed eyes and teeth. Then comes the
storm, and when you think you are going to Rome
it will suddenly throw you among a barbarous people,
ignorant of your language and customs, who will for ever
deprive you of your liberty. Or, if the storm does
not do that, it will beat up the waves, and one moment
shoot you up to heaven and the next plunge you into
hell ; it will burst your sails, break your rudder and
mast, and leave you to perish. Pirates, too, will come
along, rob you, and then take you captive or send you
to the bottom of the sea ; or you may run aground or
on to the rocks, and an adverse wind may catch you
just as you are entering the harbour and keep you out
at sea till your provisions are exhausted and you die

---

[1] Mat. Par., *Chron. maj.*, iv, 96. On Feb. 8, 1240, Frederick
banished a canon who tried to raise the people of Sulmona against
him. *Cf. Cod. diplom. Sulm.*, p. 65. *Cf.* pp. 74, 75, 79.

[2] Ap. H.-B., v, 1077 ff. It has been analysed by Macaulay, and
we have availed ourselves of his work.

of hunger and thirst. Moreover, there is at sea an utterly abominable danger which no one can escape. The food and the continuous rocking constantly provoke you to vomit, so that what you take in with disgust you give forth with pain. Besides, the ship is small, and yet is the abode of many ; and hence sick and healthy are all so crowded together that all suffer.[1] The wretched traveller is soon brought to death's door, and is at length thrown into the sea before life is extinct. Out of a thousand passengers hardly one escapes death or a mortal disease, as the faces of those coming off a boat clearly show.

In the present instance, worse than the sea is the Emperor, all powerful on land and sea, a man more cruel than Herod, and more impious than Nero.[2] As he has not spared his own son he will not spare you.

If, however, by some unlooked for chance you succeed in getting to Rome, you must fall a victim to its factions or to its climate. There you will meet with " intolerable heat, putrid water, coarse food, an atmosphere almost palpable, swarms of mosquitoes, countless scorpions, and beneath the city caverns full of poisonous reptiles which exhale noxious vapours, so that of those who delay in Rome scarce ten out of a thousand escape death." If by some miracle you escape these dangers, how are you going to compass your return journey ? And if you do not return, and so many churches are widowed, will not the resulting evil be greater than that which you were sent for to remedy ? The fact is that the important business for which you are summoned is the existing situation between the Pope and the

---

[1] At times, as here, the picture painted by our anonymous author is too realistic to be reproduced.

[2] The character here given of Frederick is very scathing : " Prodigus in pena, parcus misericordia, furore repletus, pietate deficiens, verbo falsus, opere imperfectus, viciis deditus, etc." P. 1080.

emperor, and, as the Apostolic See entered into the struggle " with a cruel and powerful Prince " without consulting you, ought it not to finish it without bringing you into such dangers? Besides, as the Emperor cannot be put down without great expense, it will be expected that you will share the expenses of the actions against him which you sanction.[1] Seeing, therefore, that no reason of absolute necessity has been put forward why we should brave such dangers, " I think it better not to obey rather than perish." [2]

The Pope prepares a fleet for the prelates.

No doubt this special but not very loyal or manly pleading had its full effect on such as were of like character to its writer, but some of the points which it emphasized had already appealed to the Pope. Gregory was fully aware of the unscrupulous character of the man with whom he was dealing, and he fully realized to what dangers those would be exposed who should attempt to reach Rome through the territories where the Emperor held sway. He accordingly wrote to Gregory of Romagna, his representative in Genoa, which as we know was an ally of the League and the Pope, and bade him arrange in secret with the Genoese for a sufficient number of ships to convey the prelates safely to Rome and back.[3]

[1] The Pope is going to play upon you : " ut sitis organa sonantia juxta deductionem et libitum organiste." P. 1083.

[2] " Ego tamen quantum sufficio, pensans et ponderans universa, in premissis elegendis arbitror non parere potius quam perire, nisi causa manifesta et necessaria primitus exprimatur ex qua causatum debeat obedientie vinculum inviolaviliter observari." These are the last words of this able but not high principled document.

[3] Ep. of Oct. 13, 1240, ap. H.-B., v, 1052 ff. He had learnt by experience, he said, that the Genoese usually charged 200 pounds a month for an armed galley, but he bade his agent to try for a more favourable quotation. *Cf.* the legate's answer of Dec. 6, ap. *ib.*, p. 1061, and the whole series of documents (littere super apparatu navigii) in the *Regist.*, iii, p. 427 ff., or in Rodenberg, i, p. 684 ff. *Cf.* C. Imperiale, *Genova e le sue relazioni con Federico II.*, Venice, 1923.

To pay the Genoese and, in general, to carry on this *Papal* bitter struggle with the Emperor, the Pope had great *money difficulties.* need of money. Yet, as owing to the seizure of his territories by his enemies his needs became greater, his ordinary sources of revenue became smaller. To raise the money of which he stood in immediate want he had to have recourse to the merchant-bankers (the *mercatores*), and to repay them, he had to tax the clergy in the different countries, and borrow money from them. To pay his Italian, and especially his Roman, creditors (lest they should embroil the city), he borrowed money from some of the great abbeys of France, Benedictine and Premonstratensian, on the security of a subsidy of a fifth from the English Church ; for he desired to keep the subsidy he had asked from the French clergy " for the greater needs of the Church." [1]

The subsidy from the English Church on which Gregory relied was a fifth of its revenues. The legate Otho laid before our bishops and some of the nobles of the land the pecuniary necessities into which the Pope had been

[1] *Cf.* the documents of Nov. 1240 (Super pecunia mutuanda ecclesie Romane a prelatis subscriptis) addressed by Gregory to James Pecoraria, his legate in France, and to Otho, his legate in England, ap. *Reg.* iii, 421 ff., or Rodenberg, i, 693 ff. As Gregory pointed out, he was struggling " for the defence of the faith, and of ecclesiastical liberty." Gregory's nephew also, Alexander IV., writing to the king of Hungary (ap. Theiner, *Mon. Hung.*, i, p. 239, Oct. 14, 1259), points out to him that his predecessor was engaged in struggling to prevent Frederick from first crushing the Church, and afterwards her children, and then getting himself revered above all " as a sort of monstrous idol of desolation— veluti immane desolationis idolum." (With the ruins of cathedrals, churches, etc., in Belgium and France before his eyes let anyone to-day, June, 1915, compare the aims of Wilhelm II. of Germany.) " In his (Gregory's) efforts to defend his own liberty and the liberty of his children, the Church was so overwhelmed with debt . . . that its resources have not been able to rid it of the load." Needless to say that Frederick did all he could to prevent Albert von Behaim from getting the same subsidy from Germany. *Cf.* his instructions to the city of Worms on the subject. Ap. H.-B., v, 1130 ff.

driven in his fight for the rights of the Church, and to repel the aggression of the Emperor, and he asked for the fifth to relieve them. The demand was a heavy one, and in many quarters caused much murmuring, especially as in the comparative peace of their own land many of our Churchmen did not realize the gravity of the questions for which the Pope was contending. However, the money was paid, and Gregory obtained the means to carry on the contest.[1]

Frederick prepares to seize the prelates coming to the Council, 1241.

Finding that, despite his threats, prelates from different parts of Christendom were making their way to Rome, Frederick ordered all his subjects to seize them, and even to plunder them for their own benefit.[2] He further bade the maritime cities prepare ships to attack those of the Genoese.[3]

Some of the bishops embark at Genoa.

As the bishops advanced on their journey, the dangers they had to face from the Emperor became more apparent. They found evidence of his determination to hinder their reaching Rome, and they heard from some that " in his grasping ambition, he was like Lucifer or Antichrist aspiring to the monarchy of the world for the ruin of the Christian faith." [4] Accordingly the

---

[1] Mat. Par., *Chron. maj.*, iv, pp. 9, 10, 15 ; *Ann. de Dunstap.*, p. 154 *R. S.* As a further means of obtaining aid against Frederick, Gregory authorized his envoys in the different countries to commute the vows which men had made to fight in the Holy Land into vows to fight " in defence of the Church against Frederick," on condition that they were prepared to spend the same amount of money in each case. Ep. of Feb. 12, 1241, ap. H.-B., v, 1095.

[2] Ep. Feb. 1241, ap. *ib.*, p. 1089.

[3] Letter of Feb. " magistris portulanis," ap. *ib.*, p. 1090. *Cf.* Ric. of S. Ger., 1241.

[4] Mat. Par., *Chron.*, iv, p. 119. We do not know how many of our bishops left England to go to the Council. We know, however, from a letter of Richard of Cornwall (ap. Mat. P., *l.c.*, iv, p. 144) that " some of our bishops " were among those captured by the emperor, and that bishop Grosseteste was anxious to go " in order to show as far as in him lay the obedience that was due to the Roman Church,

bishop of Norwich and some other English prelates, " listening to the advice of the French, turned aside from their journey, and, betaking themselves to safe places, cautiously awaited the issue of events."

However, other prelates and envoys, including some from England, pushed on to Nice whence the Genoese fleet was to convey them first to Genoa in order to join the prelates and envoys from Lombardy, and thence to Rome (March, 1241). Here also many decided to go no further. The fleet did not seem to them powerful enough, and so they sent on their representatives and remained behind themselves.[1] But, along with the two legates, James and Otho, the more courageous embarked and reached Genoa in safety.

Meanwhile every effort had been made both by the Emperor and his allies, the Pisans, to induce the Genoese not to fulfil their contract to convey the envoys to Rome. But the Genoese had declared that " the Commune of Genoa had ever (toto tempore) honoured the Roman Church . . . and were prepared to serve it in defence of the liberty of the Church and of the Christian faith." [2] Failing with the Genoese, Frederick endeavoured to impose upon the delegates who had arrived in Genoa. He offered them a safe conduct if only they would proceed to Rome not by sea but by land after they had seen him. He was only anxious, he declared, to put his case before them, as the Pope had grievously ill-treated and

and to show it that reverence and honour to which he was bound." " The infirmity of our body," however, compelled him to beg the legate Otho to excuse him to the Pope for his " involuntary but necessary absence " from the Council. *Cf.* his letter to Otho, ap. *Rob. G. Epp.*, p. 313 *R. S.* Grosseteste was enthusiastic in his devotion to Gregory, not merely because he was Pope (and he declared his conviction that no man could see salvation unless he paid the Pope the homage—the debitum subjectionis—that was his due), but because of his exceptional gifts of mind and heart. *Cf. ib.*, p. 123.

[1] *Ann. Genuenses*, ap. *R. I. SS.*, vi, 486.   [2] *Ib.*

slandered him, and had summoned his open enemies
to the Council. He could not come to them as the
protracted siege of Faënza had rendered him short of
money, and the approach of the Tartars and other
important matters were completely engrossing his
attention.[1] But the bishops and envoys of the nations
were not to be so easily entrapped. Declaring that
"no reliance could be placed on the cavilling words of
a man who had been excommunicated,"[2] they embarked
with confidence on the great galleys of Genoa.

Capture of
the prelates
and the
envoys,
1241.

Very triumphant, amidst the loud blare of trumpets
and the joyous shouts of the sailors, was the departure
of the ships from the lovely harbour[3] on St. Mark's day
(April 25), and loud was the boasting of the Genoese
sailors who heartily despised their foes, and even the
exhortations of the Pope and the prelates to be on the
safe side.[4]

Meanwhile, with instructions to its commander "to
capture, sink, or kill" the prelates, Frederick had sent
a strong fleet under his bastard son, Enzio, to join that of
the Pisans. Even though knowing this, the Genoese

[1] Mat. P., *l.c.*, pp. 121–3. It was in the previous year that the terrible
Tartars, of whom more hereafter, made their first inroad into Europe,
and at the moment King Conrad was preparing to meet them in
Germany. According to Matthew Paris, some believed that Frederick
himself had brought about the Tartar invasion. They contended that
the letter which the emperor issued on that subject contained false-
hoods, and that the secret doings and ways of the Tartars were redolent
with imperial suggestions. The imagination of these worthies further
inspired them with the notion that Frederick had induced them to
invade Hungary in the hope that its king might fly to him and do
homage to him in return for his help. *Ib.*, p. 119 f.

[2] *Ib.*, p. 124.

[3] *Ib.* "In clamore tumultuoso nautarum et clangore buccinarum
mare Tirenum sulcaverunt." *Cf. Ann. Gen.*, *l.c.*, p. 488.

[4] As late as March 16, 1241, the Pope wrote to urge Gregory of
Romagna to see that there were rather too many than too few
ships—"cum sit melioris cautele in presentis necessitatis articulo in
navigio abundare." *Cf.* Mat. P., *l.c.*

would not wait for reinforcements, but gallantly and foolishly sailed on to meet their foes. The two fleets met " near the isle of Giglio about ninety miles distant from Porto Pisano." Hopelessly outnumbered, the Genoese were completely defeated (May 3). Out of their fleet of twenty-seven ships only five escaped. The rest were taken or sunk. Among the persons captured were the three legates, Cardinals James Pecoraria, Otho, and Gregory of Romagna ; among the killed or drowned was the archbishop of Besançon, and among those who escaped was the English envoy, John of Lexinton.[1]

Exactly how many important prisoners were made by the imperial forces is not clear. Frederick himself in his usual boastful style says that besides the legates, " there were captured also many archbishops, bishops, abbots, priors, priests, proctors of various bishops over a hundred in number, and ambassadors of the rebellious Lombard cities . . . All these are locked up in our prisons." [2] However many were captured, it is certain that those who were captured were very badly treated both during their captivity and whilst they were being conveyed to Naples and Apulia. The severity of their sufferings resulted in the death of several of them.[3]

[1] Mat. Par., *l.c.*, p. 125, who makes the ludicrous mistake of converting *stolium* (fleet) into its commander " Stollius " ; *Ann. Gen., l.c.*, 489 ; *Chron. de rebus in Ital.*, p. 185 ; *Chron. Sic.*, ap. H.-B., i, p. 906 ; *Chron. Reg. Colon., Cont. V.*, p. 279, whence we learn that there were on board the Genoese fleet many envoys of the German bishops, and many letters from the bishops who escaped (ap. H.-B., v, 1119), Frederick, (ap. *ib.*, p. 1123), the Pope, etc.

[2] Ep. of May to the princes, ap. *ib.*, p. 1127. *Cf.* ep. to the king of England, *ib.*, p. 1125. Certain Cistercian abbots who were captured wrote to say that apart from the three legates, and not counting abbots, etc., the emperor had only in his prisons " three archbishops and six bishops." Ep. of *c.* May 15, ap. *ib.*, p. 1122, and a letter of Gregory (June 14, ap. *ib.*, p. 1136) is addressed to three archbishops and six bishops.

[3] Card. Jas. Pecoraria was among those who, " owing to their

The violence of the emperor, however, did not succeed in breaking the spirit of the prelates. The bishops who had escaped wrote to the Pope, and bade him give them what orders he would, because despite all difficulties they would remain firm and constant. They urged the Pope to take more drastic steps against the tyrant for his atrocious crime, assuring him that " under his rule the Church would never enjoy peace and tranquillity." [1]

Nor were all the secular Princes of Europe disposed to acquiesce in the Emperor's lawless conduct.[2] Our own Richard of Cornwall, on his return from the Holy Land, made an effort, a vain one, to obtain the release of the captives.[3] King Louis of France also took steps to obtain their release; and when Frederick attempted haughtily to disregard his representations also, the saintly monarch gave him to understand that the kingdom of France was not so weak that it could be driven about by any spurs of his. Thereupon, we are told, " through fear of offending the King of France, he, much against his will, liberated all the captives " [4]—a thing which, as we shall see, he did not do for some years.

obedience," " gained the palm of martyrdom." Mat. Par., *l.c.*, iv, 129. *Cf.* Albert von Behaim, p. 76. " Frederick cannot be acquitted of ungenerous harshness to his illustrious prisoners " is the very moderate comment of Mr. Macaulay, p. 15. In connexion with this capture of the general council, the writer just cited calls attention to the inaccuracy of Milman's account of this transaction in his *History of Latin Christianity*, thereby helping to substantiate the highly unfavourable criticism passed on that author's accuracy in an early vol. of this work.

[1] Ep. of May 10, 1241, ap. H.-B., v, 1119 ff.

[2] Mat. P., *l.c.* He quotes Ovid, *Ars Amator.*, ii, 390 (" Gloria peccati non repetenda sui est "), in support of his assertion.

[3] *Ib.*, pp. 144 and 147 f. *Cf. Ann. de Theokesber.*, p. 120 *R. S.* According to M. P., Richard failed through the obstinacy of the Pope. Whereas the superior diplomacy of Frederick, and his at least equal obstinacy had as much to do with the failure.

[4] Will. of Nangis, *Chron.*, an. 1241, p. 193, ed. Géraud. " Regnum Franciæ non erat debilitatum ut se permitteret ejus calcaribus perurgeri." See also his *Life* of St. Louis, ap. *R. F. SS.*, xx, p. 332, and the letter to

Meanwhile, however, everything seemed to go well with Frederick. Soon after the capture of the prelates, his allies the men of Pavia defeated with great loss the Milanese with their captain, the legate Gregory of Montelongo (May 11).[1] This further success decided the emperor to abandon his offensive in Lombardy and to turn his "victorious armaments" against Rome. "Thither," as he told the Princes, "under our mighty standards are we called by a more prosperous fortune by which any remaining rebels against us may be laid low, and, the head of sedition being humbled, its members may wither away."[2]

Accordingly, "with a great force of Germans, Lombards, and men from the Kingdom,"[3] Frederick began his march towards Rome about the beginning of June.

Whilst the emperor was concerned with his march on Rome, the Pope was occupied with the interests of the captive prelates. He wrote to console them in their misfortunes, assuring them that, though not actually in fetters himself, he shared their sufferings. He expressed, however, regret that he had not hitherto been able to do anything to mitigate these sufferings, and was afraid that he would not be able to effect anything in that direction.[4] We have it, however, on good, if late, authority, that Gregory did strive to effect the

Frederick advances on Rome.

Gregory disposed for peace.

Frederick of certain archbishops of France which is assigned to Oct. 2, 1241, ap. H.-B., vi, pt. ii, p. 897. Frederick's panegyrist, the so-called Nicholas of Jamsilla, pretends that his patron liberated the princes of his own clemency, and "magis Deo quam sibi satisfaciens liberatos abire permisit." Ap. *R. I. SS.*, viii, p. 496.

[1] *Cf.* ep. of Fred., of the end of May, ap. H.-B., v, 1128.

[2] *Ib.*

[3] See the ep. of brother Bartholomew, O.P. of June, 1241, ap. H.-B., v, 1146 f.

[4] Ep. of June 14, *ib.*, p. 1136.

release of the imprisoned captives. He sent a Dominican prior to the Emperor in their behalf. But the envoy met with the reception which the Pope expected. He was told that a wise man paid no heed to the prayers of an enemy, and was sent away without accomplishing anything.[1] Nevertheless Gregory did not cease his efforts for the liberation of the illustrious captives. He was able to assure them only a few days before he died that he was seeking ways to secure their freedom, and that he would not rest till he had been gladdened by the sight of them.[2]

Frederick
is invited to
Rome.

It was in the interests of the captive bishops that the Pope asserted that he was ready to make any terms with Frederick which were consistent with the honour of God, the liberty of the Church, and the peace of Christendom, if only he would approach the Church with a contrite heart.[3] It was in their interests that peace negotiations were actually set on foot.

But Frederick was as little disposed as the Pope to give up what he contended were his rights ; and he was encouraged in his resolve not to give up his claims not merely by the capture of the prelates and the defeat of Montelongo, but by the increase in the power of his party in Rome. It had been strengthened by the adhesion of one of the most distinguished of the cardinals, John Colonna (or of Colonna, de Columpna, as he is

[1] The authority is that of the fifteenth century historian, Pandulf Collenutio, in his *Vita Frid. II.*, cited by H.-B., v, 1147 n., who adds that C. is an author deserving of the highest credit.

[2] Ep. of July 31, 1241. He exhorts the captives " certe spei fiduciam habituri, quod pro liberatione vestra, quin immo nostra confusione tollenda, vias querimus, remedia cogitamus . . . nec enim a laboribus corpora, nec manus ab auxiliis deducemus, donec in vestris consolemur aspectibus." Ap. *Reg.*, iii, p. 555.

[3] *Cf.* epp. of June 19, and the first of July to the duke of Carinthia (ap. H.-B., v, 1138) and to the king of Hungary (*ib.*, p. 1148 n.). See also the letter just quoted of brother Bartholomew.

called in the sources). Owing to some disagreement with Gregory, the cardinal formally went over to the Emperor's party in January, 1241, and at once put into a state of defence the Mausoleum of Augustus,[1] his fortress within the City, and his other fortresses outside the City. Feeling sure, therefore, of substantial support in Rome, Frederick informed the Senate that he intended to visit Rome, to make peace with the Pope, if possible, in order that he might be freer to go to fight the Tartars. The Romans must therefore be ready to support him.[2] It was his intention to leave in Rome " signs of his power and of his clemency . . . of his power if he found its people obstinate rebels, of his clemency if he found them disposed to good." [3] He evidently hoped to be able to compel the Pope to make peace on terms of his own choosing.[4]

When, by the month of July, the Emperor was before Reati, he received an urgent message to advance on Rome from Cardinal Colonna, who had meanwhile left the City, and had betaken himself to Palestrina, which he made his headquarters, and from which he proceeded to act against the Pope.[5] Frederick at once

[1] The Lagusta, as Ric. of S. Ger., an. 1241, calls it. The region in the neighbourhood of the mausoleum was often called *In Augusta, Agosta, Lagusta*, etc. *Cf.* Rodocanachi, *Les Monuments de Rome*, p. 98, Paris, 1914. According to Mat. Par., *Chron. Maj.*, iv, pp. 58-9, the quarrel between the Pope and the cardinal was due to difference of opinion as to the treatment of Frederick. However, when he speaks of his death in 1244, M. P. calls him " a vessel full of all kinds of pride and insolence . . . and the fosterer of discord between the emperor and the Pope." *Ib.*, p. 287.

[2] Ep. of June 20, ap. H.-B., v, 1130. *Cf.* his letter to the king of Hungary, ap. *ib.*, p. 1143.

[3] Ep. of brother Bartholomew, *ib.*, p. 1147.

[4] *Cf.* a letter of Peter della Vigna to a friend, July 1241, ap. *ib.*, p. 1157.

[5] Ric. of S. Ger. " Monticellum et Pontem Lucanum contra Romanos recipit in odium Papæ."

acted on the cardinal's suggestions, letting him know,
however, that he was astounded that plans of such
extreme audacity should come from a cardinal and a
priest. Still, so the emperor assured his new ally, he
was a man after his own heart, and it was only necessary
for him to combine constancy with his boldness when
his sovereign should begin to carry out the daring plans
he had conceived.[1]

The Emperor cannot seize Rome.

By August Frederick had reached Tivoli, and began
to lay waste the country round Rome. But he could
not make his way into the City. The Pope and the
Romans were again more than a match for him.
Gregory had named a new Senator, Matteo Rosso
(Matthaeus Russus or de Rubeis), who proved to be
loyal, capable, and energetic. He had at once laid
siege to Colonna's fortress, the Mausoleum of Augustus
(July) ; but just before it fell into his hands, his lord,
Pope Gregory IX., had ceased to be.[2]

The death of Pope Gregory, 1241.

The capture of the prelates, the defeat of Montelongo,
enforced residence in Rome during the summer heats,
and lastly, the news that was brought to him that
Frederick had seized near Montefortino in Campania
a castle in which were a number of the Pope's relatives,
and had hanged them all [3]—these causes brought about
the rather sudden death of Gregory on August 22. He
was buried in St. Peter's near the body of the first Gregory
in front of the Sacristy.[4]

[1] Ep. of July, ap. *ib.*, p. 1155.

[2] Ric. of S. Ger., an. 1241, p. 153 f.

[3] *Chron. maj.*, iv., 163. He died, says the continuation of Otto
of Frising, "multis tribulationibus ab ipso (Frederick) pressus."
P. 354, ed. Pertz. In Gregory's *vita*, c. 23, we are told he left Reati
"ex causa reumatis." *Cf. infra*, p. 322.

[4] *Chron. Minor Ephord.*, an. 1241 ; Nic. de Carbio, *Vit. Inn. IV*,
c. 5. From a letter of Philip of Perugia, who was present on the occasion,
we learn that a funeral service was celebrated for the deceased pontiff
at Perugia. Ap. *M. G. SS.*, xxxii, p. 683.

Leaden bulla of Gregory IX. showing, as usual,
the heads of SS. Peter and Paul on the reverse.

Of this great Pope whose strenuous life came to an
end under such tragic circumstances, one of the noblest
bishops of the thirteenth century, our own Robert
Grosseteste, bishop of Lincoln, speaks in the highest
terms. He declared that the remarkable brilliancy
of the Pope's virtues powerfully stimulated his devotion
to his person. The Pope's burning zeal for souls, his
almsgiving, his love for religious, his solicitude for all
the churches and kingdoms, carried away everyone
with admiration and love for him.[1]

The opinion entertained about Gregory, and thus
expressed to him during life by impartial and highly
revered Churchmen, was shared by secular rulers. One
of these [2] whilst announcing his death, assured his correspondents that Gregory's deeds proved what a worthy
pastor and splendid ruler he had been. In his endeavour
to save his flock from the ravages of the wicked, he had
not hesitated to yield up to God that soul which had
been so grievously afflicted in his struggles for the right.

The ruler, however, who had been the cause of
Gregory's death, mockingly told the kings of the earth
that he who had scorned all thought of peace in the hope
of causing universal dissension, had failed to cross the
limits of the avenger "August" after having aimed at
offending the "Augustus." But, he continued, the emperor
will strive with all his power that a successor be elected
to Gregory who will correct his evil-doings. To such
a Pope he will offer his goodwill and protection for the
defence of the Catholic faith and of ecclesiastical liberty,

---

[1] Ep. 35, 1236 ?, p. 123 *R. S.*

[2] Ap. H.-B., vi, p. 101. In the MSS. this ruler is said to have been
"the emperor." But in view of Frederick's later expressions about
Gregory, it is generally agreed that the letter in question must have
been the work of some other ruler.

inasmuch as it was for this purpose that he had received the sceptre of Empire.[1]

---

[1] Ep. written at the end of August from Grottaferrata whither he had retired on the death of Gregory. Ap. H.-B., vi, p. 1165. It is interesting to learn from Frederick himself what was the duty of the Roman emperor. " Ei (the right kind of Pope) omnimodam bene-volentiam, defensionem, et patrocinium impensuri ad tuitionem catholice fidei et ecclesiasticæ libertatis ; cum ad hoc . . . imperii sceptrum susceperimus."

CHAPTER V.

ROME AND THE PATRIMONY.

If Gregory's pontificate was one long struggle against foes both at home and abroad, it was due in the main to the ambition of one man, the emperor Frederick II. The preceding pages have given in some detail the narrative of the Pope's struggle with the Empire, and incidentally some notices of his struggle with a certain section of the Roman people, that section which well-nigh throughout the whole of his reign the emperor kept in his pay. The present chapter will give in greater fullness the story of Gregory's relations to the City and to the Patrimony generally.

Frederick never ceases to attempt to preserve an imperial party in Rome.

Not all the trouble, however, with which Gregory was faced in Rome was brought about by Frederick. Some of it was the work of the turbulent Romans themselves in search either of gold or of power, and some of it was aggravated, if not caused, by Patarene heretics. Their usual avarice (gratia questus) was responsible for the first of the annoyances which the City caused Gregory. He had left it in the month of June to avoid passing the summer months in its unhealthy surroundings. Whilst he was sojourning in his native hill-town of Anagni, a certain individual, supported by a party of the Romans, feigned himself to be the Pope's vicar, took up his stand by the portico of St. Peter's, and for money professed to absolve from their vow of taking the Cross such Crusaders as came to him. At length, however, the impostor was seized by the Senator of the City, and after communication with the Pope, was duly punished.[1]

A sham Pope, 1227.

[1] Ric. of S. Ger., p. 127, ed. Gaudenzi.

Gregory
is compelled
to leave the
City, 1228.

He returns,
1230.

He protects
the fabrics of
the Churches
of Rome.

This took place in the first year of Gregory's pontificate. Before that year came to a close he had excommunicated Frederick, and soon after its close had the mortification of seeing his adversary gain over a number of the Romans, including the powerful Frangipani.[1] The violence of the imperial party, aggravated by Gregory's destruction of certain fortified palaces which were at once a menace to his palace at the Lateran, and an obstacle to its outlook,[2] caused the Pope to leave the City (April, 1228).

A serious inundation of the Tiber, however, and the miseries that followed it, caused the Romans to bring back the Pope to his City in triumph (Feb., 1230).[3] During the next six years, though at peace with the Empire, and though he contrived to do much for the City, Gregory was for most of the period at war with it.

Immediately on his return Gregory is supposed to have made his Seneschal, Anibaldo Anibaldi, Senator. If, however, the new Senator gratified the Pope by framing severe laws against heretics,[4] he did not please him by the ready way in which he gave the lime-burners or the *mamorarii* (marble cutters, sculptors, mosäicists) permission to burrow among the ruins of pagan Rome for marble, even at the risk of damaging existing churches and other public buildings.[5] At least, therefore, such

[1] *Cf. supra*, p. 222.

[2] *Vit. Greg.*, c. 6.

[3] *Supra*, p. 239. This inundation carried away the Pons Æmilius, at this period known as the Pons Senatorum (The Bridge of the Senators) or St. Mary's Bridge from the church of St. Mary Egiziaca hard by, and now called Ponte Rotto as there is only one arch of it left. Gregory rebuilt it " at great expense." *Vita*, c. 14.

[4] Ap. *Reg.*, i, nn. 540–1, p. 352 f., Feb., 1231. *Cf.* n. 659, p. 419, May 22, 1231, in which the podestàs of the province of Milan are ordered to inscribe among the statutes of their towns the constitutions against heretics issued by the Senator of the City.

[5] Ep. of July 23, 1231. " Ad effodiendos muros ecclesiarum seu domorum suarum non mittat de cetero cavatores."

remains of antiquity as were in the neighbourhood of the churches were protected by Gregory, inasmuch as he prohibited the search for marbles in their neighbourhood, and ordered the " rectors of the City," in case his decree was set at naught, to excommunicate both those who carried out the excavations and those who ordered them.[1]

Another letter addressed to " the Rectors of the City " informed them that, after careful examination of the constitutions submitted to him, he had suppressed certain burial clubs, and had decided that with the exception of a guild or fraternity of clerics in connexion with burials, no other such fraternity was to be allowed in the City. As mention is made of certain feasts (convivia) in connexion with the meetings of these guilds, we may presume that, as in the case of wakes, disgraceful scenes sometimes took place at them, and caused their suppression.[2]

Gregory's care for the churches of Rome arose not merely from the fact that he was its bishop, but because, as its sovereign, he had a care for the whole city, and was, moreover, a man of artistic tastes. Salimbene tells us that he was a lover of music and song;[3] and the buildings which he erected in various parts both for his own use and for that of the poor present him to us not merely as a considerate, but as a magnificent ruler. Among the palaces which Gregory built was

Burial Guilds suppressed.

Gregory's work for the City, etc. (a) Palaces.

---

[1] *Ib.* Those were to be excommunicated " qui ex nunc temerariam manum ad ecclesiarum . . . parietes apponere presumpserint fodiendos." Ap. Rod., i, p. 360. Unfortunately this regulation of Gregory was not observed in the days of the Renaissance, and we find that permission was often given to excavate even in close vicinity to churches, provided, however, that the excavations were made under the superintendence of two of the *Magistri Viarum. Cf.* Rodocanachi, *Les Monuments de Rome,* p. 65 f.

[2] Ep. of Apr. 8, 1233, ap. Rod., i, 419. *Cf. ib.,* p. 391.

[3] *Chron.,* p. 184.

a large one at Assisi close by the convent of the Friars Minor. This was erected by him " both in honour of St. Francis, and that he himself might dwell therein when he came to Assisi." [1] During the wanderings, which successive expulsions from Rome forced upon him, he not unfrequently resided at Reate (Rieti). Finding, however, that that somewhat moist place [2] did not suit his rheumatism, he sought out a pretty spot at Interamna (Terni) where the Nar and Velino join their waters, and thereon built " a commodious palace not unworthy of the needs of a Pope." [3]

(b) Churches.   Passing over his improvement of the Lateran palace,[4] his patronage of the Cosmati marks him out as one of the many Popes who, by their encouragement of art, kept alive that Roman school [5] whence issued the artists who brought about the revival of painting, and helped to make the thirteenth century the most artistic of the centuries. With the aid of the Cosmati family and probably with that of the Vassalletti, he continued the decoration of the cathedral of his native city of Anagni. Its beautiful paschal candlestick of white marble adorned with ribbon mosaics bears upon it an inscription which tells us that Vassalletto made it.[6]

[1] Ib., p. 160.

[2] In another place, c. 16, the author of the Vita Gregor., whom we are here quoting, says that the abundance of the waters about Reate (i.e., the rivers Velino and Turano) made it a cool resort in summer.

[3] Vita, c. 23.

[4] Ib., c. 11. Cf. Reg. iii, p. 247, n. 5184, where Gregory speaks of the goldsmiths (aurifices) who dwelt in the Lateran Palace.

[5] As bearing upon the importance of the Roman school of art to which we have repeatedly drawn attention, we may cite an assertion of Barbier de Montault : " I have now—May, 1856—in my possession the names of some hundred mediæval artists which I have found in Rome itself or in its environs." La Cathédrale d'Anagni, p. 60 n., Paris, 1858.

[6] " Vassalleto me fecit." The episcopal throne of the church of St. Andrew in the same city is inscribed : " Vassalet(o) de Roma me fecit." Cf. Parker, Mosaic pictures in Rome, p. 92.

If, however, there is no proof that this noble piece of work was executed during Gregory's pontificate, inscriptions state that Magister Cosmas laid the mosaic pavement of the upper church of the Cathedral and, with the aid of his sons Luke and James, the pavement of the crypt, and that in the year 1231 he re-erected the altar of the crypt.[1]

In Rome Gregory continued the work of Innocent III. and Honorius III. on the basilica of St. Peter, and renewed the mosaics of its façade, thereby renewing a work accomplished by his namesake Gregory IV. in the ninth century. His work survived till the destruction of this portion of the ancient basilica in the days of Paul V. (1606). Fortunately Grimaldi has preserved a description of Gregory's work. Our Saviour, he records, in the act of imparting His blessing, was seen seated on a throne in the centre of the picture. Our Lady was on his right, St. Peter on his left. Gregory himself in his chasuble and pallium was represented in diminutive form in accordance with the fashion of the time, as kneeling at the feet of the Saviour offering him a golden medal. Below the Pope were the words " Gregorius Papa VIIIL." Grimaldi proceeds to state that by Cardinal Pallotto, the arch-priest of St. Peter's, by whose orders he drew up the description of the mosaic, the figure of Pope Gregory, along with one of Innocent III., was given to Cardinal Carlo Conti, who belonged to their family.[2] The faces of the two figures are still preserved.

---

[1] " Magister Cosmas hoc opus fecit." " † Anno Dni. M.CCXXXI . . . per manus Magistri Cosme civis Romanus fuit amotum altare gloriosissimi martyris presulis Magni." *Ib.*, p. 100, or in full, ap. Crowe and Cavalcasselle, *A Hist. of Painting*, p. 86 n. *Cf.* de Montault, *l.c.*, p. 42.

[2] *Cf.* E. Müntz, *Recherches sur . . . J. Grimaldi*, p. 255 ff., Paris, 1877 ; and Ciampini, *De sacris ædificiis*, p. 37, with plate ix ; Alfarano,

St. Eusebius'.   Gregory also completely renovated the ancient church of St. Eusebius; and, as we may learn from an extant inscription, he consecrated his new church, and also, " with his own hands," its high altar in the month of March, 1238.[1]

It was not, however, only to the fabrics of the churches that the Pope turned his attention.   He presented to St. Peter's a bell which surpassed all the other bells in the City in size and quality of tone,[2] and he distributed to various churches sacerdotal vestments remarkable

De Basilic. Vat., p. 31 ; and especially Grisar, *Analecta Romana*, diss. xi, and plates xi, xii. A full page coloured illustration of Gregory's mosaic painted before the destruction of old St. Peter's (1606) may be seen in *Cod. Barb. Lat.*, 4410, f. 28, in the Vatican library.   See also *Cod. Bard. Lat.*, 2733, f. 120 ; f. 131 v, and especially f. 133–4.

[1] The inscription, which is given in Armellini, *Le Chiese di Roma*, p. 809, or better in Marucchi, *Basiliques de Rome*, p. 343, finishes thus :

> " Statuens ut om(n)i anno
> A quarta feria majoris edomade quadra
> Gesime usque ad octavam D(omin)ice Resurrecti
> Onis hance eccl(esi)am visitantes millis annis (*sic*)
> Et centu(m) viginti dieru(m) de iniunta sibi peni
> Tentia indulgentiam consequantur."

The crudeness of the Latin and the mention of 1,000 years' indulgence make me wonder if the inscription as it now stands can be contemporary, the more so as I find that the Vernon MS. of *The Stacions of Rome* (*c.* 1370), which shows no disposition to lessen indulgences, while professing acquaintance with the inscription, names a much more modest indulgence.   Speaking of St. Eusebius, the patron of the church, the poem continues :

> " Hit is writen in a ston
> I wol you telle or ye gon.
> Pope Gregori ther he dude stonde
> The churche de halewed with his honde
> And yaf pardoun as I ow say
> An hundred yer and fifti day
> And threo yer more I ow telle
> Forte abate the peynes of helle."

P. 15, ed. F. J. Furnivall.

[2] *Vita,* c. 14.

for the beautiful texture of their silken material, for the perfection of their dye, and for being shot with gold and adorned with gems.[1]   A reliquary of gold, silver, and precious stones which he made for a large portion of the true Cross was, with the silver case that contained it, reckoned to be worth over a thousand marks of the finest silver.

Nor was the liturgy forgotten by this indefatigable Pontiff. To encourage devotion to our Lady he prescribed that the " Salve regina misericordie " should be said every Friday at Vespers, and at Compline (in nocte) the antiphon " Beata Dei genitrix Maria " and the prayer " Deus qui de beate Marie." And to him is also due the ringing of the bell before the consecration at Mass.[2]   Finally, we are assured that he gave away a number of (liturgical) books, written out in very elegant style and tastefully illuminated.

For the general needs of the City we have already seen (c) Public works. how he rebuilt the Senator's bridge,[3] and improved the drainage. Besides, on more than one occasion supplying the poor in times of famine with food and money,[4] he built for them what his biographer calls " a noble palace," [5] and, at Anagni, a hospital.[6]

Whilst in the midst of all these works, so useful for The Romans and Viterbo, 1231.

[1] *Ib.*, c. 29.   The best of these vestments is said to have been worth a thousand pounds.   He also presented to the churches many finely wrought altar coverings.

[2] *Ib.*   " Instituit . . . quod ante corpus Domini, cum idem conficitur campana pulsetur."

[3] Lanciani, *The Golden days of the Renaissance in Rome*, p. 53, London, 1906, regards it as probable that the Torre delle Milizie, the " best specimen of a mediæval baronial tower," was built by Gregory. If so, it was certainly built by him to overawe the turbulent Romans.

[4] *Cf.* e.g. *ib.*, c. 27.

[5] *Ib.*, c. 11.   *Cf. Reg.*, iii, p. 327, n. 5311, for a papal grant to the famous hospital of the Holy Ghost to buy clothes for the poor who went there.

[6] Ep. of March 21, 1234.   *Reg.*, n. 1839.

the City, Gregory once more got into trouble with those
for whom he was doing so much. On June 1 he went
into the country and took up his residence at Reate.
Then the trouble began. Infected with the fever for
subduing their weaker neighbours, then rampant throughout all Italy, the Romans were consumed with a passion
for conquering the people of Viterbo. We have seen
that the quarrel between these two cities brought
difficulties to Innocent III., but that at length he
brought about a peace between the two cities.[1] From
the Chronicle of Viterbo, however, it is clear that
fighting still went on between them, and as Viterbo
had often afforded an asylum to the Popes when
driven from Rome, they were known to look
upon it with favour. Accordingly, when in November,
1231, the Romans heard that the Emperor had sent
help to Viterbo, they attributed his interference to
Gregory, and " to defend the Republic " imposed heavy
taxes on the Churches of the City " in hatred of the
Pope." [2] Gregory, however, just as Innocent III. had
done before him, did not relax his efforts to make peace
between the belligerents, both of whom were injuring
the property of the Church, until at length the desired
consummation was effected [3] (April, 1233). It was
brought about principally by Gregory's money, for
he compensated both parties for the damage they had
inflicted on each other. He expended twenty thousand
pounds in this way, saying that it was better to preserve
the lives of men than coins.[4]

---

[1] *Supra.* vol. xi, p. 73 ff.

[2] Ric. of S. Ger., p. 140.

[3] *Cf.* ep. Greg. of Aug. 10, 1233, ap. Rod., i, p. 445 ; *Cron. di
Viterbo*, ed. Egidi, ap. *Archiv. Rom. di storia*, vol. xxiv, p. 243 (1902),
Ric. of S. Ger., p. 145 ; *Vita*, c. 15.

[4] *Vita, l.c.* " Sanctius judicans vasa viventia quam metalla servare."
Cf. Lib. Cens., i, p. 477, n. 219. According to Gregory's biographer

Gregory had difficulties in Campania also with the Romans. Not content with trying to subdue Viterbo in Roman Tuscany, the Romans also made expeditions into Campania in order to harass the Pope for his support of Viterbo. In July, 1232, they appeared before Monte-fortino, but for money were induced to return home.[1] They could not, however, do without the Pope. Even before the treaty of peace with Viterbo was concluded, they sent to him a deputation of their principal citizens headed by the Senator in order to induce him to return. This he did to their great joy in the month of March, 1233.[2]

The Romans attack cities in Campania, 1232.

But this dearly bought peace was not of long duration. When the Senator John Poli went out of office in November, the relations between the Pope and the Romans went from bad to worse. Headed by the new Senator, Luke Savelli, and by others of the Senatorial class, such as Parenzi and John Cinthius,[3] the Romans, i.e., the faction of these nobles, rose in open rebellion. They would be masters in the city and out of it. In the City they demanded the unrestricted right of electing

A very serious rebellion of the Romans, 1234.

(*ib.*), the Pope's difficulties during this struggle between Rome and Viterbo were increased by the Senator John Poli and other nobles who had been bribed by Frederick.

[1] Ric. of S. Ger., p. 144. " Per interventum pecunie, Romam reversi sunt."

[2] *Ib.*, p. 145 ; *Vita*, c. 18. Even in 1230 when he had left Rome merely for the summer vacation, the Senator had recalled him in Nov., Ric. of S. Ger., p. 139. As usual on his return Gregory gave money to the greedy Romans. " Ipsorum esuriem non modice pecunie refecione pacavit."

[3] Parenzi was Senator in 1224-5, and J. C. for a time in 1237. *Cf.* ep. Greg., *c.* July, 1234, ap. Rod., i, p. 479. *Cf. Vita*, c. 27, which tells of the origin of this upstart : " per quam (the Church) de rusticano tugurio pretorium senatoris ascenderat." Men who rise rapidly in this way, being generally in want of money, are very open to bribery. Gregory's biographer calls him " corruptibilem senatorem" and says he was bribed by the Emperor.

the Senator and of coining money, and of receiving themselves the tax on baking ovens, and on the pasturage of cattle. They claimed also as a strict due the papal grant of 5,000 pounds, and insisted that the Pope should not excommunicate any Roman citizen or lay the City under an interdict ; and that clerics should in every way be subject to the lay tribunals. Outside the city— quite heedless of the curse against such as remove their neighbours' landmarks (termini, Deut. xxvii, 17)—the Romans, at the bidding of their senator, in order to give outward expression of their intention to usurp the civil authority of the Pope, did what Matthew Paris declared to be " a new and unheard of thing." [1] They set up large new boundary-stones, and inscribed thereon the new districts which they proposed to bring under their jurisdiction. They wished to wrest from the Pope the whole Patrimony of St. Peter ; and as further proofs of their determination, they sent justiciaries into Tuscany and the Sabina to exact oaths of fidelity, and erected a strong fortress at Montalto near Civita Vecchia.

Gregory leaves the city and excommunicates the Senator, etc., 1234.

Towards the end of May, Gregory, unable to withstand the new Senator, Luke Savelli, left the city; and, for the repudiation of the treaty made between Clement III. and the City in 1188,[2] he excommunicated the Senator, " and all the consiliarii of the City," by whose advice it had been discarded. They were excommunicated for building the fortress at Montalto, for exacting oaths to the prejudice of the Roman Church, and for erecting boundary-stones (termini) on its territory in Campania, in the Maritima and in Tuscany.[3]

---

[1] In one of his additions to Roger of Wendover, ap. *Chron. maj.*, iii, 303 f. *Cf. Vita*, c. 19, and the dossier in the Register (ii, p. 289 ff.) which bears the title " Acta pacis inter Ecclesiam et Romanos initæ."

[2] *Cf. supra*, vol. x, p. 347.

[3] Ep. *c.* June, 1234, ap. Rod., i, p. 479.

Not content with this, Gregory urged the Emperor [1] and different princes, clerical and lay, to come to the assistance of the Church thus outraged by its subjects.[2] Further, " on account of the malice of the Romans," he ordered the bishops of France and England to seize in his name and for his use all the ecclesiastical revenues which non-resident Roman clerics held in those countries.[3] He, moreover, exhorted the cities of the Patrimony to stand firm against the Romans ; [4] absolved them from any vassalage which the Romans might profess to claim from them ; [5] and begged the Lombards to allow imperial troops from Germany to pass through Lombardy to his assistance.[6]

The appeals of the Pope were not issued wholly to deaf ears. If he did not meet with the response he might have wished, he met with sufficient. Among those of greater importance who answered his appeal was the energetic Peter des Roches, bishop of Winchester, who had donned the steel hauberk before he had put on the silken chasuble, and who, under Cœur de Lion himself, had learnt the art of war.[7] What, however,

He takes other steps against them, 1234-5.

The Emperor and others come to the help of the Pope.

---

[1] In his previous trouble with the Romans he had asked his help. Ep. of July 24, 1232, ap. *ib.*, p. 381.

[2] In writing to different German bishops for military help he was able to assure them that the emperor himself was prepared to come " magnificently " to his assistance. Ep. Nov. 25, 1234, ap. *ib.*, p. 496. *Cf.* ep. of Nov. 27 to the lay Princes of Germany. *Ib.*, p. 497. *Cf. Ann. Erphord.*, an. 1235, p. 89. In writing to the bishops of France, ep. Dec. 5, 1234, Gregory declares that there is not a spark of gratitude in the Romans, *ib.*, p. 501. *Cf. ib.*, p. 503, to the Spanish princes.

[3] Ep. of Dec. 9, 1234, ap. *ib.*, p. 503. *The Annals of Tewkesbury*, i, p. 94 R. S., inform us that in England this deprivation was carried into effect.

[4] Ep. Jan. 2, 1235, *ib.*, p. 505, to the people of Velletri.

[5] Epp. Jan. 2, 1235, *ib.*, p. 506 ; March 5, 1235, *ib.*, p. 514 ; March 18, 1235, *ib.*, p. 517, to various cities.

[6] Ep. May 20, 1234, *ib.*, p. 473.

[7] Roger of Wendover, *Chron.*, 1235.

was of more importance, Gregory secured the support
of the Emperor, who at the moment, owing to the
rebellious conduct of his son Henry in Germany, and
owing to his wish to secure the hand of Isabella of England,
was in need of the Pope.[1] Accordingly, with his son
Conrad, he came to Reate to offer his services to him,
both because as Emperor he was the official defender
of the Church, and because as King of Sicily the Pope
was his suzerain (May).[2] Although, according to the
papal biographer, Gregory had reason to mistrust the
emperor, he accepted his proffered assistance, and put
in command of his own troops who had to act with
the Emperor, the cardinal deacon of S. Maria in Cosmedin,
the Cistercian, Raniero Capocci.[3] Some time in July
the allied forces laid siege to Rocca Rispampini, which
had given much trouble to Innocent III.[4] If we are to
believe Gregory's biographer, no progress was made
with the siege because the Emperor was in collusion
with the enemy, and, surrounded by falcons instead of
by arms, was more of a hunter than an emperor, and
used his "victorious eagles" for catching birds.[5] Whether
fact or prejudice prevails in these statements, certain
it is that, after besieging it in vain for some two months,

---

[1] Cf. supra, pp. 249 ff., 260.

[2] " Reate non concitus nec invitatus advenit, Ecclesiecausam, quam
ut advocatus ex imperii debito et vassallus ex homagio regni Sicilie
gemino tenebatur defendere juramento . . . sucipiens." Vita, c. 20.
Cf. Ric. of S. Ger., an. 1234, p. 146.

[3] Vita, ib.

[4] Cf. supra, vol. xi, pp. 104 and 107.   R. R. is about eight miles
from Viterbo and near Toscanella.

[5] Vita, c. 20. The papal biographer is especially bitter against the
emperor in this passage. " Hic majestatis titulum in officium venature
commutans, non armis decoratus et legibus, sed canibus et avium
garrulitate munitus, factus de imperatore venator . . . in capturam
avium solicitabat aquilas triumphales."

he allowed his " victorious eagles " to fly with him back into the kingdom (Sept., 1234).[1]

Fortunately, however, as far as the needs of the Pope were concerned, certain German knights " full of zeal for the liberty of the Church " remained behind at Viterbo. Against this rival city there poured forth from Rome in the month of October a large army of Romans,[2] fresh from destroying many of the houses of the Pope's partisans,[3] and full of the same mistaken confidence with which they had advanced against Tusculum in 1167. They suffered the same fate as their countrymen of that date. They were ambushed by the Germans, were totally routed, and retreated precipitately to the " Campus Rotundus," some ten miles from Rome.[4]

Great defeat of the Romans, 1234.

The immediate result of this victory was the recovery of the Sabina by the Church, and the somewhat more remote result was that the Romans began to long for peace.[5] The new Senator (1234-5), Angelo Malabranca, was not so much of a firebrand as Savelli, and by the spring of 1235 negotiations for a peace were well forward. A settlement was finally agreed to (April 12) on the Capitol in presence of the Romans, people who had been duly summoned thither by banner and trumpet.[6] Accordingly, a few days later, the Senator issued the following document in the name of our Lord Jesus

Peace between the Pope and the Romans, 1235.

---

[1] *Ib.* The mode of expression is that of the *Vita.* The fact is also vouched for by Ric. of S. Ger.

[2] According to Roger of Wendover, an. 1234, they numbered " as is said " a hundred thousand men. But these numbers cannot be relied upon.

[3] *Reg.,* ii, 291, n. 3018.

[4] *Ib. Cf. Vita,* c. 21 ; Ric. of S. Ger. ; *Annal. S. Rudbert,* ap. *M. G. SS.,* ix, p. 786. *Le Corniche di Viterbo,* and the notes thereto, ann. 1234-5, ed. Egidi.

[5] *Chron. reg. Colon., Contin. IV.,* p. 265.

[6] *Acta pacis,* ap. *Reg.,* ii, n. 3022. *Cf.* n. 3026.

Christ and to the honour of God and the Roman Church :
" We, Angelo Malabranca, by God's grace illustrious
Senator of the bountiful City, in virtue of an authoritative
decree of the sacred Senate, and of a publicly acclaimed
mandate of the Roman people assembled on the Capitol
in full numbers by sound of bell and trumpet, and in
response to propositions set forth by the venerable
cardinal bishop Romanus of Porto and S. Rufina, and by
the cardinal priests, John of Colonna of S. Prassede, and
Stephen of S. Maria in Trastevere, regarding the discord
between the Roman Church our Mother and our most holy
Father the Supreme Pontiff on the one hand, and on the
other the Senate and people of Rome—promise, in the
name of the said Senate and people, to make satisfaction
in accordance with the mandate of the lord Pope with
regard to the fortress and hostages of Montalto, to the
oaths exacted in the time of the Senator Luke Savelli
and with regard to the boundary stones erected in his
time in the Patrimony and in the lands of the vassals
of the Church." They also promised satisfaction for the
spoliation of the Lateran and the houses of some of the
cardinals, and many other important points ; and they
agreed not to drag Roman clerics before civil tribunals,
and not to harass them ; not to interfere with those who
came to see the Pope, and not to tax the clergy. They
further agreed to preserve perpetual peace with the
Emperor and his followers, and with all the supporters
of the Church.[1]

A week or two before this capitulation was agreed upon,
the Emperor had written to let the Pope know that he was

[1] Ap. *Reg.*, ii, p. 300, n. 3032 (*c.* April 16, 1235), where it is printed
more exactly than in Rodenberg, etc. *Cf.* Ric. of S. Ger., an. 1235.
Later on whilst Anibaldi and Oddo Colonna were senators an attempt
was made by the Romans to break away from this treaty, but it was
reaffirmed during the same period. *Cf.* their decree of March 4, 1241,
ap. *ib.*, n. 3042.

not opposed to his making peace with the Roman people. At the same time, however, he bade him not make a useless peace, seeing that though he had to go to Germany to oppose his rebellious son, he would not leave the Church defenceless.[1] The terms of the peace, which involved a surrender on the part of "the Romans" of all the objects for which they had contended, were certainly not "useless," and one of its concluding clauses which we have just quoted proves that Gregory did not forget the one who had helped him, even if that help had been given only in a half-hearted manner.

Though Gregory was now nominally at peace with the Romans, and felt in a position to return money which had been sent him or had been raised by taxation of the churches to carry on the war against them,[2] he did not return to the City. There was still sedition there.

The Emperor fans trouble in Rome.

In order to prevent the Pope from having a free hand to help the Lombards, Frederick continued his underhand policy of maintaining a party in Rome against him. Some time during the year 1236 he succeeded in buying the Frangipani who had hitherto for the most part supported the Popes. Gregory, however, took prompt measures against the traitors ; and their stronghold the Turris Cartularia, near the Arch of Titus, was stormed and destroyed (1236).[3]

Peter Frangipane goes over to the Emperor, 1236.

The Senator Angelo Malabranca, who was not only favourable to the Pope, but also a strong man, was succeeded by John of Poli (1236-7),[4] who was seemingly

---

[1] Ep. March 27, ap. H.-B., iv, pt. i, p. 535. " Quod si pax ad honorem et exaltationem Ecclesie provenerit ut optatur, quod in oculis vestris gratius fuerit faciatis."

[2] Ep. of June 16, 1235, ap. *Reg.*, ii, p. 86, and *Vita*, c. 21.

[3] *Vita*, c. 24. *Cf.* Ric. of S. Ger., an. 1236, p. 148. " Hoc anno Petrus Frayapane in urbe Roma pro parte imperatoris guerram movet contra papam et senatorem."

[4] If we are to follow Ric. of S. Ger. we should have to suppose

not a strong man.   At any rate, whatever was his character, " the Roman people," i.e., the imperial faction under the leadership of John Cinthius,[1] attacked the Senator.   John of Poli retired " to his tower," and for a time there was civil war in Rome.   Cinthius, however, proved the stronger, and at length John of Poli consented to resign his office into the hands of his rival. All powerful for a moment, Cinthius caused the City to be guarded to prevent the return of the Pope.   But his triumph was short-lived.   Gregory's friends stormed the Capitol, and sent James Capocci and others to invite the Pope to return to their distracted and impoverished City.[2]

Gregory returns to Rome, 1237.   Despite the opposition of most of the cardinals, Gregory accepted the invitation, and was received by the fickle people " as though he was a newly elected Pope," October, 1237.   " The clergy," we are told, " sang his praises, the people rejoiced at his coming, and the widow and the orphan were made happy by it.   The Greek joined in the general applause, and the Jew acclaimed him.   Both men and women and the people of every degree were glad at his home-coming." [3]   And well might they be glad, for the Pope proceeded to spend over a hundred thousand pounds to relieve their needs.[4]

Further troubles in Rome, 1238.   Frederick, however, was determined to retain influence in Rome.   No sooner had Gregory left Rome to avoid the

that John of Poli did not become senator till May, 1237, instead of November, 1236.

[1] Gregory's biographer says that Frederick " corruptibilem senatorem corrupit . . . ut regressum summi pontificis impediret." *Vita*, c. 27.

[2] Mat. Par., *Chron. maj.*, iii, p. 407, says that the Romans had discovered that the Pope's absence from the city, which with his wonted inaccuracy he sets down as having lasted *ten* years, had caused them a great loss of money.   He also says that they passed a decree (sancientes) that he should not in the future leave the city in the same way.

[3] *Vita*, c. 27 ; Ric. of S. Ger., p. 148 f. ; Mat. Par., *l.c.*

[4] *Vita*, *ib.*

summer heat (June, 1238) than the Emperor's party, supplied with fresh funds, were to the fore again. But the Senator, "Oddo Petri Gregorii,"[1] remained loyal to the Pope, laid siege to their fortresses, one of which was perhaps the Septizonium,[2] a stronghold of the Frangipani, and reduced their towers to ruins, and their owners to subjection.

Gregory was, therefore, able to return in peace to Rome in October. On the retirement of the Senator Oddo in the following month, two Senators were chosen instead of one.[3] It was possibly to stiffen the authority of John of Poli that Oddo Colonna was added to him.[4] Whether that was the fact or whether, as seems to be less likely, the imperial faction had been strong enough to procure the nomination of a second Senator, it is certain that

[1] Not John de Judice, as the *Vita*, c. 28, mistakenly says.

[2] The papal biographer says that the Senator brought to ruin the towers of the rebels and "operosi marmoris tabulata palatia nobile vestigium prioris etatis." *Vita, ib.* The reference may, of course, be to some other building on the Palatine Hill or elsewhere.

[3] Ric. of S. Ger., an. 1238.

[4] Gregorovius, *Rome*, v, pt. i, p. 194, supposes that when there were two senators "one was put forward by the Ghibelline (imperial) faction, a custom which afterwards became the rule." He cites two passages from Mat. Par. to support his view. But the first refers to the year 1237. It runs : " In the same year (1237), by the management (procurante) of the emperor Frederick, another senator was created at Rome, in order that, by the united skill and power of two senators, the insolence of the Romans might be suppressed, and by their counsels the city might be kept in greater peace, and be more easily ruled." In this passage (*Chron. maj.*, iii, 386) there is evidently but a confused memory of the usurpation of John Cinthius. The second passage from the year 1240 says (*ib.*, iv, 30), " One senator in the third year before this had been created at Rome by the authority of the emperor." Supposing with Gregorovius that the resulting date is 1238, while it is certain that in that year (1238–9) there were two senators, it is possible, but perhaps not probable, that, when the Pope chanced to be the dominant factor in Rome, the imperialists could nominate a second senator. The senators named by Gregorovius for this period must be checked by Halphen, *L'administration de Rome*, p. 174 f.

Gregory's influence in Rome remained henceforth paramount till the day of his death.

It was in the March of the year 1239 that the final struggle between the Pope and the Emperor began by the latter's excommunication. The result of Frederick's exasperation at this drastic act was not immediately felt in Rome, and Gregory left it as usual (July) to pass the summer months among the hills. During his absence, however, there was a small imperialistic demonstration which, according to Gregory's biographer, had a very dramatic termination. During the mid-August procession of the image of our Saviour,[1] whilst it was being placed for a brief space in the atrium of the Church of St. Maria Nova,[2] a band of hired imperialists greeted the figure with blasphemous shouts of " Behold the Saviour. Behold the Emperor comes ! " [3] At that moment, we are told, the great tower of the Frangipani, the Turris Chartularia, " built out of the blood of the poor and the tears of the widow," and recently repaired at the Emperor's expense,[4] fell with a great crash and crushed the blasphemers to death.

In the month of November Gregory returned to the city to meet an expected attack on it on the part of the Emperor himself, who, on his excommunication, is said to have threatened to turn the basilica of St. Peter into a cattle-shed, to devote its altar to the use of his horses, and to reduce the Pope to such beggary that he should have thorns for a crown and ashes for bread.[5]

[1] Cf. supra, vol. ii, p. 302 f.

[2] " Quasi quietis beneficium receptura." Vita, c. 42.

[3] " Ecce Salvator, veniat imperator ! " Ib.

[4] " Turrim dicti Petri frangibilis Frangipanum, cujus, potentia Petri credebat humiliare primatum, sumptibus propriis refici procuravit." Ib. Cf. Ric. of S. Ger. A document of June 2, 1238, shows the said Peter Frangipane enrolling partisans for the emperor. Ap. H.-B., v, p. 208 f.

[5] Vita, c. 41. On his excommunication he at once " per totam

As we have already seen, the Emperor's attempt on The Emperor appears before Rome, 1240 and 1241.
Rome was duly made in the early part of 1240, and
foiled by the Pope's appeal to the religious sentiments
of his people.[1] If Frederick's spirits were somewhat
damped by this failure, they were revived next year by
his capture of the General Council and by the desertion
to his side of cardinal John of Colonna, who placed at
his service his fortress of the Mausoleum of Augustus,
and captured for him papal towns in Campania. Again,
then, did he appear before Rome (August, 1241), but
though before he left its neighbourhood he was able to
announce to the world with thorough satisfaction that his
great enemy was no more, he was not able to force his
way into the city.[2] He had to be content to oppress the
Roman Church from without the walls of Rome.

Before proceeding to say a word or two about Gregory's
relations with the Patrimony generally, we may surely
pause to note that the narrative of his connexion with
Rome shows how completely he was justified in including
among the reasons for the excommunication of Frederick
his efforts to undermine papal authority in its capital.

Turning from Gregory's dealings with Rome to his Administration of the Patrimony.
dealings with the States of the Church at large, we may
note that while his administration of it did not differ
from that of his immediate predecessors, documents
which have survived bear out his own assertion that he
improved Peter's Patrimony.[3] Apart from protecting it
against wholesale usurpation on the part of the Emperor,
and against partial usurpation by cities or barons,[4]

Ytaliam equitavit bona destruendo." *Ann. S. Vincent. Metensis,*
ap. *M. G. SS.,* iii, p. 159.

[1] *Supra,* p. 299.

[2] *Supra,* p. 317.

[3] *Cf. supra,* p. 289.

[4] *Cf.* Theiner, *Cod. Diplomat.,* i, nn. 141, 151, 158.

and recovering lost rights in the Duchy of Spoleto [1] and over Mt. Fumone,[2] we find him acquiring by purchase fresh rights over Puza in the Sabina, Miranda, Paliano, and Serrone and Gualdo (Cattaneo).[3] Gregory was, too, the recipient of the lordship of Rocca Carlei, near Miranda, given him by the lady Alifanda,[4] and of the suzerainty of all that Uguccio Dadei possessed in the dioceses of Citta di Castello, Montefeltro and Sarsina.[5]

Banking.

The *Liber Censuum* (Taxbook) of the Roman Church, which has furnished us with most of the documents concerning the facts just cited, also supplies us with a few regarding Gregory's monetary transactions. We learn from it that one of those who supplied the Pope with money was cardinal John of Colonna,[6] and we may perhaps hence be inclined to wonder whether money difficulties may have been at the bottom of the disagreement between the Pope and the Cardinal. The same volume also lets us know that one at least of the banking firms employed by Gregory was that of Angelerius Solaficu and company of Sienna, merchant-bankers, also employed by our King Henry III.[7] On March 26, 1233, the Pope issued a statement in which he declared that, having examined the accounts between Solaficu, once our banker (campsor), and his partners on the one hand, and the papal treasury on the other, relative to moneys

[1] *Lib. Censuum*, i, pp. 534 and 543 ff., where there is a regular *dossier* regarding papal rights in the duchy.

[2] *Ib.*, p. 471.

[3] *Ib.*, pp. 535, 537 ff. ; 483 ff. ; a great many documents concern the acquisition of Paliano, a fortified town near Palestrina, and Serrone not far from Paliano ; and p. 546 ff.

[4] *Ib.*, p. 472.

[5] *Ib.*, p. 448 U. D., received his property back as a fief, for which he paid an acknowledgment.

[6] *Ib.*, p. 477.

[7] *Cf. Italian Bankers and the English Crown*, by R. J. Whitwell, ap. *Trans. of the R. Hist. Soc.*, vol. xvii (1903), p. 195.

received and expended for the Roman church by the said company, he found that the claims of both had exactly balanced.[1] Gregory's Register reveals the further fact that the Florentine bankers were those who were especially favoured by him [2]—a fact which had no doubt a great deal to do with the Florentines securing the first place in the banking world.

[1] *Lib. C.*, i, p. 12*.
[2] *Cf.* Reg., vol. ii, nn. 2764–6, 3534–7, 4180, 4198 ff., 4242, 4264.

CHAPTER VI.

THE BRITISH ISLES.

Sources.—To those already mentioned add various important thirteenth century monastic annals published by Luard in four volumes under the title *Annales Monastici.* Vol. i contains the Annals of Margan, Tewkesbury and Burton. The last-named *annals* are especially valuable from the number of official documents incorporated in them. But they are by no means always inserted under their proper dates. Vol. ii those of Winchester and Waverley. Vol. iii those of Dunstable and Bermondsey ; and vol. iv those of Osney and those of one of its Canons Regular, Thomas Wykes. The last-named is regarded by his editor as " one of the most interesting and trustworthy historians of his time." Preface, p. xxxv ; cf. p. xix. Cf. also the similar estimate of his German editor, Pauli, ap. *M. G. SS.,* xxviii. He is especially useful as the only important author who took the royalist side in the Barons War.

Since the days of Lingard, a growing distrust of Matthew Paris has been showing itself among historians. To the opinions already cited, *supra,* vol. xii, p. 156 n., and xi, p. 56 f., add Balan, *Storia di Gregorio IX.,* i, p. 482 n. ; Tont, *Political Hist. of England,* iii, 452 ; and C. V. Langlois, in E. Lavisse's *Hist. de France,* who speaks (vol. iii, pt. ii, p. 84 n.) of M. P. as " toujours hostile à la cour de Rome," and p. 92, " qui force la note suivant son habitude." Hence it is fortunate that to check his account of St. Edmund, Archbishop of Canterbury, we have lives of him by four contemporaries, who will be named in the text. Three of the lives and other documents concerning the saint have been published for the first time by Dom W. Wallace at the close of his valuable book, *St. Edmund of Canterbury,* London, 1893. Other Lives of St. Edmund by Frances de Paravicini, London, 1898, etc., have not the historical value of the life just mentioned. With regard to Blessed Boniface of Savoy, modern criticism has shown the falseness of the picture which Paris presents to us of that great Archbishop. *Cf.* J. Strickland, writing in Italian, " Ricerche storiche sopra il B. Bonifacio di Savoia," ap. *Miscellanea di Storia Italiana,* 3rd series, i, p. 349 ff.,

Turin, 1895 ; and Rev. H. Thurston, " Blessed Boniface of Savoy," ap. *The Tablet*, October 18, 1913. A simple *Vita de' beati Umberto e Bonifacio di Savoia* in Italian and French was published at Turin in 1839.

WHEN Gregory became Pope there was already seated on the throne of England King Henry III., one of the monarchs who have occupied it for the longest time, but one whose weakness and consequent obstinacy of character brought trouble both on the Church and on the State. His weakness of character caused him to lean on others, often on such as were quite unworthy of his confidence, or on foreigners (Poitevins) looking after their own interests, on whom it was unwise to rely. His weakness of intellect led him to embark on schemes which involved him in debt, and caused him to tax his subjects to the point of rebellion. In private life, however, he was amiable and unassuming, so that Dante, his younger contemporary, could describe him as " the King of simple life and plain." [1]

It was about the time that Gregory became Pope that Henry emancipated himself, legally, at any rate, from the control of his tutors and guardians,[2] and assumed full responsibility for his acts. In this action he received the support of his suzerain, the Pope, who decided that Henry, though a minor, was to be allowed to administer the realm ; for, said Gregory, from what he has heard, there does not appear to be " any reason to prevent the King's ordering the kingdom and its affairs both usefully and prudently." [3]

Throughout his long reign Henry received from Rome a measure of support which might perhaps be considered excessive were it not remembered that Henry and

Marginal notes:
Henry III., King of England, 1216-72.

Henry receives considerable support from the Pope.

[1] *Purg.*, vii, p. 131.
[2] *Cf. supra*, pp. 130 ff.
[3] Rymer, *Fœdera*, i, 190.

Gregory stood to each other as vassal and suzerain, and that in accordance with the ideas of the age, this very relation rendered it incumbent on the Pope to do all he could for his royal vassal. He did not, however, forget that Henry was his spiritual son, and so, while exhorting him to walk in the footsteps of his ancestors in revering " his Mother, the Holy Roman Church," and " to help us who by God's providence are called to rule it,"[1] he urged him to learn to know and to serve God.[2]

He further strove to protect the young king's property by interesting Archbishop Langton in his rights ;[3] and, by forbidding tournaments, whereat conspiracies were often hatched, he greatly strengthened Henry's authority and helped to keep his realm at peace.[4] If Henry was thus backed by the authority of Pope Gregory, one reason was that he was at pains to ask for his aid. For instance, when thanking him for his exertions in obtaining the release of his kinsman, Otho, Duke of Brunswick, he took occasion to beg him, " as every Christian Prince has at some time to implore the favour of the Apostolic See," to promote his interests whenever the opportunity offered.[5]

Gregory helps to keep England at peace abroad.

Gregory also exerted himself most successfully throughout the whole of his pontificate in maintaining peace between France and England, now checking the King of France,[6] and now Henry.[7] Louis was strictly forbidden to interfere with Henry's oversea dominions, and the English King was urged to do all he could to maintain

[1] Ep. of March 23, 1227, ap. *Reg.* i, p. 4, n. 3.
[2] Record Office, Papal bulls, Bundle 35, n. 30, cited by Gasquet, *Henry III.*, p. 111.
[3] *Cf. ib.*, n. 23.
[4] Ep. of Feb. 27, 1228, ap. Rymer, i, 189.
[5] Ep. of Apr. 4, 1229, ap. *Close Rolls of Henry III.*, i, pp. 234–5 *R. S.*
[6] Ep. of May 25, 1227, ap. *Reg.*, i, p. 44.
[7] Ep. Apr. 15, 1230. *Ib.*, p. 274.

the truce.[1] As long, therefore, as Gregory reigned, there was but little breach of the peace between England and France.

He also strove to make the Welsh keep the truce which they had made with Henry,[2] and his exertions were instrumental in preventing war between England and Scotland. On January 4, 1235, he wrote to Alexander II., king of the latter country,[3] to say that " he would ever toil that peace might be preserved between him and Henry . . . in the hope that great advantage would accrue to the two kingdoms from such a peace." He therefore urged Alexander to observe the agreement which his predecessor William had made with Henry's predecessors, Henry II. and John, and which the King of England had begged the Pope to confirm by his " apostolic authority." Trouble between the two kingdoms did not, however, cease by reason of these first efforts of the Pope. Nevertheless, desirous "that the gate of discord should be closed," Gregory bade Otho, cardinal-deacon of St. Nicholas *in carcere Tulliano*, at that time his legate in England, labour to effect a lasting peace ; [4] and, a little later,[5] he rebuked Alexander for not observing the

Gregory keeps the peace between England and Scotland.

---

[1] See Henry's letters of June 8, 1228, and Apr. 5, 1229, in which he declares that he will obey the Pope in the matter of the truce. Ap. Rymer, i, pp. 191 and 194 ; and *ib.* p. 211 for Henry's letter of May 10, 1234. *Cf.* epp. of May 14, 1233, ap. *Royal Letters*, i, p. 551 *R. S.*, wherein tne kings of England and France are urged to turn their thoughts " to Him who is the true peace," and for the sake of the Crusades to refrain from war against each other. A letter of Nov. 6, 1234, to St. Louis, ap. *ib.*, p. 557, is to the same effect. See also the *Patent Rolls*, Henry III., ii, p. 213 ff., an. 1228, in which Henry treats of the truce with France, " sicut a d. Papa Gregorio IX., nobis est injunctum."

[2] Bliss, *Calendar of Papal Let.*, i, p. 153.

[3] Ap. Theiner, *Mon. Hibern. et Scot.*, p. 29, or Rymer, i, p. 215.

[4] Theiner, *ib.*, p. 34. Ep. of March 24, 1237. *Cf. ib.*, for a letter of March 27 to Henry urging him to follow Otho's counsel in the matter of the Scottish difficulty.

[5] Apr. 27, 1237, ap. Rymer, i, p. 371.

oath he had taken to Henry with regard to homage. Then, declaring that he was bound " to take a more special care of the kingdom of Scotland because the Church of Scotland was directly dependent upon the Roman Church " as its sole mother and metropolitan," he named Otho legate in Scotland.[1] By the industry of that able ecclesiastic, the Kings of England and Scotland with their barons met at York, and came to a satisfactory agreement (September 14, 1237). To ensure its observance the King of Scotland and his barons were called upon to submit themselves to the authority of the Pope in the matter, so that, if they should not observe the treaty, he might compel them to keep it by canonical penalties. To this condition Alexander and his nobles agreed, and they notified the Pope that they were willing that he should entrust this power of compulsion to certain of the suffragans of Canterbury.[2] " Final concord " between Henry and Alexander was thus secured.

Other papal favours for Henry.　The great indebtedness of Henry and of England to Gregory did not end here. He forbade Romanus, his

---

[1] Theiner, *ib.*, or *Reg.*, ii, p. 633, May 7, 1237. " Hinc est, quod cum circa Regnum Scotie eo majorem curam gerere teneamur, quo fortius ecclesia Scoticana Romanam ecclesiam solam matrem et metropolitanam nullo medio recognoscit," etc. The letter is dated May 7, 1237. Bliss, *Calendar of Papal Registers*, i, p. 161, has completely missed the meaning of this passage. He speaks of the Scottish Church, " which does not recognize the Roman Church as its sole mother and metropolitan." *Cf. supra*, vol, ix, p. 371. The documents concerning these peace negotiations may also be seen in the *Calendar of Documents relating to Scotland*, i, pp. 230–2, 246–8.

[2] Rymer, i, pp. 374 and 377. *Cf.* Mat. Par., *Chron. Maj.*, iii, 413 f., *re* this " finalis concordia inter Angliæ et Scotiæ reges," as it is called. See also *Chron. de Mailros*, ad an. 1237. Gregory also endeavoured to keep the peace between England and Wales, and we find him bidding the archbishop of Canterbury compel Llewellyn, lord of Wales, to observe the truce made between him and king Henry, in order that there should be peace throughout the world for the sake of the Holy Land. *Calendar of Papal Letters*, Apr. 27, 1236, i, p. 153.

legate in France, without special mandate from himself, to excommunicate Henry or his brother Richard,[1] and he allowed the King to employ bishops as his counsellors.[2] Further, with a view to protect the King's property, he absolved him from certain oaths. During his father's quarrels with the barons, the royal demesnes had been largely usurped, and at the time of his coronation the youthful king had been compelled to swear not to disturb the usurpers. On Henry's appeal to Gregory regarding this state of things, the Pope reminded him that at the time of his coronation he had sworn to maintain the rights of his crown and to recover such as had been unlawfully alienated. Then, under pressure which might well shake even a strong man, the youthful monarch had been forced to alienate some of his liberties, possessions, and other crown rights, under oath not to attempt to reclaim them. Under the circumstances the Pope decided that Henry must keep his first oath notwithstanding his second one, as that was unlawful.[3]

Furthermore, Gregory issued numberless regulations which, while they primarily concerned ecclesiastics, all tended to the betterment of the country, as they were all calculated to improve that class which at this period had such paramount influence in it. He ordered the reformation of certain monasteries, so that they might be in a better condition to help the poor ; he forbade clerics to be justices or sheriffs, so that they might not have to be partakers in the shedding of blood ; and he prohibited

[1] May 27, 1227, ap. *Royal Letters*, i, p. 548.
[2] July 20, 1231, ap. *ib.*, p. 549.
[3] Ep. of Jan. 10, 1233, ap. *ib.*, p. 551. *Cf.* ep. of July 20, 1231, and June, 1235, ap. Rymer, i, pp. 200 and 299. On July 20, 1231, he also granted a petition of the king that his barons should not, when summoned by papal letters, be bound to go to places without the realm to which they could not pass without danger or without crossing hostile territory. Ap. *ib.*, p. 201.

churches and sacred places being turned into houses of merchandise.[1]

The ecclesiastics of England were not behind the King in agitating for an acknowledgment of their claims by the Pope ; and in some cases at least they secured redress from him. The principal grievances, apart from taxation, of which they complained were " papal provisions " [2] and the granting of benefices to Italians. Although Gregory enjoined the Archbishop of Canterbury, St. Edmund, to warn the English not to take it amiss if foreigners obtained honours and benefices in England,[3] he nevertheless granted them certain concessions in this matter. He decreed, for instance, that, unless special mention were made of this particular document, English prelates might bestow vacant benefices, which were normally in their gift, but which had once been held by Italians, on any suitable persons, without regarding the law that such benefices were reckoned to be at the disposal of the Pope.[4] So much for livings already in the possession of Italians. With regard to the future, he conceded that, when any benefice in

---

[1] *Cal. of P. L.*, i, p. 155.

[2] *Cf. supra*, p. 161.

[3] *Cal. of P. L.*, Apr. 3, 1234, i, p. 140.

[4] *Ib.*, Apr. 15, 1230, p. 123. This concession was, however, not unfrequently rendered void by the phrase : "notwithstanding the indult granted to the English in regard to benefices of Italians." *Cf. ib.*, May. 7, 1236, p. 154. Gregory was really only confirming a constitution of Honorius III. After pointing out to the archbishop of Canterbury that it was but fair that foreigners who were doing the work of the Church in a country should occasionally receive benefices therein, he added : " But because at times on the departure of such beneficed persons, they have left successors without consulting the patrons of the benefice, we, wishing to remedy this, and to prevent the patron's generosity irom causing them loss, decree that, when Italians have held a benefice, and are definitely leaving the country, the said benefice shall freely return to its patrons, to be conferred by them on a suitable candidate." Let this be proclaimed throughout England. Ep. of Feb. 26, 1221. *Cf.* Potthast, p. 6569.

England was bestowed by a mandate from the Pope, the English prelates were not to be bound to grant it, unless again special mention were made of this privilege.[1]

These concessions were no doubt, partly at least, due to the action of a league brought into existence in 1231 by Sir Robert Twenge, a Yorkshire knight who took the name of William Wither. Irritated that his right to present to a living had been rendered nugatory by papal provisions, he banded together some eighty men into the league " of those who would rather die than be put to shame by the Romans." Blaming the Pope and his legates for ordering Romans to be intruded into English livings, and the bishops for carrying out their orders, they threatened the latter, if they interfered, to treat them as they intended to treat the intruders. Then they proclaimed a " boycott " of the foreigners, and declared that such as did not observe it would be liable to the same penalties as were to be inflicted on the Romans. After this, seemingly with the connivance of some persons in authority, bishops or lay members of the King's council,[2] members of the League, going about masked, began to rob the Roman clerics and to plunder their property, especially their corn, which they sold for the benefit of the poor. This " indiscreet presumption " was, however, not allowed to run its

---

[1] *Ib.*, May 11, 1237, p. 162. *Cf.* the *Annals of Tewkesbury*, p. 75.

[2] The justiciar Hubert de Burgh was pointed out as one of the principal allies of the league, seeing that its members sometimes produced royal letters to justify their outrages. If they were not forgeries, they must have been procured from some person in high authority. According to the *Patent Rolls* of Henry III., iii, pp. 28–9, 1232 ? *R. S.*, the king " found on inquiring that the said trespasses were done by H. de B. during the time of his justiciarship." Hubert, however, received a letter from the Pope (June 9, 1232) in which Gregory praised his devotion to the Roman Church. " Devotionis insignia et grata obsequia quae . . . humiliter ecclesiæ Romanæ nostris temporibus exhibere curasti ? " Ap. *Royal Letters*, i, p. 549. *Cf. infra*, p. 349, n. 1, for a vindication of Hubert.

course with impunity. On February 10 the Bishop of London and ten other bishops excommunicated the perpetrators of these acts of violence,[1] and as this seemingly did not improve the situation there came indignant letters to the King and others from Rome.

The letter to the King begins by reminding him of all that the Popes have done for him ; and, in speaking of what Innocent III. in particular did for him, Gregory takes occasion to tell him that he himself, though then in a subordinate position, had had much to do with that Pope's action.[2] Despite then all the blessings that the Holy See has procured for him, its messengers (cursores, carrying letters sealed with our bullæ, and treating as well with what was for the good of the land as with the punishment of offenders, are cruelly ill-treated, even, as it is said, with your connivance. The violent manner in which Italian, nay, even so it is said, English clerics have been treated makes one almost believe that the days of Nero have returned. Especially is it shameful that such conduct has remained so long unpunished. The King's excellency, then, should atone now for past dilatoriness by more energetic action, or else nothing will prevent the Pope from vindicating the outraged honour of the Roman Church.[3]

Other letters followed, blaming the bishops for not giving the Pope immediate notice of what had happened, and ordering them to deal with the malefactors.[4]

[1] Roger of Wendover, *Chron.*, 1231, iv, pp. 228–33, ed. Coxe ; ep. Grosseteste, 3.

[2] Rymer, i, p. 203. " Nobis tunc in minori officio constitutis ipsum negotium ex tunc utiliter procurantibus." June 7, 1232.

[3] *Ib.*, or ap. *Reg.*, i, p. 503 ff.

[4] *Reg., ib.,* p. 506. One such letter burning with eloquent indignation may be read in Raynaldus, an. 1232, n. 28 f. ; or fuller in the *Annales de Burton,* i, p. 239 f. *R. S.* Other mandates from the Pope on the same subject are to be found in the British Museum, *Addit. MSS.,* 15353, ff. 133–40, cited by Gasquet, *Henry III.,* p. 134.

These letters had the desired effect. Inquiries were at once set on foot, by means of which many of the guilty, both principals and their abettors, were discovered. Among the latter were even bishops and royal officials, of whom many sheriffs were at once seized and imprisoned. Twenge surrendered himself to the King, who, in accordance with the Pope's mandate, bade him go to Rome for absolution. In view, however, of the provocation the knight had received, Henry furnished him with letters to the Pope, in order that his contentions might receive careful consideration.[1]

Long before Twenge could have reached Rome, the Pope, convinced of the gravity of the situation, directed the Archbishop of York and others to publish his decision that the rights of patrons, whether clerical or lay, were not to be contravened without his special orders (July 28, 1232).[2] This mandate was of some advantage to England inasmuch as it limited the action of papal agents in the country ; but it did not go far enough or was not observed well enough to satisfy the malcontents. However, it appears to have been some years before Twenge went to Rome to plead his cause.[3] But, when he did go, he took with him a letter from many of the Barons of England complaining of the way their rights of patronage were ignored. The barons suggest that the Lord in Peter's berth must be asleep, as " justice and judgment are the establishment of his throne " (Ps. xcvi, 2), and these are in danger of perishing by that violation

Twenge goes to Rome, 1239.

---

[1] Wendover, *l.c.*, pp. 240-3. *Cf.* the apology of Lawrence of St. Albans for Hubert de Burgh, ap. Mat. Par., *Addit.*, vi, p. 72 *R. S.* It may be noted incidentally that charges against Hubert of complicity in this affair are triumphantly disposed of by Lawrence.

[2] Ap. *Royal Letters*, i, 550, or ap. Archbishop Gray's *Register*, p. 166, ed. Camden Soc.

[3] These facts are furnished by Mat. Par., *Chron. Maj.*, iii, p. 609 ff., under the year 1239. But there is reason to believe that the events there set forth really belong to an earlier year. *Cf. ib.*, n. 6, p. 610.

of rights of patronage which is being practised in England. The letter concludes with a threat to invoke the power of the King, if their immemorial customs are not guaranteed. To this strong letter Gregory replied that when he had caused a cleric from Italy to be presented to Twenge's church, he did not know that the right of patronage over it belonged to a layman. He, therefore, now withdrew his nominee, and, renewing letters already sent to England, he pronounced it " by these presents to be unlawful for any one henceforth, by the authority of the Apostolic See, to bestow churches in England, of which laymen are patrons, without their consent." [1]

In leaving this question of " provisions " we may again call attention to the fact that they were not by any means all granted on papal initiative. They were often granted by the Pope to oblige the King [2] or some other important person in Church or State who was desirous of rewarding in this easy way some faithful servant or favourite, just as it was often at the request of one or the other that he granted dispensations for clerics to hold more than one benefice. [3]

Taxation.

Great irritation was also caused in England during Henry's reign by the taxes levied by the Pope and by the King. At all times and by all men there is impatience of taxation, and that, too, even when the taxes are imposed and levied regularly and in every way according to recognized law, and for purposes which the taxpayer approves in the main, and from which he reaps personal advantage. When all or many of these saving features

[1] Ib., p. 613. Cf. Mat. Par., Hist. Anglorum, ii, pp. 337-41, 352.
[2] Cf., e.g., Cal. of Pap. Let., i, pp. 235, 252 (a provision granted " at the request of the count of Burgundy "), p. 257. Cf. the case of John Mansel, ap. Mat. Par., l.c., iv, 152-4.
[3] Cf., e.g., ib., i, pp. 186-7.

are absent from imposed taxes, an opposition to them
is at once aroused which may lead to any extremes.
Now, during the reign of Henry III., and indeed during
the Middle Ages generally, these saving features did not
by any means always accompany the taxes imposed by
Pope or King. Consequently, their imposition, unprecedented and ill-regulated as it often was, brought about
many unhappy consequences. Still, in considering the
taxation of his reign, we must be on our guard against
judging of it exclusively according to the account of it
left to us by Matthew Paris. With that narrow-minded
partisan, money was a regular obsession, a veritable
King Charles' head.[1] By referring frequently to the same
tax, and by gratuitously imputing the performance
of various acts to pecuniary motives, Paris would lead
one to suppose that ruinous wringing of money from the
nation by Pope and King was .much more regular and
systematic than it was in fact. Indeed, as far as taxation
by the King was concerned, " of all the Kings since the
Conquest, Henry received the least money from the
tenants of the Crown." [2] Nevertheless his taxation
brought him much odium, as the money raised by it was
often wasted on foreign favourites, or on wars in France,
which brought neither profit nor glory. Similarly the
taxes imposed by papal authority were often unpopular,
partly because the urgent reason of their imposition
was not easily appreciated by a people who were quite
free from imperial oppression whether in Church or
State ; partly because they came as an addition to

[1] I once began to count up the number of times which Matthew Paris
mentions money, but soon gave up the attempt, as he mentions it at
every turn. It is very unsafe to make general statements, but I can
say, not indeed that he puts money before his readers more than any
other general historian, but that he does so far more than any other
chronicler whom I have ever read.

[2] Lingard, *Hist. of England*, ii, p. 237, ed. 1874.

Grosseteste
on pecuniary
help for the
Pope.

unpopular regal taxes ; and partly because they were
often collected by foreign agents whose methods were
not unfrequently very irritating.[1]

It required a broad-minded, enlightened bishop, like
Grosseteste of Lincoln, to realize the issues at stake,
and to feel that it was necessary for all her children
to help their mother the Roman Church, seeing that,
in her struggle against Frederick, she was really fighting
for the liberty of the whole Church of God. Hence,
when asked by Henry by what authority he raised
a tallage for the Pope, he replied : " What our fellow-
bishops and we ourselves do in this matter is no matter
for wonder ; but it would well deserve the greatest
wonder and the utmost indignation if, even unasked and
unordered, we did not do this and more than this.   For
we see our spiritual Father and Mother (the Pope and
the Roman Church), whom we are much more bound to
honour, obey, and help than our earthly parents—we
see them exiled, hemmed in on every side by persecution
and tribulation, stripped of their patrimony, and in want
of decent means of support." [2] These words were
not written until 1246, but they could for the most part
have been written during the pontificate of Gregory IX.,
and are the more important that they are the words
of one who would not remain quiet in the face of any
abuse, did it proceed from Pope or King, and who, as
a matter of fact, freely opposed not indeed the system
of Provisions in itself, but its abuse, and boldly protested
against papal taxation when it became excessive.   And

[1] Mat. Par., *Chron. Maj.*, iv, p. 35, an. 1240, names one Pietro Rosso
with special abhorrence.

[2] Ep. 119, p. 341 *R. S.* Compare what Gregory himself says : " The
patrimony of Blessed Peter is overrun with tyrannical cruelty, our
fortresses have been invaded, and our faithful people slaughtered by
impious Saracens." *S. Osmund. Reg.*, ii, 145, cited by Wallace, *Life of
St. Edmund*, p. 217.

so, whilst distinctly declaring that " the lord Pope and the holy Roman Church have the power of freely disposing of all ecclesiastical benefices," [1] he loudly proclaimed that " whoever abused that power was building for hell-fire," and that " he was abusing that power who did not use it for the furtherance of faith and charity." [2] Hence, too, whilst declaring that it was the right and duty of the Pope to regulate and purify the whole Church,[3] still, when it was discovered that foreign ecclesiastics in this country drew a revenue of 50,000 marks,[4] which was more than the total revenue

[1] Ep. 49 of 1238, p. 145, " Veraciter scio d. Papæ et sanctæ Romanæ Ecclesiæ hanc esse potestatem, ut de omnibus beneficiis ecclesiasticis libere possit ordinare."

[2] Ib. Cf. his strong letter of protest (an. 1253) when asked to give a canonry of Lincoln to a nephew of Innocent IV., Frederick of Lavagna, whom he regarded as altogether unworthy. " Provisions of that sort," he said, " were not for edification, but for destruction, and hence cannot be made by the blessed Apostolic See." Ep. 128, p. 437. In some MSS. this letter is addressed by mistake " to the lord Pope Master Innocent." But the proper address is given in the Annals of Burton, i, p. 311 R. S. " Robertus, Dei permissione Lincoln. Ep., Cantuariensi Archidiacono et magistro Innocentio Dni, Papæ Scriptori salutem." Besides the address, " reverendi Domini," in the course of the letter, shows it was addressed to two persons. It should, moreover, be added that the authenticity of this letter is strongly called in question by Smith, Church and State, p. 110 ff.

[3] Cf. his pamphlet of 1239 (?), ep. 127, p. 357 ff., against the chapter of Lincoln, the object of which was to prove that the power of a bishop in his diocese was like that of the Pope in the Universal Church : " Quemadmodum et d. Papa in universali ecclesia, et unusquisque episcopus in sua diocesi," p. 389.

[4] Cf. ep. of Innocent IV. of May 22, 1253, ap. Calendar of Papal Let., i, p. 286. Cf. Mat. Par., Chron. Maj., and his usual inaccuracy. He says that in 1245 Henry found that the said revenue amounted to 40,000 marks, a sum greater than " the annual revenue of the whole kingdom of England " (iv, 419) ; and in 1252 he says that bishop Grosseteste found that the alien clerical revenue (evidently the valuation referred to by the Pope) was " more than 70,000 marks," and that the revenue of the king (" redditus regis merus ") was not a third part of that sum (v, p. 355). From data which he gives elsewhere (v, 627) it is clear that the king's revenue was either about 24,000 or 30,000 marks,

of the King, he was indignant, because he not unnaturally regarded the sum as unmistakably proving that the system of Provisions was being abused.

The views of Grosseteste were also those of his friend St. Edmund, Archbishop of Canterbury. Though the Saint was so opposed to the "provided" Italians that he once accepted a benefice "for fear some Roman, or someone like the Romans (who care nothing about the sheep except for their milk and wool), should lay greedy hands upon it,"[1] yet, when it was a question of helping the Pope in his needs, "he cheerfully paid whatever demands were made upon him without a murmur or word of remonstrance."[2]

The clergy pay a tenth to the Pope, 1229. The first tax levied for Gregory IX. was in 1229. King Henry, in order to get his way in an election for the see of Canterbury (which will be dealt with presently), through his agents in Rome offered the Pope a tenth of all the revenues of England, Ireland, and Wales, clerical and lay, to enable him to carry on his war with the Emperor. In order, therefore, to claim the promised tenth, Gregory dispatched to England his chaplain Stephen, who asked for it at a general assembly at Westminster (Apr., 1229).[3] The lay nobility, however, would not listen to the nuncio's pleading in his master's behalf, but the clergy, after much deliberation and no little grumbling, agreed to pay the tenth, "being afraid that they would incur excommunication or interdict if they opposed the apostolic commands."[4]

according as the phrase "postquam coeperat esse regni dilapidator" refers to his accession or to his coming of age.

[1] See his *Life*, by the monk Eustace, printed in full by Wallace, ap. his *St. Edmund of Canterbury*, p. 564. *Cf. ib.*, p. 308.

[2] Wallace, *ib.*, p. 313.

[3] *Ann. de Burton*, p. 245, and Roger of Wendover, *Chron.*, pp. 184 and 200 ff., ed. Coxe.

[4] *Ib.*, p. 201. Gregory had already asked for the tenth at the close of 1228. See his letter to the bishop and chapter of Salisbury of

This tax " ad opus Papae " was based upon the actual value of the clerical property, as well movable as immovable.[1] Following the directions of the chaplain Stephen, a regular assessment of it was made under oath by some of the canons or monks in each cathedral or monastery, and collectors of the tax were duly appointed. These measures, seemingly new, in part at least, caused loud complaints ; but, as a recent student of taxation concludes, " it may be questioned whether the assessment was as severe as the outcries of the chroniclers would indicate."[2]

The unpopular tax of 1229, rendered more so by the drastic methods used in its collection which are said to have forced some of the clergy to pledge the sacred vessels,[3] was followed some years later by an appeal

Dec. 20, ap. *Register of St. Osmund*, ii, p. 144 ff. *R. S.* He told the bishop that after the Patrimony had been invaded, he took up arms to repel invasion, and to secure ecclesiastical liberty. He then reminds his correspondents, " quod non est rebus parcendum, ubi universaliter ecclesia tam acriter impugnatur." We have not noticed "the tax " of 1238, as it was no more than a suggestion on the part of the Pope that the English clergy should give a thirtieth for three years for the support of the Latin empire of Constantinople. See his letters ap. Bliss, *Calendar*, i, 166, 177, 185. *Cf.* Mat. Par., *Chron.*, iii, p. 480 f.

[1] *Ann. de Burton*, p. 364 f., *R. S. Cf. Ann. de Theokesber.*, p. 77.

[2] S. K. Mitchell, *Studies in Taxation under John and Henry III*, p. 78. New Haven, Yale University Press, or Oxford, 1914. *Cf.* F. M. Powicke's review of this work in *The Eng. Hist. Rev.*, July, 1918. For ourselves we have to say that, useful as is Mr. Mitchell's work, it is not too lucid on account of the insertion of details which do not immediately concern the point at issue.

[3] Roger, p. 203. According to an addition of Matthew Paris, *Chron. Maj.*, iii, 188 f., the vessels were pledged " to most wicked usurers who called themselves merchants " whom Master Stephen brought along with him. Under the year 1235, he adds (*ib.* iii, 331 f.) that, when Roger, bishop of London, wished by excommunication to suppress them, they had influence enough at Rome to cause him to be " peremptorily " summoned abroad to explain his conduct. Unwilling, says Paris, to expose the shame "of his father," he gave way to the merchants. In this story it must be noted that we know nothing of what the

for pecuniary aid for the crusades (1234). Again,
according to an addition made by Matthew Paris to
Roger of Wendover,[1] mere nuncios who came from
Rome for the money, acting as though they were legates,
wrung it from everybody so tyrannically that once more
" an infinite number " were reduced to beggary.

Taxes of the year 1240. But the most serious tax imposed upon the Church
of England by Pope Gregory was in the year 1240 when
the legate Otho was in the country. In that year, as we
have seen, the unfortunate Pontiff was in the greatest
difficulties ; and his piety alone saved himself and Rome
from falling into the hands of Frederick.[2] Thus
straitened, he had no other resource but to appeal to the
countries to which he had access, and which were in a
position to help him. Of these England was the one
to which he would most naturally turn. It was one of
the vassal states of the Church ; it was well disposed
towards the Holy See, and it was wealthy.

Passing over a supposed demand on the part of the
Pope that the bishops should reserve the first three
hundred vacant benefices for Romans, as Matthew
Paris, who stands alone in mentioning this demand,
makes it rest on a merely *rumoured* compact between
the Pope and the Romans,[3] we have to record that he

" mercatores " had to say for themselves. *Cf. Ann. de Dunstap.*, p. 114 ;
Ann. de Theokesberia, p. 73, and *Ann. de Waverleia*, p. 305.

[1] *Ib.*, p. 279. " Infinitos extorres redierunt et mendicantes."
If Matthew Paris were to be taken seriously in his accounts of papal
and regal impositions, we should have to believe that the country
was " ruined " by them over and over again during the pontificates of
Gregory IX. and Innocent IV. At least on one occasion Gregory
returned money which had been sent to him for a certain purpose and
which he did not need when it came. *Vit. Greg.*, c. 21.

[2] *Cf. supra*, p. 299.

[3] He says that " ut dicebatur," a most iniquitous compact was made
between the Romans and the Pope, by which the latter, in return for
their help, agreed to give their relations as many benefices as possible

did ask for twenty per cent of the revenues of the English Church (1240).[1] Despite the legate's explanation of the Pope's difficulties, there was no little opposition to this heavy demand. It was contended that the money was to be used for the shedding of Christian blood, and against the Emperor who was the brother-in-law and ally of the King of England and who, if money were raised against him in England, would endeavour to seize and to punish Englishmen whom he might capture on their way to Rome. Besides, when the tenth had been granted in 1229, a protest was made against such exactions in the future. Moreover, the country was much impoverished at the moment by the departure of many Crusaders who had taken a great deal of money with them. If, as was said, the whole Church was in danger, a general contribution should be raised which should be arranged by the General Council that report whispered was about to be held.[2] However, by the diplomatic skill or artfulness of the legate and his agents, the demand of the fifth was at length agreed to.[3]

Unfortunately, however, the unpopularity of the levies of 1229 and 1240 was not lessened by the conduct of those who were concerned with raising them. The minor Roman officials were, some of them at least,

in England, and that, in consequence, he sent letters to certain bishops giving them the order mentioned in the text. *Chron. Maj.*, iv, 31. Of these letters there is no trace anywhere.

[1] *Ann. de Dunstap.*, p. 154 ; Mat. Par., *ib.*, pp. 9–11.

[2] *Cf.* these and other reasons given by the bishops, the Berkshire rectors and others, ap. Mat. P., *ib.*, pp. 37–43. The Annals of Burton give what is practically the same document as coming from " each and all the rectors of the churches of England." P. 265 ff., *R. S.*

[3] M. P., *ib.*, 15, 35, 43, for the submission of the bishops, abbots, and rectors respectively. Paris' account of this transaction is very broken and confused. A fuller analysis of this protest is given by Smith, *Church and State in the Middle Ages*, p. 25 ff.

overbearing, and the legate Otho was exacting regarding his procurations.[1]

Discovery of some of the coins raised by this tax. It seems highly likely that some of the money raised by Otho's agents on this occasion has since been found. In 1902 a leaden vessel containing about twelve thousand silver coins was found in the digging of the foundations of a new bank in the High Street, at Colchester. The coins belonged to the currency of Henry II., Richard I., and Henry III., and as many as one hundred and fifty-five to that of William the Lion of Scotland.

Thirty years earlier a like hoard had been found in an old grange of the abbey of Eccles, near Manchester. In this collection were two hundred pieces of silver belonging to William.

Another hoard was found in France, and again William's coins were prominent.

The deposits were made between 1230 and 1248, probably in 1240.

The English hoards were connected with houses of religion, and many of the coins came from ecclesiastical mints.

It would appear that these collections were part of the money raised by Peter Rubeus (Pietro Rosso) on the Border, and his colleague, another Peter, in Ireland. It is supposed that the two met at Eccles when they fled on hearing the news that Gregory IX. was dead or dying, and that they hid portions of the papal money in different places on their way to Dover whence they sailed to

---

[1] No doubt the fact is that the struggle in which the Pope and the emperor were engaged forced them into abusing their positions in raising money. If the Pope stretched his prerogatives, so did the emperor. "Circumstances forced him (Frederick) to drain the country (the kingdom of Sicily) of its wealth in order to sustain his war against the Papacy and the Lombard towns, and in his hands the instrument of government which had been forged by the Norman kings became a thing of penetrating tyranny." H. Fisher, *The Mediæval Empire*, ii, p. 199, London, 1898.

France.   A fourth hoard found in a Church at Sudbourne, in Suffolk, would seem to show that they made an attempt to sail from there.[1]

For some three years one of the most important persons, if not the most important person, in the realm of England was the legate *a latere*, Otho, cardinal-deacon of St. Nicholas, quite " a second Pope."[2]   He had been sent into the country at the urgent request of Henry, who had wanted John of Colonna as legate as early as 1230.[3]   That weak King's reliance upon Peter des Roches, bishop of Winchester, and other foreigners had deservedly roused great opposition against him. Towards the close of 1233 the bishops threatened to excommunicate Peter and other chief advisers of the King.[4]   Peter thereupon appealed to Rome.[5]   Meanwhile, as time went on, and it became known that the King was asking for a legate, there was much indignation on the part of some ; even, " it was said," on the part of St. Edmund, archbishop of Canterbury.[6]   But Richard, the earl marshal, one of the leaders of the lay opposition to the King's foreign favourites, when it was urged by the royal advisers that the Pope had a great regard for the King, and, at their request, was about to send a legate who would excommunicate all the King's enemies, replied : " I am glad to hear what they say respecting the Pope, for the more regard he has for the King and the kingdom the more will he wish him to govern his kingdom and his subjects according to the laws of justice. . . . And I am

The legate a latere, Otho de Torengo, cardinal-deacon of St. Nicholas in carcere Tulliano, 1237–40.

---

[1] This account of these hoards of money is taken from *The Tablet* of Sat., Nov. 10, 1906.

[2] " Otto legatus immo alter papa." The monk Eustace in his biography of St. Edmund, ap. Wallace, p. 570.

[3] Royal letters, n. 310, June, 1230, vol. i, p. 379.

[4] Roger of Wend., iv, p. 277.

[5] *Ib.*

[6] " *Dictum est autem*," Mat. Par., iii, p. 395.

glad that the legate is coming, for the more people there
are to hear the justice of our cause, the more will the
enemies of justice be put to shame." [1]

As the bishops continued to press the King on the
subject of his foreign favourites,[2] and were not checked
by letters from Rome urging them to proceed " against
the disturbers of the peace " (1234),[3] Henry continued
to urge the Pope to send him a legate. He hoped with
his aid to crush the bishops, who were the leaders of the
party opposed to the foreigners, whose influence increased
still more after his marriage with Eleanor, daughter of
Raymund of Provence. For some time the Pope turned
a deaf ear to Henry's request ; and, when the King sent
fresh messengers, Gregory still declined to send a legate.
He reminded Henry that once before, when at his request
a legate had actually been appointed, he had asked for
the revocation of the appointment.[4]

Our King, however, continued to press. " We throw
ourselves with all confidence on the Apostolic See, our
tender mother, whenever we see our royal dignity in
any difficulty, inasmuch as she has ever compassionate
regard for us, her devoted son." [5]

The Pope at last gave way, and wrote to tell Henry, as
well as the bishops of England, Wales, and Ireland,
that he had dispatched Cardinal Otho, " a great and
honourable member of the Church," as legate to those
countries, and exhorted the King to receive him in such
a way as to show his devotion to the Roman Church.[6]

---

[1] *Ib.*, p. 288. " Item de legato, placet quod veniat."

[2] *Cf.* Mat. Par., *Chron. Maj.*, iii, p. 286 ff.

[3] *Cf.* Epp. of March 11 and Apr. 3, 1234, ap. *Royal Letters*, i, p. 554 ff.
The Pope urges the bishops " ut laicos regni . . . quos pacis ejusdem
esse constiterit turbatores . . . per censuram ecclesiasticam, nomina-
tim, compescant."

[4] Epp. of Aug. 21, 1236, ap. *Reg.*, ii, p. 467, nn. 3298 f.

[5] *Royal Letters*, n. 421, ii, p. 13, May 25, 1236.

[6] Epp. of Feb. 12, 13, 1237, *ib.*, p. 563 ff.

Otho was already known in England, which he had The arrival of the legate Otho in England, 1237. visited (1226) as papal nuncio in the days of Honorius III., and if the news of his appointment angered many,[1] still many, besides the King, rejoiced when it was known that he was on his way to England. He was met at Paris by messengers of several of the bishops, who offered him presents of scarlet cloth and costly cups. As his galley approached the shores of England, about the end of July, and not, as Matthew Paris says, " about the feast of St. Peter and Paul," some went out in boats to meet him ; and, when he landed, he was met by the bishops " with processions and the music of bells," and by King Henry who, " bowing his head to his knees," conducted him " into the interior of the country." [2] Then, according to Matthew Paris, our weak monarch " resigned himself entirely to the will of the Romans, and especially to the legate . . . so that he seemed to worship his very footsteps, and he always declared that he could not, either in public or in private, transact any business of the realm without the consent of his lord the Pope or of the legate." [3]

At first, at any rate, Otho conducted himself most Wins general goodwill. admirably, even according to the writer just quoted. He says that the legate, " contrary to the usual custom of the Romans," by " refusing for the most part the valuable presents offered to him, calmed by his well-ordered conduct the angry feelings which had been conceived against him." [4] Those presents, however,

---

[1] Mat. Par., ib., iii, 395 f. See above.

[2] " Parisius in obviam ei obtulerunt telas escarleti et vasa pretiosa nuntii diversorum episcoporum." Cf., about the date, Wallace, St. Edmund, p. 212.

[3] M. P., iii, p. 412. To these sentiments Henry gave expression over and over again. Cf. ib., iv, pp. 4, 8, 19, an. 1240.

[4] Ib., iii, p. 403. The Close Rolls of Henry, iv, p. 33, show the legate's refusal of a number of silver vessels, presents from the king.

which he did receive, he accepted with a smiling face, mindful, continues Paris, of the dictum of Seneca that if it is a sign of avarice to take all that is offered to one, and of churlishness not to accept anything, it is a sign of friendly feeling to accept something.[1]

His good work for the country. During the three years of Otho's stay in England he did a great deal of good both in the political and in the religious order. He did much, for instance, for the peace of the land. He first promoted peace among the warlike nobles themselves,[2] and then strove to keep the peace between them and the King (1238).[3] Further, in accordance with instructions received from the Pope,[4] he brought about a meeting between the Kings of England and Scotland, and succeeded in effecting a peace between the two countries.[5]

The Council of St. Paul's, 1237. But the most important thing done by Otho was in the direction of Church reform. Not long after his arrival the legate wrote to all the prelates in England, bidding them assemble in St. Paul's on November 18 to hear the papal letter read which conferred on him full legatine power, and in his presence to hold a council for the reformation of the English Church.[6] Accordingly, soon after the octave of the feast of St. Martin, the prelates

---

[1] *Ib.*, p. 412. Yet such is the spitefulness of Paris that, when he first tells us of the legate's refusing certain presents, he pretends that he nevertheless ordered them to be kept for him. " Sed quae non recepit, jussit sibi reservari," iii, p. 395.

[2] *Ib.*, iii, p. 403 f.

[3] *Ib.*, 475 ff. He was also so far successful in his efforts to curb the king's extravagant expenditure that Henry promised only to dispose of the grant of a thirtieth made to him on Jan. 13, 1237, by the legate's counsel. Ep. Nov. 28, 1237, ap. *Patent Rolls*, Henry III., vol. iii, p. 205.

[4] *Reg.*, ii, p. 605 f., March 24 f., 1237 ; *ib:*, p. 633 f., May 7 and 10. In the letter of May 7, the Pope declares that he is bound to have a special care of the Scottish Church as " it recognizes the Roman Church as its sole mother, and metropolitan without any intermediary."

[5] Mat. Par., iii, 413.

[6] *Ib.*, iii, 404, 414.

of England appeared before the legate, who was seated in great state on a lofty throne which had been prepared for him at the west end of the cathedral. After a message had been proclaimed from the King forbidding the legate " to attempt to decree anything against the dignity of the crown," master Atho, one of Otho's clerks, arose with the Register of the Pope in his hands, and read from it a decretal which clearly set forth that the legate's statutes would have the force of law even after his departure from the country.[1] Then with a voice " like a trumpet," the legate, having addressed the assembled prelates, " ordered his decrees to be read distinctly and in a loud voice." These decrees, given incorrectly by Matthew Paris,[2] but more correctly by our great canonist Lyndwood, embraced many subjects, the sacraments, the celibacy of the clergy, their dress, the administration of justice, etc., all bearing on the general reformation of the English Church.

These legatine constitutions, together with those of Cardinal Ottoboni published later in Henry's reign, were commented on by such English canonists as John of Ayton or Acton (between 1333 and 1348), and William Lyndwood (1430), and became the immovable foundation of English Canon Law—"immovable" because no ecclesiastical authority in the country had any power to alter them.[3]

About this time, to Henry's great dismay, the Pope

Henry begs the Pope not to recall the legate, 1238.

[1] Mat. P., iii, p. 419. "Attho . . . aperto libro autentico, scilicet registro d. Papæ, ad majorem auctoritatem . . . quandam decretalem legit . . . per illam asserens manifeste, quod etiam post recessum ejus sua statuta perpetuæ firmitatis robur debeant optinere."

[2] *Ib.*, p. 421 ff.

[3] Such is the definite assertion of Lyndwood. "Et verum est quod constitutiones legatinas non poterit archiepiscopus tollere, quia inferior non potest tollere legem superioris." Lyndwood, *Provinciale*, p. 154, gl. ad. v. *adjciendo*, ed. Oxford, 1679. On Lyndwood, see chap. i of F. W. Maitland's *Roman Canon Law in the Church of England.*

sent word to the legate to return to him. The King at once dispatched a letter to Gregory (March 6, 1238), entreating him to consider " the divers perils to the King and this realm which may result from the recall of the legate," and begging him to grant that the legate may continue " to fill his office in England until the King's affairs, so well begun by him, are brought to a happy issue, and the tranquillity of England to which he was in all things necessary, as Peter Sarracenus (the King's envoy) will set forth, is more strongly established for the future by his control." [1]

The King's petition was granted, and Otho remained to the great advantage of the realm.

Otho issues regulations for the reform of the Benedictines, 1238.

Following up his efforts for the reform of the Church of England in general, Otho endeavoured, in accordance with his commission from Rome, to reform the English Benedictines. Accordingly, on the anniversary of the important council of London, he met the abbots " of the Black Order " whom " by the authority of the Pope " he had ordered to assemble at London in St. Martin's Church (Nov. 18, 1238). He there promulgated a number of reformatory decrees " which his holiness the Pope, after due deliberation, had ordained for the reformation of the order." [2] Somewhat later (Feb. 20, 1239), at an assembly of the bishops of the country, which he had ordered to meet in London, Otho again publishep the new regulations which the Benedictines had to observe. On this occasion, however, he had tempered " the indiscreet rigour " of many of them. [3]

---

[1] *Patent Rolls*, Henry III., vol. iii, 235 *R. S.* " In like manner," we are told, " it is written by letters close to the Pope, and to the cardinals that they interpose their prayers."

[2] Mat. Par., *ib.*, iii, p. 449. The decrees are given by Paris. The Pope himself was working for the general reform of the whole Benedictine Order. *Cf. Regist.*, ii, p. 317 ff.

[3] *Ib.*, p. 524.

All this splendid work, accomplished by the legate in the cause of peace, law and order, and reform, was more than enough to have caused the memory of cardinal Otho to have been long held in benediction in this country. However, not to mention a few personal weaknesses,[1] the reputation,[2] or rather the popularity of Otho suffered somewhat in consequence of his having to raise funds for the needs of the Pope. When the legate arrived in England, the emperor Frederick had begun his campaign against the Lombards, and communication with Rome had already become difficult. Gregory was accordingly even then conscious of a loss of revenue, and that consciousness was increased by the loss of Ferrara and Sardinia. After his excommunication of Frederick in the spring of 1239, he could again have written : " The patrimony of Blessed Peter is overrun with tyrannical cruelty, our fortresses have been invaded, and our faithful people slaughtered by impious Saracens." [3]

In consequence, the Pope's need of money became acute. Otho was therefore commissioned by Gregory to try to procure some for him from England, and,

[1] He appears to have been perhaps a little fond of going about with an over fine retinue, and was solicitous about obtaining prebends for his clerks. *Cf.* Mat. Par., iii, p. 446 ; Grosseteste's *Letters*, nn. 49, 52, 74.

[2] Even according to Matthew Paris, Otho's reputation was good. " Otto, fama referente, vir discretus extitit et modestus, necnon et juris peritus." *Hist. Anglorum*, ii, p. 398. Mr. Luard, *Relations between England and Rome*, p. 66, notes that " the very strong anti-Papal bias that characterizes Matthew Paris, has perhaps blinded subsequent historians to the work effected by the legate and to the best points of his character . . . His returning to his prison at Naples, from which Frederick had allowed him temporary freedom in order to be present at the conclave which elected Celestine IV., not only proved the innate nobleness of the man, but conciliated even Frederick."

[3] The letter whence this extract is taken was really written in 1228, Dec. 20, to the bishop and chapter of Salisbury, ap. *Register of St. Osmund*, ii, p. 144 f. *R. S.*

if we had not the various monastic annals to enable us to check the narrative of Matthew Paris, we should be led to suppose that Otho was engaged in raising money all the time he was in England. No doubt the fine retinue with which he went about the country took some keeping up, and the " procurations " which he demanded for that purpose were heavy,[1] but he only demanded one subsidy for the Pope, and that was not until Frederick had furiously attacked the Patrimony (Jan., 1240) after his excommunication.[2] He asked for a fifth of the ecclesiastical revenues of the country.[3] The demand, no doubt, was considerable, and there was in many quarters, as we have shown, a great deal of opposition to it ; but, as there was no one " who opposed himself like a wall to the legate in behalf of the opponents (of the tax)," [4] it was gradually, if reluctantly, paid.[5]

Departure of Otho, 1241.

This levying of the fifth for the Pope was one of the last acts of Otho as papal legate in England. His great ability caused him to be wanted in Rome. As early as October 18, 1237, cardinal John Colonna had written to tell him to get ready to return " as he was necessary

---

[1] Mat. P., *Chron. Maj.*, iii, p. 567, an. 1239 and p. 620 about *the same incident.* *Cf.* iv, p. 55.

[2] King Henry regarded the persecution as sufficient justification for the tax. In his *Close Rolls*, iv, p. 361, we read this : " Quia ecclesia Romane magnam persecutionem patitur ad presens ita quod nonnulli ad ipsius oppressionem magis quod ad ejus exaltationem nituntur, nos indempnitati et commoditati ejusdem ecclesie providere volentes, etc."

[3] Such is the assertion of Mat. P., *ib.*, iv, 10, 15. Most of our annalists simply say that he levied a tax. *Cf. supra.*

[4] *Ann. de Burton*, p. 366. *Cf. ib.*, p. 257 ; and *Ann. de Theokesber.*, p. 115.

[5] *Ann. de Wigornia*, " Tam conventuales quam parochiales ecclesiæ dederunt subsidium Papæ," p. 432, ap. *Ann. Monast.*, vol. ii, *R. S. Cf. Ann. de Dunstap.*, p. 154, which state that the tax was paid when Otho was leaving England : "in cujus recessu solutum tallagium suprascriptum." *Cf.* Mat. Par., *Chron.*, iv, pp. 9, 35 ff., 55.

for his mother the Church."[1]   In fact Gregory recalled
him several times during the years 1238 and 1239 ; but,
as often as he recalled him, Henry contrived to induce
the Pope to leave him in England.[2]   At length, however,
in 1240 a peremptory summons from Rome bade the
cardinal come thither as soon as ever possible, in order
that his wisdom might help the preparatory work for the
General Council which the Pope had summoned.[3]
Regretting that he could not detain his friend any longer,
Henry gave him a royal send-off, accompanying him
to the sea-coast.   At Dover, laying aside the insignia
of his legatine office, Otho left England (Jan. 7, 1241)
to fall with the money he had collected into the hands
of Frederick, against whom he had worked so successfully.

Among those in this country who had frequent relations Archbishops
with Pope Gregory, and also with his legate Otho, were of
naturally the archbishops of Canterbury. With Stephen Canterbury.
Langton, who died (July 9, 1228) some fifteen months (1) Richard
le Grant.
after Gregory became Pope, that Pontiff had no dealings
of any peculiar importance.   On his death the monks
of Christchurch elected one of their own number, Walter
of Eynsham.[4]   His election was, however, objected to
both by the King and by the bishops on the ground
that his poor character and intellect rendered him unfit

---

[1] Ep. ap. Mat. P., iii, p. 444 ff.

[2] Mat. P., iii, p. 473, an. 1238, 525 f., *cf.* p. 530 f., an. 1239.

[3] *Ib.*, iv, p. 55 ; *Ann. de Theok.*, p. 116 ; *Ann. de Wintonia*, p. 88 ;
Ann. de Waverleia, p. 328. According to Matthew Paris, *ib.*, p. 84,
whose testimony as we have seen is not borne out by facts, Otho
during his stay in England had ruined its Church, and left the country
regretted only by the king, and by those whom he had fattened on its
provisions. See, on the contrary, the splendid eulogy pronounced on
him by Abbot Alexander Neckam, quoted by Fordun, *Scotichronicon*,
l. ix, c. 54. "Qui marsupia non exhaurit . . . cujus memoria in
benedictione est."

[4] A full account of his election is given ap. Gervase of Canterbury,
Gesta regum contin., ii, p. 115 ff. R. S.

to be archbishop. The matter was referred to Rome. Walter's ignorance and worse conduct were proved; and Gregory himself appointed to the vacant see Richard le Grant, chancellor of Lincoln, who had been recommended by the King's envoys,[1] because, as he said, the Church of Canterbury being noble, ought " to have a noble prelate, a discreet and modest man, and one taken from the bosom of the Roman Church." [2]

When news of the Pope's choice reached England, Richard was consecrated in the presence of the suffragans of Canterbury by the bishop of Rochester in the church of the Holy Trinity in that city. But, as his pallium had not yet arrived from Rome, the historian takes care to inform us that his powers were limited. " He was allowed either to confer Holy Orders or to consecrate churches," [3] but not to exercise any *archiepiscopal* function.

Richard's dispute with the King.

The pontificate of the new archbishop, though short, was not destined to be peaceful. He was soon in difficulties with the King both with regard to matters spiritual and temporal. Unable to get justice from Henry, Richard went to Rome, and complained to the Pope that the justiciar, Hubert de Burgh, unjustly detained Tunbridge Castle, that he ruled the kingdom without reference to the other magnates, and that

---

[1] *Cf. Ann. de Dunst.*, p. 116; epp. of Gregory of Jan. 19, 1229, ap. Bliss, *Calendar*, i, p. 120; Roger of Wendover, ann. 1228 and 1229, iv, p. 170 f., and 184 ff., ed. Coxe; Mat. Paris, *Hist. Anglorum*, ii, 309 f. These historians declare that the Pope was moved to quash the election of Walter because the king offered him a tenth to maintain his war against the emperor.

[2] Roger, *ib.*, p. 185.

[3] *Ib.*, p. 204. The pallium arrived from Rome on Nov. 23. *Ib.*, p. 205. Among the *Royal Letters*, i, p. 336, there is an interesting letter from Master Philip de Arden to Ralph, bishop of Chichester and Chancellor. Philip writes that the Pope asked him whom the king would like to have as archbishop if Walter's election were annulled, and that he mentioned the bishop's name. He also says that he urged the establishment of secular canons at Canterbury.

he had made an unlawful marriage. He, moreover, complained that bishops and other prelates, acting as judges, decided even capital cases, and that some of the clergy held more than two benefices with the cure of souls. Although Richard's wisdom, eloquence, and dignified presence enabled him to worst the King's agents, and to obtain what he desired from the Pope, his work was in vain, for he died on his return journey, Aug. 3, 1231.[1]

As soon as the news of Richard's death reached England the monks, having, in accordance with custom, obtained the royal permission (September 24), proceeded to elect a successor to him. Looking, according to a foreign historian, "more for the favour of an earthly monarch than for that of the king of heaven," [2] they unanimously elected Ralph Neville, bishop of Chichester, the King's chancellor. Some of their number, along with some clerks of the King and of Ralph, were at once sent to Rome to obtain the Pope's confirmation of their choice. This, however, the monks could not obtain. Ralph was declared by Gregory to be a courtier and illiterate, and his election was therefore annulled.[3] Then, "rather by favour than by right, the chapter of Canterbury were granted the right of holding another election, on condition that the election was canonically made in a short time and that the elect were sent to Rome for examination." [4]

Another disputed election to the see of Canterbury.

[1] Roger, *ib.*, 219 f., 225 f. The words concerning the archbishop's "statura elegantissima," etc., are an addition of Paris, iii, p. 205.

[2] Will. of Andres, *Chron.*, c. 250, ap. *M. G. SS.*, xxiv, p. 771.

[3] Roger, iv, p. 228.

[4] " De gratia potius quam de jure predicto Cantuariensi capitulo fuit iterum electio indulta, ita tamen ut infra certum et brevem terminum canonice eligerent et suum electum apostolico examini destinarent." Will. And., *l.c.* ; *cf.* Roger, *ib.* The monks were warned by the king not to do anything against his prerogatives by reason of the papal mandate. *Cf.* his letter to them of March 11, 1232. Ap. *Roy. Letters*, i, p. 406.

A fresh election resulted in the monks choosing their prior John as the new archbishop. Accepted by the King, he was rejected at Rome on account of his age and simplicity.[1] The next candidate, Master John Blund, chosen by the monks, was also rejected by the Pope, because, among other matters, he had held, contrary to the decree of the Lateran council, two benefices with the cure of souls.[2]

Grieved, however, that " a metropolitan see of such importance " had been so long vacant, Gregory bade the monks return home with their rejected candidate, and elect Edmund Rich, treasurer of Salisbury, whom he had ascertained by careful inquiry made all over England to be the most suitable candidate for the vacant see.[3] The

---

[1] Roger, *ib.*, pp. 234, 243. From Wendover it is clear that William of Andres was mistaken in ascribing John's rejection to his unwillingness to bribe the Roman curia.

[2] Rog., *ib.*, pp. 248, 267 ; Will., *l.c.* According to the Annals of Osney, p. 74 *R. S.*, John Blund was rejected because it was feared that the whole power of the land would fall into the hands of Peter des Roches, who, it had been proved, had given money to John. Some colour may perhaps be lent to this view by the subsequent conduct of the Pope towards John, if indeed that were not caused by a wish to soothe his feelings. One document addressed (June 8, 1233) to Master John, "called Blund," canon of Chichester, declared that the cancelling by the Pope of his election to the see of Canterbury was not to be considered an obstacle to his being elected to a bishopric. Another of the same date restored to him the Church of Horsley, resigned by him because he was holding it and Bertun without a dispensation ; and permitted him to hold a prebend of Chichester as well as these churches. Bliss, *Calendar*, i, p. 135. Hitherto, it is interesting to note, the prior and monks had borne the expenses of the archiepiscopal elections, but, by papal authority, they had added the 612 silver marks which Blund's election had cost them to the debts of the already heavily indebted see. However, on the protest of St. Edmund, Gregory finally decided that, in accordance with his petition, the expenses should be divided between the see and the monastery. Bliss, *ib.*, pp. 146–7.

[3] "Cum . . . ad Gregorium P. ix, illi metropoli preficiendi pastoris esset provisio devoluta, per totam faciens Angliam diligenter inquiri . . . quis tantum honus levare sufficeret," etc. Roger Bacon's *Life*

monks accordingly followed the Pope's advice, and in September, 1233, elected St. Edmund.[1] The royal and papal assent to the election followed in due course, and the Saint was consecrated on April 2, 1234, after having received the pallium from Rome.[2]

The new Archbishop was one of the sweetest characters that ever sat on the throne of Canterbury. According to Matthew Paris, his devotion to St. John the Evangelist appears to have produced a striking similarity between them. This likeness manifested itself in their virginity of body and soul, their theological science, their preaching, and in their being dear to God and man.[3] The opinion entertained of him by men in general may conveniently be gathered from Gregory's letter to the suffragans of Canterbury confirming his election to its see, for the character there given of him is in accordance with that which the papal agents had after careful inquiries reported to their master.

St. Edmund Rich.

Whereas we have had presented to us the election which our beloved sons the chapter of the Church of Canterbury have canonically and harmoniously made of our beloved son, Master Edmund, treasurer of Salisbury, a man of conspicuous rectitude of conduct, eminently endowed with literary accomplishments, and prudent in management of temporal affairs, to be Archbishop of Canterbury, we, having carefully scrutinized that election as was befitting, inasmuch as no difficulty ought to be put in the way of matters rightly settled, by the advice of our brethren have decided to confirm his election in the firm hope and confidence that he, by preserving order and controlling disorder in

of St. Edmund, ap. Wallace, p. 608. *Cf.* Rog., *ib.*, p. 267, and a letter of Greg. IX. of Apr. 3, 1234, ap. *Roy. Let.*, i, p. 556.

[1] *Cf.* the monk Eustace's *Life* of the Saint, ap. Wallace, p. 554.

[2] Roger, *ib.*, 298 ; *Life* of Eustace, *l.c.*, p. 555 ; Bertrand, c. 48, p. 1804 ; Bliss, *Calendar*, i, pp. 137–8 ; *Reg.* Greg., i, p. 957 f., nn. 1742–3, Feb. 3, 1234. *Cf.* Bliss, *Calendar of Papal Let.*, i, p. 174, for a privilege allowing the Saint under certain conditions to wear his pallium outside his province.

[3] *Chron. maj., Addit.*, vi, 127.

the same church, and improving himself by the merit of his life, and others by his example like a star set in the firmament of the same church through the carefulness of his ministry may by God's grace promote its spiritual and temporal welfare. And, since one is bound to honour one's earthly father, how much more ought the spiritual father to be honoured in proportion as the spirit excels the flesh, and souls are more estimable than bodies ; hence we command you all by these apostolic letters that you humbly submit yourselves to the father and pastor of your souls and that you take care scrupulously to obey his salutary counsels and precepts, etc. Given at the Lateran, December 22, in the seventh year of our pontificate (1233).[1]

Edmund's difficulties with the legate and with the Pope.

Later on, however, when in consequence of many appeals to Rome in which he was concerned, Gregory had come to know more of the Saint, he declared with jesting truth that he should have been a monk.[2] The fact was that, with his gentleness, his asceticism, and his love of learning, Edmund was not equal to coping with a weak King made to do the will of unscrupulous men,[3] with turbulent barons, and with unruly monks, whose possession of the right to elect the archbishop threw them into the midst of intrigues of every kind. The Saint's difficulties were, moreover, increased, possibly by a little obstinacy of his own, certainly by the position of the Pope. As the oppressive hand of the first Frederick prevented Alexander III. from giving wholehearted

[1] This letter is given by Raynaldus, *Annales Eccles.*, an. 1233, n. 64. The translation is that of Wallace, p. 599, who also gives from the *Liber Censuum*, i, p. 449 (*cf. ib.*, 286) the oath he took to the Pope. He shows that it is practically the same as the oath now taken by the archbishops of Westminster.

[2] " Ait papa jocose vultuque sereno : ' bene scires monachus esse.' At ipse : ' Utinam his executus (? exerutus) sollicitudinibus bonus monachus essem.' " *Life* by the contemporary monk Eustace, ap. Wallace, p. 558.

[3] " Quum igitur ignorans elenchum, se leviter trahi permittit ad inconveniens incurrendum, rex, licet Christianissimus, sinistris quorundam consiliis adquiescens, sacrum antistitem attemptavit, nec potuit ab incepto movere." *Life* by Robert Bacon, ap. *ib.*, p. 610.

support to St. Thomas Becket, so the violence of the second Frederick equally prevented Gregory from cordially assisting the reforming efforts of St. Edmund.[1] The legate Otho was also a thorn in the side of the Archbishop. "Inasmuch," says the Saint's biographer, Eustace,[2] "as Otho was desirous of pleasing the King, it happened that, when he saw that his heart was turned away from the Archbishop, and that the Saint's enemies were multiplied on every side, he strove to please the many. Accordingly, in virtue of his authority, he annulled the acts of the Archbishop, absolving those whom he had excommunicated by name (specialiter), and those whom the archbishop had absolved the legate anathematized."

Nor, as we have seen, did St. Edmund receive from the Pope that support which he believed he had a right to expect in his efforts to preserve the peace of the realm, and to reform the monks of Canterbury.

After his marriage with Eleanor of Provence (Jan., 1236), Henry replaced his former favourites by Provençals. Uncles of the queen had a great influence over him. Of these, William, bishop-elect of Valence, hoped to succeed to the influence of Peter des Roches, bishop of Winchester, and Boniface of Savoy, afterwards beatified by the common voice of the people, was destined to succeed St. Edmund himself as archbishop of Canterbury.

Henry III. and his foreign favourites.

Henry's attempt to rule the country in the interests

---

[1] In the Lambeth MS. (No. 135) of the *Life* of St. Edmund by Bertrand there are certain additions to the edition which Martene published in his *Thesaurus Novus Anecdot*, vol. iii. Among them is one giving reasons why the archbishop left England (1240), in which it is said that "the Church of Rome, which ought to have supported him, was at that time in such a plight as not to be able to help itself." Ap. Wallace, p. 330. It is also so stated in the *Life*, ap. Martene, c. 73, p. 1822 f.

[2] Ap. *ib.*, p. 568, *cf.* Bertrand's *Life*, pp. 1810, 1822.

of these foreigners soon created great discontent ; and as
the archbishop thought the way to peace was for him to
support the national party, whilst Gregory believed that
it was to be secured by his adhering to his vassal Henry
and his advisers, it was only to be expected that Edmund
would at times not receive more encouragement from him
than he had from his legate.[1]

St. Edmund
and the
monks of
Canterbury,
1235.

The whole of the pontificate of St. Edmund was
embittered by his quarrels with the monks of Canterbury.
There is no doubt that at this period the discipline of
many of the grand old Benedictine houses was not exactly
as it should have been.   A spirit of worldliness had brought
about such a widespread relaxation that Gregory had
ordered a general visitation not only of the monasteries
in England, but throughout all Europe.[2]   This he did,
because as he said, writing of the religious houses of the
diocese of Canterbury in particular, they had " seriously
fallen off in spiritual and temporal matters . . . Lest,
therefore, if we should suffer them to go uncorrected, we
should seem to take their faults on ourselves, we have
appointed special visitors, reformers, and correctors . . .
to visit those monasteries in that district which are known
to be subject immediately to the Church of Rome, and
we have granted them full authority, in their visitation

---

[1] Eustace, l.c.   Bertrand, c. 73, p. 1822, says that Rome " which is
the head and mistress of all the churches, ought to have helped the
Church of Canterbury like the other churches, but her own difficulties
hindered her.   Unde cum consuluisset d. papam vir beatus, quid
vellet eum facere, mandavit ei pacem principis sui cum discretionis
studio conservare."   Cf. Gregory's letter of Apr. 3, 1234, to the
Saint, ap. Royal Letters, i, p. 556, and one of Feb. 15, 1235, exhorting
him to patience.   Needless to say, the Saint did not always fail to
win the support of the Pope.   His brother Robert Rich tells us how on
one occasion the monks had to leave the papal presence condemned " by
God and by his Vicar."   Life, ap. Wallace, p. 622.

[2] Ep. of June 9, 1232, ap. Roger of Wend., iv, 258 ff.   Cf. Ann. de
Theokesber, p. 89, and de Dunstap., 132.

of those places, to correct and reform the abuses which they may be certain require reformation and correction." [1]

Unfortunately in his zeal for reform, both in the Church and in the State, St. Edmund did not always proceed in his work with tact. Because the monks of Christ-Church and others certainly stood in need of some reform, the saintly archbishop would appear to have supposed that he might use all means that were in themselves lawful to effect that reform. Hence was he led at times to disregard some of the recognized privileges of the monks. This course of action not merely dragged him into costly lawsuits, and resulted in his losing cases at Rome to which both parties ever turned,[2] but brought about the failure of his efforts at reform, and no doubt helped to beget in him that feeling of hopelessness of doing any good which ultimately led him to leave the country.

The archbishop's quarrels with the monks may be divided into two groups separated by his visit to Rome in 1238. For these two groups there are two sets of authorities. One was printed for the first time by Dom Wallace,[3] and the other was inserted in the Continuation of the Chronicle of Gervase of Canterbury.[4] The authorities printed by Wallace consist of " The Judges' report of the process between the archbishop and the Chapter of Christ-Church " and " The final composition between the Archbishop and the Chapter of Canterbury." The Chronicle, on the other hand, furnishes us with a sort of

First quarrels with the monks.

---

[1] *Ib.*

[2] Especially the monks. To impede the action of St. Edmund they had constantly on their lips : " We appeal from you to the lord Pope, placing ourselves and our spiritual and temporal concerns under the protection of God, and the lord Pope and the Roman Church." Gervase, *Contin.*, ii, p. 159.

[3] Ap. his *Life of St. Edmund*, p. 488 ff. The documents of this group belong to the year 1237.

[4] Gervase, vol. ii, p. 130 ff. *R. S.*

memorandum or Journal from November, 1238, to May, 1239. Despite these authorities, however, we are not too well informed as to all the subjects in dispute between the archbishop and the monks. We are dependent upon monks for our knowledge of the history of our country at this period,. and as some of the things done by the monks of Canterbury during the dispute were not reputable, the chroniclers " out of reverence for so noble a Church " [1] prefer to keep silence about the controversy.

Let it suffice here to state that the first cause of quarrel between the archbishop and the monks seems to have been in connexion with certain liberties [2] which the latter maintained had been taken from them by St. Edmund. One, however, of the charters which the monks brought forward to establish their claims, proved to have been tampered with,[3] and it became necessary for the Pope to intervene. He appointed arbitrators with instructions to effect a friendly settlement if possible ; but, if they were unable to effect this, to refer the matter to him.[4] At first the archbishop would not appear before the judges, and even seems to have invoked the aid of the King ; [5] so that when his biographers complain that the monks attacked him in the temporal as well as in the spiritual

[1] *Ann. de Waverleia*, p. 320.

[2] The monks complained that the archbishop had wronged them in the matter of certain of their possessions and perquisites from them, and in their right of presentation to certain churches. See the *Report*. Cf. Eustace, *Life*, ap. Wallace. " Monachi . . . quasdam suas libertates ipsum, ut dicebant, conventum specialiter contingentes, quas archiepiscopales occuparant, constanter reposcebant."

[3] *Cf.* the *Life* by the Monk Eustace, ap. p. 565 f. See also Wallace, p. 280 f., and a letter of Gregory, ap. *ib.*, p. 499.

[4] See Gregory's letter of Dec. 22, 1235, ap. the *Report*, p. 488.

[5] See Henry's letter forbidding a question of advowsons to be tried in the courts Christian, and maintaining that such questions " never have been held in our realm except in our court." Letter of March 14, 1237, ap. *Report*, p. 490 f.

courts, it would seem that the saint had himself set them the example.[1]

Nevertheless, the dispute dragged on, despite the King's forbidding the question of presentation to livings to be decided in ecclesiastical courts ; for the Pope ordered the judges to go on with the case, notwithstanding this prohibition.[2] At length, however, the archbishop, for the sake of peace, offered certain concessions which the monks agreed to accept, and for which the Saint declared he would try in person to secure papal sanction.[3] The peace compact, dated December 18, 1237, was agreed to by both parties on condition that the Pope and the King would give their consent to it.[4]

To secure the adhesion of Gregory to the compromise the archbishop set out for Rome in December, 1237.[5] When Edmund arrived in the Eternal City he was greatly distressed to find that the monks of Christ-Church were already there, and were endeavouring to repudiate the compromise to which they had agreed, and had allied themselves to such as they found in Rome with grievances against him.[6] The Saint would not, however, go out of his way to gain his cause ; nay, he even did things which were not to his interest. He, for instance, showed that he was not pleased when he had to appear before the Pope after the hour of Compline, as he was wont not to talk after that time ;[7] and, as he was not in the habit of attending banquets, he would not make an exception even when it was the Pope himself who invited him[8] to one.

St. Edmund in Rome, 1238.

---

[1] See Rob. Rich, *Life*, p. 621. " Pro juribus bellum in utroque foro (monachis) inferentibus." *Cf.* p. 622.

[2] See his letter of Feb. 26, 1237, ap. *Report*, p. 419 f.

[3] *Cf.* Eustace, *Life*, p. 566 f. ; and the *Composition*, p. 495 f.

[4] The *Composition*, p. 498.

[5] On the question of the date see Wallace, p. 256.

[6] *Cf.* Eustace, *Life*, p. 567 ; and Robert Rich, p. 622, ap. Wallace.

[7] Eustace, pp. 558, 567.

[8] See the Saint's *Life* by his chamberlain Bertrand, ap. Wallace, p. 262.

"The archbishop and the monks pleaded their case in the presence of the Pope,"[1] who on one occasion at least, before the close of the dispute, was so ill that he had to lie down on a couch.[2] But, if Edmund was successful on some counts,[3] he was not so on others. He could not bring to a head principal points in dispute between the Christ-Church monks and himself. Decision was deferred, and the Saint returned to England (Aug., 1238), "crest-fallen, dejected, and impoverished."[4]

Fresh trouble with the monks of Christ-Church on his return, 1238.

On his return his difficulties did but increase. Though even the legate Otho, who is generally believed to have been hostile to Edmund, approached the monks and begged them to "obey their pastor and father, their most holy archbishop," he could not bring the community as a whole to withdraw from the position they had taken up.[5] It cannot, however, be denied that the archbishop contributed to the continuance of the quarrel. We have seen in a previous volume that archbishop Baldwin, with a view to depriving the monks of their privileges, especially that of electing the archbishop of Canterbury, strove to found a collegiate church at Hakington near that city, in order to secure a new cathedral. This, and a similar attempt by archbishop Hubert Walter, had been quashed

We are assured that the Saint's absence on this occasion saved him from seeing a most distressing sight, to wit, the assassination of a cardinal's nephew before the eyes of the Pope.

[1] *Ann. Wav.*, p. 320 ; Rob. Rich, *Life*, p. 622.

[2] Gervase, *Contin.*, ii, pp. 183–4 *R. S.* The account of this affair in Matthew Paris (*Chron. maj.*, iii, 492) is confused.

[3] R. Rich, *l.c.* " Quibus (charges made by the monks against the Saint) nullatenus admissis, sed a Deo et suo vicario de fratrum consilio turpiter ejectis," etc. *Cf.* Bertrand, c. 54, p. 1808. "Audientia benigna conceditur et quod ab eo (the Pope) petible petitur favorabiliter impetratur."

[4] Wallace, p. 266, seemingly quoting a contemporary biographer of the saint. Still we are assured by Bertrand, *l.c.*, that he returned. " Præsidiis apostolicis munitus, et roboratus consiliis."

[5] Eustace, p. 566.

by Innocent III.[1] Despite this clear papal judgment on
the matter, Edmund reopened the whole question, and
decided to build a similar church at Maidstone.[2] He
succeeded, indeed, in obtaining papal sanction for his
scheme ; [3] but the monks contrived to frustrate it by the
support of the King, who had now turned against the
archbishop.[4]

Distressed at the little support he received from Rome,
and feeling that " the action of the King and of the
legate Otho prevented him from fulfilling the duties of
his office," [5] St. Edmund, who had many other quarrels
with other monks and with nobles which we here pass
over,[6] left the kingdom towards the close of September,
1240, and retired to Pontigny where he died soon afterwards (November 16, 1240). Other reasons are given
for the archbishop's flight besides those named in the
Annals of Winchester. Such are the injuries which
surrounding nobles were suffered to inflict on him,[7]
his conviction that the Pope could not help him,[8] and his
being told by Gregory to keep on good terms with the
sovereign who was thwarting his work.[9]

St. Edmund retires to Pontigny, and dies 1240.

[1] Cf. supra, x, p. 304 ff.

[2] Cf. Gervase, Contin., ii, p. 132 ; cf. p. 174, and documents on this
subject, ap. Wallace, pp. 509–14 ; Bliss, Calendar, i, 172–4.

[3] Cf. ep. Greg. of June 6, 1239, ap. Wallace, p. 509 ff. ; Bliss, ib.,
pp. 182, 189. Cf. Wallace, p. 303 ff.

[4] On his former dutifulness to the Saint see Roger of Wend., an. 1234,
iv, 298 f. For the intervention of the King see the Annals of Dunstable,
pp. 150–1, and Bertrand, l.c.

[5] Annal. de Wintonia, p. 88, ap. Annal. Monast., ii, R. S. Cf.
Bertrand, c. 55, and Rob. Rich, " Vir Dei nolens cum rege contendere
. . . cum debitum pastoris officium, quamquam ad ecclesiæ libera-
tionem manus ejus fuisset extenta, premissis obstantibus, minime
potuit adimplere." Ap. Wallace, p. 622.

[6] Details of them will be found in Wallace, and in Gasquet, Henry III.
and the Church.

[7] Rob. Rich, Life, p. 621.

[8] Cf. supra, Mat. Par., Chron., iv, 14, 32.

[9] Wallace, p. 330. It was largely the opposition of the King, but

The monks
of Christ-
Church are
absolved
from
censures,
and elect
Boniface of
Savoy.

Before he went abroad, the archbishop had inflicted various ecclesiastical censures upon the monks of Christ-Church. Of these they had hitherto taken no notice, inasmuch as they contended that they were not bound by them because they had appealed to Rome. When, however, St. Edmund died, and it became a question of electing another archbishop, they realized that it would be prudent to obtain public absolution from the censures, as they knew that there were very many who were ready to take advantage of any excuse for challenging their exclusive right to elect the archbishop of Canterbury. Sending accordingly to Rome, they obtained the desired absolution by the aid of a large sum of money and the support they received from the King and the legate. They asked for and received the absolution *ad cautelam* only.[1]

When the monks had been duly absolved (May 4, 1241),[2] and had obtained the licence of the King, they met together to elect a new archbishop, and " as far as it lay with them" provided a pastor for the Church in the person of " the noble lord Boniface of Savoy, the administrator of the diocese of Belley." Praising him for his illustrious

certainly no question of papal taxes, as suggested by Matthew Paris, that caused the retirement of the archbishop. *Cf.* Bertrand, cc. 54–5, who says that the King had been prejudiced against him, and " sic inter ipsum et regem orta contentione gravi super jure Cantuariensis ecclesiæ et libertatis."

[1] Eustace, p. 568. *Cf.* Mat. Par., *Chron.*, iv, 103, and the letter of the Pope (March 6, 1241) authorizing, " without prejudice to archi-episcopal rights," the provisional relaxation of the interdict, etc., laid upon them by the late archbishop. Ap. Bliss, *Calendar*, i, p. 194, or ap. Gervase, *Contin.*, ii, pp. 192–3. " Volumus tamen ut nullum propter hoc futuro Cantuariensi pontifici præjudicium generetur." See also other documents on the absolution of the monks, ap. Gervase, *ib.*, p. 193 ff.

[2] *Cf.* Gervase, *ib.*, pp. 194–6.

birth and good life, the monks begged the Pope to confirm their choice.[1]

Unfortunately, the envoys dispatched to Rome to obtain the Pope's confirmation of the election were captured by the emperor Frederick with the rest of the prelates who were on their way to the general council (1241).[2] Owing to this accident they were unable to obtain the desired confirmation before Gregory's death. The brief pontificate of Celestine IV., and the troubles that ensued thereon prevented the monks and King Henry[3] from obtaining what they desired till September 16, 1243. On that day Innocent IV. informed the suffragans of the church of Canterbury, "the mirror of the kingdom of England which is most dear to the King of Kings and to the apostolic See," that, considering the good name and fame of Boniface and his illustrious birth, he, "of the plenitude of his power," freed him from his relation to the church of Belley, and "by special favour" granted him to the church of Canterbury.[4]

Perhaps the best work done by Gregory IX. for the

The election confirmed by Innocent IV., 1243.

The coming of the Franciscans and Dominicans.

[1] "Eum tam generis nobilitas naturalis quam ejusdem conversationis honestæ bonitas specialis commendaverint, etc." The letter of the monks asking for papal confirmation of their election, Feb. 1, 1241, ap. Gervase, ib., p. 186 f. Cf. the many other documents on the election, ap. ib.

[2] Ib., p. 198.

[3] Cf. the King's letters of Feb. 17, 1243, to the Pope begging him to confirm the monks' choice. Patent Rolls, Henry III., vol. iii, p. 400 R. S.

[4] Ep. ap. Gervase, ib., p. 198 ff. As the praise given to Boniface by the Pope is in accordance with that given him by the monks, we need not attach any weight to the assertion of Matthew Paris that the monks did not know anything about his abilities or character, and that, "as was said" (ut dicebatur), he was, compared with his predecessors, incompetent for such a position. Chron., iv, 104. In one MS. of M. P. this assertion is much modified. When, however, he implies that Henry put pressure on the monks to elect his uncle, he is no doubt speaking accurately enough. On Matthew's prejudices against Boniface more will be said under Innocent IV.

good of the world in general and of England in particular, was the encouragement and direction which he gave to the Orders of SS. Francis and Dominic. It was with our country in the thirteenth century as it is in our own time. In the midst of wealth and splendour of many kinds, there was much that was mean and sordid, and though knowledge made great strides in the thirteenth century, there was ignorance in plenty as well of things divine as human. Moreover, what was worse, there were not at hand in the beginning of the century, means adequate to cope with the existing corruption—a corruption which was not lessened by the relaxation which had crept into some of the older religious Orders. But Francis and Dominic had inspired their followers with ideals calculated to leaven the sodden masses. To go about among the poor and the ignorant, to console, comfort, elevate, and instruct them for Christ's sake was the noble ambition of the Franciscan and the Dominican.

It was in 1221 that the Dominicans came to England; and, as one of the Franciscan writers tells us, it was " in the year of the Lord, 1224 . . . on the Tuesday after the feast of the Nativity of the Blessed Virgin (September 8), which that year fell upon a Sunday, the Friars Minor first arrived in England, landing at Dover." [1] Straightway, the Minorites, especially, betook themselves to the abodes of the poor, " and there they lived on charity, doing for the lowest the most menial offices, speaking to the poorest the words of hope, preaching to learned and simple such sermons—short, homely, fervent, and emotional—as the world had not heard for many a day." [2] Their sanctity and self-sacrifice appealed to our countrymen. Many joined their ranks, particularly the ranks of

[1] Thos. of Eccleston, *De adventu FF. Minorum in Anglian*, c. 1.
[2] Jessopp, in his charming essay " The coming of the friars," p. 44.

St. Francis,[1] and many of our greatest bishops like Stephen Langton and Robert Grosseteste showed them the greatest consideration.[2]

Besides their own virtues, the Friars had to support them the influence of the Pope. He had given them a working organization, and he furnished them with his recommendation. At first, indeed, the brethren (the Franciscans) " having the firstfruits of the Holy Spirit, served the Lord not so much by the observance of human constitutions as by the free outpouring of their piety," being content with their Rule, and the very few statutes which were made the same year that the Rule was confirmed.[3] But as time went on and the Order increased in numbers, and spread into different countries, many new relations were necessarily formed, and new questions arose which called for answers. Many such answers were supplied by Gregory, as we have seen, and his explanation or Exposition of the Rule was brought to England " for the first time " by Brother John Naverius.[4]

Moreover, in the very first year of his reign, he issued a decree giving faculties to the priests of the Dominican Order everywhere to preach the word of God, to hear confessions, and to enjoin penances.[5] He followed this up (September 28) by a circular letter in which he ordered

---

[1] The fourth Minister-General, Brother Albert of Pisa, commended " the English above all other nations in that they were zealous for the Order." Eccleston, ib., c. 12, al. coll. 13.

[2] Of Langton, Nicholas Trivet, himself a Dominican, writes : " Toto suo tempore religionem fratrum Prædicatorum et officium prosecutus est gratia et favore." Annal., an. 1221, p. 209, ed. Hog. Grosseteste, speaking, as he says, from personal experience (" ex contactu propinquo multiplicis experientiæ "), wrote most enthusiastically to Gregory about the burning zeal of the Friars Minor " ad fulciendum ruinosa," etc. Ep. 58, p. 179 ff., R. S. Cf. epp. 34 and 59.

[3] Eccleston, ib., c. 4. or coll. 5, ed. Little. Father Cuthbert's trans.

[4] Ib., c. 7 or coll. 8.

[5] Ep. of Sept. 27, 1227, ap. Potthast, 8042.

the prelates of the whole Church " graciously to receive the
brethren of the Order when they were fulfilling their
duties as preachers, and the people intrusted to their
care devoutly to hear the word of God as spoken by the
Friars Preachers." [1]

With this notice regarding Gregory's interest in the
Friars in England we must conclude what we have to say
about his activities in this country, for a glance at the
Calendar of Papal Letters will show that we could
scarcely treat of them all. We will, however, just direct
attention to his decision in behalf of the monkish chapter
of Rochester in their three years' dispute with St. Edmund; [2]
to his bull wherein he forbade the erection of any chapel
within the abbey grounds against the will of the monks ; [3]
and his indignation at the audacity of the dean and
chapter of Lincoln for daring to pretend to jurisdiction
over Stephen, cardinal-deacon of St. Hadrian, on the
ground that he was a fellow canon, whereas it is univer-
sally known that a cardinal is subject only to the Pope. [4]

Ireland.

Gregory's dealings with Ireland are mostly concerned
with the ordinary matters of Church government, and do
not call for any special comment. We may, however,
note that, in the interests of the Irish people, Gregory
continued the work done by Honorius in his efforts to
obtain details as to the origin of certain *customs* which
king Henry wished to use for his advantage, but which
some [5] at least of the bishops of Ireland regarded as
intolerable. It was in vain, however, that they would
seem to have tried to secure the presence of a papal

[1] Pot., n. 8043.

[2] *Cf. Annales Roffenses*, ap. Wharton, *Anglia Sacra*, i, p. 348.

[3] *Reg. S. Osmundi*, i, pp. 384–6, R. S.

[4] *Cronica Buriensis*, ap. *Memorials of St. Edmund's Abbey*, iii, p. 27 ;
cf. p. 28, R. S.

[5] Ep. of Jan. 4, 1235, ap. Theiner, *Monument. Hib.*, p. 30. *Cf.*
supra, p. 151.

legate to inquire into them. The king contrived to block their request at Rome.[1]

These royal *customs* were no doubt of the same species as those which St. Thomas of Canterbury gave his blood to wash away. That some of them at any rate were resisted in Ireland with the support of the Holy See, we have proof in a letter sent by Gregory to the archbishop of Cashel (December 13, 1231),[2] in which the Pope encouraged him not to suffer ecclesiastics to submit to lay tribunals—a submission which, as all know, was one of the points aimed at by that statement of Plantagenet *customs* known as the Constitutions of Clarendon.

As the other connexions between Ireland and Rome, Scotland. including the payment of the papal *aids* of 1229 and 1240, were much the same as those which bound England to Rome, they may here be passed over, and we may turn to Scotland.

Through the exertions of the Pope, as we have already taken notice, peace was preserved between that country and England. This peace was made through the agency of Cardinal Otho (1237). After he had brought it about, he told the king, Alexander II., that he was desirous of

---

[1] *Close Rolls*, Henry III., vol. iii, p. 167, R. S.

[2] N. 69, Dec. 13, 1231, ap. *ib.*, p. 28. On these documents, several of which he gives in full with an English translation, Mr. M. Nevins (*Ireland and the Holy See in the Middle Ages*, p. 202) remarks : " If one thing more than another has struck me in reading these Papal records from Theiner's most valuable work, it is the even-handed justice meted out by the Popes to both sides. The Irish when they rebel are severely admonished ; but, on the other hand, when the English treat them unjustly none more than the Popes denounces such doings and censures the conduct of the English and their king." *The Close Rolls, Henry III.*, i, p. 588, furnish us with a letter (May 22, 1231) of Henry to the Pope in which he begs him, " under whose protection we ought to stand secure," not to suffer him to be deprived of that custom by which he had the guardianship of bishoprics " in our country of Ireland " during their vacancies.

visiting Scotland as papal legate, seeing that Pope
Gregory had informed the Scottish monarch that he had
been sent to the Scottish Church as well as to the English.[1]
Alexander, however, like most kings, did not want
interference from without; and so, desirous of keeping
Otho out of the country, answered him, if we can trust
Matthew Paris, with more force than truth : " I do not
remember to have seen a legate in my country,[2] nor that
it was ever necessary for one to be summoned there,
thanks be to God ; and there is not now need of one, for
all goes well. Neither was any legate allowed ingress into
that kingdom during the time . . . of my ancestors, and
I will not allow it as long as I am able. However, since
report pronounces you to be a man of sanctity, I warn
you that, if you should chance to enter my territories
. . . ungovernable, wild men dwell there . . . whom I
could not restrain if they were to attack you." On
hearing this the legate moderated his desire to enter
Scotland, and remained with the English king, " who
obeyed him in everything." [3]

Considering, however, that what Alexander is here
supposed to have said about papal legates never having
been in Scotland is wholly false, that the Scottish
chroniclers know nothing about this truculent speech,
and that Otho himself went into Scotland two years
later, there is no doubt that this speech, like so many other

[1] See the Pope's letter of May 10, 1235, to the Scottish King, ap.
Theiner, *l.c.*, p. 35. Gregory told the King that he did not think it
proper that when, through his legate Otho (virum experte providentie
et magna morum preditum honestate), he was visiting England, he
should fail to visit Scotland, which was directly subject to the Holy
See. *Cf. supra*, p. 343.

[2] It is scarcely probable that Alexander would have told such a
barefaced lie, as he had seen the legate James hold a council at Perth
in 1221.

[3] *Chron. maj.*, iii, 414.

speeches given us by Matthew Paris, is, to say the least of
it, largely an invention of that author.

He goes on to say that a relative of the legate went
with the king into Scotland, and that the latter, in order
that he might not seem wholly rebellious, conferred the
honour of knighthood and some lands on him.

However all this may be, in September, 1239, the legate Otho in
again (i.e., if he had ever made one before) made an Scotland,
attempt to enter Scotland; and again, according to the 1239.
sole evidence of Paris, there was trouble with the king.
According to him, Alexander only allowed him to enter
his kingdom on the intercession of English and Scotch
nobles, and after he had signed a paper to the effect that
his entry into the country should not form a precedent.
Paris then adds that the legate collected money, arranged
all ecclesiastical matters to his liking, and when the king
was in the interior of the country, suddenly left it without
his permission, carrying off the aforesaid paper with him.[1]
Of all this the Chronicle of Melrose does not appear to
know anything; but it does know what Matthew Paris
did not at least choose to tell us, namely, that Otho held
a council at Edinburgh (October 19), and that he left
Scotland about the feast of All Saints (November 1).[2]

For the sake of mentioning one of the most distinguished David de
men at this time in Scotland, we will say a word Bernham.
regarding David de Bernham, at one time Alexander's
chamberlain.

In 1238, there died William of Malvoisine, bishop of
St. Andrew's, who by the authority of the legate John
of Salerno had been allowed to be translated thither

[1] *Chron. maj.*, iii, 568.

[2] *Chron. de Mailros*, an. 1239. Fordun, *Scotichronicon*, l. ix, c. 54,
says that Otho entered Scotland for the *first* time in 1239. He goes
on to quote with approval Neckam's eulogy of Otho.

from the see of Glasgow (1202).[1] On his death there was a desire to translate to St. Andrew's, Geoffrey bishop of Dunkeld. But as translations from see to see were not wont to be easily allowed by Rome, Gregory would not consent to the choice and bade the canons elect another candidate.[2] Then, in the quaint language of the old Scottish chronicle,

> " Than chesyed thai Dawy off Barname
> Ane honest clerk and off gud fame,
> That to the Pape was welle lykand." [3]

Gregory in due course approved of this election, and bade the bishops of Glasgow, Caithness, and Brechin receive from David the oath of fealty to the Roman Church, and then consecrate him.[4] Duly consecrated in the following year (1240), he at once made great efforts to do his duty, as his *Pontificale* shows.

No document has preserved for us the decrees which were issued by Otho's synod at Edinburgh, but as the *Pontificale* used by the energetic bishop of St. Andrew's

---

[1] Wyntoun, *Cronykil*, l. vii, c. 8, vol. ii, p. 229, ed. Laign.
> " And the translatyowne off that
> Wes that tyme done be a Legat,
> That cald than wes Jhon be name,
> At the instans off the Kyng Willame."

The reader will notice yet another legate in Scotland. *Cf. supra*, vol. xii, p. 16.

[2] *Cf.* his letter of Feb. 12, 1239, ap. Theiner, *l.c.*, n. 98, p. 30 ; *cf.* n. 100. See also Fordun, *Scotichronicon*, vi, 42, and Wyntoun, *ib.*, c. 9, ii, 244.
> " . . . Bot till hym (Geoffrey) the Pape
> Be na way grawnt wald hys gud will."

[3] *Ib.*

[4] Ep. of Oct. 1, 1239, ap. Theiner, *l.c.*, p. 39. " Recepturi ab eo prius pro nobis et ecclesia Romana fidelitatis solite juramentum." The English reader will find a " free translation " of this document in W. Lockhart's *The Church of Scotland—The Life of David de Bernham*, p. 29 ff. By mistake Mr. Lockhart dates the letter from Avignon instead of Anagni. *Cf.* the accurate and valuable work of Bishop Dowden, *The Bishops of Scotland*, p. 12 ff., Glasgow, 1912.

records the names and dates of no less than one hundred and forty churches and chapels between the years 1240 and 1249,[1] we may perhaps conclude that one of its decrees concerned the consecration of chapels; that indeed in general its decrees were like those of the council in London;[2] and that, in any case, David de Bernham made strenuous efforts to fulfil the duties of his sacred office.[3]

[1] On this interesting document and its list, see Lockhart, p. 42 ff.

[2] The first of the decrees of the council of London laid it down that "all cathedral, conventual, and parochial churches . . . were to be consecrated within two years." Mat. Par., *Chron.*, iii, 421 f.

[3] He was prepared to run considerable risks in the cause of duty. Summoned by name along with the bishop of Glasgow to attend the council convoked by Gregory, he did not hesitate to obey the summons (1240), though he knew the danger he was running and though in consequence "many lamented his departure." *Chron. de Mailros.*, an. 1240. As a matter of fact, he did not get beyond France. With many other English and French bishops he "returned home," because they found . "that they could not reach the Apostolic see without incurring the danger of being killed." *Ib.*, an. 1241.

CHAPTER VII.

MISCELLANEOUS DOINGS OF GREGORY. THE GREEK
CHURCH AND THE LATIN EMPIRE OF CONSTANTINOPLE.
THE CRUSADE. FOREIGN MISSIONS. HERESY, ETC.

Robert
Courtenay,
Emperor of
Constanti-
nople.

LIKE so many of his predecessors, Gregory was deeply
interested in the Greek Church; and, like Innocent III.
and Honorius III., in the preservation of the Latin empire
of Constantinople. When "the queen of cities" was
stormed by the Latins and became the capital of a
Latin empire (1204), Innocent was deeply grieved. He
felt that, at any rate as far as religion was concerned, the
Frankish conquerors had committed a great wrong and
made a ghastly blunder. In the political order, however,
he thought that some good had been effected. With
many other Western statesmen, he believed that with
Constantinople in the hands of the Franks, the cause of
the Crusades would be greatly helped; and, even in the
sphere of religion, he hoped, whatever he might have
feared, that in time good would result, and that the Greek
schism might thereby be brought to an end. Accordingly
he strove with the whole energy of his vigorous nature to
prop up the Latin Empire, weak from its very beginning,
and to organize the Latin Church within its boundaries.
His policy was continued by his successors, and when the
weak and vicious emperor Robert, the successor of Peter
of Courtenay, came to Gregory IX. (1228) to beg help
from him against his barons, justly incensed by his vices
and his weakness, the Pope gave him some money, and
than blandly bade him return to his city.[1]

---

[1] Dandolo, *Chron.*, l. x, c. 5, ap. *R. I. SS.*, xii, p. 344. What
Matthew Paris (*Chron. maj.*, iii, 386) refers to "an emperor" in 1237
should be said of Robert in 1228. *Cf.* Baldwin of Avesnes, *Chron.*,
ap. Kervyn de Lettenhove, *Istore de Flandres*, ii, p. 676. "Li Apostoles

As Robert died on his return journey (1228), his little Baldwin II.
brother, aged ten, became the emperor Baldwin II. As the and John of Brienne.
empire was beset on all sides by enemies, the barons chose
the aged titular king of Jerusalem (John of Brienne),
then commander of the papal troops,[1] to be the emperor-
regent.[2] Their choice was naturally approved by the
Pope, seeing that John was a devoted adherent of the
Holy See, and it was under his direction that the terms
of John's regency were drawn up.[3] Gregory also confirmed the arrangement that in due course the daughter
of John should marry the youthful emperor.[4] With such
troops as he could collect, and with the blessing of the
Pope, the valiant and energetic octogenarian set sail for
Constantinople in 1231, sure at least of the support of
Gregory,[5] who is said to have excommunicated Theodore,

---

le reconforta, et li donna dou sien, et puis le pria tout que il l'en fit
raler vers Constantinoble." Before the year 1284 there appeared
under the auspices of Baldwin of Avesnes (†1289) an extensive chronicle
in French going down to the year 1281, and made up fragments of
early authors. It has been published under the title of *Chronicon
Hanoniense*, ap. *M. G. SS.*, xxv. Abridgments and continuations
of it were soon made, and have been published by K. de L. in the work
noted above.

[1] *Cf. supra*, p. 234.

[2] G. Acropolites, *Ann.*, c. 27, pp. 47–8, ed. Bonn.

[3] Mouskes, *Chron.*
    "Teus (tel) fu li consaus ordenés
     De l'apostole, et les barons
     De Grèse, etc."
Line 28090 ff. *Cf.* Richard of San Germano, *Chron.*, an. 1231. Epp.
Greg. IX. (Apr. 9, 1229), ap. *Reg.* i, p. 175 f.

[4] *Cf.* the document (Apr. 9, 1229) printed at length in Tafel, and
Thomas, *Urkunden der Republik Venedig*, ap. *Fontes RR. Austr.*, Abt. ii,
xiii Band, ii Theil, p. 265 ff., Vienna, 1856.

[5] Already in 1227 (Apr. 7), Gregory had began to grant favours to
the tottering empire of Constantinople by allowing ecclesiastical
revenues to be diverted to its use, *Reg.*, i, 27. How he endeavoured
to smooth the way for John's entry into his kingdom by begging for him
the aid of the Hungarians, etc., may be seen in his letters of May 8
and 9, 1231, ap. *Reg.*, i, 417 f.

despot of Epirus, and all the adversaries of the emperor of Constantinople.[1]

Hardly had John of Brienne settled in his new capital when the emperor of Nicæa, John Vatatzes, and his patriarch, Germanus II., began to think of reunion between Rome and the Greek Church. Whether their motives were political, and they were animated by the hope of preventing Gregory from giving whole-hearted support to Brienne, or whether they were spiritual, and they were really desirous of ecclesiastical unity, is not certain. They appear certainly to have been moved by the virtues of some Franciscan friars, who appeared at their court.[2] At any rate, the Patriarch Germanus by the hands of these friars sent letters to the Pope and the cardinals on the subject of unity. The long one to Gregory was written in the spring of 1232, and was thus addressed : " To the most holy and most excellent Pope, Rector of Old Rome and of the Apostolic See, Germanus, by Divine mercy archbishop of Constantinople,[3] the

---

[1] Muralt, *Chronog. Byzantine*, ii, p. 341, n. 11. *Cf. ib.*, p. 343 f. On the fall of the Byzantine empire in 1204, one of its fragments was seized by a Greek who founded the Despotate of Epirus.

[2] Salimbene tells us of the affectionate respect which later on Vatatzes displayed to the Franciscan John of Parma, *Chron.*, p. 304, ap. *M. G. SS.*, xxxii. The same author (p. 324) says that Vatatzes himself declared that the Greeks wished to be united to Rome. " Qui (the Greeks) Romane ecclesie, ut Vattacius scripsit, reconciliari desiderant." *Cf.* Mouskes, who declares that Theodore Angelus Comnenus, Vatatzes, and John Asen (" Que Todres, Vatace, et Auscens ") promised that they and their men would submit to Rome (l. 29873 f.).

> " Et il kerroient et lor oume
> L'Apostole et la loi de Rome."

Phil. Mouskes' description of Gregory is very quaint :

> " Et li preudom papes Grigores,
> Ki n'ot cure de vainnes glores."—L. 30413 f.

[3] Though residing at Nicæa he styled himself " archbishop of Constantinople."

New Rome." [1] After a prayer for union, the Patriarch expressed a hope that the Pope who " had obtained the primacy of the Apostolic See," would " descend a little from the height of his glory " and hearken to his words. He then told the Pope how the five friars had called his attention " to the long-standing schism " in what ought to be the seamless garment of Christian unity ; and so, even at the risk " of seeming to injure the primacy of your Fraternity " or " of appearing to wish to seize the rights of the first-born," he proceeded to urge Gregory to find out whether it was the fault of the Greeks or of the Latins that they were disunited, to apply the right remedy, and to bring about unity. He then declared that many would submit to the Pope " did they not fear the unjust oppressions and the unwarrantable exactions of money which you practise, and the undue service which you require." And in this connexion he instanced the persecutions to which the Greeks were at the moment being exposed in Cyprus.[2] " Are these things good, most holy Father, successor of the Apostle Peter ? "

[1] This and the following letters are given among others by Massi, *Concil.*, vol. xxiii, p. 59 ff., and by Matthew Paris (*C.M.*, iii, p. 448 ff.), who, however, assigns them to the wrong year (1237), and introduces them by absurd remarks about the Greek Church rising against the avarice of Rome, expelling their emperor (he appears to be thinking of the departure of the emperor Robert in 1228), and showing only obedience to archbishop Germanus II. *Ib.*, p. 446 ; *cf.* p. 386. It is possible, too, that he may be confusing with this " expulsion " the voluntary departure of Baldwin II. in 1236 to seek help from Europe. Nicephorus Blemmydas also, in his autobiography (*Diegesis*, ed. Heisenberg, Leipzig, 1896), assures us that it was Germanus who first approached the Pope on the subject of reunion. C. 14, p. 64. Blemmydas was one of the Greeks who disputed with Gregory's envoys. He also opposed the Latins under Innocent IV.

[2] He complained that there the Greek churches were shut up (" sigilla januis ecclesiarum impressa," p. 452), and some of the Greeks martyred. On these Cypriot affairs, see Hackett, *A history of the orthodox Church of Cyprus*, p. 89, who throughout his work shows his preference for the Greek rather than for the Latin. Whatever

For these strong words Germanus then asked pardon,
"for they are," he said, "the groans of a heart in anguish,"
and he concluded by praying that the God of peace would
send to them, "who are the shepherds of His rational
sheep," the angel of peace so that they may be able to
salute one another with the kiss of peace.

Germanus also addressed a letter " to the most holy,
discreet, and illustrious cardinals, the glory of the
Apostolic See." He exhorted them to gird themselves " to
destroy the hedge of the old animosity existing between
the church of the Greeks and that of the Latins," and

was done by the Latins in Cyprus, Gregory himself was most considerate to the Greeks in southern Italy and Sicily, where, as we know
from our own Roger Bacon, among others, there were "many Greek
Churches and a number of people subject to them." *Opus tertium*,
p. 33 ; *Cf. Compend. studii*, p. 434 R. S. The Pope strictly forbade
their rites to be disturbed. *Reg.*, i, p. 498, n. 798 ; *cf.* p. 720. A
Greek original of this letter of Germanus may be read, ap. Sathas,
Bibliotheca Medii Aevi, ii, p. 46 ff. It should be noted that its date
is not certain. Whilst on the subject of Gregory and the Greeks
in Italy, we may notice an article by the Rev. T. A. Lacey,
" Gregory IX. and Greek Ordinations," ap. *The Church Historical
Society's* publications, n. 33, London, 1898. The article concerns
a reply sent by Gregory to the archbishop of Bari (*Reg.*, i, p. 460,
n. 740) regarding certain Greek customs connected with the sacraments.
The Pope declared that those were not baptized in whose case there
had been used the formula " baptizetur talis in nomine Patris, et
Filii et spiritus sancti." This formula Mr. Lacey translates : " so
and so *is* baptized in the name of the Father, etc." Such, however,
is not the exact translation : it should be : " Let so and so be baptized
in the name," etc. This formula (though acknowledged as valid by
the Church later on), as not giving an obvious declaration of the fact
of the baptism, was regarded by the Pope as doubtfully valid. That
he thought it might be valid is clear from a remark which he makes
towards the close of his letter to the effect that he is following " the
safer course " in rejecting it—" nos, quod tutius est sequentes."
With regard to such as are ordained outside the prescribed times, he
declared that they were validly ordained, but that the archbishop
should insist on the observance of the appointed seasons for ordination.
Finally, he condemned the custom of the use by priests who were
travelling of a kind of corporal blessed by a bishop in place of a portable
altar stone.

then to bind together in unity the parts which have been thus separated. He begged them to put aside all feelings of pride which might raise themselves up in opposition to brotherly union in order that there might be no more schism between them. Then, after laying the blame of the separation on the rapacity of the Roman Church,[1] he pleaded for an examination into the existing state of things, so that unity might be restored, " for we all, Greeks and Latins, were once in the same faith, and subject to the same canons. We were at peace with one another, we fought for one another, and we confounded the enemies of the Church. Did I not revere the great Apostle Peter, who was the head of Christ's apostles, and the rock of the faith," I would remind you how this rock was once shaken even by the words of a weak woman. It is indeed a fact, he urged in conclusion, that many great nations think as do the Greeks, as for instance the Ethiopians, and the Syrians, " and others who are greater and more worthy, such as the Iberians, the Lazi, the Alans, the Goths, and the Chazars, the countless multitudes of the Russians, and the victorious kingdom of the Blachi (Wlgarorum, Bulgarians)." But may God again collect us all in the unity of that faith in which from ancient times there was a general agreement.

To this communication from Germanus, Gregory, after consultation with the cardinals, replied [2] that he was making preparations to send him some religious of tried knowledge who would bring him the words of life, and more fully

Reply of Gregory, 1232.

---

[1] He returned to this accusation later on, not understanding the legitimate position which the feudal system and the historical development of Europe had given to the Pope of Rome. " Regna vobis tributo subjicitis."

[2] His letter began : " Gregory, bishop, servant of the servants of God, to his venerable brother, Germanus, archbishop of the Greeks, health and the apostolic benediction." Ap. Mat. Par., *Chron.*, iii, p. 460. This letter is dated July 26, 1232.

make known to him the will of the Apostolic See. Meanwhile, courtesy required that he should reply to the archbishop's letter. Gregory then proceeded to draw out at some length the primacy of the Popes. Just as, he said, the fullness of sensation (plenitudo sensuum) is in the head, whence it flows into the other members of the body, so from *Peter* (the *rock*, that is, on which the Lord built his Church) as from " the primate of primates " must flow upon the faithful the means of salvation, and the remedies for scrupulous doubts.[1] " As there is one Lord," continued the Pope, " one faith, one baptism, one origin (unum principium) and one body of the church militant, and as a body with many heads is a monster, and one without a head is incapable (headless), it follows that its Lord . . . should name a successor to rule the whole Church." Hence, He prayed that Peter's faith might not fail and that he might confirm the faith of his brethren (St. Luke, xxii, 32) ; and so it follows that all questions of faith must be referred to the see of Peter.[2]

Then, in contradistinction to the origin of the schism set forth by Germanus, Gregory laid down that the Greek Church seceded " from the unity of the Roman See," and, as a consequence, " immediately lost ecclesiastical liberty, and, from being free, became the bondwoman of the secular power, so that, by a just judgment of God, she who was unwilling to recognize the primacy of Peter, had, however, against her will, to submit to the dominion of the State." [3] After more to the same effect,

---

[1] " Sic tres fidelium ordines in ecclesia . . . (prælati, continentes et conjugati) a Petro—petra, super quam . . . ecclesiam suam aedificavit Dominus—et suæ salutis debent postulare remedia, et . . . a mentis suæ tenebris dubietatis scrupulos removere." *Ib.*, p. 461.

[2] " Ex quo colligitur evidenter quod ad sedem Petri omnis quæstio fidei referenda sit."

[3] Since Gregory wrote these words nearly 700 years have passed. During those long ages the Patriarchs of Constantinople have refused

the Pope reminded Germanus that on the one hand " in defence of ecclesiastical liberty the Roman Pontiff with his brethren opposed himself like a wall in behalf of his fellow bishops and their subjects against heretics, schismatics, and tyrants," and that on the other hand by the action of the Greeks " ecclesiastical authority (ordo) being parcelled out among opposing nations in the East,[1] is confounded, episcopal power is trodden underfoot, and there is not one of their dear ones to console them, because, being as it were without a head, they will not return to the head of the Church. " Return, return, O Sulamitess, return, return, that we may behold thee (*Cant.* vi, 12) ; for then, indeed, can brother be helped by brother."

After the dispatch of this letter, it took the Pope some time to select suitable men to be sent to Nicæa to

Delegates sent to Nicæa, 1233.

to recognize the " primacy of Peter," and all the time have they remained the slaves of the secular power, for the most part that of the Sultans of Turkey. On this subject of ecclesiastical liberty being linked up with union with Rome, Ffoulkes, *Christendom's Divisions*, part ii : *Greeks and Latins*, has pertinently remarked (p. 237), " Churches in communion with Rome have remained in communion with each other and formed one corporate body, and their independence of the civil power has been in exact proportion to their dependence on the Pope ; churches out of communion with Rome, on the other hand, have never united with each other—never otherwise than subject for any length of time to the civil power ; never otherwise than peculiar and isolated in their faith. So it has been in practice, ever since the church took possession of the world, for some reason or other. The alternative has lain practically between one or other of the two central powers—the temporal sovereign, be he one or many, or the Pope."

[1] In 1235 this very Germanus to whom Gregory was writing acknowledged the independent ecclesiastical authority of the bishop of Ternovo : "Τότε καὶ ὁ Τρινόβου ἀρχιερεὺς ὑπὸ τὸν τῆς Κωνσταντινοπόλεως τελῶν αὐτονομίᾳ τετίμηται καὶ πατριάρχης ἀναγορεύεσθαι κέκριται." George Acropol., *Annal.*, c. 33, p. 55. As time went on, the Patriarchs of Constantinople had to acknowledge more and more independent churches in the east. To-day the *Orthodox* Church is subject to some twelve different heads. *Cf. supra*, vi, 162, and that excellent book, *Turkey in Europe*, by Ulysses, i.e., Sir G. Elliot.

promote the work of reunion. At length, as members of
the new Orders of friars had evidently made a good
impression upon the Greeks, Gregory selected two
Franciscans and two Dominicans, among whom was the
Englishman, the Minorite, brother Haymo of Faversham.[1]
In the letter of recommendation which Gregory sent with
them " to the venerable archbishop of the Greeks," [2]
he laid down that it was expedient for all to read or to
hear the Scriptures, as what was written therein was
written for the guidance of men in all ages. He then
declared, with a view to meeting the Greek animadversion
on the temporal power possessed by the Western Church,
that according to the Gospels both swords belonged to
the Roman Pontiff, but that the Church herself only
used the spiritual sword, entrusting the material sword
to the secular power to be used in her behalf. Finally,
to clear another Greek objection out of the way, he concluded by observing that the sacrifice of the Mass could
be celebrated with either leavened or unleavened bread,
as in either case there was simple bread, and by expressing
a hope that all of them would soon be singing : " Behold
how good and how pleasant it is for brethren to dwell
together in unity " (Ps. cxxxii).

Conferences
at Nicæa,
1234.

The papal envoys arrived at Nicæa in January, 1234,
and though they held many conferences with the patriarch,
supported by that book-hunter and book-lover, Nicephorus Blemmydas, and others, they could not induce the
Greeks to acknowledge either that God the Holy Ghost
proceeded from the Father and from the Son, or even
that Mass could be lawfully celebrated with unleavened
bread.[3]

[1] Cf. the letter of Gregory of May 17 or 18, 1233 ; Eccleston, De
advent frat., c. 5, or coll. 6, p. 35, ed. Little ; and Lives of the Brethren,
Eng. trans., p. 185.

[2] Ep. of May 17 or 18, 1233, ap. Mat. P., iii, p. 466 ff.

[3] They were evidently not very sincere with regard to this latter

Seeing that the envoys of Gregory have left us a very complete account of their mission, we may use it with advantage, as it will enable us to understand what was the general course and issue of the many attempts at reunion between the Greek and Latin Churches that were made during the Middle Ages.

Of the envoys two were Dominicans and two were Franciscans, and one of them was, we are assured, skilled " in the literature of the Greeks," [1] and read in Greek such quotations as he made from it. Before they reached Nicæa, which they did in the evening of the first Sunday after the octave of the Epiphany (January, 1234), they were met by deputies from the Patriarch and the emperor John Vatatzes, who expressed their satisfaction at their coming. On their arrival in the ancient city they were taken, in response to their request to be led to the Cathedral, to that famous Church in which had been held the first General Council of Nicæa, and in which they beheld with wonder frescoes depicting the Fathers who had attended it.

Then, after they had explained that they were not legates who had been sent to a council, but simply envoys who had been sent to the patriarch in consequence of his letter to the Pope, they presented their credentials to Germanus.[2] On receiving them into his hands, he kissed the leaden bulla attached to them, and turning to the clergy who were standing by, exclaimed " Peter, Paul," in reference to the figures of the heads of those two

point, as they endeavoured to recover by stealth from the papal envoys the written declaration which they had made with regard to it. See the Latin envoys' account of all these proceedings in Mansi, *Concil. Ampliss. collect.*, t. xxiii, p. 279 ff., or ap. Hefele, *Hist. des Conciles*, v, pt. ii, p. 1568 ff., ed. Leclercq. *Cf.* ep. Greg., ap. *Reg.*, n. 4110, March 17, 1238. On Blemmydas, see his own works, ed. Heisenberg, Leipzig, 1896, and also Miss A. Gardner's useful book, *The Lascarids of Nicæa*, p. 164 ff., and p. 278 ff.

[1] Mansi, xxiii, p. 290.
[2] *Ib.*, p. 279.

apostles which were stamped upon the seal.[1] After this the papal envoys were escorted with great honour by the clergy and people to the place which had been nominated by the emperor for their abode. Before leaving them, the Greeks begged them to state the questions which it would be most desirable to discuss, and were told in reply that they would be glad to know why the Greek Church, which like all Christians all over the world had been subject to the Roman Church, had withdrawn from its obedience. According to the envoys' account the Greeks were not at first willing to reply, but at length said the reasons were twofold—the question of the Procession of the Holy Ghost and that of the Azyms. It was, therefore, agreed to discuss these two points.

A Greek priest does not accept the Latin Mass.

Meanwhile, an incident occurred which nearly brought the friars' mission to an abrupt termination. A church had been assigned for their exclusive use close to their residence, and when they said Mass next morning we are told that a number of Latins, Franks, English, and others came to assist at it.[2] Not long after it was over, one of the Latins came to the monks in tears to say that his *papa* or Greek priest had excommunicated him for being present at it. The monks at once complained to the Patriarch, and after some demur the offender was brought before them by some of his fellow priests. They then stripped him of his priestly garments, and paraded him through the town until the envoys interceded for him, as they had been informed that he had acted in ignorance.

Discussion on the Procession of the Holy Ghost.

At length, on the Thursday, the monks betook themselves to the imperial palace for the discussion, and opened it by asking for the Greek belief regarding the Latin use of unleavened bread in Mass—" de nostro

---

[1] *Cf.* p. 441, for an illustration of the bulla of Gregory IX.
[2] Mansi, *l.c.*, p. 280.

sacramento altaris." The Greeks, however, record the envoys " pertinaciously insisted " that the question " of the Procession of the Holy Ghost " should be first considered. To this the monks at last agreed, and the discussion was opened by the *Chartophylax* (the keeper of the records) "who at that time was the treasurer of the patriarchal Church." When the Latins declared that they believed in the propositions which he put forth, i.e., in the unbegotten Father, in His only Son, and in the Procession of the Holy Ghost from the Father, the Chartophylax cried out that there was no difference between them. If then, said the monks, this is your opinion apropos of the doctrine of the Blessed Trinity, and we are of opinion that there is no difference between us regarding the Sacrament of the Altar, then there is no cause for schism, and " the Greek Church has unjustly and without cause separated itself from the obedience of the Roman Church." Thereupon, the emperor himself, who was present, said, after some consultation, that the Patriarch would like to know about the addition which you have made to the Creed. The question of the *Filioque* having been thus started, the conference adjourned till the following day, when it was reopened after Mass. The Greeks, of course, tried to show that the Latins had really added something new to the Nicene Creed, and the Latins that they had merely added an explanation or natural development such as the Greeks themselves recognized had happened with regard to the Creed of Constantinople, which they accepted. The monks then proceeded to cite Greek Fathers to show that it was the faith of the Greek Church itself that the Holy Ghost proceeded from the Father and from the Son, making their quotations from " a large number of Greek books which they had brought with them from Constantinople."

Pressed by the monks as to whether they believed

that the Holy Ghost did not proceed from the Son, the
Greeks replied : " we do not believe that He proceeded
from the Son," from which words clearly " from the Son
alone " might be understood. The Latins, however,
pointed out that the Greeks had not replied to their
question, which was whether they held that the Holy
Ghost did not proceed from the Son—in any way.

It was in this discussion that, according to his own
account, Nicephorus Blemmydas, who is no doubt the
one to whom the monks allude as " a certain philosopher,"
intervened in aid of his hard-pressed co-religionists.[1]
He insisted that the Holy Ghost " was sent through the
Son," but did not proceed from Him.[2]

Though the monks assure us that the emperor often
said " excellent, καλῶς " to their points, the discussion
dragged on for days. The Greeks would not give way on
the question of the Procession, and on the question of
the azyms the Greek Patriarch declared that he would
like to consult the Patriarchs of Alexander, Jerusalem,
and Antioch, before giving an answer. On this the papal
envoys said they would wait at Constantinople till the
middle of March for the Greek reply to their contentions.

The monks
take
temporary
leave of the
Emperor.

Accordingly, when the Latins went to take leave of the

[1] *Cf.* his *Diegesis*, c. 13, p. 63 ff., ed. Heisenberg.

[2] He spoke of the Holy Spirit as " δι᾿ υἱοῦ χορηγούμενον " or
" παρεχόμενον " or " πεφηνὸς," but not " δι᾿ υἱου ἐκπορευόμενον " ;
i.e., he contended that the Holy Ghost proceeded from the Father,
but was sent (apparere vel præberi per Filium) through the Son. Two
discourses of his, however, on the Procession of the Holy Ghost are
printed in Raynaldus at the end of the year 1256. A Latin version
accompanies the Greek original. He there lays down that the Holy
Ghost proceeds from the Father, *through* (per) the Son, but not from
(ex) the Son ; not ἐκ τοῦ Υἱοῦ, but δι᾿ Υἱοῦ. He asserts: " Τὸ δὲ τὴν
τοῦ ἁγίου Πνεύματος ἐκπόρευσιν δι᾿ Υἱοῦ εἶναι παρα πατρος " is " δόγμα
κοινὸν ἀνατεθειμένον τῇ ᾿Εκκλησίᾳ." *Oratio sec.*, n. 3, p. 533, ed. Paris,
1887. Other works of N. B. on this abstruse subject may be read
ap. Migne, *Pat. Græc.-Lat.*, t. 142.

emperor, he asked them under what conditions could the
Greek Patriarch be reconciled to the Roman Church.
By believing and preaching what that Church believed,
was the answer of the envoys. They added, however, that
the Roman Church would not insist on their chanting the
Creed with or without the addition of the *Filioque*,
provided that the same obedience was paid to her that
had been paid before the schism. But, said the emperor,
if the Patriarch consents to obey the Pope, will he give
him back his jurisdiction (jus suum). On condition,
replied the monks, that he will give that obedience which
is due to his mother, we believe that he will obtain greater
consideration from the Pope and the Roman Church than
he has any idea of.

After this, the papal envoys made their way back to
Constantinople to await the conclusions of the Greeks.
But about the middle of March, the Greek Patriarch,
instead of sending his written reply, begged the monks
to come to a council. As they had not been commissioned
to appear before a council, the envoys demurred for some
time, but at length agreed when the Patriarch promised
that, if they came, " he would with great pleasure betake
himself to the Papal court." [1] It was not, however, till
after Easter that the Council was ready to meet the
envoys at Nymphæum, a place on the coast of Bithynia
near the mouth of the river Oxines, where Vatatzes
usually spent the winter.

The envoys return to Constantinople, and then revisit the Greek patriarch.

At this assembly the Greeks, instead of giving the
promised reply anent the question of the Procession of
the Holy Ghost, proposed to reopen both that question
and the one regarding the azyms. However, after various
delays, the latter question was brought forward for
discussion.

The Council of Nymphæum, 1234.

You condemn our practice of celebrating with un-

[1] "Cum magna lætitia rediremus ad curiam."

leavened bread, said the envoys, as is clear first from your
writings, which are full of the heretical assertion that
only leavened bread can be used for the Mass ; secondly,
from the fact that, when questioned on the subject, you
abstained from giving an answer lest your heresy should
stand confessed ; thirdly, from your deeds, as you wash
your altars after a Latin has celebrated at them, as though
they had been defiled ; fourthly, from the fact of your
forcing Latins to abjure the rites (sacramenta) of the
Roman Church, if they would receive the sacraments with
you ; fifthly, from your having erased the name of the
Pope from your diptychs, and we know that you never
eject any but heretics or excommunicated persons ; and
sixthly, from your excommunicating him once a year, as
we have been told by those who have heard you. To this
formidable indictment the Chartophylax replied simply
by denying that they excommunicated the Pope, and by
a retort," With regard to the other things for which you
blame us you ought not to be surprised, seeing that when
the Latins took Constantinople they broke into churches,
threw down altars, stole the gold and silver from them,
tossed the relics of the Saints into the sea, trampled the
holy images underfoot, and turned the Churches into
stables." Here the Patriarch himself intervened by
asking : " If you wonder why we erased the name of the
Pope from our diptychs, why, I ask, has he erased mine
from his ? " The envoys replied that he could not have
done that as the name was never there. And if, they
continued, the matter be looked into, it may be asked
who was the first to begin the erasing of names. As they
received no reply to this, they turned to the Greek counter-
charges, and pointed out that the Roman Church was in
no way responsible for them, but that, if done at all, they
were the work of wicked excommunicated lay persons
acting on their own authority. But, they urged, what

you do is done by your patriarchs, bishops, and inferior clergy, as you yourselves acknowledge.

As the dispute had now waxed too hot to be productive of good, the Latins declared that they would return to the Pope, and accordingly went to the emperor to tell him what had occurred, and to take their leave of him. But as he was " astute and far-seeing—astutus et providus in agendis," he began to made excuses for his people, and said that the affair would not have taken so disagreeable a turn if he had been present. He added that he would send an embassy and presents to the Pope, as he wished him to be his friend. The monks, however, assured him that the Pope would only be his friend if he would return to the Unity of the Church. But, replied he, a schism which has lasted now nearly three hundred years cannot be healed in a moment. I will, therefore, speak to the prelates, and I beg you to answer their queries.

When the monks, therefore, once more appeared before the Greeks, it was only to hear that it was their belief that Mass offered with unleavened bread was wholly invalid. Afterwards the Greeks presented the envoys with a very short paper [1] condemning the azyms, dated April, and drawn up by the Chartophylax " of the most holy great Church of God of Constantinople, by order of the patriarchs of Constantinople and Antioch, and the other prelates with them."

In return the monks presented the Council with a signed summary statement on the double Procession of the Holy Ghost.[2] Then after the monks had offered some criticism of the Greek paper, pointing out that $\dot{\alpha}\rho\tau o\nu$ did not necessarily mean fermented bread, the two parties separated, and the Latins asked the emperor's leave to depart. He, however, appears to have been really anxious

[1] Ap. Mansi, xxiii, pp. 298-9.
[2] Ib., pp. 299-301.

to bring about a union, but obviously not for reasons of faith, and suggested the following compromise. The Latins were to give up the *Filioque*, and the Greeks would give way on the question of the Azyms. But prompt and decisive was the reply of the monks : " Understand that the lord Pope and the Roman Church will not give up a single jot or tittle of the faith." [1]

The last conference between the two parties was held on a Friday, and to the great regret of the emperor only ended in their calling one another heretics.

Departure of the monks.

Early the next morning, the monks set out for the harbour without even saluting the Greek prelates or asking their blessing. Afterwards reproached with this conduct, the envoys replied that they felt that the Patriarch would understand their reasons for acting as they did.

The monks, however, had not gone far when they were overtaken by emissaries from the bishops, their own paper was returned to them, and they were asked to return that of the Greeks, and accept letters to the Pope in its place. This they declined to do. In the midst of the dispute which took place thereon, the Chartophylax himself came up, and ordered their Greek attendants to leave the monks unless they gave up the required document. On their continued refusal to surrender the paper, their attendants left their packages of books on the ground and went off with the Chartophylax. Unable to carry all their books themselves, the papal envoys took with them what they could, and, leaving the rest in charge of the imperial officer who was accompanying them, continued their journey alone. They had made

[1] " Hoc scitote quod d. Papa et ecclesia Romana non dimittent unum jota de fide sua." They then repeated that faith : " Corpus Christi confici potest ita in azymo sicut in fermentato," and " Spiritum Sanctum procedere a Filio sicut a Patre."

some six or seven miles of the six leagues to the shore
when the officer overtook them, and begged them to
return to their last halting-place, promising that all that
had been said or done would be revoked. There they
were again met by the Chartophylax, who at once searched
all their books and baggage. Finding at length the
paper which he had been seeking, he simply said, " I have
got it," and left. But the monks had already translated
it into Latin, and so to-day it may be read in their
diary.[1]

As there was no real wish for reunion on the part of the
Greeks generally, these conferences then had the same
abortive ending as those inaugurated by Innocent III.,
when he sent to Constantinople cardinal Benedict
(1205–7),[2] and then cardinal Pelagius (1213–16),[3] and
as the " reunion " scheme of the Patriarch of Nicæa
Manuel I. Sarantenos, during the pontificate of Honorius
III.[4] (1220).

Political complications—alliances between the king of

[1] Mansi, xxiii, p. 307. The diary is followed by a full profession
of faith drawn up by the Council of Nymphæum which was sent to
Pope Gregory. *Ib.*, p. 307 ff. The corresponding statement of the papal
envoys on the Procession of the Holy Ghost is given both in Greek and
Latin. *Ib.*, p. 61 ff.

[2] The chief authority for the " reunion " work of Benedict is said
to be the report of the Greek interpreter, Nicholas of Otranto, which
has been published with a Russian translation by Bishop Arsenij
Novgorod, 1896, *Des Nikolaus von Otranto . . . drei Aufzeichnungen
über Gespräche der Greichen mit den Lateinern.*

[3] On his work see the report of Nicholas Mesarites, bishop of Ephesus.
It gives the Greek version of the doings of Pelagius, but has only been
published by bishop Arsenij in a privately printed Russian work.
Cf. W. Norden, *Das Papsttum und Byzanz*, p. 216.

[4] *Cf.* Gardner, p. 112 f. There is no need to discuss the diplomatic
approaches made to Rome by Theodore Angelus of Epirus and
Thessalonica, nor even the submission of Manuel, Despot of Epirus,
to Gregory IX. (*cf. Reg. Greg.*, i, p. 491, ep. of Apr. 1, 1232) ; for,
even if sincere, it had no result, as the power of Manuel was shortlived.
Cf. Gardner, p. 142 ; Miller, *The Latins in the Levant*, p. 95.

Bulgaria or Frederick II.¹ with Vatatzes against the empire of Constantinople—prevented the reopening of "reunion" negotiations during the pontificate of Gregory, though Vatatzes appears to have made fresh overtures to him just before his death.² We shall have to wait till the reign of Gregory X. before we find any kind of tangible result from these frequently renewed attempts at healing the Greek schism.³

Help for the Latin Empire of Constantinople.   The alliance just alluded to between Frederick II. and Vatatzes, and that between John Asen II. of Bulgaria and Vatatzes, also against Constantinople, no doubt kept the mind of the emperor of Nicæa from thoughts of the spiritual needs of his people, and turned it to thoughts of political gain. He accordingly directed all his energies towards the recapture of Constantinople ; and Gregory, after excommunicating him, turned his attention to its defence, principally for the sake of safeguarding the faith in the East.⁴ It was in the same year as the conference on reunion (1234) that Vatatzes concluded an alliance against John of Brienne with John Asen II., the powerful ruler of Bulgaria. Ratifying it by marrying his little son to the daughter of Asen (1235), he carried on the

¹ Hence Gregory's biographer (C. 22) does not hesitate to lay the failure of the reunion negotiations at the door of " that so-called Catholic Prince." He also tells us that Gregory returned most of the presents which Vatatzes had sent him, with the exception of some carpets which he distributed to the patriarchal churches of the City.

² *Reg.*, iii, 353, Feb. 10, 1241.

³ *Cf.* Bousquet, *L'Unité de l'Eglise et le Schisme Grec*, p. 195 ff., Paris, 1913, though this work is rather apologetic than historical.

⁴ *Cf.* ep. of March 17, 1238, ap. *Reg.*, ii, p. 902 f. " Ne frustra sit nobis evellendi et plantandi celitus.collata potestas (Jer., xxiv, 6), contra dictum Vatacium seismaticum et ejus fautores, qui excommunicati a nobis semel in annis singulis nuntiantur ; quia ipsorum vulnera sanare hujusmodi non potuit medicina, non tam pro subsidio Constantinopolitani imperii quam pro corroboranda et defendenda fide catholica in partibus Orientis, multos principes, barones et milites signo crucis fecimus insigniri."

war with renewed vigour against John, who had begun
to attack the Nicæan Empire in 1233. Alarmed by this
combination against him, John turned among others to
the Pope. Nor did he appeal in vain. Letters poured
forth from the pontifical chancery to various kings and
especially to Béla IV., king of Hungary, as he was the
sovereign who was nearest to the empire, urging them to
help the Latin empire against the schismatics, Vatatzes
and Asen. Letters were also sent to bishops in Hungary
and in France, the country of Baldwin and John of
Brienne, authorizing them to commute the vows of such
as were ready to march against the enemies of the latter instead of against the Saracens in Palestine (December 1235).[1]

Although with the aid of the Venetians and others,
Brienne gained a preliminary success against his enemies
(1275),[2] the situation of Constantinople was still so serious
that the young Baldwin left the City, and came to the
West to obtain further succour (1236). Again did the
Pope bestir himself for the threatened Empire; and, in
letters addressed to rulers and peoples both in France and
in England, he pointed out the probable evil consequences
of its fall. "The body of the Eastern Church would,"
he urged, "be rent in pieces with schisms; great
hindrances would be placed in the way of rendering help
to the Holy Land; the Lord's field would be oversown
with the thorns and briars of heresies, and the position of
all the Latins in the East would be endangered." Vatatzes
had already taken many cities, and, as the Greeks "hate
the Latins more than they do the heathen," there would
be a grave danger of the loss of the Holy Land. Gregory
accordingly endeavoured to raise an army which was to

---

[1] *Reg.*, ii, p. 217 f.   *Cf.* epp. of Jan. 12–16 (p. 232 f.) and of May 24,
1236 (p. 391).

[2] Mouskes, l. 29039 ff.; Dandolo, x, 5, n. 15, ap. *R. I. SS.*, xii,
p. 349.

set out in March, 1238.[1] He also strove to provide it with funds.[2] Hence he tried hard to induce the English clergy to contribute to the cause a thirtieth of their revenues,[3] and if he himself did not raise much from them, Baldwin, who visited England, got money from our king.[4]

Meanwhile, the aged John of Brienne died (March, 1237), whilst Baldwin was in the West seeking help. This would have been followed by the immediate destruction of the Latin rule in Constantinople had it not been for a temporary defection of the Bulgarian monarch from the Emperor of Nicæa,[5] and for the action of Gregory who succeeded in impressing on Vatatzes the danger of his pursuing his plans against Constantinople, by assuring him that there was an army of Crusaders ready in Europe to avenge any attempt against it.[6]

[1] Cf. Reg., ii, p. 512 ff., for letters of Dec. 8, 1236, to bishops in France and Hungary.   Cf. ep. May 10, 1237, ib., p. 639 f. ; epp. of May 21, p. 659 f., May 31 and June 1, p. 672 f. ; Oct. 30, ib., p. 804 ff., and ap. Calendar of Papal letters, i, 166, addressed to the bishop of Winchester, etc. ; Jan. 8–12, 1238, p. 852 ff. ; Jan. 27, p. 875 ff. ; March 22, p. 955 f. ; Oct. and Nov., 1240, iii, p. 320 ff.

[2] Reg., ii, 779, 781, for epp. of Oct. 6, 1237 ; epp. of Dec. 19, 1238 ; Jan. 23, 1239, p. 1210.

[3] Epp. of Nov. 24, 1238, ap. Calendar of P.L., i, p. 177.   Cf. Mat. Par., Chron., iii, 386, and 469, on the wish "of the Pope and the whole Church" to send crusaders to help the emperor of Constantinople, though, as we have noted before, he says much that is inaccurate on these relations between Rome and Constantinople.

[4] Paris, ib., p. 480, an. 1238.   Cf. Ann. de Wav., p. 318.

[5] About the beginning of the year 1237 Asen wrote to the Pope to express his devotion to the Roman Church, and his readiness to help John of Brienne.   See the letters of Gregory of May 21, 1237, ap. Theiner, Mon. Hungar., i, p. 155.   After some months of negotiation we find the Pope calling on the Hungarians to march against "the treacherous" Asen.   Epp. of Jan. 27, and Aug. 8, 1238, ap. ib.

[6] Epp. Greg., of March 12 and 17, 1238, ap. Reg., ii, 918 and 902. One of the reasons given by Gregory for excommunicating Frederick in 1239 was his endeavouring to prevent "reparatio imperii Romaniæ." Mat. Par., iii, p. 536.   Cf. Mouskes, Chron., l. 29392 ff. ; 29506 ff.
    "Papes Grigories li douna
        Del sien, et moult promis li a."

Though Gregory did not succeed in this matter altogether as he could have wished, as he had to face the opposition of Frederick II., who contrived to prevent much of the destined help from reaching Constantinople,[1] still aided by the resources procured by Gregory's co-operation, with which he returned to his imperial city (1238),[2] Baldwin contrived to prolong the feeble life of the Latin Empire till 1261.

Though the needs of the Latin Empire of Constantinople and the preaching of a *crusade* in its behalf largely turned the thoughts of Gregory from the Holy Land, he did not fail to give much attention to it. He was, however, for many years hampered by the ten years' truce which had closed the ignominious crusade of the Emperor Frederick II. in 1229. For some time, therefore, he had to content himself with endeavouring to keep peace among the Christians themselves in the Holy Land.[3] But at length towards the close of the year 1234, after having himself with great feeling preached the Cross publicly to the Romans,[4] he addressed letters to the Kings of France and England and others reminding them that as he held the place of our Lord on earth, it was his duty to stir up the faithful to fight the battles of the Lord, and hence, as the truce made by Frederick was running out,

The Crusades, 1229–41.

Cf. ll. 29580–29622 ; 29855 ff. ; 30405 ff. ; 30547 ff. ; and Alberic Trium. Font., *Chron.*, an. 1239, ap. *M. G. SS.*, xxiii, p. 946.

[1] Ep. of May 21, 1237, ap. *Reg.*, ii, p. 659 f. Letters of the same date show that Gregory had reason to know that the fickle Bulgarian monarch was to abandon his offensive alliance against Constantinople ; *ib.*, pp. 660–1. *Cf.* Muralt, *Chronog. byzant.*, p. 353. History shows that the crooked Bulgarian policy which we are witnessing to-day (Autumn, 1915) is a regular feature of their conduct. *Cf.* Bousquet, *Hist. du peuple Bulgare*, p. 80, Paris, 1909.

[2] Mat. Par., iii, 517 f. ; G. Acropol., *Ann.*, c. 37, p. 62 ff.

[3] Röhricht, *Regest. reg. Hierosol.*, addit., nn. 1071a and 1079b, etc.

[4] *Cf. Vita*, c. 21. He enrolled at the same time many of the Romans.

he had ordered the crusade to be preached everywhere, so that Christendom might not be found unprepared. All must then begin to gird themselves for the fray.[1]

Preachers, Franciscans and Dominicans especially, supported by " able masters of theology," were also appointed by the Pope to preach the Cross "throughout all the world ".[2] By the eloquence of such men as St. Edmund Rich [3] no little enthusiasm was roused in our own country, and many nobles " assumed the cross ", including Richard, Earl of Cornwall, the King's brother.[4] At first there was a difficulty in restraining the enthusiasm of the Crusaders, and Gregory had to urge the bishops to forbid them to start for the Holy Land " before the general passage appointed by the Roman Church." [5] Then there were efforts made by different persons for different reasons to divert or damp the enthusiasm. The Pope, as we have seen, wanted some at least of the Crusaders to go to the aid of the Latin Empire of Constantinople instead of to the Holy Land. The Emperor, because he was at war with the Lombards, and could not control the movement himself, was not anxious that it should succeed,[6] and exerted himself to get the starting of the expedition delayed from the August of 1238 to

[1] Epp. of Nov. 6, 1234, ap. *Reg.*, i, 1172 f. *Cf.* ep. of Nov. 17 to the people, *ib.*, p. 1180 ff. *Cf.* ep. of Sept. 4, 1235, to the English people, ap. Rog. Wendover, iv, p. 327 ff., ed. Coxe.

[2] R. W., *ib.*, pp. 330-1.

[3] " Verbum pro crucis negocio de mandato summi pontificis non sine fructu multiplici seminavit." *Vit. S. E.*, by Eustace, p. 553, ap. Wallace. *Cf.* Rob. Rich, p. 619, *ib.* ; and Bertrand, c. 34, p. 1799. Knowing the Saint to be "crucis amatorem," the Pope committed to him "legationem crucis cum grandi privilegio."

[4] *Cf.* Mat. Par., an. 1236, iii, 368-9, 373 f.

[5] Ep. to the bishops of England of Oct. 28, 1235, ap. *Calendar of Papal Let.*, i, p. 149.

[6] Hence the earnest efforts made by the Pope in Nov., 1237, to induce the Emperor to help the Crusaders who were to start on the feast of St. John the Baptist (Aug. 29), 1238. *Cf. Reg.*, ii, 801 ff.

the same date in the year 1239, i.e. the feast of St. John the
Baptist, 1239. He was anxious, he said, that all necessary
preparations should be made as the burden of the
liberation of the Holy Land rested on him more than on
any other Prince.[1] Finally, our own King was anxious
that in the midst of his difficulties his brother should not
leave the kingdom ; and so Gregory put all the pressure
he could on the Earl and others to prevent his departure,
or, at least, the departure of all the English lords at
once.[2]

But many both in this country and in France were
anxious to fight for the liberation of the Holy Land,
and not for anything else. They were, moreover,
urged to set out thither immediately and not to delay.
It was true that the ten years' truce made by Frederick
did not expire till 1239, but advices from Palestine informed
them that the Moslems had broken the truce, and had
captured and killed many pilgrims.[3] It was also pointed
out that discord had arisen among the Saracens, and that
one of them, the Sultan of Damascus, had promised
to receive baptism and put his territory under Christian
suzerainty.[4]

In face of this there was nothing left for it but that the
Pope should give his blessing and money to those who
wished to set out.[5] Accordingly, first the French (1239),
under Theobald of Champagne, and then the English

Departure of English and French for the Holy Land, 1239–40.

[1] See his letter of Feb. 11, 1238, to Richard of Cornwall, ap. Mat.
Par., iii, 471. *Cf.* p. 627 f.

[2] *Cf.* a series of letters of Apr. 1238, ap. *Cal. of P.L.*, i, p. 170 f.

[3] Ep. sent to Theobald IV., king of Navarre and Count of Champagne,
by the authorities in Palestine. Oct. 6, 1238, ap. Röhricht, *Regest.*,
pp. 282–3.

[4] Alberic, ap. *M. G. SS.*, xxiii, p. 945, and Mat. Par., iv, 65.

[5] With the letters of Nov., 1239, ap. *Cal. of P.L.*, i, pp. 184–5, *cf.*
those of Apr., 1238, ap. *ib.*, p. 170 f. The Pope assigned to Richard
all the money which had been collected in England for the Crusades.
See also Wykes, *Chron.*, p. 87, R. S.

(1240), under Richard of Cornwall, left Europe for the Holy
Land. But, although discord among the Ayubites at
home, and continued attacks from without by their new
Tartar enemy had weakened the power of the Saracens,
unfortunately want of discipline among the Crusaders,
and differences between the great military orders, prevented
anything very substantial from being effected either by
the French or the English. The former returned in 1240,
and the latter in the following year.[1]

Spread of the
faith and
Catholic
unity in (a)
the East.

In the midst of the pressing difficulties of every kind
in which Gregory passed most of his pontificate, he did not
fail to watch over the propagation of the faith, which was
going on in the East and in the West. In the East, where
there was at this time a widespread desire for union with
Rome,[2] the knowledge of Christ, or of his One Church, was
being spread by the new zeal of the sons of SS. Francis and
Dominic, and the Pope not only granted them privileges
which would help them in their work of conversion, but
endeavoured to secure for them the protection of such
Eastern potentates as the King of Georgia,[3] the Caliph of
Bagdad,[4] and the Sultans of Iconium (Konich), Aleppo,
and Damascus.[5] Both the Sultan of Iconium and the
Sultan of Damascus professed great sympathy with the

---

[1] Cf. Will. of Tyre, Contin., l. xxv, c. 29–34, and 36, ap. Migne,
Pat. Lat., t. 201, p. 1028 ff. ; and various letters ap. Mat. Par., an.
1240, iv, 25 ff., 138 ff.

[2] Cf. e.g., the narrative of the Dominican Richard, who at this time
went into the East to seek for the original home of the Hungarians.
He not unfrequently, he says, met peoples who declared : " quod cito
fieri debeant Christiani et ecclesiæ Romane subesse," p. 251. Cf.
pp. 252, 254. De facto Hungariæ Magnae, p. 248 ff., ed. Endlicher, in
Rer. Hung. Mon., or ap. Theiner, Mon. Hung., i.

[3] Regist., nn. 1217, 1220, vol. i, pp. 692–3 ; nn. 2429–30, ib., p. 1267 f.,
and 4400, vol. ii, p. 1054 ; or ap. Eubel, Bullar. Francisc. Epit., nn. 102,
104, 106–7, 111.

[4] Regist., n. 1337, i, p. 750.

[5] Ib., n. 1099, p. 632.

Christian cause in the East, and proclaimed their willingness to help it.[1] But as far as these princes, at any rate, were concerned, there was seemingly more question of political than religious gain, as may be seen almost certainly in the case of the Sultan of Damascus, who was simply looking for the military support of the Franks.[2]

If, however, the friars had no great success with secular rulers, they secured the return to Catholic unity of Ignatius II., patriarch of the Jacobites, or Syrian Monophysites (One-nature heretics).[3] This had been the special work of Prior Philip, a Dominican, who reported the conversion to the Pope and to his confessor, Godfrey. The latter, in a circular letter, preserved by Matthew Paris,[4] and addressed to all the Dominicans in England and France, embodied the report of Philip. It set forth that the Divine mercy was " bringing back to the obedience of the Pope and to the unity of our holy mother, the Church, the nations which have been long withdrawn from that unity. For in this year the patriarch of the Oriental Jacobites, a man venerable at once from his learning and character as well as from his age, came, with a large number of archbishops, bishops, and monks of his nation, to worship in Jerusalem." When the Catholic faith had been explained to him he abjured his heresy, swore obedience to the Holy Roman Church, and gave to the writer his profession of faith inscribed " in Chaldaic and Arabic characters." The authority of the convert patriarch, continued Philip, " extends over Chaldæans, Medes, Persians, and Armenians " in some seventy provinces, " now to a great extent ravaged by the

The Jacobites.

---

[1] *Re* the former, see *ib.*, nn. 2433 and 2473 ff., pp. 1264 and 1279 f. The latter, as we have seen, even expressed his readiness to be baptized. *Cf. supra.*

[2] Mat. Par., iv, 79, an. 1240.

[3] On him, see Le Quien, *Oriens. Christ.*, ii, coll. 1392 ff.

[4] *Chron.*, iii, 396 ff., an. 1237.

Tartars." The example of Ignatius, continued Philip, was followed by two archbishops. Of these one was the Jacobite patriarch of Jerusalem who had been intruded into that see by the aggressive Jacobite patriarch of Alexandria, Cyril III.;[1] the other was a Nestorian. Their sees were in Syria and Phœnicia. The prior further reported that the head of the Nestorians " in greater India, in the kingdom of Prester John, and in other kingdoms of the Far East " had also promised to return to ecclesiastical unity, as had also the patriarch of the Egyptian or Coptic Jacobites " who are wont to go much further from the truth than the Orientals." The sight of all these peoples ready to embrace the faith has caused us, declared the prior, to make all the brethren study Armenian and other Oriental languages, and now " they speak and preach in them, especially in Arabic,[2] which is the most generally spoken tongue." It remained for the Pope " to provide for the gathering together and for the peace of those who were returning to the Church."

With a view to carrying out the recommendation herein contained, Gregory wrote kindly to the prelates named in Philip's letter,[3] and did his best to provide for their needs.[4]

[1] Hence his acceptance of the Catholic faith is assigned by some to his desire to obtain the help of the Latins against Ignatius, the outraged Jacobite patriarch of Antioch, under whose jurisdiction the Jacobite see of Jerusalem had remained for some six hundred years. Cf. J. M. Neale, *Patriarchate of Alexandria*, ii, p. 299 f. ; Raynaldus, *Annales*, an. 1237, n. 87. From the foregoing and the corresponding matter in the text, it will be seen that the phrase of Godfrey " unus Jacobinus de Egipto " means " a Jacobite from Egypt," and not, as translated by Giles, " the Jacobin bishop of Egypt." On the action of Cyril III. (Laklak), cf. Bar Hebræus, *Chron. eccles.*, i, p. 658 f., ed. Abbeloos.

[2] In connexion with Arabic, Paris notes (*ib.*, p. 403) that even their ecclesiastical Arabic was not understood by the ordinary people.

[3] Epp. of July 1237, ap. *Reg.*, ii, p. 719 f.

[4] *Ib.*, p. 914, for epp. of March 9, 1238 ; and a letter of June 7,

The movement towards Rome in the Coptic Church at this period was partly the result and partly the cause of a literary awakening which then took place in its midst. That this movement was regarded as natural, by some of the Copts at least, may be gathered from the way in which Ibn-al-Assal (al-Safi), the second of three brothers, all with literary tastes, speaks of the position of the Pope in the Church in his abridgment of the canons promulgated at the Coptic Synod held at Cairo in 1230.[1] He says that just as there are four cardinal points and four Gospels, so there are four patriarchs. " The first is he who sits on the chair of St. Peter in Rome, as the Apostles have laid down," and he adds that, as the patriarch has authority over the bishops dependent upon him, so " the lord of the see of Rome has power over all the patriarchs as their Prince and Chief, as St. Peter himself, indeed, to whom power has been given over all the pastors of Christianity and over all peoples, for he is the Vicar of Jesus Christ over all the Church." [2]

The Coptic Church.

Gregory was also called upon to work for the spreading of the faith in Africa. We have already noted that the famous battle of Las Navas de Tolosa in Spain (1212) broke the Moorish power in that country.[3] The defeated Almohade sovereign, An Nasir (En-Nacer), was succeeded by unworthy sons, of whom Yahya was deposed by the learned El-Mamoun, the governor of Seville. With the aid of twelve thousand Castillian cavaliers, whom he obtained from St. Ferdinand III. of Castile, he crossed over into

(b) Africa (Morocco).

1238, giving jurisdiction in certain circumstances to Jacobite priests over Latins.

[1] On Ibn-al-A., see *Encyclopédie de l'Islam, sub voce*, Paris, 1918, and I. Guidi, *Fetha Nagast*, p. v ff., Rome, 1899. His *Il libro dei Canoni* (in Arabic) was published in Cairo, 1908.

[2] Ap. Guidi, l.c., p. 30. See G. Macaire, *Hist. de l'église d'Alex.*, Cairo, 1894.

[3] *Supra*, vol. xii, p. 177. Cf. Merrâkechi, *Hist. des Almohades*, p. 279 f., ed. Fagnan, Alger, 1893.

Africa, seized Morocco, and practically put an end to the
power of Yahya. To keep his Spanish auxiliaries, El-
Mamoun (1227–†1232) had to agree to a Christian Church
being built in Morocco, and to a bishopric being established
first at Fez, and then at Morocco.[1] It was to El-Rechid,
the son of the successful usurper, that Gregory wrote on
May 27, 1233. Expressing a hope that "Miramolinus"[2]
would some day embrace the Christian faith, the Pope
thanked him for the way in which he had received the
Friars Minor, and particularly Brother Agnellus, bishop
of Fez. At the same time he took care to inform "the
commander of the faithful" (Miramolinus) that, if he
ceased to favour them, he would not suffer the Christian
cavaliers to remain in his service.[3] Gregory consecrated
Brother Agnellus himself, and assured all the faithful of
Christ dwelling in Morocco that he was delighted "that
the Church of Morocco, hitherto barren, had now become
fruitful."[4] According to Mas Latrie, "the faithful"
here spoken of are the remnant of the old Christian
population of *Africa* (i.e., North Africa from Egypt to
the Atlantic Ocean), which, after the extinction of the
more easterly sees of Gummi and El-Kala,[5] came under the
spiritual sway of the bishop of Morocco. This see was
therefore styled by Innocent IV., who tended it very
carefully, "the only daughter of the Roman Church in
those parts."[6]

[1] On El-Mamoun, see Mas Latrie, *Les relations des Chrétiens avec l'Afrique*, pp. 72 f., 124 f. ; and Rosseeuw St. Hilaire, *Hist. d'Espagne*, iv, p. 102 ff. El-Mamoun, whose full name is said to be "Abou'l Ola-Idris E.-M.," is called by St. Hilaire "abou Ali."

[2] *Supra*, vol. xii, p. 178 n.

[3] Ep. of May 27, 1233, ap. Mas Latrie (in full), *l.c.*, p. 10, pt. ii ; *Reg.*, i, 754.

[4] Ep. of June 12, 1237, ap. M. L., p. 11 f. ; *Reg.*, ii, 689.

[5] *Cf. supra*, vol. vii, pp. 193–5.

[6] Ep. of Oct. 31, 1246, ap. Wadding, *Annal. Minor.*, 1246, § 14, t. iii, p. 150. *Cf.* the whole series of letters of the Pope on this Church of Oct., 1246, ap. *Regist.*, i, nn. 2242–51, ed. Berger.

In the West the indefatigable Friars had penetrated (c) Europe into Russia.[1] At this period the Russian principalities and Russia. were going all to pieces through internal dissensions, and through the external pressure of the Tartars, of whom the old Russian chronicle of Novgorod says naively : " God alone knows who they are, and whence they came out. Very wise men know them exactly, who understand books ; but we do not know who they are." [2]

Among others who appear to have been terrified by the Tartars was the Grand Knyaz (Prince or Duke) of Vladimir (Volodimir), Georges II. (1212–38),[3] who exercised some kind of suzerainty over the independent city which produced the Chronicle just quoted, and with which he was frequently at war. At any rate, when the lesser Knyazes were boldly telling the Tartars who demanded tribute that " only when none of us remains then all will be yours," [4] Georges appears to have lacked the courage to face them. Flight, however, availed him not. " It happened when he reached the river Sit, they overtook him, and there he ended his life (1238). And God knows how he died, for some say much about him." [5]

Whether, then, because he hoped for Western help or because he was affected by the words of the preachers, Georges expressed a desire to return to Catholic unity. Addressing him as " the illustrious King of Russia," Gregory reminds him that by the will of Christ there is to be but one sheepfold, of which St. Peter and his successors

[1] See Gregory's letters " to the provincial prior of Poland and to the Friars Preachers dwelling in Russia," March 15, 1233, ap. Turgeneff, *Hist. Russ. Mon.*, p. 35, and *Regist.*, i, pp. 668–9.

[2] Eng. trans. by Michell and Forbes, p. 64, ed. Camden Soc., London, 1914. This chronicle, which runs from 1016–1471, was written " by a series of ecclesiastics in the archiepiscopal palace."

[3] Otherwise, Georgi (Gyurgi or Yuri) Vsevolodvich. On Georges, see Rambaud, *Hist. de Russie*, pp. 95 ff., 128 f.

[4] *Chron. Novgor.*, p. 81.

[5] *Ib.*, p. 83.

have the charge, and tells him that, as he understands that he wishes to enter that fold, he should cease to follow the customs and rites of the Greeks and Ruthenians, and adopt those of the Latins. Should he thus submit himself " to the sweet dominion of the Roman Church, the mother of all the faithful," she will account him " a great Prince in the Church of God, and love him as a special son." [1] No doubt the Tartar invasion prevented any tangible result from following the overtures of Georges; and, as in the case of the Greeks, we shall have to wait for the pontificate of Innocent IV. (1247) before we find any sign of even a passing Russian reunion with Rome. [2]

Spread of the faith in Livonia, Prussia, etc.

Giving a few references to prove that Gregory followed in the footsteps of his predecessors and worked for the further spread of the faith in Livonia [3] and Prussia, [4] and that he helped on the conversion of the Cumani, [5] a Tartar horde that first appeared in Russia and on the Danube in the eleventh century, we may conclude our notices of his efforts to sow the good seed of the Gospel by adding that he strove to convert the Saracens whom the policy of Frederick had settled at Lucera. [6]

[1] Ep. of July 18, 1231, ap. Turgeneff, p. 30, or *Regist.*, i, p. 433, n. 684.

[2] *Cf.* Romanet du Caillaud, *L'Eglise Russe Catholique*, L. iii, c. 4, " Retour momentané de la Russie au Catholicisme en 1247."

[3] Turgeneff, *l.c.*, has collected the papal documents that bear on Livonia. Cf. Robinson, *The Conversion of Europe*, 513–9.

[4] With regard to this country, Gregory was mainly concerned to procure warlike aid against the pagan Prussians, who were for ever endeavouring to exterminate their Christian brethren. *Regist.*, i, p. 323, n. 492 ff. ; and p. 846 ff., n. 1534 ff.

[5] *Reg.*, i, p. 107, n. 185 ff.; p. 209, n. 344 f. ; p. 1142, n. 2120. Gregory worked through the Kings of Hungary for the conversion of the Cumani. Their final conversion is assigned to Louis I., King of Hungary, 1370.

[6] *Reg.*, i, p. 848, n. 1540. Frederick promises his co-operation, *ib.*, p. 925, n. 1682.

And now, leaving the affairs of France (including those of the Albigensians) and those of the Tartars to be dealt with under the pontificate of Innocent IV., and necessarily passing over completely many interesting concerns in which Gregory took a part, our biography of him may be terminated by a notice of the rapidly increasing severity against heretics.[1]

During Gregory's pontificate we find that heretics were being assailed by regular forces in the field, by popular outbreaks and by more or less new forms of law. But under whatever names these heretics were known, they appear in the main to have been branches of the impure, anti-social, and inhuman sect known as the Cathari, enemies of the Church, the State, and Society at large.[2] *Heretics attacked by regular forces and by popular outbreaks.*

Though the persecution of heretics began under the first Christian emperors,[3] its development in the Middle Ages was commensurate with the growth of those Manichæan sects which may be conveniently called Cathari or Albigensians. Its development was therefore most marked between the years 1150 and 1250.

During the pontificate of Gregory, as we have just said, proceedings were taken against them by three methods, by regular forces, by popular outbursts, and by law. We have now to add that the first and third of these methods had his sanction.

The great centre of the Cathari, where they were known as Bogomils,[4] was Bosnia. Innocent III. and his successor had made efforts to root them out of that country; but, *The Bogomils attacked.*

---

[1] L. Auvray's little paper, " Un acte de la légation du card. Jean Halgrin," Rome, 1896, gives some detail of the ordinary church work of Gregory. It deals with the delimitation of the dioceses of Sigüenza and Osma in Spain (1229). The paper is an extract from *Mélanges d'archæol.*, t. xvi.

[2] *Cf. supra*, vol. x, 144 ff., 257 ff. ; xii, 36 ff., 218 ff.

[3] *Supra*, vol. x, p. 266.

[4] *Supra*, vol. xii, p. 36 ff.

though Gregory took under his protection those who were converted to the faith,[1] and though he sent Dominican missionaries among the people,[2] he had to complain that " the number of the perfidious had so increased in Bosnia and the neighbouring provinces that the whole land, like a trackless desert, was mourning and languishing . . . and had become the lair of the dragon and the feeding ground of the ostrich." [3] To cope with the evil, he first sent as his legate into Bosnia and the surrounding districts the Prior of the famous Carthusian monastery of St. Bartholomew, on the wild plateau of Trisulti. In sending him, Gregory described him " as a man after his own heart, a friend of God, powerful in word and work, who, imitating the poverty of the poor Christ, does not in his burning zeal shrink from going to those parts clad in despicable garb in order to free souls deceived by the fraud of the devil." [4]

Peaceful means were, however, useless; and at length Gregory felt himself obliged to call upon Colomann, " King of the Ruthenians and Duke of the whole of Slavonia," [5] powerfully to gird himself to bring back Bosnia to the light of Catholic faith (1234).[6] He was the

---

[1] *Cf.* epp. of Oct. 10, 1233, ap. Theiner, *Mon. hist. Hungariæ,* i, p. 120, nn. 100–2.

[2] E.g., *ib.,* n. 305, Dec. 22, 1238.

[3] Ep. Feb. 13, 1234, ap. *ib.,* pp. 122–3.

[4] *Ib.*

[5] In one case he is called " Haliciæ Rex," i.e., King of the province of Halitz (or Halicz), which corresponds more or less with the modern Galicia. Colomann was a son of Andrew II., King of Hungary ; his brother was Béla IV., King of Hungary (1235–70).

[6] Ep. n. 218, Oct. 14, 1234. " Ad convertendum in robore tue fortitudinis infectos macula heretice pravitatis, te versus partes Sclavoniæ ita . . . potenter accingas, quod . . . sedentes in perfidie tenebris ad lucem catholice properare fidei non postponant." *Cf.* nn. 220–1, and ep. 301, Dec. 22, 1238. Gregory congratulates him for striving " ut de Bosna partibus, deletis pravitatis heretice maculis, ibidem fulgeat lumen catholice puritatis." Ap. Theiner, *ib.*

more moved to try force because the Bogomils are said to have deposed (1232) the Catholic Ban Stephen,[1] the son of Ban Calin, and to have set up the Bogomil Matthias Ninoslav.[2] This was followed by the defection to the "insensate" doctrine of Bogomilism of the bishop of Bosnia.[3] Ninoslav at first contrived to secure the favour and support of Gregory ; [4] but when the Pope was better informed of his doings and opinions, or when political opponents of Ninoslav had deceived him with regard to them, he confirmed to Colomann the cession of Bosnia made to him by his father,[5] and, as we have said, encouraged him to take possession of it. With the aid of Sebislav, son of the deposed Ban Stephen, who was Knez or governor of Oussora, a district of north Bosnia on the borders of Hungary,[6] Colomann succeeded at length in reducing the power of Ninoslav, and in winning the praise of the Pope.[7]

Fortune, however, favoured the party loyal to Ninoslav, including the Bogomils, who through their opposition to invasion from without confounded their religion with their nationality, and regarded themselves as the national

[1] *Cf. supra*, vol. xii, p. 43 f., for the submission to Rome of Culin's son.

[2] So say Coquelle, *Hist. du Monténégro et de la Bosnie*, p. 81 ff. ; and Prince Lazarovich-Hrebelianovich, *The Servian People*, ii, 464. But through his want of knowledge or disregard of the papal letters the Prince makes many mistakes. Hence he supposes it was the King of Hungary who invaded Bosnia on this occasion. It was, however, as we have seen, Colomann.

[3] Ep. of May 30, 1233, ap. Theiner, *ib.*, p. 113. "Ad doctrine incidit amaritudinem insensate." The bishop declared that he had erred "through simplicity."

[4] Epp. of Oct. 10, 1233, ap. *ib.*, nn. 100-2, p. 120.

[5] Ep. Aug. 9, 1235, n. 229, ap. *ib.*, p. 133.

[6] See a number of papal instruments in behalf of " Zibisclao de Woscura nato quondam Stephani Bani de Bosna," ap. Theiner, *ib.*, p. 147.

[7] Ep. of Apr. 26, 1238, n. 289, p. 162, and ep. of Dec. 5, 1239, ap. *ib.*, p. 172, n. 310.

party. The invasion of the Tartars caused the Hungarian
Prince to turn his attention to the East, and Ninoslav
returned to power. The work of Colomann was quite
undone, and Innocent IV. had to write that " the church
and diocese of Bosnia . . . had wholly lapsed into heretical
depravity " [1] ; and, even if Ninoslav before he died " lived
as a Catholic, " [2] in " heretical depravity," Bosnia
remained. While, therefore, it cannot be claimed that
armed intervention did much to stop the spread of heresy
in Bosnia, it must be remembered that the dearth of
documentary evidence relative to early Bosnian history
makes it very hard to say how much of the resistance
offered to Colomann was political and how much religious.
Probably Bogomilism gained ground because it was really
resisting attempts at political, nearly as much as at
religious, domination ; for Colomann was perhaps as
desirous of breaking Bosnia's wish for independence as
he was eager to stop the spread of heresy. And, as many
nobles in Languedoc became Albigensians to keep themselves independent of the King of France, so the Bosnians,
or at least many of them, became Bogomils because they
wished to keep themselves aloof from the Hungarians,

[1] Ep. of Aug. 26, 1247, ap. Theiner, *ib.*, n. 382, p. 204.
[2] In ep. of March 27, 1248, ap. *ib.*, p. 206, Innocent forbids Ninoslav
and his country to be disturbed because "he understood " that it
was "owing to necessity " that he had favoured the Bogomils against
his enemies, but that "a fide nequaquam deviet orthodoxa, sed
tamquam catholicus vivat." *Cf.* ep. n. 386. Prince L.-H., *l.c.*,
p. 466, reminds us that Ninoslav obtained from Rome the privilege that
the Servian and Croat Catholics might use the Slavonic tongue in their
church services, and the Glagolitza characters in their writings. "This
was a re-establishment of the state of things . . . prior to the council
of Spalato in 1059 when the Pope had supplanted the use of the
Slavonic tongue by the Latin." But *cf. supra*, vol. vi, p. 352 ; and
vol. iii, p. 245 f. It was Innocent IV. who granted the desired
permission : "dummodo sententia ex ipsius varietate littere non
ledatur." Ep. of March 29, 1248, ap. Smičiklas, *Cod. Diplom. regni
Croatiæ*, etc., vol. iv, p. 343.

and because their rulers regarded a difference of faith as a sign of independence.[1]

But if the Bogomils of Bosnia ultimately triumphed over the Crusaders who were sent against them, the fate of the Albigensians of Provence, as we shall see later, and that of the Stedingers of the Weser was very different. In the thirteenth century there dwelt in what is now the Duchy of Oldenburg a brave independent people known as the Stedingers.[2] To keep them in subjection the local magnates kept various garrisons in their midst. The soldiers of these garrisons, as so very often happens under similar circumstances, conducted themselves in a very loose way towards the women of the country. The Stedingers flew to arms, expelled the garrisons, and, from being oppressed, became oppressors. Not only would they not pay any dues either to the Church or the State, but they became a terror to the surrounding districts, and attracted all the lawless spirits to them " on account of their liberty." [3] Moreover, besides being enemies of the civil authorities, they were also said to be enemies of the Church. They, too, were accused of holding Manichæan doctrines, of being Cathari.[4] Writing to the bishops of Lübeck, and Minden, Gregory says that he has been informed

The Stedingers, 1234.

---

[1] *Cf.* Coquelle, *l.c.*, p. 87.

[2] Most exact geographical details about them will be found in the important *Historia Monast. Rastedensis*, written towards the close of the thirteenth century. Ap. *M. G. SS.*, vol. xxv. The said monastery was situated near Oldenburg, and its *Historia* is quite the best authority for the Stedinger question.

[3] *Cf.* the *Hist. M. R.*, pp. 504–5. A curious, if not fabulous, example of the misconduct of the ruling authorities of the Church towards the Stedingers is given by the fourteenth century author, William of Egmond, *Chron.*, an. 1234, pp. 7–9, ed. Hordijk, Amsterdam, 1904.

[4] Baldwin of Ninove expressly calls them " Katari." *Chron.*, ap. *M. G. SS.*, xxv, p. 542. Baldwin's indifferent universal chronicle which went down to 1294 was continued to 1304. And we are assured that " Catharorum perversitas quam plura Theotonie loca infecit." *Ann. Neresheimenses*, an. 1231, ap. *ib.*, x, p. 23.

not only of the horrible cruelties and devastations practised by the Stedingers (Scethinci, Stedinchi) in their raids, but that they are devoted to the Black Art, consulting witches and demons, and performing magical practices with waxen images.[1] Their savage raids caused attacks to be made upon them at different times (1229, 1233), but without success. At length Gerhard, archbishop of Bremen, explained the situation to the Pope, and asked his help.[2] Gregory accordingly ordered a crusade to be preached against them,[3] and offered the same indulgences to those who took part in it as to those who went to Palestine.[4] Floris IV., Count of Holland, Henry, Duke of Brabant, and many others took the Cross,[5] and the unfortunate Stedingers were completely subdued (May–June, 1234).[6] The survivors, many of them at least, would appear to have been desirous of being reconciled to the Church. At any rate, Gregory bade Archbishop Gerhard absolve them from excommunication after they had given sufficient guarantee of their good faith (August 21, 1235).[7]

Popular outbursts against the Luciferians.

Very different to the brave Stedingers was what Alberic

[1] " Querunt responsa demonum, cerea simulacra faciunt et in suis spurcitiis erroneas consulunt phitonissas." Ep. of June 17, 1233, ap. Rodenberg, i, p. 436. *Cf. ib.*, for ep. of Oct. 29, 1232. Some, without reason, apply to the Stedingers the vile practices mentioned in a letter of June 13, 1233 (*ib.*, p. 433), to the archbishop of Mainz.

[2] *Hist. M. R.*, p. 506.

[3] " Crux contra Stedingos ubique auctoritate apostolica prædicatur." *Ann. Stadenses*, an. 1233, ap. *M. G. SS.*, xvi, p. 361.

[4] *Cf.* Gregory's letters just cited.

[5] *Chron. de orig. duc. Brab.*, an. 1234, ap. *M. G. SS.*, xxv, p. 410.

[6] In addition to the authorities already cited, see especially Emo, *Chron.*, ap. *M. G. SS.*, xxiii, p. 515 ff. See also Mat. Par., *Chron. maj.*, iii, 267, who calls these heretics " Catini "; *Ann. de Theokesber.*, p. 93; and *Chron. reg. Colon., Cont. IV.*, an. 1234. Lovers of the marvellous will find curious details of their slaughter in Joh. Longi, *Chron. S. Bertini*, ap. *M. G. SS.*, xxv, 840.

[7] Potthast, n. 9992.

" of the Three Fountains " calls " the pestiferous sect of
the Luciferians." [1] And if we are to believe what is said
of its votaries they may well be described as
" pestiferous." The charges brought against them are
of the same type as were afterwards brought against the
Templars, and as are even now from time to time brought
against certain classes of Spiritualists or of continental
Freemasons, who are *said* to offer liturgical service to
Satan. The doctrines and practices ascribed to the
Luciferians were, as Pope Gregory declared, " contrary
to reason, opposed to any kind of piety, hateful to every
human heart, and inimical to all things of earth and of
heaven, against which not only ought men who have the
use of reason to rise in arms, but even the very elements
that lack it, as this plague is much worse than their
natural deficiencies." [2] The idea that sane men would
ever do the things which are laid to the charge of the
Luciferians could scarcely be entertained for an instant,
did not the curious repetition throughout the ages of the
assertion that they actually have been practised by certain
sectaries make one recognize that one should pause before
refusing off-hand any credence to them.

The charges against the Luciferians are set forth in The
the letter of Pope Gregory just cited. It is addressed to practices.
the archbishop of Mainz (Sigfrid III.), and is based upon
reports which were sent into him by Sigfrid, Brother
Bernard, once a papal penitentiary, and others, [3] and
which had been drawn up in connexion with a council
which had been held at Mainz in the presence of the King
and of the bishops and princes of the realm.

[1] *Chron.*, an. 1233, ap. *M. G. SS.*, xxiii, p. 931.
[2] Ep. of June 13, 1233, ap. Rodenberg, i, p. 432 f., or better ap.
Reg., i, p. 780.
[3] The substance of some of these reports and some other hearsay
evidence on the Luciferian doings is given by Alberic, " Trium
Fountium," *Chron.*, *l.c.*, p. 931 f.

The Luciferian novice is said to have kissed a sort of toad and to have allowed its tongue and saliva to enter his mouth. Then there appeared to him a man of ghastly pallor, all skin and bones, but with coal-black piercing eyes ; and when the novice had kissed this icy cold apparition, all memory of the Catholic faith left him. A banquet followed this performance, and after it a black cat is stated to have showed itself, to which obscene reverence was paid. The presiding *Magister* then said : " Spare us," while another asked : " Who has commanded this ? " On the answer, " the chief master," a fourth added : " And we must obey." The lights were then extinguished, and unspeakable orgies are said to have followed.   On their close there came forward " a man," from his loins upward all fiery, and thence downwards, " so they say," inserts the Pope, " all hairy like a cat." To this shining *thing* the Magister presented a portion of the novice's clothing, saying : " Master, what has been given to me, I give to thee." " Well have you often served me," replied the monster, " . . . to your charge do I entrust what you have given me."

Noting that something more really horrible than the above, anent the profanation of the sacred species, is added by the Pope, we may certainly cease to wonder that, if there was any truth at all in this description of the practices of the Luciferians, respectable people felt justified in wishing to exterminate them.

Conrad of Marburg joins in persecuting the Luciferians.

At any rate, whether the charges against the Luciferians were solidly founded on fact, or whether they were the outcome of ludicrously distorted imaginations, they were accepted as true by many who were neither fools nor knaves, as well as by the extravagantly superstitious. An indignant people rose up against these sectaries. Their leaders were at first a certain Conrad Dorso, or Torso, who though a Dominican was not in sacred orders (laicus totalis), and a secular named John, who, according to the chronicler we are quoting,[1] was a one-eyed deformed scoundrel. These two began by attacking those of the heretics who belonged to the poorer classes, and, as some of them confessed their views, and refused to to retract them, they burnt them with the assistance of the mob. This, says our chronicler, was well done, " because they were worthy of death." Finding, however, that the masses were with them, the pair went about denouncing anybody, and found judges ready to condemn men on their bare assertion that they were heretics.[2] The clergy, we are told, were much distressed at this lawless state of things, but they could do nothing, as the pair had won over King Henry and the nobility by undertaking to denounce rich people whose goods they could confiscate. Moreover, to increase their spiritual influence, they attached to themselves the famous Conrad of Marburg, the harsh confessor of St. Elizabeth of Hungary, everywhere well known for his learning and personal purity of life. He was one of those disagreeable persons who in some way contrive to unite an exact observance of the letter of the law to a cold unfeeling disposition, and who really seem to believe that they can resemble the sweet Saviour of mankind, and yet not have within them a drop of the milk of human kindness. He was a judge without mercy, says the chronicler.[3] Thus strengthened by the adhesion of Conrad, many of the Friars sided with them, and took their orders from them, " though they had no mandate from the Apostolic See."

At length, however, the trio over-reached themselves. They flew too high, and accused of heresy Henry, Count

Rome is appealed to.

---

[1] The author of the contemporary *Annales Wormatenses*, ap. *M. G. SS.*, xvii, p. 39, or ap. Böhmer, *Fontes*, ii, p. 175.

[2] " Et quia semper vulgus istis injustis judicibus ubique adherebat, prevaluit ubique voluntas eorum." *Ib.*

[3] On Conrad, *cf.* Montalembert, *Hist. de S. Elizabeth,* chaps. x, xvii.

of Sein, a man who was at once virtuous and rich.[1] He
had influence enough to have his case tried by the Council
of Mainz, to which we have already alluded (July, 1233),
and then referred to Rome. The case was accordingly
laid before Gregory, who was very much shocked by what
had happened, and in great grief said : " I am astonished
that you have borne this injustice so long without
reporting it to me. We would not have this state of things
last any longer, and annul all that has been done." [2]

The murder of Conrad and others, 1233.

Meanwhile, Conrad and his fellow judges were murdered
by the relatives of some of those whom they had done to
death. " The Germans," said the Pope, in the hearing of
the messengers who brought him the news, " have ever
been violently mad (furiosi), and now they have got
frantic judges." The murder of Conrad rather complicated
the situation,[3] though it did not prevent the Pope from
decreeing not merely that in all trials for heresy the proper
forms of law must be observed, but that all clerics would
become " irregular " who were to give any kind of consent
to, or even to see, trials conducted except in conformity
with the law.[4]

Imperial decrees against heretics, 1232-3.

These religious disturbances in Germany, and the
evidence brought to light as to the doctrines and practices
of the various denominations of Cathari, naturally called

[1] They accused him "equitasse in cancro." *Ann. W.*

[2] *Ann. Wormat., l.c.*

[3] By indignant letters of Oct., 1233, Gregory ordered the bishops
to excommunicate the murderers of Conrad ; nn. 560 and 561, ap.
Rod., i. *Cf. ib.,* n. 647, ep. of July 26, 1235, where he laid down the
penance which the murderers had to perform if they wished for absolution for their crime. Gregory was bound to act strongly against
them as he had himself given Conrad a commission to proceed against
heretics. *Cf.* ep. of June 10, 1233 ; n. 533 in Rod.

[4] *Ann. Worm., ib.* Alberic, *l.c.,* in concluding his narrative of the
death of Conrad, adds that from a vision seen in Germany it may be
conjectured that he was damned. *Cf. Chron. reg. Colon., Cont. IV.,*
an. 1233, p. 264 f. ; and *Annal. Erphord. Frat. Prædic.,* ann. 1233–4,
p. 84 ff., ed. Holder-Egger.

Frederick's attention to the spread of these baneful heretics in his dominions. Accordingly, in February, 1232, he issued a decree against them,[1] and incidentally against all heretics. He placed them under the ban of the Empire, ordered the perpetual confiscation of their goods, and that the officials of the Empire should take an oath to do all in their power to root them out of their districts. The imperial legislation also placed the heretics under various civil disabilities. They could not become magistrates of any kind, could not make wills, succeed to property, etc.[2]

As this legislation did not produce the desired effect, the Emperor, as " the chief defender " of the Christian faith, issued in the following year a much more drastic decree.[3] He ordered that, especially in places where the heretics were supposed to lurk, a justiciary and " some

[1] Hence the decree begins : " Incipiunt capitula constitutionis contra *Patarenos* (as the Cathari were named in Italy) edite per D. Fridericum." Ap. Huillard-Bréholles, *Hist. Dip. Frid.*, ii, vol. iv, p. 298. The decree mentions by name " Catharos, Patarenos, Speronistas, Leonistas, Arnaldistas, Circumcisos." It closes with an order for the destruction of the meeting-houses of the Patarenos. " Adicimus . . . quod domus Patarenorum receptatorum, defensorum, et fautorum eorum, sive ubi docuerint aut manus aliis imposuerint, destruantur." *Ib.*

[2] *Cf.* corresponding legislation on the part of the Pope, ap. *Reg.* i, n. 539, and on the part of the Senator of Rome, Anibaldi, ap. *ib.*, nn. 540–1 and 659. *Cf. Statuti di Roma I.*, ii, p. 3, ed. Re, 1880, for a Senatorial decree of 1363 approving the statute of Anibaldi. The statutes of Bologna (1246) against heretics were put forth according "to the form of the Statutes of the Lord Pope Gregory." Ap. Vacandard, *The Inquisition*, p. 112 n.

[3] June 15, 1233, ap. H.-B., iv, p. 435. As early as March, 1224, he had passed a constitution imposing the penalty of fire on any convicted heretic throughout the whole of Lombardy. Ap. *Regist. Greg.*, i, p. 348, n. 535, or H.-B., ii, p. 421. Later (Apr. 29, 1227, ap. *Reg.*, i, n. 54) we find Gregory calling on the Podestàs and peoples of Lombardy to put into force the ecclesiastical and imperial laws against heretics. Milan was the special home of the Patarenes and even of the Luciferians. *Cf. Ann. Marbach.*, an. 1231 ; and Mat. Par., *Chron.*, iii, 375.

venerable prelate " should search them out, and condemn to the flames such as were clearly convicted of heresy.[1] This decree applied to the whole Empire laws already enacted for Lombardy (1224) and Sicily (1231) ; and, as the Emperor expressly stated when drawing up his Sicilian code, it was conceived in the spirit of the ancient imperial legislation,[2] which, as we know, decreed the death penalty against the Manichæans, the precursors of the Cathari,[3] and which, through its revived study at this period, profoundly affected the treatment of heretics in every country of the West.

Further, in order that his general decree might run in Italy as in the rest of his dominions, Frederick begged the Pope, " to whom it belonged to remove any evil that threatened the Christian religion," to co-operate with him, so that the madness of the heretics might be struck down with the two swords which were in their hands.

To this request Gregory returned a very qualified assent. He was, indeed, glad to hear, he said, that the Emperor was zealous for the faith, and he would certainly give him suitable support in his efforts " to destroy the contagion of so baleful a pest." The Emperor must, however,

[1] *Cf.* his commission to the bishops of Caserta to search out the Patarenes and their supporters, ap. Richard of San Germano, *Chron.*, an. 1233, p. 145. It is always the Patarenes that are prominently mentioned in all these decrees. There can be no doubt that their dangerous doctrines and practices were the cause of all this legislation against heretics in general.

[2] The first title of the Sicilian Code (" Inconsutilem tunicam," " concerning heretics and the *Patarenes* ") especially states that the crime of heresy " as is set forth in the ancient laws " is a crime against society (inter crimina publica) worse than high treason, and that the officials of the kingdom must take cognizance of it as of any other crimes. Then, alluding to the Patarenes in particular, it decides that they must be burnt. " Presentis nostre legis edicto damnatos mortem pati Patarenos decernimus quam affectant, ut vivi . . . comburentur." Ap. Huillard-Bréholles, *l.c.*, iv, p. 5 ff.

[3] *Cod. Theod.*, xvi, 5, 7, 18, ap. Boyd, *The eccles. edicts of the Theodosian Code*, p. 55.

take care in future not to commit to the flames men who
were not heretics but merely his own personal enemies,
as in fact had already happened, to the great grief of the
Pope and others, to the general scandal and to the
dishonour of God.[1]

This letter is not a proof that Gregory was opposed to Action of
the infliction even of the death penalty upon the Cathari.[2] Gregory.
As a matter of fact, he was convinced that their
" insensate " doctrine had to be rooted out by force, and
he constantly stimulated the zeal both of clerical and lay
authorities against heretics.

He decreed (February, 1231) that Cathari, Patarenes,
poor men of Lyons, etc., after being condemned by the
Church, were to be handed over to the secular tribunals,
there to be punished with the punishment which was due
(animadversione debita). Such, moreover, as aided them
in any way, were also to be excommunicated ; and, if they
took no steps to have the excommunication removed,
they were to become " infamous " (infames) and incapable
of holding any public office and of electing others thereto
or of giving evidence. They were also to be deprived of
the right of making wills or of inheriting property, and
acts performed by them in any official capacity in which
they might be were to be held as null and void. Those who

---

[1] Ep. of July 15, 1233, ap. Rod., i, p. 444. *Cf. Chron. reg. Colon.,
Contin. IV.*, an. 1233, p. 254.

[2] Even in 1231 some Patarenes (nonnulli Paterorum) were burnt
at Rome " as unconvertible," while others were sent to do penance
at Monte Cassino or La Cava. *Cf.* Ric. of St. Germ., *Chron.*, an. 1231.
We do not, however, know on whose initiative this was done. If the
execution of these Patarenes was sanctioned by Gregory, he thereby
went much further than his great-uncle, Innocent III., who never
decreed the death penalty. *Cf.* Vacandard, *The Inquisition*, pp. 59,
61-3, 216, 226. The spread of heresy in Rome (" occulto meatu
proficiens ") is assigned by the biographer of Gregory (c. 14) to his
absence from the City, and he assigns the persecution of them to the
Senator.

were strongly suspected of heresy must prove their innocence under pain of excommunication, and if they remained under the excommunication for a year they were to be condemned as heretics. Laymen were forbidden to hold public or private disputations on the Catholic faith ; and, not to mention all the Pope's regulations and threatened penalties, sentence of excommunication was to be passed on such as did not denounce heretics or their secret conventicles, or such as " dissented " from the ordinary habits of life of their neighbours.[1]

Gregory orders his statutes against heretics to be published, 1231.

The next step taken by the Pope was to order the hierarchy to publish his decrees against heretics, once a month, and to try to induce the local civil authorities to adopt and put in force the constitutions against them proclaimed by Anibaldi, the Senator of Rome.[2] Many cities followed the example of the city of Rome, and heretics were in some of them sent to the stake.

Dominicans appointed to help the Bishops in dealing with heretics.

But it was felt by the supreme authorities both in the Church and in the State that it was not enough to issue decrees against heretics who threatened their very existence, and who propagated their subversive doctrines in secret. Accordingly, Frederick II. ordered that, though the heretics were to be examined by ecclesiastics, they were to be sought out like other malefactors by his officials ; [3] and the chroniclers show that he put this decree into force.[4]

The Church, too, had ordered that the heretics were to

[1] Ap. *Regist.*, i, n. 539, p. 351. It is to be noted that Gregory himself never directly decreed the death penalty against heretics.

[2] Ep. of June, 1231, to the archbishop of Salzburg and his suffragans, ap. Potthast, 8753. The decrees of Anibaldi were noted above.

[3] " Per officiales nostros, sicut et alios malefactores, inquiri ac *inquisitione* notatos (the Paterenes), . . . a viris ecclesiasticis . . . examinari jubemus." The Sicilian Code, ap. H.-B., *l.c.*, iv, p. 6.

[4] " Imperator pro capiendis *Paterenis* apud Neapolim mittit Reginum archiepiscopum et Riccardum . . . marescalcum suum." Ric. of S. Germ., *Chron.*, an. 1231, p. 140, ed. Gaudenzi.

be sought out, and Lucius III., with Frederick I.,
Barbarossa (1184), and then the Lateran Council had
put this duty on to the bishops.[1] But they proved to be
either too hard worked or too indifferent to carry out this
new duty, so that Gregory appointed others to help them.
" We," he wrote to the bishops of southern France,
" seeing you wrapt in the whirlwind of cares, and scarce
able to breathe under the pressure of overwhelming
anxieties, think it well to divide your burdens, that they
may be more easily borne. We have therefore determined
to send preaching friars against the heretics of France
and the adjoining provinces, and we beg, warn, and
exhort you . . . to receive them kindly, and to treat them
well, giving them . . . favour, counsel, and aid that they
may fulfil their office." [2]

This entrusting of the duties of inquisitors to the
Dominicans is very simply put before us by one of the
earliest of their records.[3] " The order of Preachers having
been specially founded by St. Dominic in Toulouse for the
main end of combating heresy and schism, after the
brethren had now for nearly forty years waged incessant
war against the like, and manfully battled with tyrants
who befriended the teachers of heresy, suffering untold
hardships in their ministry . . at last Pope Gregory IX.
entrusted the office of the inquisition to them for the
suppression of heresy and its abettors, in consequence

---

[1] Cf. supra, vol. x, p. 261 ff.

[2] Ep. of Apr. 13, 1233, ap. Potthast, n. 9143. In the text we have
copied Vacandard's extract from this letter. The Inquisition, p. 123.
Cf. two letters of Apr. 19 and 20 ; one, ap. P., n. 9152, to the Dominican
Robert, known as the Bugre (Bulgarian), because he was a converted
Patarene, exhorting him with the aid of the secular arm if necessary
(" advocato ad hoc, si necesse fuerit, brachio seculari," ap. Reg., i,
n. 1253) to root " heretical depravity " out of La Charité in the diocese
of Orleans. Cf. P., n. 9153.

[3] The Vitae Fratrum., pt. v, n. 1, Eng. trans.

of which they were exposed to very many and grave dangers." [1]

When Inquisitors had been duly appointed, Gregory instructed them as to the procedure they should follow. Arrived in a city where heretics were supposed to be, they were " to summon the bishops, clergy, and people, and preach a solemn sermon on faith. Then," continued the Pope, " select certain men of good repute to help you in trying the heretics and suspects denounced before your tribunal. All who on examination are found guilty or suspected of heresy must promise to obey the commands of the Church, if they refuse you must prosecute them according to the statutes which we have recently promulgated." [2]

Though Gregory did not fail to impress upon Conrad and the other Inquisitors that, while punishing the guilty they must take care not to injure the innocent,[3] there is no doubt that by means of the Inquisition both secular and ecclesiastical authorities were able with impunity to perpetrate a very great deal of injustice and cruelty. The letters of the Pope, indeed, show that in all his legislation he had no other end in view but the salvation

[1] The *Vitae* go on to tell of the murder of some of the brethren in 1242 " for the faith of Christ, and obedience to the Church of Rome." The brief contemporary chronicle of the Inquisitor, Brother William Pelissus, also tells of the sufferings the Dominicans had to endure from being boycotted (an. 1235, p. 33, ed. Molinier, Anicii (Le Puy), 1880), to being put to death, *ib.*, p. 55 ff. *Cf.* pp. 5, 18, 26, and especially p. 15. " Reprimebantur autem illis temporibus in terra illa catholici, et persecutores haereticorum in multis locis occidebantur." It will be seen from these passages and from Will of Puylaurens, c. 40, that the heretics often killed the accusers of their brethren.

[2] Quoted by Vacandard, *l.c.*, p. 124, and Böhmer-Ficker, *Regest. Imper.*, v, pt. ii, n. 6878, from Kuchenbecker, *Analecta Hassiaca*, iii, p. 73.

[3] " Attentius provisuri ut puniatur sic temeritas perversorum, quod innocentie puritas non ledatur." Ep. of Oct. 21, 1233, addressed to the Archbp. of Mainz, to Bro. Conrad, etc., ap. Rod., i, p. 451.

of souls and the good of humanity. Unfortunately, however, in common with all the great rulers of his age, he was so shocked at the enormities of the Patarenes and of some of their branches, like the Luciferians,[1] that, with them, he came to the conclusion that the extremest penalties were required to check the propagation of their dogmas, detrimental at once to soul and body, to Church and to State. Hence, in laying down that heretics were to be punished by the secular authority, " with the punishment which was due," he sanctioned, indirectly only it is true, the death penalties which that authority now decreed against them.

Had he been able to foresee the evils which were to flow later on from a formally established *Inquisition*, and to realize how in some countries it would become an agency which the State would use purely and simply for its own ends, he would perhaps not have approved of the legislation of Frederick II. against heretics, nor have himself issued any drastic measures against them, or encouraged civil authorities to make and put in force decrees against them. Perhaps if he had been a prophet

[1] The sea saved our own country from many heretical as well as from other troubles. Alberic (ap. *M. G. SS.*, xxiii, 932, *Chron.*, an. 1233) says that one of the leaders of the Luciferians was going to bring his vile teachings into England, when he was drowned in crossing the Channel " and was joined to the master he served." Again we must remind our readers that not all the heretics who were persecuted at this time held the impossible tenets of the Patarenes. Unfortunately, however, the persecuting of the Patarenes involved the principle of the lawfulness of persecution, and caused more harmless sects to suffer along with the noxious disciples of Manes. The great majority, however, of those who were proceeded against were Manichæans of some description. Hence in the guide issued in 1242 for the direction of the Inquisitors of Aragon, we find that, after it has been stated that " heretics are those who persevere in their errors," the example given is the sect of the *Insabbatati*, "who say that it is never lawful to take an oath, to obey either ecclesiastical or civil authorities, or to inflict corporal punishment." The guide has been printed in full by Douais, *L'Inquisition*, p. 275 ff., Paris, 1906.

he might, while believing that the burning of certain men
" terrified many heretics," have doubted whether the
act was ultimately " for the exaltation of the faith of
Jesus Christ." [1]

However this may be, Gregory, who had the same ideas
as St. Louis IX. and Frederick II. as to the proper way
to treat heretics who secretly spread teachings which were
fatal to law and order, was not a prophet. Nor was he
destined to have a long experience of the effect of the
repressive measure against heretics which he issued, and
of the means which he sanctioned for their discovery.

At least from the year 1238 [2] he had been ill, and
frequently confined to bed, lying on which he not
unfrequently, like the first great Pope of his name,
transacted business. A naïve story simply told by
Brother Jordan [3] furnishes us with an example of one of
Gregory's bedchamber audiences. The Franciscans of
Saxony, as, indeed, of many other parts, had been unduly
harassed by the *visitors*, who had been sent to them by the
despotic Elias of Cortona. At last there was nothing for
it but an appeal to Rome. Brother Jordan was accordingly
sent to make it ; but, after he had saluted the, Pope, who
was lying sick on his bed, he and his companion were told
to go. To this, however, Jordan had no mind, but with a
joyful face (jocunde) he approached the bed, and drawing
forth the Pope's bare foot from beneath the clothes, he
kissed it, exclaiming to his companion : " We have no
such relic as this in all Saxony." And when Gregory again

---

[1] Bro. Will. Pelissus in his Chronicle, p. 21, speaking of certain
heretics, says : " Qui conbusti fuerunt ad terrorem multorum
hæreticorum et exaltationem fidei Jesu Christi."

[2] *Cf.* the *Chron.* of bro. Jordan, n. 63. That he was ill again in
Feb., 1239, we learn from a letter, ap. Gervase, *Gesta*, ii, pp. 183-4,
R. S. These two references show the Pope granting audiences though
he had to lie in bed.

[3] *Ib.*

expressed his wish that they should leave him, the simple
Brother said : " No, my lord, we have not come to ask
you for anything just now. For through you we have all
manner of good things, and are completely happy ;
for you are the father, protector, and corrector of our
Order. We have only come to see you." This was, of
course, irresistible. Gregory sat up in bed delighted, told
the brothers that he knew what they had come about,
and would attend to their wishes.

The bad state of the Pope's health was aggravated both
by his enforced stay in Rome owing to Frederick's
blockade of the City, and by the news which reached him
of the Emperor's treatment of his relatives. His enforced
stay in Rome compelled him to endure the summer heats
in the unhealthy City, and prevented him from using the
baths of Viterbo, which lessened his gout or rheumatism.[1]
Then, says Matthew Paris, " the principal grief with which
the heart of the Pope was pierced, and which brought him
to his death was that the Emperor, just after the feast of
the Assumption (August 15), had taken a castle belonging
to the nephews and other relations of the Pope, near
Montefortino, in the province of Campania, which the
Pope had reconstructed (with the money of the Crusaders
is the, no doubt, gratuitous assertion of Paris himself)
for the protection of his relatives.[2] The Emperor,

---

[1] " Calculosus fuit . . . (et) caruit balneis quibus solebat Viterbii
confoveri." Mat. Par., *Chron.*, iv, p. 163. *Cf.* the diatribes against
Frederick by Albert von Behaim (?), ap. Höfler, *A. v. B.*, p. 63, and
p. 77. In the latter place we read a denunciation of Frederick for
daring to besiege in the City his spiritual Father and temporal Lord,
" quem ibidem conclusum nimii ardoris cauma peremit, eo quod
salubriori aura foveri consueverat in æstate." On the baths of
Viterbo and Gregory's use of them, see Pinzi, *I monumenti di Viterbo*,
pp. 183, 204.

[2] He had already threatened not only the Pope but his relatives,
if he were excommunicated. See a letter ap. Höfler, *Albert v. B.*,
p. 62.

however, having been informed of this circumstance, surprised and destroyed the castle, and " hanged all its inmates, and in testimony of his destruction of it left standing a half-ruined tower, in order that the memory of the *offence* and of his revenge might never die." [1]

Seeing that his illustrious patient was overcome by disease and the sorrow caused by this brutality, Richard of Wendover, a canon of St. Paul's, Gregory's English physician, was fain to tell him that he could do no more for him. Grateful for his services, the Pope gave him what he regarded as his most precious treasure, a crucifix which contained a number of relics. Richard in turn bequeathed the cross to the Abbey of St. Albans, and its great historian, Matthew Paris, tells us that the figure was of ivory and the cross itself was also covered with ivory.[2]

Death and burial of Gregory, 1241.

Gregory " of the great name " [3] died on August 22, 1241, and, amid the general grief of the Romans, was buried in St. Peter's.[4] When speaking of the election of Innocent IV., some important personage called the attention of the world to the fact that by the death of Gregory the Church had lost " a noble and venerable ruler." " For from his deeds and the fruits of his works, it may most certainly be seen what a useful shepherd and what a desirable ruler was Pope Gregory IX. of revered memory. To the best of his power did he preserve the flock entrusted to him from the assaults of the wicked,

---

[1] *Ib.* According to Richer of Senones (†1267), *Chron.*, l. iv, c. 8, ap. Böhmer, *Fontes III.*, or *M. G. SS.*, xxv, Frederick had already hanged a brother of Gregory.

[2] *Chron. maj.*, v, 299.

[3] " Magni nominis." *Ann. Gotwicenses*, an. 1227, ap. *M. G. SS.*, ix.

[4] *Cf.* Nicholas de Carbio, *in vit. Inn. IV.*, c. 5 ; and the letter of the Senator of Rome to Innocent IV., ap. *Albert v. Behaim*, p. 138, ed. Höfler.

nor did he shrink from giving his life for his sheep, until the day when he resigned it into Abraham's bosom, and gave back to Our Lord the soul which in the midst of conflicts he had so sorely tried." [1]

[1] The MSS. assign this letter of 1243 to the Emperor. " Imperator universis regni fidelibus." But Huillard-Bréholles, *Hist. Diplom. Fred.*, vi, p. 101, who printed it, and all others are agreed that its substance shows clearly that it was not written by Frederick. It was perhaps the work of Henry III. or St. Louis IX.

CELESTINE IV.

Gules a lion rampant argent holding a tower or.

CELESTINE IV.

A.D. 1241.

Sources.—In addition to those already mentioned there may be noted three documents first printed by Hampe. The principal one, while primarily connected with the election of Innocent IV., incidentally gives us much information regarding Celestine's election. The remaining two are concerned with an effort to obtain a benefice for a cleric of cardinal Sumercote. K. Hampe, *Ein ungedruckter Bericht über das Konklave von* 1241 *im römischen Septizonium*, Heidelberg, 1913. According to some of the authorities which treat of Celestine's death, he was never invested with the pallium, and never issued a bull—" nec bulla functus " [1] " habuit neque bullam." [2] At any rate, if he did issue one, neither bull nor, needless to add, Register of his has come down to us.

Works.—I have not been able to examine his biography by V. Castiglione who calls him a nephew of Urban III.; *Celestino IV. papa, milanese, nipote di P. Urbano III., Crivello milanese, conservato alla famiglia ed alla patria.*, Turin, 1661.

WHILST Gregory was fighting his last fight with death, Frederick was laying waste the Campagna with fire and sword. At length,[3] as the Emperor looked down on Rome from his headquarters at the Greek monastery of Grottaferrata, the news reached him that the great man whom he regarded as the bitterest of his foes was no more.[4] He at once with exultation proclaimed the fact to the kings of the earth. His " victorious army " with which " for the sake of making peace " he had marched to the

Frederick announces Gregory's death, 1241.

---

[1] *Cron. S. Petri Erford. Mod.*, an. 1241, p. 237. " Qui (the Pope statim morbo correptus . . . nec pallio, nec infula vel bulla functus, xvii die, iv scilicet Idus Novembris (Nov. 10), diem clausit extremum."

[2] Nic. de Carbio, *Vit. Inn. IV.*, c. 5.

[3] According to Mat. Par., *Chron.*, iv, p. 161, Gregory's death was concealed from the people for some days.

[4] Ric. of S. Ger., *Chron.*, ad an. 1241.

boundaries of Rome, had learnt that he who had refused peace, and who had " flouted the August one, had therefore not been able to pass in life the limits of August." [1] He went on to express a hope that God would give to the Apostolic See a man after His own heart, who would correct the misdeeds of his predecessor, and bring peace to the world—peace which is all the more necessary now that the Tartars are sweeping everything before them, and aiming at the complete destruction of the Christian name. Provided that the new Pontiff does not imitate the views of his predecessor,[2] we will be his devoted son, and with his help and that of the Princes of the world, will " magnificently " oppose and crush the haughtiness of the Tartars.

A lengthy conclave.

When Gregory died there appear to have been only fourteen cardinals.[3] Of these, Otho, cardinal deacon of St. Nicholas, in carcere Tulliano, who had been legate in England, and James Pecoraria, cardinal bishop of Praeneste, were prisoners of Frederick, while Thomas and Peter of Capua seem to have been away from Rome. The following ten cardinals, then, were in or near the City when Gregory died.[4] Geoffrey Castiglione, bishop of Sabina ; Romanus Bonaventura, bishop of Porto, Vicar of the City ; Rinaldo Conti, bishop of Ostia, afterwards Pope Alexander IV. ; the cardinal priests, Sinibaldo Fieschi, of St. Lawrence in Lucina, vice-chancellor, afterwards Pope Innocent IV., and John of Colonna ; Stephen Fitzcount or de Normandis of S. Maria in

---

[1] " Vix ultoris Augusti metas excederet, qui (Gregory) Augustum offendere nitebatur." Ep. of August, 1241, ap. H.-B., v, pt. ii, p. 1166.

[2] " Dummodo predecessoris crimen et odium non sequatur." Ib.

[3] Felten, P. Gregor. IX., p. 386, gives 16, but James de Vitry, according to Eubel, Hierarchia Cath., p. 6, died in 1240, and of a certain Guido said to have been cardinal-deacon of St. Eustachius there does not appear to be any authentic record, and it is known for certain that Robert Sumercote was card.-deacon of St. Eustachius at this time.

[4] Cf. Chron. S. Petri Erford. Mod., an. 1241, p. 236.

Trastevere, and the cardinal deacons Gilles de Torres, of SS. Cosmas and Damian, a Spaniard, afterwards archbishop of Toledo ; Rainerius Capocci of Viterbo, a Cistercian, of S. Maria in Cosmedin ; Robert Sumercote, of Ummarcote, an Englishman, of St. Eustachius ; Richard Anibaldi, of St. Angelo, a Benedictine, nephew of Rinaldo Conti.

We have already seen that John of Colonna, cardinal priest of S. Prassede, left Rome not many months before Gregory died, and formally attached himself to the Emperor. It would seem, however, that on Gregory's death, he must have returned immediately to the City, sent, no doubt, by his imperial master, "who," as he said, " was intent on striving with all his might that a friend of peace and one zealous for justice might be placed in the Church of God." [1] Frederick, that is, in plain language, sent John back to the City that he might have another partisan in the College of Cardinals.

Immediately after Gregory's death the cardinals in Rome were enclosed in what Carbio calls the prison (in cacerali ergastulo) of the Septizonium [2] by the Senator Matteo Rosso, of the Orsini, one of Gregory's nominations,[3] " in order that," says the chronicler, " though unwillingly they might proceed to elect a Pope."[4]

The cardinals are shut up in the Septizonium.

----

[1] "Ad quod (the peace of the world, etc.) . . . totis conatibus insudamus, ut pacis amico et justicie zelatore in Dei Ecclesia substituto," etc. Ep. of Aug., 1241.

[2] Or, as Mat. P. calls it, " the Palace of the Sun—in palatio quod Regia Solis dicitur." Cf. Chron. Siculum, ap. H.-B., i, pt. ii, p. 907, and Carbio, Vit. Inn. IV., c. 5.

[3] Ric. of S. Ger., Chron., an. ad 1241. It is possible that the Senator was a relative of the Pope. At any rate, Pietro Rosso, of whom mention has been made above, is described by Mat. P. (ib., p. 160) as a relative of the Pope. The Senator is called Russus or Rubeus in the chronicles. See the genealogical tree of his family, ap. Gregorovius, Rome, v, p. 215.

[4] Ric. of S. G., l.c.

The Senator acted in this prompt manner as he knew that Frederick had many adherents among the cardinals, and that if forcible measures were not taken, he would from his heights above Rome impose his will both on the City and on the Church.

According to Matthew Paris, and, indeed, according to what might have been expected under the circumstances, the ten cardinals, when they assembled to elect a successor to Gregory, could not come to any agreement. Then, again, according to the same authority only, they begged the Emperor to allow the two imprisoned cardinals to return to Rome on his own terms, " in order that the welfare of the universal Church, which depended mainly on the election of a Pope, might not be impeded by him." [1] It happened that our own Richard of Cornwall, on his way back to England after his return from his expedition to the Holy Land, chanced to be staying with the Emperor, and Paris falsely states that it was through his entreaties that Frederick agreed to allow the two cardinals to proceed to Rome, on condition that they should both return to their place of confinement, unless, indeed, one of them was elected Pope. [2]

[1] *Chron.*, iv., p. 164.

[2] *Ib.* That this statement of Paris that cardinals James and Otho took part in this election is false may be gathered not only from what has already been said and what will be said in a following note, but from the fact that Frederick bluntly refused the request of the King of France to liberate them, saying that "he would keep in straits (in angusto) those who had endeavoured to put the Augustus into straits (qui ad Cæsaris augustias nitebantur)." Ep. of Sept., 1241, ap. H.-B., vi, p. 1 ff. When in May, 1243, Frederick did at length release cardinal James, he proclaimed his action in so doing to the world as an act of utterly unprecedented magnanimity. *Cf.* several letters of June, 1243, ap. H.-B., vi, pp. 90–7. Besides, Richard of San Germano, *Chron.*, an. 1241, p. 154, mentions the bringing at this time of the two cardinals as far as Tivoli, but no further. *Cf.* also *ib.*, an. 1242, p. 155. Moreover, under the circumstances, it is not likely that Frederick would increase the strength of the cardinals opposed to him, by sending

It would seem, then, that at first five of the cardinals elected the Milanese, Geoffrey Castiglione, who is said to have been the candidate favoured by the Emperor.[1] Three of the others, including Rinaldo Conti, bishop of Ostia, who " according to custom had the first voice in the election of a Pope," chose Romanus, whose election was opposed by the Emperor. As this party also included Sinibaldo Fieschi, it is easy to see which section was the one in favour of carrying on the policy of Gregory IX.

Week followed week, but Geoffrey could not get the required majority of two-thirds. The emperor, therefore, finding that on account of the opposition of the Senator and the Romans, he could not force his way into Rome in order to exert military pressure in behalf of his candidate, retired to Apulia. Before his departure, however, at the request of Richard of Cornwall, he proclaimed that, in consequence of the death of his adversary Pope Gregory, no ecclesiastic was to be disturbed, " owing to the widowed state of the Roman Church." [2] Moreover, if anyone is prepared to believe Paris' story about the two cardinals, it was before his departure that Otho and James returned to their prisons, because they saw no hope of the cardinals agreeing on a candidate [3]—as if, in any case, the Senator would have allowed them to leave the Conclave.

them James and Otho. For, as he told one of the Princes of Germany, " the cardinals were about to promote to the Apostolic See one who would bring the other sword to his support and that of the empire." Ep. of Sept., 1241, ap. H.-B., vi, p. 5.

[1] We say "it is said " because the only historian who asserts this is Matthew Paris, whose whole narrative is obviously inaccurate ; for, though he tells us that cardinals Otho and James were enclosed with the ten, he does not assign them any share in the election of either Geoffrey or Romanus, but says that James died "about this time." He did not die till June, 1244.

[2] Mat. Par., iv, p. 166.

[3] Mat. P., iv, p. 170, who says that Otho returned to set free the hostages who were taking his place.

Cardinal
Sumercote
dies there.

The close confinement during the heats of August
and September, and the hardships which they had to
endure,[1] began to tell on the health of the cardinals, and
Sinibaldo was reduced to death's door, and on September
26 the English cardinal died.[2]   At last, however, the
necessary majority was obtained, and on October 25,
after a vacancy of over two months, the apostolic chair
was filled by Geoffrey Castiglione as Celestine IV.[3]

Election of
Geoffrey
Castiglione
as
Celestine IV.

However, there appear to have been many lively scenes
before the election of this " old and infirm " prelate was
agreed to as a compromise.   It is said that both Geoffrey
and Romanus retired when it was found that neither had
the required majority, and that " the cardinals," i.e.,

[1] *Cf.* the letter of the cardinals who fled to Anagni on Celestine's
death.   Hampe, p. 27 ff.

[2] Nich. de Carbio, *Vit. Inn. IV.*, c. 5. Mat. Par., p. 168, says
" it was reported " that he was poisoned by his rivals lest he should
be elected Pope.   But see two letters printed by Hampe, p. 31 ff.,
showing the affection and esteem of the cardinals for Robert.   They
speak " quem ad dictum cardinalem affectum habemus, qui nobis
vivit post funera."   There is then no more truth in the report than in
his mere statement that another cardinal died in the same way.   But
no other cardinal died at this time in any way.   Luard in a note to
this passage says that Paris probably referred to Romanus " who
died about this time."   But he did not die till 1243.   Nor again,
despite Mat. P., p. 172, did Richard Anibaldi die about the time of
the election of Celestine IV.   He did not die till 1276 !   We have
already said enough to show the carelessness of Matthew Paris.   He
also leads us to infer that not only were the castles of John of Colonna
seized by the Romans, but that he himself was torn from the
Septizonium and thrown into prison (iv, p. 168).   We know, indeed,
that his fortress of the Mausoleum of Augustus was seized by the
Senator (Ric. of S. G., *l.c.*), and that he himself, though he came to
Rome " on the security of the Senate " (Cardinals' letter in Hampe,
p. 27), was at length cast into prison ;   but it is not likely that he was
dragged from the Septizonium.   As a matter of fact he was seized
after the election of Celestine.   *Cf. Chron. de reb. in Ital.*, p. 187,
ed. H.-B.

[3] Mat. Par., iv, 172 ;   Ric. of S. G. ;   " mittens de celesti cœnaculo
Celestinum," says the sovereign who announced to his subjects the
election of Innocent IV.   Ep. of 1243, ap. H.-B., vi, p. 102.

seemingly the imperial party, elected a new candidate
who did not belong to the sacred college.[1] Rumour of
this action reached the Romans. Accordingly, fearing
the election of a strong partisan of Frederick, they
demanded to know the name of the new candidate.[2]
When this request was refused, they had recourse to
violence [3] and pressure ; and, if we can fully trust the
ex parte statement of the imperialist cardinals who fled
from the City after Celestine's death, the Romans resorted
to pressure of even the most indecent and revolting kind [4]
to prevent the election of " an outsider." Among other
things the Senator threatened to dig up the body of
Gregory and place it in their midst if they did not produce
" a mitred Pope " from amongst themselves.[5]

At length, wearied out with the heat and with the
absence of every comfort, and with the presence of every
form of discomfort, all the cardinals agreed in electing
the aged and infirm Geoffrey, as a kind of compromise,
conjecturing that he had not long to live. The new Pope,

Geoffrey
Castiglione.

[1] *Ann. Stadenses*, ap. *M. G. SS.*, xvi, p. 367.

[2] *Ib.*

[3] " Nec silendum est, quod gravis comminatio . . . facta fuit si
eligeretur extraneus, de quo suspicio haberetur." The election
document, ap. Hampe, p. 30.

[4] " Annon super testitudines nostris capitibus imminentes
a custodibus decubantibus in eisdem urina sepius fundebatur, que
per rimas et crepidines super unius fratris nostri cubiculum, velud
olens locium, et de altera ; ubi sua purgamenta sternebant, mixta
imbribus super alterum noctibus defluebat." *Ib.*, p. 29. There is
much more to the same and even worse effect. The Continuator of the
Gesta Regum of our own historian Gervase of Canterbury had heard
something at least of these doings. " Cardinales a Romanis civibus
ad eligendum papam *turpiter* et miserabiliter coartantur." Vol. ii,
p. 201, R. S. Moreover, a letter of Frederick to Louis IX. perhaps
suggests that these outrages were directed against the cardinals of the
imperial party " violentas manus extendunt . . . ad cardinales,
dilectos amicos nostros." Ep. of June, 1243, ap. H.-B., vi, 95. *Cf.*
also *Ann. S. Rudberti*, ap. *M. G. SS.*, ix, p. 788.

[5] *Ib.*, p. 30.

a man distinguished for " his character and learning," [1]
is said by modern authors to have been the son of John
Castiglione and Cassandra Crivelli, sister of Urban III.,
and at one time, as a Canon, to have held the chancellorship
of the Church of Milan.   Resigning this office, he is
believed to have been a Cistercian of Hautecombe in
1187.[2]   In 1227, he was named cardinal priest of St.
Mark by Gregory IX. in his first nomination of cardinals,
and, some twelve years later (1239), he became cardinal
bishop of Sabina, in which capacity he showed himself the
champion of the poorer clergy.[3]

Death of
Celestine,
1241.

It would appear that Celestine must have been at the
point of death when he was elected.   At any rate, he is
not known by any public act to have given any proof that
he had profited by the experience which he had gained as
one of the legates of his great predecessor.[4]   After
seventeen days' pontificate, this " estimable old man " [5]
died on November 10, without having even received the
pallium.   He was buried in St. Peter's on the following
day [6] by such of the cardinals as remained in the city ;
for no sooner had he died than most of the cardinals,
including of course those of the imperial party, fled from
Rome to escape coercion.

[1] Mat. Par., iv, 172.   *Cf.* Roland of Padua, *Chron.*, ap. *M. G. SS.*
xix, 78, who calls him a "skilled theologian."

[2] *Cf.* Ciaconius, *Vitæ Rom. Pont.*, i, p. 687 ; Novaes, *Elementi della
storia de' Sommi Pontefici*, who adds that he was educated by
St. Galdinus ; and that in the monastery of Hautecombe he wrote
a History of the Kingdom of Scotland.   Hautecombe (Altacomba)
was founded by Amadeus III. of Savoy "on the Lac du Bourget as
the family Abbey."   Orton, *The House of Savoy*, p. 60.

[3] "Negocia pauperum clericorum frequenter et diligenter intuitu
misericordie promovit aput P. Gregorium." *Chron. minor Erphord.*,
an. 1243, ap. *M. G. SS.*, xxiv, p. 199.

[4] *Reg. Greg. IX.*, i, 179.   Ep. of May 16.

[5] Geoffroy de Courlon, *Cron. Senon.*, p. 528, ed. Julliot.

[6] *Cf.* ep. Inn. IV., ap. Rod., ii, p. 2, July 2, 1243.

INDEX

Abel, king of Denmark, 296.
Acre, 225.
Adelasia, the Lady of Torres, 280 f.
Adenulf de Mathia, 170.
Africa, faith in, 417.
Agnes, Bl., of Bohemia, 196 ff.
Alans, the, 395.
Albert of Pisa, O.M., 192 f., 294.
Albert von Behaim, 295, 307 n.
Albigensians, 45, 144 f., 158 ff., 421 ff.
Alexander II., king of Scotland, 116, 148 f., 343, 385 f.
Alexander IV., 185 n., 192, 198, 307 n.
Alice (or Alix), queen of Cyprus, 248.
Amalricus (Aimeric, or Amaury), hist., 2.
Anagni, 322.
Ancona, march of, 97, 224, 234, 242, 260, 279, 293, 299.
Andrew, king of Hungary, 26 f., 55.
Angelica, Porta, 18.
Anibaldi, Ric., card., 445.
Anibaldo Anibaldi, senator, 320, 332 n., 431 n., 434.
Annales Genuenses, 167.
Annales Monastici, 340.
Annales Pisani, 167.
Annales S. Justini Patavini, 167.

Anthony, St., of Padua, 179 n., 200 n.
Aquileia, 256 f.
Archives, papal, loss of, 89.
Ardea, 90.
Aristotle, books of, condemned, 173.
Arles, kingdom of (see Burgundy), 67 n., 259.
Art, the black, 426.
Artois, Robert of, 297.
Asen, John II., king of Bulgaria, 392 n., 408 ff.
Assisi, papal palace at, 322.
Atho, master, 363.
Auditor, 176 ; auditores, the, 6 n.
Augustus, mausoleum of, 315 f., 448 n.
Austria, 266, 271 ff., 295.
Ayton (or Acton), John, 208 n., 363.
Azzo, Marquis of Este, 97.

Bagdad, 29.
Baldwin II., emp., 285 n., 391, 393 n., 409 ff.
Baldwin of Avesnes, hist., 391 n.
Baldwin of Ninove, hist., 425 n.
Bankers, 107 ff., 338.
Baptism, valid formula of, 394 n.
Baptistery, Lateran, 91.
Bartholomæus, hist., 167.
Bela IV., king of Hungary, 266 n., 409.

Printed in Great Britain by Stephen Austin & Sons, Ltd., Hertford